CASES AND MATERIALS ON FEDERAL CONSTITUTIONAL LAW

Volume V

The Fourteenth Amendment

CASES AND MATERIALS ON FEDERAL CONSTITUTIONAL LAW

Volume V
The Fourteenth Amendment

Lee J. Strang

VOLUME 5 ISBN: 978-1-4224-2889-4
VOLUME 5 EBOOK ISBN:978–0–3271–7954–2

Library of Congress Cataloging-in-Publication Data

Odom, Thomas H.
Introduction to interpretive methods & introduction to the federal judicial power / Thomas H. Odom.
p. cm. -- (Cases and materials on federal constitutional law ; v. 1)
Includes index.
ISBN 978-1-4224-2205-2 (soft cover)
1. Courts--United States. I. Title.
KF8718.O36 2008
347.73'1--dc22

2008036946

NOTE TO USERS

To ensure that you are using the latest materials available in this area, please be sure to periodically check the LexisNexis Law School web site for downloadable updates and supplements at www.lexisnexis.com/lawschool.

Editorial Offices
121 Chanlon Rd., New Providence, NJ 07974 (908) 464-6800
201 Mission St., San Francisco, CA 94105-1831 (415) 908-3200
www.lexisnexis.com

MATTHEW◆BENDER

(2013–Pub.3265)

INTRODUCTION TO THE MODULAR CASEBOOK SERIES

By now you have realized that the course materials assigned by your instructor have a very different form than traditional casebooks. The *Modular Casebook Series* is intentionally designed to break the mold. Course materials consist of one or more separate volumes selected from among a larger and growing set of volumes. Each volume is relatively short so that an instructor may "mix and match" a suitable number of volumes for a course of varying length and focus.

Each volume is also designed to serve an instructional purpose rather than as a treatise; as a result, the *Modular Casebook Series* is published in soft cover. Publication of the separate volumes in soft cover also permits course materials to be revised more easily so that they will incorporate recent developments. Moreover, by purchasing only the assigned volumes for a given course, students are likely to recognize significant savings over the cost of a traditional casebook.

Traditional casebooks are often massive tomes, frequently exceeding 1000 or even 1500 pages. Traditional casebooks are lengthy because they attempt to cover the entire breadth of material that *might* be useful to an instructor for a two-semester course of five or six credits. Even with six credits, different instructors will cover different portions of a traditional casebook within the time available. As a consequence, traditional casebooks include a range of materials that may leave hundreds of unexplored pages in any particular six-credit class. Especially for a student in a three or four credit course, such a book is hardly an efficient means of delivering the needed materials. Students purchase much more book than they need, at great expense. And students carry large, heavy books for months at a time.

Traditional casebooks are usually hard cover publications. It seems as though they are constructed to last as a reference work throughout decades of practice. In fact, as the presence of annual supplements to casebooks makes clear, portions of casebooks become obsolete very shortly after publication. Treatises and hornbooks are designed to serve as reference works; casebooks serve a different purpose. Once again, the traditional format of casebooks seems to impose significant added costs on students for little reason.

The form of traditional casebooks increases the probability that the content will become obsolete shortly after publication. The publication of lengthy texts in hardcover produces substantial delay between the time the author completes the final draft and the time the book reaches the hands of students. In addition, the broader scope of material addressed in a 1,000 or 1,500 page text means that portions of the text are more likely to be superseded by later developments than any particular narrowly-tailored volume in the *Modular Casebook Series*. Because individual volumes in the *Modular Casebook Series* may be revised without requiring revision of other volumes, the materials for any particular course will be less likely to require supplementation.

Most importantly, the cases and accompanying exercises provide students with the opportunity to learn and deploy the standard arguments in the various subject matters of constitutional law. Each case is edited to emphasize the key arguments made by the Court and justices. For instance, in many older cases, headings were added to note a new or related argument. Furthermore, the exercises following each case focus on identifying and critiquing the Court's and justices' arguments. The exercises also form the basis for rich class discussion. All of this introduces students to the most important facet of constitutional law: the deployment of standard arguments in each doctrinal context and across constitutional law doctrines.

I hope you enjoy this innovative approach to course materials.

Dedication

To Elizabeth and Saint Thomas Aquinas.

Acknowledgments

I would like to thank Tom Odom for proposing and initiating the *Modular Casebook Series*, and for inviting me to participate in the *Series*, and the University of Toledo College of Law for research leave and support. The hard work and excellent research of Paul Cordell is reflected in this Volume. Without Elizabeth's loving support, this project would not have been completed.

Preface to the First Edition

Technological improvements permit the compilation of resources in a manner unthinkable when I was a law student. Materials that permit further examination of assigned reading can be delivered in a cost-effective manner and in a format more likely to be useful in practice than reams of photocopies. The associated DVD-ROM contains full, searchable text of several of the most important resources for interpreting the Constitution, lowering the wall between doctrinal courses and research courses.

With regard to assigned reading, there is no good reason to burden students with stacks of hand-outs or expensive annual supplements. Publication through the *Modular Casebook Series* ensures that even very recent developments may be incorporated prior to publication. Moreover, if important cases are decided after publication of the latest edition of the volume, they will be included on the DVD-ROM. Cases and materials that shed additional light on matter in the hard copy casebook are also included.

I welcome comments from readers so that I may make further improvements in the next edition of this publication.

Lee J. Strang

TECHNICAL NOTE FROM THE EDITOR

The cases and other materials excerpted in this Volume have been edited in an effort to enhance readability. Citations of multiple cases for a single proposition have been shortened in many places to reference only one or two prominent authorities. In some places, archaic language or spelling has been revised. Headings were added to some of the longer decisions to permit ease of reference to various parts of the opinion. Such headings may also assist the reader in identifying a transition from one point to another.

Cases have been edited to a suitable length. In order to achieve that result, many interesting but tangential points have been omitted. The length of some opinions also hindered the inclusion of excerpts from concurring or dissenting opinions. Where such opinions have been omitted, it is noted in the text.

In editing these cases, I have not indicated the portions of cases I deleted unless such deletion with the absence of ellipses would have been misleading. However, any time I inserted material into a case, I indicated the insertion with the use of brackets.

Lee J. Strang

TABLE OF CONTENTS

TABLE OF CONTENTS

TABLE OF CONTENTS

TABLE OF CONTENTS

TABLE OF CONTENTS

Introduction to Volume 5

The Reconstruction Amendments refer to the three constitutional amendments adopted during and shortly after the Civil War: the Thirteenth, Fourteenth, and Fifteenth Amendments. This Volume addresses constitutional limitations imposed upon states by the Fourteenth Amendment. Its primary focus is on the Due Process and Equal Protection Clauses located in Section 1 of the Fourteenth Amendment, though the nearly identical limits upon the federal government in the Fifth Amendment's Due Process Clause are also discussed. Volume 5 begins with an explanation of the "state action doctrine," which limits the Constitution's reach.

A. The State Action Doctrine

1. The Rule Itself

The State Action Doctrine is relatively easy to state: "It is state action . . . that is prohibited. Individual invasion of individual rights is not the subject-matter of the amendment." *The Civil Rights Cases*, 109 U.S. 3, 21 (1883). This requirement is central to American constitutional law and has deep roots.

2. Exceptions to the State Action Doctrine

There are three commonly accepted exceptions to the State Action Doctrine: (1) the Thirteenth Amendment's prohibition on slavery and involuntary servitude; (2) the Public Functions Exception; and (3) the Entanglement Exception. The first is textually rooted and less controversial than the latter two exceptions, which are Court-created.

The State Action Doctrine is the subject of **Chapter 1.**

B. The Privileges or Immunities Clause

The Privileges or Immunities Clause is located in Section 1 of the Fourteenth Amendment. U.S. Const., amend. XIV, § 1, cl. 2. The Privileges or Immunities Clause was the focus of debate in the Reconstruction Congress, and it was widely assumed that the Clause would be the primary means of protecting newly-freed black Americans in the South. The post-Ratification history of the Clause — especially its narrow interpretation of the Clause in *The Slaughterhouse Cases*, 83 U.S. (16 Wall.) 36 (1872) — is one of the most interesting stories in constitutional law and a testament to the power of stare decisis.

The Privileges or Immunities Clause is the subject of **Chapter 2.**

C. The Due Process Clause(s)

The Due Process Clause of the Fifth Amendment, ratified in 1791, played relatively little role in the Supreme Court's antebellum jurisprudence. However, with the narrow interpretation of the Privileges or Immunities Clause in *The Slaughterhouse Cases*, 83 U.S. (16 Wall.) 36 (1872), the Fourteenth Amendment's Due Process Clause became the focus of constitutional limits on states.

1. The Incorporation Doctrine

The first primary function of the Due Process Clause is incorporation. Incorporation is the concept of the Due Process Clause of the Fourteenth Amendment serving as the vehicle through which the substantive guarantees of the Bill of Rights apply — are "incorporated" — against the states. Incorporation was, and remains, controversial, though the debates today center, not on whether the Bill of Rights should apply to the states, but primarily over whether the Due Process Clause was/is the appropriate legal mechanism to do so.

2. "Substantive" Due Process

The Fifth and Fourteenth Amendments' Due Process Clauses also serve as the source for a second important legal doctrine: "substantive" due process. This substantive facet of the Due Process Clauses holds that, in addition to the enumerated rights in the Bill of Rights, the Clauses also protect *un*enumerated constitutional rights. This doctrine had its origin in the late-nineteenth century. The Supreme Court's treatment of the doctrine is conventionally divided into two eras: classical, which lasted from the late-nineteenth century up to the New Deal, and modern, which arose during the 1960s.

The Due Process Clauses, the incorporation doctrine, and substantive due process are the subject of **Chapter 3.**

D. The Equal Protection Clause

The original Constitution did not contain an equal protection provision. The closest analogue was the Privileges and Immunities Clause in Article IV, Section 2, Clause 1, which required states to give non-state citizens the same privileges and immunities as state citizens. The Equal Protection Clause, following its seminal interpretation in *Brown v. Board of Education*, 347 U.S. 483 (1954), became a major focus of constitutional law. The Supreme Court's equal protection case law has two components: (1) standard equal protection; and (2) "fundamental rights" equal protection.

The Equal Protection Clause is the subject of **Chapter 4.**

Introduction to Volume 5

The Constitution of the United States

We the People of the United States, in order to form a more perfect nion, establish Justice, insure domestic Tranquility, provide for the common defence, promote the general Welfare, and secure the Blessings of Liberty to ourselves and our Posterity, do ordain and establish this Constitution for the United States of America.

Article I

Section 1. All legislative Powers herein granted shall be vested in a Congress of the United States, which shall consist of a Senate and House of Representatives.

Section 2. The House of Representatives shall be composed of Members chosen every second Year by the People of the several States, and the Electors in each State shall have the Qualifications requisite for Electors of the most numerous Branch of the State Legislature.

No person shall be a Representative who shall not have attained to the Age of twenty five Years, and been seven Years a Citizen of the United States, and who shall not, when elected, be an Inhabitant of that State in which he shall be chosen.

Representatives and direct Taxes shall be apportioned among the several States which may be included within this Union, according to their respective Numbers, which shall be determined by adding to the whole Number of free Persons, including those bound to Service for a Term of Years, and excluding Indians not taxed, three fifths of all other Persons. The actual Enumeration shall be made within three Years after the first Meeting of the Congress of the United States, and within every subsequent Term of ten Years, in such Manner as they shall by Law direct. The Number of Representatives shall not exceed one for every thirty Thousand, but each State shall have at Least one Representative; and until such enumeration shall be made, the State of New Hampshire shall be entitled to chuse three, Massachusetts eight, Rhode-Island and Providence Plantations one, Connecticut five, New-York six, New Jersey four, Pennsylvania eight, Delaware one, Maryland six, Virginia ten, North Carolina five, South Carolina five, and Georgia three.

When vacancies happen in the Representation from any State, the Executive Authority thereof shall issue Writs of Election to fill such Vacancies.

The House of Representatives shall chuse their Speaker and other Officers; and shall have the sole Power of Impeachment.

Section 3. The Senate of the United States shall be composed of two Senators from each State, chosen by the Legislature thereof, for six Years; and each Senator shall have one Vote.

Immediately after they shall be assembled in Consequence of the first Election, they shall be divided as equally as may be into three Classes. The Seats of the Senators of the first Class shall be vacated at the Expiration of the second Year, of the second Class at the Expiration of the fourth Year, and of the third Class at the Expiration of the sixth Year, so that one third may be chosen every second Year; and if Vacancies happen by Resignation, or otherwise, during the Recess of the Legislature of any State, the Executive thereof may make temporary Appointments until the next Meeting of the Legislature, which shall then fill such Vacancies.

No Person shall be a Senator who shall not have attained to the Age of thirty Years, and been nine Years a Citizen of the United States, and who shall not, when elected, be an Inhabitant of that State for which he shall be chosen.

The Vice President of the United States shall be President of the Senate, but shall have no Vote, unless they be equally divided.

The Senate shall choose their other Officers, and also a President pro tempore, in the Absence of the Vice President, or when he shall exercise the Office of President of the United States.

The Senate shall have the sole Power to try all Impeachments. When sitting for that Purpose, they shall be on Oath or Affirmation. When the President of the United States is tried, the Chief Justice shall preside: and no Person shall be convicted without the Concurrence of two thirds of the Members present.

Judgment in Cases of Impeachment shall not extend further than to removal from Office, and disqualification to hold and enjoy any Office of honor, Trust or Profit under the United States: but the Party convicted shall nevertheless be liable and subject to Indictment, Trial, Judgment and Punishment, according to Law.

Section 4. The Times, Places and Manner of holding Elections for Senators and Representatives, shall be prescribed in each State by the Legislature thereof; but the Congress may at any time by Law make or alter such Regulations, except as to the Places of chusing Senators.

The Congress shall assemble at least once in every Year, and such Meeting shall be on the first Monday in December, unless they shall by Law appoint a different Day.

Section 5. Each House shall be the Judge of the Elections, Returns and Qualifications of its own Members, and a Majority of each shall constitute a Quorum to do Business; but a smaller Number may adjourn from day to day, and may be authorized to compel the Attendance of absent Members, in such Manner, and under such Penalties as each House may provide.

Each House may determine the Rules of its Proceedings, punish its Members for disorderly Behaviour, and, with the Concurrence of two thirds, expel a Member.

Each House shall keep a Journal of its Proceedings, and from time to time publish the same, excepting such Parts as may in their Judgment require Secrecy; and the Yeas and Nays of the Members of either House on any question shall, at the Desire of one fifth of those Present, be entered on the Journal.

Section 6. The Senators and Representatives shall receive a Compensation for their Services, to be ascertained by Law, and paid out of the Treasury of the United States. They shall in all Cases, except Treason, Felony and Breach of the Peace, be privileged from Arrest during their Attendance at the Session of their respective Houses, and in going to and returning from the same; and for any Speech or Debate in either House, they shall not be questioned in any other Place.

No Senator or Representative shall, during the Time for which he was elected, be appointed to any civil Office under the Authority of the United States, which shall have been created, or the Emoluments whereof shall have been encreased during such time; and no Person holding any Office under the United States, shall be a Member of either House during his Continuance in Office.

Section 7. All Bills for raising Revenue shall originate in the House of Representatives; but the Senate may propose or concur with Amendments as on other Bills.

Every Bill which shall have passed the House of Representatives and the Senate, shall, before it become a Law, be presented to the President of the United States; If he approve he shall sign it, but if not he shall return it, with his Objections to that House in which it shall have originated, who shall enter the Objections at large on their Journal, and proceed to reconsider it. If after such Reconsideration two thirds of that House shall agree to pass the Bill, it shall be sent, together with the Objections, to the other House, by which it shall likewise be reconsidered, and if approved by two thirds of that House, it shall become a Law. But in all such Cases the Votes of both Houses shall be determined by yeas and Nays, and the Names of the Persons voting for and against the Bill shall be entered on the Journal of each House respectively. If any Bill shall not be returned by the President within ten days (Sundays excepted) after it shall have been presented to him, the Same shall be a Law, in like Manner as if he had signed it, unless the Congress by their Adjournment prevent its Return in which Case it shall not be a Law.

Every Order, Resolution, or Vote to which the Concurrence of the Senate and House of Representatives may be necessary (except on a question of Adjournment) shall be presented to the

Introduction to Volume 5

President of the United States; and before the Same shall take Effect, shall be approved by him, or being disapproved by him, shall be repassed by two thirds of the Senate and House of Representatives, according to the Rules and Limitations prescribed in the Case of a Bill.

Section 8. The Congress shall have Power To lay and collect Taxes, Duties, Imposts and Excises, to pay the Debts and provide for the common Defence and general Welfare of the United States; but all Duties, Imposts and Excises shall be uniform throughout the United States;

To borrow Money on the credit of the United States;

To regulate Commerce with foreign Nations, and among the several States, and with the Indian Tribes;

To establish an uniform Rule of Naturalization, and uniform Laws on the subject of Bankruptcies throughout the United States;

To coin Money, regulate the Value thereof, and foreign Coin, and fix the Standard of Weights and Measures;

To provide for the Punishment of counterfeiting the Securities and current Coin of the United States;

To establish Post Offices and post Roads;

To promote the Progress of Science and useful Arts, by securing for limited Times to Authors and Inventors the exclusive Right to their respective Writings and Discoveries;

To constitute Tribunals inferior to the supreme Court;

To define and punish Piracies and Felonies committed on the high Seas, and Offences against the Law of Nations;

To declare War, grant Letters of Marque and Reprisal, and make Rules concerning Captures on Land and Water;

To raise and support Armies, but no Appropriation of Money to that Use shall be for a longer Term than two Years;

To provide and maintain a Navy;

To make Rules for the Government and Regulation of the land and naval Forces;

To provide for calling forth the Militia to execute the Laws of the Union, suppress Insurrections and repel Invasions;

To provide for organizing, arming, and disciplining, the Militia, and for governing such Part of them as may be employed in the Service of the United States, reserving to the States respectively, the Appointment of the Officers, and the Authority of training the Militia according to the discipline prescribed by Congress;

To exercise exclusive Legislation in all Cases whatsoever, over such District (not exceeding ten Miles square) as may, by Cession of particular States, and the Acceptance of Congress, become the Seat of the Government of the United States, and to exercise like Authority over all Places purchased by the Consent of the Legislature of the State in which the Same shall be, for the Erection of Forts, Magazines, Arsenals, dock-Yards, and other needful Buildings; — And

To make all Laws which shall be necessary and proper for carrying into Execution the foregoing Powers, and all other Powers vested by this Constitution in the Government of the United States, or in any Department or Officer thereof.

Section 9. The Migration or Importation of such Persons as any of the States now existing shall think proper to admit, shall not be prohibited by the Congress prior to the Year one thousand eight hundred and eight, but a Tax or duty may be imposed on such Importation, not exceeding ten dollars for each Person.

The Privilege of the Writ of Habeas Corpus shall not be suspended, unless when in Cases of Rebellion or Invasion the public Safety may require it.

No Bill of Attainder or ex post facto Law shall be passed.

No Capitation, or other direct, Tax shall be laid, unless in Proportion to the Census or Enumeration herein before directed to be taken.

No Tax or Duty shall be laid on.Articles exported from any State.

No Preference shall be given by any Regulation of Commerce or Revenue to the Ports of one State over those of another; nor shall Vessels bound to, or from, one State, be obliged to enter, clear, or pay Duties in another.

No Money shall be drawn from the Treasury, but in Consequence of Appropriations made by Law; and a regular Statement and Account of the Receipts and Expenditures of all public Money shall be published from time to time.

No Title of Nobility shall be granted by the United States: And no Person holding any Office of Profit or Trust under them, shall, without the Consent of the Congress, accept of any present, Emolument, Office, or Title, of any kind whatever, from any King, Prince, or foreign State.

Section 10. No State shall enter into any Treaty, Alliance, or Confederation; grant Letters of Marque and Reprisal; coin Money; emit Bills of Credit; make any Thing but gold and silver Coin a Tender in Payment of Debts; pass any Bill of Attainder, ex post facto Law, or Law impairing the Obligation of Contracts, or grant any Title of Nobility.

No State shall, without the Consent of the Congress, lay any Imposts or Duties on Imports or Exports, except what may be absolutely necessary for executing it's inspection Laws: and the net Produce of all Duties and Imposts, laid by any State on Imports or Exports, shall be for the Use of the Treasury of the United. States; and all such Laws shall be subject to the Revision and Controul of the Congress.

No State shall, without the Consent of Congress, lay any Duty of Tonnage, keep Troops, or Ships of War in time of Peace, enter into any Agreement or Compact with another State, or with a foreign Power, or engage in War, unless actually invaded, or in such imminent Danger as will not admit of delay.

Article II

Section 1. The executive Power shall be vested in a President of the United States of America. He shall hold his Office during the Term of four Years, and, together with the Vice President, chosen for the same Term, be elected as follows

Each State shall appoint, in such Manner as the Legislature thereof may direct, a Number of Electors, equal to the whole Number of Senators and Representatives to which the State may be entitled in the Congress: but no Senator or Representative, or Person holding an Office of Trust or Profit under the United States, shall be appointed an Elector.

The Electors shall meet in their respective States, and vote by Ballot for two Persons, of whom one at least shall not be an Inhabitant of the same State with themselves. And they shall make a List of all the Persons voted for, and of the Number of Votes for each; which List they shall sign and certify, and transmit sealed to the Seat of the Government of the United States, directed to the President of the Senate. The President of the Senate shall, in the Presence of the Senate and House of Representatives, open all the Certificates, and the Votes shall then be counted. The Person having the greatest Number of Votes shall be the President, if such Number be a Majority of the whole Number of Electors appointed; and if there be more than one who have such Majority, and have an equal Number of Votes, then the House of Representatives shall immediately chuse by Ballot one of them for President; and if no Person have a Majority, then from the five highest on the List the said House shall in like Manner chuse the President. But in chusing the President, the Votes shall be taken by States, the Representation from each State having one Vote; A quorum for this Purpose shall consist of a Member or Members from two thirds of the States, and a Majority of all the States shall be necessary to a Choice. In every Case, after the Choice of the President, the Person having the greatest Number of Votes of the Electors shall be the Vice President. But if there should remain two or more who have equal Votes, the Senate shall chuse from them by Ballot the Vice President.

The Congress may determine the Time of chusing the Electors, and the Day on which they shall give their Votes; which Day shall be the same throughout the United States.

No Person except a natural born Citizen, or a Citizen of the United States, at the time of the Adoption of this Constitution, shall be eligible to the Office of President; neither shall any Person be eligible to that Office who shall not have attained to the Age of thirty five Years, and been fourteen Years a Resident within the United States.

In the Case of the Removal of the President from Office, or of his Death, Resignation, or Inability to discharge the Powers and Duties of the said Office, the Same shall devolve on the Vice President, and the Congress may by Law provide for the Case of Removal, Death, Resignation or Inability, both of the President and Vice President, declaring what Officer shall then act as President, and such Officer shall act accordingly, until the Disability be removed, or a President shall be elected.

The President shall, at stated Times, receive for his Services, a Compensation, which shall neither be encreased nor diminished during the Period for which he shall have been elected, and he shall not receive within that Period any other Emolument from the United States, or any of them.

Before he enter on the Execution of his Office, he shall take the following Oath or Affirmation: — "I do solemnly swear (or affirm) that I will faithfully execute the Office of the President of the United States, and will to the best of my Ability, preserve, protect and defend the Constitution of the United States."

Section 2. The President shall be the Commander in Chief of the Army and Navy of the United States, and of the Militia of the several States, when called into the actual service of the United States; he may require the Opinion, in writing, of the principal Officer in each of the executive Departments, upon any Subject relating to the Duties of their respective Offices, and he shall have Power to grant Reprieves and Pardons for Offenses against the United States, except in Cases of Impeachment.

He shall have Power, by and with the Advice and Consent of the Senate, to make Treaties, provided two thirds of the Senators present concur; and he shall nominate, and by and with the Advice and Consent of the Senate, shall appoint Ambassadors, other public Ministers and Consuls, Judges of the supreme Court, and all other Officers of the United States, whose Appointments are not herein otherwise provided for, and which shall be established by Law but the Congress may by Law vest the Appointment of such inferior Officers, as they think proper, in the President alone, in the Courts of Law, or in the Heads of Departments.

The President shall have Power to fill up all Vacancies that may happen during the Recess of the Senate, by granting Commissions which shall expire at the End of their next Session.

Section 3. He shall from time to time give to the Congress Information of the State of the Union, and recommend to their Consideration such Measures as he shall judge necessary and expedient; he may, on extraordinary Occasions, convene both Houses, or either of them, and in Case of Disagreement between them, with Respect to the Time of Adjournment, he may adjourn them to such Time as he shall think proper; he shall receive Ambassadors and other public Ministers; he shall take Care that the Laws be faithfully executed, and shall Commission all the Officers of the United States.

Section 4. The President, Vice President and all civil Officers of the United States, shall be removed from Office on Impeachment for, and Conviction of, Treason, Bribery, or other high Crimes and Misdemeanors.

Article III

Section 1. The judicial Power of the United States, shall be vested in one supreme Court, and in such inferior Courts as the Congress may from time to time ordain and establish. The Judges, both of the supreme and inferior Courts, shall hold their Offices during good Behaviour, and shall, at stated Times, receive for their Services, a Compensation, which shall not be diminished during their Continuance in Office.

Section 2. The judicial Power shall extend to all Cases, in Law and Equity, arising under this Constitution, the Laws of the United States, and Treaties made, or which shall be made, under their Authority; — to all Cases affecting Ambassadors, other public Ministers and Consuls; — to all Cases of admiralty and maritime Jurisdiction; — to Controversies to which the United States shall be a Party; — to Controversies between two or more States; — between a State and Citizens of another State; — between Citizens of different States; — between Citizens of the same State claiming Lands under Grants of different States, and between a State, or the Citizens thereof, and foreign States, Citizens or Subjects.

In all cases affecting Ambassadors, other public Ministers and Consuls, and those in which a State shall be a Party, the supreme Court shall have original Jurisdiction. In all the other Cases before mentioned, the supreme Court shall have appellate Jurisdiction, both as to Law and Fact, with such Exceptions, and under such Regulations as the Congress shall make.

The Trial of all Crimes, except in Cases of Impeachment, shall be by Jury; and such Trial shall be held in the State where the said Crimes shall have been committed; but when not committed within any State, the Trial shall be at such Place or Places as the Congress may by Law have directed.

Section 3. Treason against the United States, shall consist only in levying War against them, or in adhering to their Enemies, giving them Aid or Comfort. No Person shall be convicted of Treason unless on the Testimony of two Witnesses to the same overt Act, or on Confession in open Court.

The Congress shall have Power to declare the Punishment of Treason, but no Attainder of Treason shall work Corruption of Blood, or Forfeiture except during the Life of the Person attainted.

Article IV

Section 1. Full Faith and Credit shall be given in each State to the public Acts, Records, and judicial Proceedings of every other State. And the Congress may by general Laws prescribe the Manner in which such Acts, Records and Proceedings shall be proved, and the Effect thereof.

Section 2. The Citizens of each State shall be entitled to all Privileges and Immunities of Citizens in the several States.

A Person charged in any State with Treason, Felony, or other Crime, who shall flee from Justice, and be found in another State, shall on Demand of the executive Authority of the State from which he fled, be delivered up, to be removed to the State having Jurisdiction of the Crime.

No Person held to Service or Labour in one State, under the Laws thereof, escaping into another, shall, in Consequence of any Law or Regulation therein, be discharged from such Service or Labour, but shall be delivered up on Claim of the Party to whom such Service or Labour may be due.

Section 3. New States may be admitted by the Congress into this Union; but no new State shall be formed or erected within the Jurisdiction of any other State; nor any State be formed by the Junction of two or more States, or Parts of States, without the Consent of the Legislatures of the States concerned as well as of the Congress.

The Congress shall have Power to dispose of and make all needful Rules and Regulations respecting the Territory or other Property belonging to the United States; and nothing in this Constitution shall be so construed to Prejudice any Claims of the United States, or of any particular State.

Section 4. The United States shall guarantee to every State in this Union a Republican Form of

Government, and shall protect each of them against Invasion; and on Application of the Legislature, or of the Executive (when the Legislature cannot be convened) against domestic Violence.

Article V

The Congress, whenever two thirds of both Houses shall deem it necessary, shall propose Amendments to this Constitution, or, on the Application of the Legislatures of two thirds of the several States, shall call a Convention for proposing Amendments, which, in either Case, shall be valid to all Intents and Purposes, as Part of this Constitution, when ratified by the Legislatures of three fourths of the several States, or by Conventions in three fourths thereof, as the one or the other Mode of Ratification may be proposed by the Congress; provided that no Amendment which may be made prior to the Year One thousand eight hundred and eight shall in any Manner affect the first and fourth Clauses in the Ninth Section of the first Article; and that no State, without its Consent, shall be deprived of its equal Suffrage in the Senate.

Article VI

All Debts contracted and Engagements entered into, before the adoption of this Constitution, shall be as valid against the United States under this Constitution, as under the Confederation.

This Constitution, and the Laws of the United States which shall be made in Pursuance thereof; and all Treaties made, or which shall be made, under the Authority of the United States, shall be the supreme Law of the Land; and the Judges in every State shall be bound thereby, any Thing in the Constitution or Laws of any State to the Contrary notwithstanding.

The Senators and Representatives before mentioned, and the members of the several State Legislatures, and all executive and judicial Officers, both of the United States and of the several States, shall be bound by Oath or Affirmation, to support this Constitution; but no religious Test shall ever be required as a Qualification to any Office or public Trust under the United States.

Article VII

The Ratification of the Conventions of nine States, shall be sufficient for the Establishment of this Constitution between the States so ratifying the Same.

Go. Washington — Presidt.

And deputy from Virginia

New Hampshire
John Langdon
Nicholas Gilman

Massachusetts

Nathaniel Gorham
Rufus King

Connecticut
Wm. Saml. Johnson
Roger Sherman

New Jersey
Wil: Livingston
David Brearley
Wm. Paterson
Jona: Dayton

Pennsylvania

B Franklin
Thomas Mifflin
Robt. Morris
Geo. Clymer
Thos. Fitzsimons
Jared Ingersoll
James Wilson

Introduction to Volume 5

New York
Alexander Hamilton
Delaware
Geo: Read
Cunning Bedford jun
John Dickinson
Richard Bassett
Jaco: Broom
Maryland
James McHenry
Dan of St. Thos. Jenifer
Danl. Carroll
Virginia
John Blair
James Madison Jr.

Gouv Morris

North Carolina
Wm: Blount.
Richd. Dobbs Spaight
· *Hu Williamson*

South Carolina
J. Rutledge
Charles Cotesworth Pinckney
Pierce Butler
Georgia
William Few
Abr Baldwin

Introduction to Volume 5

The Bill of Rights

(1791)

Amendment I

Congress shall make no law respecting an establishment of religion, or prohibiting the free exercise thereof; or abridging the freedom of speech, or of the press; or the right of the people peaceably to assemble, and to petition the government for a redress of grievances.

Amendment II

A well regulated militia, being necessary to the security of a free state, the right of the people to keep and bear arms, shall not be infringed.

Amendment III

No soldier shall, in time of peace be quartered in any house, without the consent of the owner, nor in time of war, but in a manner to be prescribed by law.

Amendment IV

The right of the people to be secure in their persons, houses, papers, and effects, against unreasonable searches and seizures, shall not be violated, and no warrants shall issue, but upon probable cause, supported by oath or affirmation, and particularly describing the place to be searched, and the persons or things to be seized.

Amendment V

No person shall be held to answer for a capital, or otherwise infamous crime, unless on a presentment or indictment of a grand jury, except in cases arising in the land or naval forces, or in the militia, when in actual service in time of war or public danger; nor shall any person be subject for the same offense to be twice put in jeopardy of life or limb; nor shall be compelled in any criminal case to be a witness against himself, nor be deprived of life, liberty, or property, without due process of law; nor shall private property be taken for public use, without just compensation.

Amendment VI

In all criminal prosecutions, the accused shall enjoy the right to a speedy and public trial, by an impartial jury of the state and district wherein the crime shall have been committed, which district shall have been previously ascertained by law, and to be informed of the nature and cause of the accusation; to be confronted with the witnesses against him; to have compulsory process for obtaining witnesses in his favor, and to have the assistance of counsel for his defense.

Amendment VII

In suits at common law, where the value in controversy shall exceed twenty dollars, the right of trial by jury shall be preserved, and no fact tried by a jury, shall be otherwise reexamined in any court of the United States, then according to the rules of the common law.

Amendment VIII

Excessive bail shall not be required, nor excessive fines imposed, nor cruel and unusual punishments inflicted.

Amendment IX

The enumeration in the Constitution, of certain rights, shall not be construed to deny or disparage others retained by the people.

Amendment X

The powers not delegated to the United States by the Constitution, nor prohibited by it to the states, are reserved to the states respectively, or to the people.

Later Amendments

Amendment XI

(1798)

The judicial power of the United States shall not be construed to extend to any suit in law or equity, commenced or prosecuted against one of the United States by Citizens of another State, or by Citizens or Subjects of any Foreign State.

Amendment XII

(1804)

The Electors shall meet in their respective states and vote by ballot for President and Vice-President, one of whom, at least, shall not be an inhabitant of the same state with themselves; they shall name in their ballots the person voted for as President, and in distinct ballots the person voted for as Vice-President, and they shall make distinct lists of all persons voted for as President, and of all persons voted for as Vice-President, and of the number of votes for each, which lists they shall sign and certify, and transmit sealed to the seat of the government of the United States, directed to the President of the Senate; — The President of the Senate shall, in the presence of the Senate and House of Representatives, open all the certificates and the votes shall then be counted; — the person having the greatest number of votes for President, shall be the President, if such number be a majority of the whole number of Electors appointed; and if no person have such majority, then from the persons having the highest numbers not exceeding three on the list of those voted for as President, the House of Representatives shall choose immediately, by ballot, the President. But in choosing the President, the votes shall be taken by states, the representation from each state having one vote; a quorum for this purpose shall consist of a member or members from two-thirds of the states, and a majority of all the states shall be necessary to a choice. And if the House of Representatives shall not choose a President whenever the right of choice shall devolve upon them, before the fourth day of March next following, then the Vice-President shall act as President, as in the case of the death or other constitutional disability of the President. The person having the greatest number of votes as Vice-President, shall be the Vice-President, if such number be a majority of the whole number of Electors appointed, and if no person have a majority, then from the two highest numbers on the list, the Senate shall choose the Vice-President; a quorum for the purpose shall consist of two-thirds of the whole number of Senators, and a majority of the whole number shall be necessary to a choice. But no person constitutionally ineligible to the office of President shall be eligible to that of Vice-President of the United States.

Amendment XIII

(1865)

Section 1. Neither slavery nor involuntary servitude, except as a punishment for crime whereof the party shall have been duly convicted, shall exist within the United States, or any place subject to their jurisdiction.

Section 2. Congress shall have power to enforce this article by appropriate legislation.

Amendment XIV

(1868)

Section 1. All persons born or naturalized in the United States, and subject to the jurisdiction thereof, are citizens of the United States and of the State wherein they reside. No State shall make or enforce any law which shall abridge the privileges or immunities of citizens of the United States; nor shall any State deprive any person of life, liberty, or property, without due process of law; nor deny to any person within its jurisdiction the equal protection of the laws.

Section 2. Representatives shall be apportioned among the several States according to their respective numbers, counting the whole number of persons in each State, excluding Indians not taxed. But when the right to vote at any election for the choice of electors for President and Vice President of the United States, Representatives in Congress, the Executive and Judicial.officers of a State, or the members of the Legislature thereof, is denied to any of the male inhabitants of such State, being twenty-one years of age, and citizens of the United States, or in any way abridged, except for participation in rebellion, or other crime, the basis of representation therein shall be reduced in the proportion which the number of such male citizens shall bear to the whole number of male citizens twenty-one years of age in such State.

Section 3. No person shall be a Senator or Representative in Congress, or elector of President and Vice President, or hold any office, civil or military, under the United States, or under any State, who, having previously taken an oath, as a member of Congress, or as an officer of the United States, or as a member of any State legislature, or as an executive or judicial officer of any State, to support the Constitution of the United States, shall have engaged in insurrection or rebellion against the same, or given aid or comfort to the enemies thereof. But Congress may by a vote of two-thirds of each House, remove such disability.

Section 4. The validity of the public debt of the United States, authorized by law, including debts incurred for payment of pensions and bounties for services in suppressing insurrection or rebellion, shall not be questioned. But neither the United States nor any State shall assume or pay any debt or obligation incurred in aid of insurrection or rebellion against the United States, or any claim for the loss or emancipation of any slave; but all such debts, obligations and claims shall be held illegal and void.

Section 5. The Congress shall have power to enforce, by appropriate legislation, the provisions of this article.

Amendment XV

(1870)

Section 1. The right of citizens of the United States to vote shall not be denied or abridged by the United States or by any State on account of race, color, or previous condition of servitude.

Section 2. The Congress shall have power to enforce this article by appropriate legislation.

Amendment XVI

(1913)

The Congress shall have power to lay and collect taxes on incomes, from whatever source derived, without apportionment among the several States, and without regard to any census or enumeration.

Amendment XVII

(1913)

The Senate of the United States shall be composed of two Senators from each State, elected by the people thereof, for six-years; and each Senator shall have one vote. The electors in each State shall have the qualifications requisite for electors of the most numerous branch of the State legislature.

When vacancies happen in the representation of any State in the Senate, the executive authority of such State shall issue writs of election to fill such vacancies: *Provided*, That the legislature of any State may empower the executive thereof to make temporary appointments until the people fill the vacancies by election as the legislature may direct.

This amendment shall not be so construed as to effect the election or term of any Senator chosen before it becomes valid as part of the Constitution.

Amendment XVIII

(1919)

Section 1. After one year from the ratification of this article the manufacture, sale, or transportation of intoxicating liquors within, the importation thereof into, or the exportation thereof from the United States and all territory subject to the jurisdiction thereof for beverage purposes is hereby prohibited.

Section 2. The Congress and the several States shall have concurrent power to enforce this article by appropriate legislation.

Section 3. This article shall be inoperative unless it shall have been ratified as an amendment to the Constitution by the legislatures of the several States, as provided in the Constitution, within seven years from the date of the submission hereof to the States by the Congress.

Amendment XIX

(1920)

The right of citizens of the United States to vote shall not be denied or abridged by the United States or by any State on account of sex.

Congress shall have power to enforce this article by appropriate legislation.

Amendment XX

(1933)

Section 1. The terms of the President and Vice President shall end at noon on the 20th day of January, and the terms of Senators and Representatives at noon on the 3d day of January, of the years in which such terms would have ended if this article had not been ratified; and the terms of their successors shall then begin.

Section 2. The Congress shall assemble at least once in every year, and such meeting shall begin at noon on the 3d day of January, unless they shall by law appoint a different day.

Section 3. If, at the time fixed for the beginning of the term of the President, the President elect shall have died, the Vice President elect shall become President. If a President shall not have been chosen before the time fixed for the beginning of his term, or if the President elect shall have failed to qualify, then the Vice President elect shall act as President until a President shall have qualified; and the Congress may by law provide for the case wherein neither a President elect nor a Vice President elect shall have qualified, declaring who shall then act as President, or the manner in which one who is to act shall be selected, and such person shall act accordingly until a President or Vice President shall have qualified.

Section 4. The Congress may by law provide for the case of the death of any of the persons from whom the House of Representatives may choose a President whenever the right of choice shall have devolved upon them, and for the case of the death of any of the persons from whom the Senate may choose a Vice President whenever the right of choice shall have devolved upon them.

Section 5. Sections 1 and 2 shall take effect on the 15th day of October following the ratification of this article.

Section 6. This article shall be inoperative unless it shall have been ratified as an amendment to the

Introduction to Volume 5

Constitution by the legislatures of three-fourths of the several States within seven years from the date of its submission.

Amendment XXI

(1933)

Section 1. The eighteenth article of amendment to the Constitution of the United States is hereby repealed.

Section 2. The transportation or importation into any State, territory, or possession of the United States for delivery or use therein of intoxicating liquors, in violation of the laws thereof, is hereby prohibited.

Section 3. This article shall be inoperative unless it shall have been ratified as an amendment to the Constitution by conventions in the several States, as provided in the Constitution, within seven years from the date of the submission hereof to the States by the Congress.

Amendment XXII

(1951)

Section 1. No person shall be elected to the office of the President more than twice, and no person who has held the office of President, or acted as President, for more than two years of a term to which some other person was elected President shall be elected to the office of the President more than once. But this article shall not apply to any person holding the office of President when this article was proposed by the Congress, and shall not prevent any person who may be holding the office of President, or acting as President, during the term within which this article becomes operative from holding the office of President or acting as President during the remainder of such term.

Section 2. This article shall be inoperative unless it shall have been ratified as an amendment to the Constitution by the legislatures of three-fourths of the several States within seven years from the date of its submission to the States by the Congress.

Amendment XXIII

(1961)

Section 1. The District constituting the seat of government of the United States shall appoint in such manner as the Congress may direct:

A number of electors of President and Vice President equal to the whole number of Senators and Representatives in Congress to which the District would be entitled if it were a State, but in no event more than the least populous State; they shall be in addition to those appointed by the States, but they shall be considered, for the purposes of the election of the President and Vice President, to be electors appointed by a State; and they shall meet in the District and perform such duties as provided by the twelfth article of amendment.

Section 2. The Congress shall have power to enforce this article by appropriate legislation.

Amendment XXIV

(1964)

Section 1. The right of citizens of the United States to vote in any primary or other election for President or Vice President, for electors for President or Vice President, or for Senator or Representative in Congress, shall not be denied or abridged by the United States or any State by reason of failure to pay any poll tax or other tax.

Section 2. The Congress shall have the power to enforce this article by appropriate legislation.

Introduction to Volume 5

Amendment XXV

(1967)

Section 1. In case of the removal of the President from office or his death or resignation, the Vice President shall become President.

Section 2. Whenever there is a vacancy in the office of the Vice President, the President shall nominate a Vice President who shall take office upon confirmation by a majority vote of both Houses of Congress.

Section 3. Whenever the President transmits to the President pro tempore of the Senate and the Speaker of the House of Representatives his written declaration that he is unable to discharge the powers and duties of his office, and until he transmits to them a written declaration to the contrary, such powers and duties shall be discharged by the Vice President as Acting President.

Section 4. Whenever the Vice President and a majority of either the principal officers of the executive departments or such other body as Congress may by law provide, transmit to the President pro tempore of the Senate and the Speaker of the House of Representatives their written declaration that the President is unable to discharge the powers and duties of his office, the Vice President shall immediately assume the powers and duties of the office as Acting President.

Thereafter, when the President transmits to the President pro tempore of the Senate and the Speaker of the House of Representatives his written declaration that no inability exists, he shall resume the powers and duties of his office unless the Vice President and a majority of either the principal officers of the executive department or of such other body as Congress may by law provide, transmit within four days to the President pro tempore of the Senate and the Speaker of the House of Representatives their written declaration that the President is unable to discharge the powers and duties of his office. Thereupon Congress shall decide the issue, assembling within forty-eight hours for that purpose if not in session. If the Congress, within twenty-one days after receipt of the latter written declaration, or, if Congress is not in session, within twenty-one days after Congress is required to assemble, determine by two-thirds vote of both Houses that the President is unable to discharge the powers and duties of his office, the Vice President shall continue to discharge the same as Acting President; otherwise, the President shall resume the powers and duties of his office.

Amendment XXVI

(1971)

Section 1. The right of citizens of the United States, who are 18 years of age or older, to vote, shall not be denied or abridged by the United States or any State on account of age.

Section 2. The Congress shall have the power to enforce this article by appropriate legislation.

Amendment XXVII

(1992)

No law varying the compensation for the services of the Senators and Representatives shall take effect until an election of Representatives shall have intervened.

Chapter 1

THE STATE ACTION DOCTRINE

A. INTRODUCTION

There is no specific provision in the Constitution labeled the "State Action Clause." Instead, the State Action Doctrine is drawn from a number of constitutional provisions, applied in numerous cases, and rooted in a fundamental presupposition of American government.[1]

The State Action Doctrine is the foundational legal rule that the Constitution only applies to the government and governmental actors. Therefore, the State Action Doctrine precludes application of the Constitution to private parties. For example, if a private employer fired an employee based on the employee's out-of-workplace advocacy of a political candidate that the employer opposed, the Constitution would not apply.

EXERCISE 1:

Apply the first four forms of argument to the State Action Doctrine.

1. Looking at the Constitution's text, can you discern the textual "hooks" of the State Action Doctrine?

2. Looking at the Constitution's structure, what do you learn about the State Action Doctrine?

3. Reviewing evidence of the Constitution's original meaning, what does it tell you about the Doctrine?

4. Do the materials following adoption of the Constitution offer any insight into the Doctrine?

———

The State Action Doctrine is relatively uncontroversial, though there is significant debate over the scope of the Doctrine and its exceptions. The Doctrine is also relatively stable though, again, internal tensions within the exceptions open the possibility for future instability.

In the Supreme Court's modern case law, there are two major exceptions that play a crucial role in State Action Doctrine litigation. The first is the Public Functions

---

[1] Even though it is labeled the *State* Action Doctrine, the label applies to doctrines that govern both the federal and state (and local) governments and governmental actors.

Exception; the second is the Entanglement Exception. We will address each in turn, after reviewing the State Action Doctrine itself.

As you read the materials below, some of the issues to consider include:

What is the State Action Doctrine?

Which of the first four forms of argument — text, structure, original meaning, and post-ratification materials — support the Doctrine as constitutionally required?

What or who comes under the Doctrine's purview?

What are the reasons for or purposes of the Doctrine?

What are the exceptions to the State Action Doctrine?

From what source(s) do these exceptions arise?

What are the reasons for the exceptions? Do these reasons undercut the existence of the State Action Doctrine in the first place?

What tensions exist *within* the exceptions?

Are the exceptions appropriately articulated by the Supreme Court? Should one or both be broader or narrower? Why?

B. ORIGINAL MEANING OF THE STATE ACTION DOCTRINE

Unlike other provisions of the Constitution that you have studied, the State Action Doctrine does not originate from a particular constitutional provision. The Doctrine was a fundamental presupposition of the Constitution's Framers and Ratifiers in 1787–1789. For this reason, it is difficult to identify statements, discussions, or arguments that directly evidence the Doctrine during the Framing and Ratification of the original Constitution. In other words, the fact that the Constitution would apply only to the government was a fact so well known and undisputed, that it was rarely raised, much less discussed at length.

Numerous constitutional provisions in the original Constitution exemplify the State Action Doctrine. Surveying the original Constitution, one finds that the Constitution identifies, empowers, and limits the Federal and, to a lesser degree, the state governments. For example, Article I, § 2, cl. 1, identifies the federal House of Representatives. Article I, § 1, cl. 1, empowers the Congress to exercise "[a]ll legislative Powers herein granted." Section 9 then lists a number of limits on congressional power. U.S. Const. art. I, § 9.[2] This same pattern occurs for the President and federal judiciary. In each instance, the Constitution does not speak to private actors.

---

[2] The enumeration of powers in Section 8 also limits congressional power by granting Congress authority only in the enumerated areas.

The Reconstruction Amendments, however, are a different matter. Though the Fourteenth Amendment explicitly limited the "State[s']" ability to, for instance, "deprive any person of life, liberty, or property, without due process of law," U.S. CONST. amend. XIV, § 1, it also contained provisions not limited to state action. For instance, Section 1 affirmed that all "persons born or naturalized in the United States . . . are citizens of the United States." *Id.* § 1. Moreover, though the Equal Protection Clause prohibits "State[s]" from "deny[ing] to any person . . . the equal protection of the laws," such denial would occur when a state affirmatively acts and *fails* to enforce its laws equally. For instance, failing to enforce homicide statutes equally against black and white perpetrators would constitute denial of equal protection even though the only "action" was state *in*action.[3] As explained by Republican Senator Pool, when arguing in favor of the Civil Rights Act of 1871, "[t]he protection of the laws can hardly be denied except by failure to execute them."[4]

During congressional debates over the Reconstruction Amendments, and legislation passed pursuant to them, congressmen occasionally debated whether the Amendments limited private action, in addition to state action, and whether the federal government could regulate state action under the Amendments' enforcement provisions.[5] There is an enormous and enormously complex scholarly literature covering this issue, which is beyond the scope of this Introduction.[6]

There is evidence that the Fourteenth Amendment limited state *and* private conduct. Representative John Farnsworth articulated this motive when he stated: "Why, sir, we all know . . . that the reason for the adoption of this [Fourteenth] amendment was because of the partial, discriminating, and unjust legislation of those States under governments set up by Andrew Johnson, by which they were punishing and oppressing one class of men under different laws from another class."[7] Congress adopted the Fourteenth Amendment in response to, among other things, the pervasive private violence occurring in the South against newly-freed black Americans, and white Americans with Union loyalties.[8] This private violence was actively assisted and not punished by states.

Furthermore, Reconstruction legislation indicated that Congress believed it had the authority to regulate private conduct under the Reconstruction Amendments' enforcement provisions. For instance, the Civil Rights Act of 1866, 14 Stat. 27, § 1 (1866), the Force Act of 1870, 16 Stat. 140, § 4 (1870), the Civil Rights Act of 1871, 17 Stat. 13, § 2

---

[3] Michael P. Zuckert, *Congressional Power Under the Fourteenth Amendment — The Original Understanding of Section Five*, 3 CONST. COMMENT. 123, 142 (1986).

[4] CONG. GLOBE, 42d Cong., 1st Sess. 608 (Apr. 12, 1871) (statement of Senator John Pool).

[5] The Thirteenth Amendment, adopted in 1865, explicitly regulated private conduct.

[6] For further reading, see, e.g., Zuckert, *supra*, at 123 (arguing that the Fourteenth Amendment also applied to state inaction).

[7] CONG. GLOBE, 42d Cong., 1st Sess. 116 (Mar. 31, 1871) (statement of Rep. John Farnsworth).

[8] Michael Kent Curtis, *The Fourteenth Amendment: Recalling What the Court Forgot*, 56 DRAKE L. REV. 911, 917–27 (2008); *see also id.* at 942 ("From the 1850s through the Fourteenth Amendment debates, Republicans and others protested private violence that had been used to silence anti-slavery and Republican speech, press, petition, assembly, and religious expression.").

(1871), and the Civil Rights Act of 1875, 18 Stat. 335, § 1 (1875), all limited private action.

The most significant congressional debate over the State Action Doctrine occurred over the proposed 1871 Civil Rights Act. Known as the Ku Klux Klan Act, it was the congressional Republicans' response to depredations performed by private individuals, such as Klan members, with either the active support by, or inactive acquiescence of, southern states. The Act prohibited private action including, for example, private conspiracies to violate federal rights. The Civil Rights Act of 1871, 17 Stat. 13, § 2 (1871).

Congressmen debated whether Section 5 of the Fourteenth Amendment authorized this. An important piece of evidence in favor of the view that the Fourteenth Amendment authorized federal regulation of private conduct via the Fourteenth Amendment is that all the congressional Republicans who had voted in favor of the Fourteenth Amendment also voted for the Ku Klux Klan Act.[9] For example, Representative Garfield, who voted for both, stated that:

> [T]he chief complaint is not that the laws of the State are unequal, but that even where the laws are just and equal on their face, yet, by a systematic maladministration of them, or a neglect or refusal to enforce their provisions, a portion of the people are denied equal protection under them. Whenever such a state of facts is clearly made out, I believe the last clause of the first section [of the Fourteenth Amendment] empowers Congress to step in and provide for doing justice to those persons who are thus denied equal protection.[10]

At the same time, there was also a congressional consensus that the Reconstruction Amendments did not completely displace states and upend federalism.[11] Instead, states remained the primary source of law and Congress would step in to protect constitutional rights when states failed to do so.[12] For instance, Congressman Burton Cook, when defending the 1871 Civil Rights Act, argued that Congress had the authority to "protect and enforce every right secured to American citizens by the Constitution of the United States," but he did "not believe . . . that Congress has a right to punish an assault and battery when committed by two or more persons within a State."[13] Cook went on to say that Congress could supplant state protection of constitutional rights only when the states failed to do so.[14]

While most scholars believe that the original Constitution limited only federal and state governmental action, there is significant scholarly debate over whether the

---

[9] Zuckert, *supra*, at 148.

[10] CONG. GLOBE, 42d Cong., 1st Sess. 153 (Apr. 4, 1871) (statement of Rep. James Garfield).

[11] *See* Curtis, *supra*, at 947 (describing this consensus).

[12] *See* Zuckert, *supra*, at 141 ("Bingham did not . . . believe that the national power must supplant the states in their ordinary custody of these national principles.").

[13] CONG. GLOBE, 42d Cong., 1st Sess. 485 (Apr. 5, 1871) (statement of Rep. Burton Cook).

[14] *Id.*

Fourteenth Amendment authorized Congress to restrict private action under Section 1 of the Fourteenth Amendment.[15]

EXERCISE 2:

1.   What does this history tell us about the State Action Doctrine's meaning and scope, along with any potential exceptions?

2.   Does this history provide additional explanatory power to the State Action Doctrine's "textual hooks," or does it make the situation more murky?

3.   Why would there be less Framing and Ratification Era discussion of the State Action Doctrine than of other constitutional provisions, such as the Commerce Clause? Does this variability of the existence of historical evidence lessen the value of history to constitutional interpretation?

Below, we will review the Supreme Court's foundational articulation of the State Action Doctrine, followed by exceptions to the Doctrine.

C.   THE SEMINAL CASE

The Civil Rights Cases, 109 U.S. 3 (1883), is the foundational Supreme Court statement of the State Action Doctrine. The State Action Doctrine that it articulated is relatively uncontroversial today, though the fact that it is subject to exceptions shows that the Doctrine remains potentially in tension with other constitutional commitments.

THE CIVIL RIGHTS CASES
UNITED STATES v. STANLEY
109 U.S. 3 (1883)

BRADLEY, J.

[I]

These cases are all founded on the first and second sections of the act of congress known as the 'Civil Rights Act'. Two of the cases are indictments for denying to persons of color the accommodations and privileges of an inn or hotel; two of them are for denying to individuals the privileges and accommodations of a theater, 'said denial not being made for any reasons by law applicable to citizens of every race and color, and regardless of any previous condition of servitude.'

---

[15] *Compare* MICHAEL KENT CURTIS, NO STATE SHALL ABRIDGE: THE FOURTEENTH AMENDMENT AND THE BILL OF RIGHTS 158 (1986) ("[I]n 1871 most Republicans thought that when states failed to provide adequate protection, Congress could supply it by laws operating directly on private individuals."), *with* RAOUL BERGER, GOVERNMENT BY JUDICIARY: THE TRANSFORMATION OF THE FOURTEENTH AMENDMENT 213–20 (2d ed. 1997) (arguing that the State Action Doctrine was faithful to the Framers' vision of the Fourteenth Amendment).

The [first] section of the law referred to provide[s] as follows: 'Section 1. That all persons within the jurisdiction of the United States shall be entitled to the full and equal enjoyment of the accomodations, advantages, facilities, and privileges of inns, public conveyances on land or water, theaters, and other places of public amusement; subject only to the conditions and limitations established by law, and applicable alike to citizens of every race and color, regardless of any previous condition of servitude.'

[II]

Has congress constitutional power to make such a law? Of course, no one will contend that the power to pass it was contained in the constitution before the adoption of the last three amendments. The power is sought in the fourteenth amendment, and the views and arguments of distinguished senators, advanced while the law was under consideration, claiming authority to pass it by virtue of that amendment, are the principal arguments adduced in favor of the power. We have carefully considered those arguments, as was due to the eminent ability of those who put them forward, and have felt, in all its force, the weight of authority which always invests a law that congress deems itself competent to pass. But the responsibility of an independent judgment is now thrown upon this court; and we are bound to exercise it according to the best lights we have.

The first section of the fourteenth amendment is prohibitory in its character, and prohibitory upon the states. It declares that 'no state shall make or enforce any law which shall abridge the privileges or immunities of citizens of the United States; nor shall any state deprive any person of life, liberty, or property without due process of law; nor deny to any person within its jurisdiction the equal protection of the laws.' It is state action of a particular character that is prohibited. Individual invasion of individual rights is not the subject-matter of the amendment. It has a deeper and broader scope. It nullifies and makes void all state legislation, and state action of every kind, which impairs the privileges and immunities of citizens of the United States, or which injures them in life, liberty, or property without due process of law, or which denies to any of them the equal protection of the laws.

It not only does this, but, in order that the national will, thus declared, may not be a mere *brutum fulmen*, the last section of the amendment invests congress with power to enforce it by appropriate legislation. To enforce what? To enforce the prohibition. To adopt appropriate legislation for correcting the effects of such prohibited state law and state acts, and thus to render them effectually null, void, and innocuous. This is the legislative power conferred upon congress, and this is the whole of it. It does not invest congress with power to legislate upon subjects which are within the domain of state legislation; but to provide modes of relief against state legislation, or state action, of the kind referred to. It does not authorize congress to create a code of municipal law for the regulation of private rights; but to provide modes of redress against the operation of state laws, and the action of state officers, executive or judicial, when these are subversive of the fundamental rights specified in the amendment. Positive rights and privileges are undoubtedly secured by the fourteenth amendment; but they are secured by way of prohibition against state laws and state proceedings affecting those rights and privileges, and by power given to congress to legislate for the purpose of carrying such prohibition into effect; and such legislation must necessarily be predicated upon such supposed state laws or state proceedings, and be directed to the correction of their operation and effect.

And so in the present case, until some state law has been passed, or some state action through its officers or agents has been taken, adverse to the rights of citizens sought to be protected by the fourteenth amendment, no legislation of the United States under said amendment, nor any proceeding under such legislation, can be called into activity. Of course, legislation may and should be provided in advance to meet the exigency when it arises, but it should be adapted to the mischief and wrong which the amendment was intended to provide against; and that is, state laws or state action of some kind adverse to the rights of the citizen secured by the amendment.

Such legislation cannot properly cover the whole domain of rights appertaining to life, liberty, and property, defining them and providing for their vindication. That would be to establish a code of municipal law regulative of all private rights between man and man in society. It would be to make congress take the place of the state legislatures and to supersede them. In fine, the legislation which congress is authorized to adopt in this behalf is not general legislation upon the rights of the citizen, but corrective legislation . . . .

[III]

An inspection of the law shows that it makes no reference whatever to any supposed or apprehended violation of the fourteenth amendment on the part of the states. It proceeds *ex directo* to declare that certain acts committed by individuals shall be deemed offenses, and shall be prosecuted and punished by proceedings in the courts of the United States. It does not profess to be corrective of any constitutional wrong committed by the states. It applies equally to cases arising in states which have the justest laws respecting the personal rights of citizens, and whose authorities are ever ready to enforce such laws as to those which arise in states that may have violated the prohibition of the amendment. In other words, it steps into the domain of local jurisprudence, and lays down rules for the conduct of individuals in society towards each other, and imposes sanctions for the enforcement of those rules, without referring in any manner to any supposed action of the state or its authorities.

If this legislation is appropriate for enforcing the prohibitions of the amendment, it is difficult to see where it is to stop. Why may not congress, with equal show of authority, enact a code of laws for the enforcement and vindication of all rights of life, liberty, and property? The truth is that the implication of a power to legislate in this manner is based upon the assumption that if the states are forbidden to legislate or act in a particular way on a particular subject, and power is conferred upon congress to enforce the prohibition, this gives congress power to legislate generally upon that subject, and not merely power to provide modes of redress against such state legislation or action. The assumption is certainly unsound. It is repugnant to the tenth amendment of the constitution, which declares that powers not delegated to the United States by the constitution, nor prohibited by it to the states, are reserved to the states respectively or to the people.

In this connection it is proper to state that civil rights, such as are guarantied by the constitution against state aggression, cannot be impaired by the wrongful acts of individuals, unsupported by state authority in the shape of laws, customs, or judicial or executive proceedings. The wrongful act of an individual, unsupported by any such authority, is simply a private wrong, or a crime of that individual; an invasion of the rights of the injured party, it is true, whether they affect his person, his property, or his reputation; but if not sanctioned in some way by the state, or not done under state authority, his rights remain in full force, and may presumably be vindicated by resort to the laws of the state for redress. An individual cannot deprive a man of his right to vote, to hold property, to buy and to sell, to sue in the courts, or to be a witness or a juror; he may, by force or fraud, interfere with the enjoyment of the right in a particular case; he may commit an assault against the person, or commit murder, or use ruffian violence at the polls, or slander the good name of a fellow-citizen; but unless protected in these wrongful acts by some shield of state law or state authority, he cannot destroy or injure the right; he will only render himself amenable to satisfaction or punishment; and amenable therefor to the laws of the state where the wrongful acts are committed.

HARLAN, J., *dissenting*.

[I]

The substance and spirit of the recent amendments of the constitution have been sacrificed by a subtle and ingenious verbal criticism. 'It is not the words of the law but the internal sense of it that makes the law. The letter of the law is the body; the sense and reason of the law is the soul.' Constitutional provisions, adopted in the interest of liberty, and for the purpose of securing, through national legislation, if need be, rights inhering in a state of freedom, and belonging to American citizenship, have been so construed as to defeat the ends the people desired to accomplish, which they attempted to accomplish, and which they supposed they had accomplished by changes in their fundamental law. By this I mean only to express an earnest conviction that the court has departed from the familiar rule requiring, in the interpretation of constitutional provisions, that full effect be given to the intent with which they were adopted.

Before the adoption of the recent amendments it had become the established doctrine of this court that negroes, whose ancestors had been imported and sold as slaves, could not become citizens of a state, or even of the United States. Still further, between the adoption of the thirteenth amendment and the proposal by congress of the fourteenth amendment, on June 16, 1866, the statute-books of several of the states had become loaded down with enactments which, under the guise of apprentice, vagrant, and contract regulations, sought to keep the colored race in a condition, practically, of servitude. To meet this new peril to the black race, that the purposes of the nation might not be doubted or defeated, and by way of further enlargement of the power of congress, the fourteenth amendment was proposed for adoption.

The assumption that this amendment consists wholly of prohibitions upon state laws and state proceedings in hostility to its provisions, is unauthorized by its language. The first clause of the first section is of a distinctly affirmative character. In its application to the colored race, previously liberated, it created and granted, as well citizenship of the United States, as citizenship of the state in which they respectively resided.

The citizenship thus acquired by that race, in virtue of an affirmative grant by the nation, may be protected, not alone by the judicial branch of the government, but by congressional legislation of a primary direct character; this, because the power of congress is not restricted to the enforcement of prohibitions upon state laws or state action. It is, in terms distinct and positive, to enforce 'the *provisions* of *this article*' of amendment; not simply those of a prohibitive character, but the provisions, — *all* of the provisions, — affirmative and prohibitive, of the amendment. If any right was created by that amendment, the grant of power, through appropriate legislation, to enforce its provisions authorizes congress, by means of legislation operating throughout the entire Union, to guard, secure, and protect that right.

It is, therefore, an essential inquiry what, if any, right, privilege, or immunity was given by the nation to colored persons when they were made citizens of the state in which they reside? There is one, if there be no others — exemption from race discrimination in respect of any civil right belonging to citizens of the white race in the same state. [S]uch must be their constitutional right, in their own state, unless the recent amendments be 'splendid baubles,' thrown out to delude those who deserved fair and generous treatment at the hands of the nation. Citizenship in this country necessarily imports equality of civil rights among citizens of every race in the same state.

If, then, exemption from discrimination in respect of civil rights is a new constitutional right, secured by the grant of state citizenship to colored citizens of the United States, why may not the nation, by means of its own legislation of a primary direct character, guard, protect, and enforce that right? It is a right and privilege which the nation conferred. It did not come from the states in which those colored citizens reside.

This court has always given a broad and liberal construction to the constitution, so as to enable congress, by legislation, to enforce rights secured by that instrument. The legislation congress may enact, in execution of its power to enforce the provisions of this amendment, is that which is appropriate to protect the right granted. Under given circumstances, that which the court characterizes as corrective legislation might be sufficient. Under other circumstances primary direct legislation may be required. But it is for congress, not the judiciary, to say which is best adapted to the end to be attained. 'Let the end be legitimate, — let it be within the scope of the constitution, — and all means which are appropriate, which are plainly adapted to that end, which are not prohibited, but consistent with the letter and spirit of the constitution, are constitutional.' *McCulloch v. Maryland*, [17 U.S. (4 Wheat.) 316 (1819)].

[II]

It was perfectly well known that the great danger to the equal enjoyment by citizens of their rights, as citizens, was to be apprehended, not altogether from unfriendly state legislation, but from the hostile action of corporations and individuals in the states. And it is to be presumed that it was intended, by that section, to clothe congress with power and authority to meet that danger. If the rights intended to be secured by the act of 1875 are such as belong to the citizen, in common or equally with other citizens in the same state, then it is not to be denied that such legislation is appropriate to the end which congress is authorized to accomplish, viz., to protect the citizen, in respect of such rights, against discrimination on account of his race.

There has been adverse state action within the fourteenth amendment. In every material sense applicable to the practical enforcement of the fourteenth amendment, railroad corporations, keepers of inns, and managers of places of public amusement are agents of the state, because amenable, in respect of their public duties and functions, to public regulation. It seems to me that a denial by these instrumentalities of the state to the citizen, because of his race, of that equality of civil rights secured to him by law, is a denial by the state within the meaning of the fourteenth amendment. If it be not, then that race is left, in respect of the civil rights under discussion, practically at the mercy of corporations and individuals wielding power under public authority.

For the reasons stated I feel constrained to withhold my assent to the opinion of the court.

EXERCISE 3:

1. What arguments did the Court use to support its conclusion that the Fourteenth Amendment applied only to "state action"?

2. The Court suggested that Congress had the authority under Section 5 to enact "corrective" legislation; what did the Court have in mind?

3. Construct an argument that, by a failure to proscribe private, racially discriminatory conduct, states met the State Action Doctrine's requirements.

4. Later, in **Chapter 2**, you will read *The Slaughter-Houses Cases*, 83 U.S. (16 Wall.) 36, 39 (1872). Compare the reasons for its holding given by the Court eleven years earlier in that case. What similar arguments did the Court make?

5. The Supreme Court drew a line between private conduct — that the Fourteenth Amendment did not proscribe — and state action. What is the line the Court drew? What rule or factors did the Court identify to aid application of the distinction?

6. What meaning did the Court give to Section 5 of the Fourteenth Amendment?

7. The Court stated: "We have carefully considered those arguments, as was due to the eminent ability of those who put them forward, and have felt, in all its force, the weight of authority which always invests a law that congress deems itself competent to pass." What weight, if any, did the majority give to Congress' constitutional judgment? De minimis? Significant? Determinative? What is the right amount of weight to give a congressional constitutional judgment?

8. Articulate criticisms of the State Action Doctrine.

9. Explain the State Action Doctrine's possible virtues.

10. Relatedly, from the perspective of a proponent of the State Action Doctrine, what would be some of the negative consequences of *not* having the Doctrine?

11. The Court noted, elsewhere in its opinion, that Congress could directly control private conduct through its other powers, such as the Commerce Clause. Congress has frequently resorted to this avenue to do just that. For example, Congress passed the 1964 Civil Rights Act pursuant to its Commerce Clause powers. The Civil Rights Act of 1964, Pub. L. No. 88-352, 78 Stat. 241, § 201(c). This facet of Congress' Commerce Clause authority was covered in Volume 3.

12. The majority utilized a "slippery-slope" argument to claim that, if Congress had the authority under Section 5 to enact the challenged law, then Congress could totally displace states. This argument has been and continues to be used in many doctrinal areas, especially in the Commerce Clause and Tenth Amendment contexts. The Supreme Court will advance an interpretation of the scope of Congress' powers, and then bolster that interpretation by resort to the "slippery-slope." *See, e.g., United States v. Lopez*, 514 U.S. 549, 564 (1995) ("Under the theories that the Government presents . . . , it is difficult to perceive any limitation on federal power, even in areas such as criminal law enforcement or education where States historically have been sovereign. Thus, if we were to accept the Government's arguments, we are hard pressed to posit any activity by an individual that Congress is without power to regulate.").

13. What did Justice Harlan mean when he referred to the "letter" and the "spirit" of a law? How are they different? Is it a real distinction? Is it legitimate for judges to employ it?

14. Justice Harlan argued that the Court's interpretation of the Fourteenth Amendment — as limited to authorizing Congress to proscribe only state action — frustrated the American People's intent. In what way? Is he correct? If so, what follows?

15. Why did the majority not review the legislative history of the Fourteenth Amendment? Does its failure to do so undermine its ruling?

16. Justice Harlan relied on the Fourteenth Amendment's text to rebut the majority's claim that Congress' power was limited to prohibiting illegal state action. Articulate Justice Harlan's argument. Are you persuaded?

17. Justice Harlan contended that, when it comes to the issue of what means Congress may utilize to "enforce" the Fourteenth Amendment, "it is for congress, not the judiciary, to say which is best adapted to the end to be attained." Is that true? Why? Are there any limits to Justice Harlan's reasoning?

18. Justice Harlan claimed that one reason to reject the majority's interpretation was that it would lead to the Fourteenth Amendment having little or no legal impact. Is that true? Has the Fourteenth Amendment had little impact because of its limitation to state action?

19. As we will see, one of the exceptions to the State Action Doctrine is the Public Functions Exception. In short, this exception states that private action is state action, for purposes of the Constitution, when the private party is performing a "public

function." Justice Harlan articulated this exception (though it was not called that until much later). Describe Justice Harlan's use of the exception.

Since *The Civil Rights Cases*, the State Action Doctrine has remained a fundamental facet of American constitutional law. *See* James M. McGoldrick, The Civil Rights Cases: *The Relevancy of Reversing a Hundred Plus Year Old Error*, 42 St. Louis U. L.J. 451, 464–66 (1998) (providing reasons why *The Civil Rights Cases* have retained viability). The primary debate has been, and continues to be, whether and to what extent exceptions to the Doctrine should exist. We turn to that subject, below.

D. EXCEPTIONS TO THE STATE ACTION DOCTRINE

The sole textual exception to the State Action Doctrine is the Thirteenth Amendment, which has had relatively infrequent invocation. As a result, the State Action Doctrine remained a powerful limit on the Fourteenth Amendment's scope until the early twentieth century, when the Supreme Court began slowly to articulate exceptions to the Doctrine.

The Court's creation and expansion of exceptions grew dramatically during the Warren Court, leading prominent scholars to speculate that the Court would overrule *The Civil Rights Cases. See, e.g.*, Charles L. Black, Jr., *Foreword: "State Action," Equal Protection, and California's Proposition 14*, 81 Harv. L. Rev. 69, 84–91 (1967) (describing how the Supreme Court had significantly undermined the Doctrine). However, in the early 1970s, the Supreme Court initiated a trend of restricting the exceptions. This trend continued through the 1980s. We will not cover the complex evolution of the Supreme Court's case law in detail. For more information on the evolution of the State Action Doctrine and its exceptions, see G. Sidney Buchanan, *A Conceptual History of the State Action Doctrine: The Search for Governmental Responsibility*, 34 Hous. L. Rev. 333 (1997); G. Sidney Buchanan, *A Conceptual History of the State Action Doctrine: The Search for Governmental Responsibility*, 34 Hous. L. Rev. 665 (1997); Terri Peretti, *Constructing the State Action Doctrine: 1940–1990*, 35 Law & Soc. Inquiry 273 (2010).

Today, there are two fairly firmly entrenched, precedent-based exceptions to the State Action Doctrine. The first, the Public Functions Exception, is relatively narrow in scope, and has remained relatively unchanged since *Jackson v. Metro Edison*, 419 U.S. 345 (1974), reprinted below.

The other exception, frequently labeled the Entanglement Exception, though narrowed during the 1970s, has experienced greater variability. This unsettledness is best exemplified by *Brentwood Acad. v. Tennessee Secondary Sch. Athletic Ass'n*, 531 U.S. 288 (2001), which is discussed in the notes at the end of this **Chapter**.

As you review the material below, determine whether the exceptions to the State Action Doctrine carved out by the Supreme Court are faithful interpretations of the Constitution, and whether they are articulated at the appropriate level of breadth.

1. The Thirteenth Amendment

The Thirteenth Amendment was ratified in 1865. Its prohibition on "slavery" and "involuntary servitude" applies to both governmental and private parties. *Jones v. Alfred H. Mayer Co.*, 392 U.S. 409, 413 (1968). Because the Thirteenth Amendment's application to private actors is infrequently litigated, we will not discuss it further.

2. The Public Functions Exception

The Supreme Court, in a series of cases beginning with *Nixon v. Condon*, 286 U.S. 73 (1932), began to limit the State Action Doctrine with an exception that today is known as the Public Functions Exception. Not surprisingly, these early cases involved challenged activity that was closely intertwined with paradigmatically state activity, such as the operation of elections, which was at issue in *Nixon*.

The most important of these early cases was *Marsh v. Alabama*, 326 U.S. 501 (1946). There, Marsh challenged, on First and Fourteenth Amendment free speech grounds, her arrest for trespass. She proselytized in violation of a company-owned town's prohibition. Alabama prosecuted Marsh for criminal trespass. The State argued that there was no state action since the company was a private party not subject to the Fourteenth Amendment. The Supreme Court ruled that the First and Fourteenth Amendments applied because operation of a town is a state activity.

The Court continued to expand the Public Functions Exception's scope until 1972, when the Court reversed course and began narrowing the exceptions. *See Lloyd Corp. v. Tanner*, 407 U.S. 551 (1972) (ruling that a private shopping center was not a state actor); *Moose Lodge No. 107 v. Irvis*, 407 U.S. 163 (1972) (ruling that a private fraternal organization was not a state actor). Below is the key case defining the Exception's scope today.

JACKSON v. METROPOLITAN EDISON COMPANY
419 U.S. 345 (1974)

Mr. Justice Rehnquist delivered the opinion of the Court.

Respondent Metropolitan Edison Co. is a privately owned and operated Pennsylvania corporation which holds a certificate of public convenience issued by the Pennsylvania Public Utility Commission empowering it to deliver electricity to a service area which includes the city of York, Pa. As a condition of holding its certificate, it is subject to extensive regulation by the Commission. Under a provision of its general tariff filed with the Commission, it has the right to discontinue service to any customer on reasonable notice of nonpayment of bills.

Petitioner Catherine Jackson is a resident of York, who has received electricity in the past from respondent. Until September 1970, petitioner received electric service to her home in York under an account with respondent in her own name. When her account was terminated because of asserted delinquency in payments due for service, a new account with respondent was opened in the name of one James Dodson, another occupant of the residence, and service to the residence was resumed. There is a dispute as to whether payments due under the Dodson account for services provided during this period were ever made. In August 1971, Dodson left the residence. Service continued thereafter but concededly no payments were made. Petitioner states that no bills were received during this period.

On October 6, 1971, employees of Metropolitan came to the residence and inquired as to Dodson's present address. Petitioner stated that it was unknown to her. On the following day, another employee visited the residence and informed petitioner that the meter had been tampered with so as not to register amounts used. She disclaimed knowledge of this and requested that the service account for her home be shifted from Dodson's name to that of the Robert Jackson, later identified as her 12-year-old son. Four days later on October 11, 1971, without further notice to petitioner, Metropolitan employees disconnected her service.

Petitioner then filed suit against Metropolitan in the United States District Court for the Middle District of Pennsylvania under the Civil Rights Act of 1871, 42 U.S.C. § 1983, seeking damages for the termination and an injunction requiring Metropolitan to continue providing power to her residence until she had been afforded notice, a hearing, and an opportunity to pay any amounts found due. She urged that Metropolitan's termination of her service for alleged nonpayment, action allowed by a provision of its general tariff filed with the Commission, constituted "state action" depriving her of property in violation of the Fourteenth Amendment's guarantee of due process of law.

The District Court granted Metropolitan's motion to dismiss petitioner's complaint on the ground that the termination did not constitute state action and hence was not subject to judicial scrutiny under the Fourteenth Amendment. On appeal, the United States Court of Appeals for the Third Circuit affirmed, also finding an absence of state action.

The Due Process Clause of the Fourteenth Amendment provides: "[N]or shall any State deprive any person of life, liberty, or property, without due process of law." In 1883, this Court in the *Civil Rights Cases*, 109 U.S. 3 [(1883)], affirmed the essential dichotomy set forth in that Amendment between deprivation by the State, subject to scrutiny under its provisions, and private conduct, "however discriminatory or wrongful," against which the Fourteenth Amendment offers no shield. *Shelley v. Kraemer*, 335 U.S. 1 (1948).

We have reiterated that distinction on more than one occasion since then. *See, e.g., Moose Lodge No. 107 v. Irvis*, 407 U.S. 163 (1972). While the principle that private action is immune from the restrictions of the Fourteenth Amendment is well established and easily stated, the question whether particular conduct is "private," on the one hand, or "state action," on the other, frequently admits of no easy answer. *Burton v. Wilmington Parking Authority*, 365 U.S. 715 (1961); *Moose Lodge No. 107 v. Irvis*, 407 U.S. at 172.

Petitioner urges that state action is present because respondent provides an essential public service required to be supplied on a reasonably continuous basis by Pa.

Stat. Ann., Tit. 66, s 1171 (1959), and hence performs a "public function." We have, of course, found state action present in the exercise by a private entity of powers traditionally exclusively reserved to the State. *See, e.g., Nixon v. Condon,* 286 U.S. 73 (1932) (election); *Terry v. Adams,* 345 U.S. 461 (1953) (election); *Marsh v. Alabama,* 326 U.S. 501 (1946) (company town); *Evans v. Newton,* 382 U.S. 296 (1966) (municipal park). If we were dealing with the exercise by Metropolitan of some power delegated to it by the State which is traditionally associated with sovereignty, such as eminent domain, our case would be quite a different one. But while the Pennsylvania statute imposes an obligation to furnish service on regulated utilities, it imposes no such obligation on the State. The Pennsylvania courts have rejected the contention that the furnishing of utility services is either a state function or a municipal duty.

Perhaps in recognition of the fact that the supplying of utility service is not traditionally the exclusive prerogative of the State, petitioner invites the expansion of the doctrine of this limited line of cases into a broad principle that all businesses "affected with the public interest" are state actors in all their actions. Doctors, optometrists, lawyers, [and] Metropolitan are all in regulated businesses, providing arguably essential goods and services, "affected with a public interest." We do not believe that such a status converts their every action, absent more, into that of the State.[16]

We conclude that the State of Pennsylvania is not sufficiently connected with respondent's action in terminating petitioner's service so as to make respondent's conduct in so doing attributable to the State for purposes of the Fourteenth Amendment. The judgment of the Court of Appeals for the Third Circuit is therefore

Affirmed.

MR. JUSTICE DOUGLAS, dissenting. [Opinion omitted.]

MR. JUSTICE BRENNAN, dissenting [Opinion omitted.]

MR. JUSTICE MARSHALL, dissenting.

I

C

The fact that the Metropolitan Edison Co. supplies an essential public service that is in many communities supplied by the government weighs more heavily for me than for the majority. The Court concedes that state action might be present if the activity in question were "traditionally associated with sovereignty," but it then undercuts that point by suggesting that a particular service is not a public function if the State in question has not required that it be governmentally operated. This reads the "public function" argument too narrowly. The whole point of the "public function" cases is to look behind the State's decision to provide public services through private parties. *See*

---

[16] The argument has been impliedly rejected by this Court on a number of occasions. *See, e.g., Civil Rights Cases,* 109 U.S. 3 (1883).

Evans v. Newton, 382 U.S. 296 (1966); *Terry v. Adams*, 345 U.S. 461 (1953); *Marsh v. Alabama*, 326 U.S. 501 (1946). In my view, utility service is traditionally identified with the State through universal public regulation or ownership to a degree sufficient to render it a "public function."

I agree with the majority that it requires more than a finding that a particular business is "affected with the public interest" before constitutional burdens can be imposed on that business. But when the activity in question is of such public importance that the State invariably either provides the service itself or permits private companies to act as state surrogates in providing it, much more is involved than just a matter of public interest. In those cases, the State has determined that if private companies wish to enter the field, they will have to surrender many of the prerogatives normally associated with private enterprise and behave in many ways like a governmental body. And when the State's regulatory scheme has gone that far, it seems entirely consistent to impose on the public utility the constitutional burdens normally reserved for the State.

Private parties performing functions affecting the public interest can often make a persuasive claim to be free of the constitutional requirements applicable to governmental institutions because of the value of preserving a private sector in which the opportunity for individual choice is maximized. *See Evans v. Newton*, 382 U.S., at 298; H[enry J]. Friendly, The Dartmouth College Case and the Public-Private Penumbra (1969). In the due process area, a similar value of diversity may often be furthered by allowing various private institutions the flexibility to select procedures that fit their particular needs. But it is hard to imagine any such interests that are furthered by protecting privately owned public utility companies from meeting the constitutional standards that would apply if the companies were state owned. The values of pluralism and diversity are simply not relevant when the private company is the only electric company in town.

II

The majority's conclusion that there is no state action in this case is likely guided in part by its reluctance to impose on a utility company burdens that might ultimately hurt consumers more than they would help them. Elaborate hearings prior to termination might be quite expensive, and for a responsible company there might be relatively few cases in which such hearings would do any good. The solution to this problem, however, is to require only abbreviated pretermination procedures for all utility companies, not to free the "private" companies to behave however they see fit. Accordingly, I think that at the minimum, due process would require advance notice of a proposed termination with a clear indication that a responsible company official can readily be contacted to consider any claim of error.

III

What is perhaps most troubling about the Court's opinion is that it would appear to apply to a broad range of claimed constitutional violations by the company. Thus, the majority's analysis would seemingly apply as well to a company that refused to extend service to Negroes, welfare recipients, or any other group that the company preferred, for its own reasons, not to serve.

I dissent.

EXERCISE 4:

1.   What is the basis of the State Action Doctrine, according to the majority?

2.   What test did the Supreme Court prescribe to determine whether private action falls within the Public Functions Exception?

3.   From where did the Court draw the Public Functions Exception test? Was this a fair reading of those sources?

4.   What activities fall under the Public Functions Exception, as articulated in *Jackson*? Is it too broad? Too narrow?

5.   Justice Rehnquist argued that a broader conception of the Public Functions Exception would lead to a slippery slope. What were the bad effects identified by Justice Rehnquist? How likely are they to come to pass? What response did Justice Marshall articulate? Who had the better of the argument?

6.   Did the *Jackson* Court's articulation of the Public Functions Exception fulfill the purposes of the State Action Doctrine?

7.   What was the scope of the Public Functions Exception, as articulated by Justice Marshall? What is the source of Justice Marshall's conception of the Exception's scope?

8.   According to Justice Marshall, why was Metropolitan Edison engaged in a public function?

9.   Justice Marshall suggested that the Court limited the Public Functions Exception because of its fear of the adverse effects of applying — sometimes costly — procedural due process norms to a vast array of private parties, such as public utilities. How did Justice Marshall know this? If it is true, is it a legitimate concern for the majority to take into account?

––––––––––

During this same period, the Supreme Court changed direction in its procedural due process case law. During the Warren Court era, the Court had broadened both what constituted the interests protected by the Due Process Clauses and the procedures necessary for government to deprive a person of life, liberty, or property. The high point of expansive procedural due process protection occurred in *Goldberg v. Kelly*, 397 U.S. 254 (1970). There, the Court ruled that welfare was a constitutionally protected "property" interest and prescribed robust procedures that states must utilize to remove a welfare recipient from the welfare rolls. The Court also moved toward ruling that there was a substantive due process right to a minimum level of material resources. *Id.* at 262–65.

A short two years later, however, the Supreme Court reversed course and significantly restricted the scope of constitutionally protected interests, *Board of Regents of State Colleges v. Roth*, 408 U.S. 564 (1972), and then, in 1976, the Court narrowed what procedures were due. *Mathews v. Eldridge*, 424 U.S. 319 (1976).

One must read Justice Marshall's dissent in light of this broader context where he was on the "losing side" and likely saw *Jackson* as of-a-piece with the Court's narrowing movement in the procedural due process context.

Since *Jackson*, there has been little movement in the scope of the Public Functions Exception. Consequently, and because of its relative narrowness, this Exception has not enjoyed widespread invocation. This is in contrast to the Entanglement Exception, discussed below.

3.   The Entanglement Exception

The Supreme Court's jurisprudence in this area is difficult to synthesize for two main reasons. First, the Court has shifted from a broad to narrow, and then to — possibly — a broader conception of the Exception, without explicitly overruling or limiting its previous cases. Second, the Exception is itself relatively amorphous; it is a catch-all. Its focus is on the relationship between a purportedly private party and the government. This is a matter of degree, dependent on a host of ever-varying factors and circumstances.

For this reason, you should think of the Entanglement Exception as involving two axes. The first axis is the *quantity* of relationships or contacts between the private party and the government. For example, does the government regulate the entity? Do the parties exchange financial resources? Has the government approved of the private party's conduct? Is there a symbolic identification of the two? The second axis is the *quality* of the relationships or contacts. Is the regulation extensive? Do either or both parties significantly profit from the relationship? Did the government's laws require the private party's conduct? Has the government symbolically adopted the private party in a conspicuous manner? *Burton v. Wilmington Parking Auth.*, 365 U.S. 715 (1961), reprinted below, exemplifies this approach.

The Entanglement Exception has experienced significant evolution since its rise to prominence during the Warren Court. Initially, the Supreme Court utilized a multi-factor test, best exemplified by *Burton*, to ascertain whether the totality of the (purportedly) private party's relationship with the government was so closely connected that its actions were the state's.

Then, beginning with *Moose Lodge No. 107 v. Irvis*, 407 U.S. 163 (1972), the Court raised the bar to find state action. We will review the key portion of *Moose Lodge* following *Burton*. The Supreme Court later seemed to lower the bar in a series of cases in the 1990s, *Edmonson v. Leesville Concrete Co.*, 500 U.S. 614, 621–22 (1991); *Georgia v. McCollum*, 505 U.S. 42, 51 (1992), but, at this point, it is not clear how many points of contact between the government and a private party, nor what quality of relationships must exist for the Entanglement Exception to apply. The Court recently amplified the unsettledness of the law in this area in *Brentwood Academy v. Tennessee Secondary School Athletic Ass'n*, 531 U.S. 288 (2001), which we will also briefly review at the end of this **Chapter**.

BURTON v. WILMINGTON PARKING AUTHORITY
365 U.S. 715 (1961)

MR. JUSTICE CLARK delivered the opinion of the Court.

[I]

In this action for declaratory and injunctive relief it is admitted that the Eagle Coffee Shoppe, Inc., a restaurant located within an off-street automobile parking building in Wilmington, Delaware, has refused to serve appellant food or drink solely because he is a Negro. The parking building is owned and operated by the Wilmington Parking Authority, an agency of the State of Delaware, and the restaurant is the Authority's lessee. Appellant claims that such refusal abridges his rights under the Equal Protection Clause of the Fourteenth Amendment to the United States Constitution. The Supreme Court of Delaware held that Eagle was acting in "a purely private capacity" under its lease; that its action was not that of the Authority and was not, therefore, state action. On the merits we have concluded that the exclusion of appellant under the circumstances shown to be present here was discriminatory state action in violation of the Equal Protection Clause of the Fourteenth Amendment.

[II]

The Authority was created by the City of Wilmington pursuant to 22 Del. Code, §§ 501-515. It is "a public body corporate and politic, exercising public powers of the State as an agency thereof." Its statutory purpose is to provide adequate parking facilities for the convenience of the public. The first project undertaken by the Authority was the erection of a parking facility in downtown Wilmington. To secure additional capital needed for its "debt-service" requirements, and thereby to make bond financing practicable, the Authority decided it was necessary to enter long-term leases with responsible tenants for commercial use of some of the space available in the projected "garage building."

In April 1957 such a private lease, for 20 years and renewable for another 10 years, was made with Eagle Coffee Shoppe, Inc., for use as a "restaurant, dining room, banquet hall, cocktail lounge and bar and for no other use and purpose." The multi-level space of the building which was let to Eagle, [is] []within the exterior walls of the structure. Eagle spent some $220,000 to make the space suitable for its operation.

The Authority further agreed to furnish heat for Eagle's premises, gas service for the boiler room, and to make, at its own expense, all necessary structural repairs [and] all repairs to exterior surfaces. The Authority retained the right to place any directional signs on the exterior. Agreeing to pay an annual rental of $28,700, Eagle covenanted to "occupy and use the leased premises in accordance with all applicable laws, statutes, ordinances and rules and regulations of any federal, state or municipal authority." Its lease, however, contains no requirement that its restaurant services be made available to the general public on a nondiscriminatory basis, in spite of the fact that the Authority has power to adopt rules and regulations respecting the use of its facilities except any as would impair the security of its bondholders.

Upon completion of the building, the Authority located at appropriate places thereon official signs indicating the public character of the building, and flew from mastheads on the roof both the state and national flags.

In August 1958 appellant parked his car in the building and walked around to enter the restaurant by its front door on Ninth Street. Having entered and sought service, he was refused it. Thereafter he filed this declaratory judgment action in the Court of Chancery.

[III]

The Civil Rights Cases, 109 U.S. 3 [(1883)], "embedded in our constitutional law" the principle "that the action inhibited by the [Equal Protection Clause] of the Fourteenth Amendment is only such action as may fairly be said to be that of the States. That Amendment erects no shield against merely private conduct, however discriminatory or wrongful." *Shelley v. Kraemer,* 334 U.S. 1, 13 [(1948)]. [P]rivate conduct abridging individual rights does no violence to the Equal Protection Clause unless to some significant extent the State in any of its manifestations has been found to have become involved in it. [T]o fashion and apply a precise formula for recognition of state responsibility under the Equal Protection Clause is an "impossible task" which "This Court has never attempted." Only by sifting facts and weighing circumstances can the nonobvious involvement of the State in private conduct be attributed its true significance.

The land and building were publicly owned. As an entity, the building was dedicated to "public uses" in performance of the Authority's "essential governmental functions." The costs of land acquisition, construction, and maintenance are defrayed entirely from donations by the City of Wilmington, from loans and revenue bonds and from the proceeds of rentals and parking services out of which the loans and bonds were payable. [T]he commercially leased areas constituted a physically and financially integral and, indeed, indispensable part of the State's plan to operate its project as a self-sustaining unit. Upkeep and maintenance of the building, including necessary repairs, were responsibilities of the Authority and were payable out of public funds. It cannot be doubted that the peculiar relationship of the restaurant to the parking facility in which it is located confers on each an incidental variety of mutual benefits. Guests of the restaurant are afforded a convenient place to park their automobiles. Similarly, its convenience for diners may well provide additional demand for the Authority's parking facilities. Should any improvements effected in the leasehold by Eagle become part of the realty, there is no possibility of increased taxes being passed on to it since the fee is held by a tax-exempt government agency. Neither can it be ignored, especially in view of Eagle's affirmative allegation that for it to serve Negroes would injure its business, that profits earned by discrimination not only contribute to, but also are indispensable elements in, the financial success of a governmental agency.

Addition of all these activities, obligations and responsibilities of the Authority, the benefits mutually conferred, together with the obvious fact that the restaurant is operated as an integral part of a public building devoted to a public parking service, indicates that degree of state participation and involvement in discriminatory action which it was the design of the Fourteenth Amendment to condemn. It is irony amounting to grave injustice that in one part of a single building, erected and maintained with public funds by an agency of the State to serve a public purpose, all persons have equal rights, while in another portion, also serving the public, a Negro is a second-class citizen, offensive because of his race, without rights and unentitled to service. But no State may effectively abdicate its responsibilities by either ignoring them or by merely failing to discharge them whatever the motive may be. By its inaction, the Authority, and through it the State, has not only made itself a party to the refusal of service, but has elected to place its power, property and prestige behind the admitted discrimination. The State has so far insinuated itself into a position of interdependence with Eagle that it must be recognized as a joint participant in the challenged activity, which, on that account, cannot be considered to have been so "purely private" as to fall without the scope of the Fourteenth Amendment.

Owing to the very "largeness" of government, a multitude of relationships might appear to some to fall within the Amendment's embrace, but that, it must be remembered, can be determined only in the framework of the peculiar facts or circumstances present.

The judgment of the Supreme Court of Delaware is reversed and the cause remanded for further proceedings consistent with this opinion.

Reversed and remanded.

Mr. Justice Stewart, concurring. [Opinion omitted.]

Mr. Justice Harlan, whom Mr. Justice Whittaker joins, dissenting. [Opinion omitted.]

Mr. Justice Frankfurter, dissenting. [Opinion omitted.]

EXERCISE 5:

1. What analysis did the Supreme Court utilize to rule that Eagle Coffee Shoppe was a state actor? Consider both the quantity and quality of private-state interaction.

2. What is the source of this test?

3. Did the Court appropriately apply its Entanglement test?

4. Could one read the *Burton* Court's analysis in a way that undermines the state action requirement itself?

5. One of the frequently leveled criticisms of the Entanglement Exception is that, as a multi-factor balancing test, its meaning, scope, and application is indeterminate. Articulate this criticism. Assuming for the moment that you agree with this criticism, is there a better test, one that better advances the Rule of Law?

6. Does the Entanglement Exception serve the purposes of the State Action Doctrine?

In the early 1970s, the Supreme Court narrowed its exceptions to the State Action Doctrine. In the Entanglement context, this occurred in *Moose Lodge No. 107 v. Irvis*, 407 U.S. 163 (1972). *Moose Lodge* involved a private fraternal organization that discriminated on the basis of race. Pennsylvania heavily regulated alcohol distribution and, consistent with its regulatory regime, granted Moose Lodge a liquor license.

The Court, in an opinion written by Justice Rehnquist — who also wrote *Jackson v. Metropolitan Edison* — reviewed each of the contacts between the Moose Lodge and Pennsylvania. The Court concluded that:

> Here there is nothing approaching the symbiotic relationship between lessor and lessee that was present in *Burton*, where the private lessee obtained the benefit of locating in a building owned by the state-created parking authority, and the parking authority was enabled to carry out its primary public purpose of furnishing parking space by advantageously leasing portions of the building constructed for that purpose to commercial lessees such as the owner of the Eagle Restaurant. Unlike *Burton*, the Moose Lodge building is located on land owned by it, not by any public authority. Far from apparently holding itself out as a place of public accommodation, Moose Lodge quite ostentatiously proclaims the fact that it is not open to the public at large. Nor is it located and operated in such surroundings that although private in name, it discharges a function or performs a service that would otherwise in all likelihood be performed by the State. In short, while Eagle was a public restaurant in a public building, Moose Lodge is a private social club in a private building.

> [T]he Pennsylvania Liquor Control Board plays absolutely no part in establishing or enforcing the membership or guest policies of the clubs that it licenses to serve liquor. There is no suggestion in this record that Pennsylvania law, either as written or as applied, discriminates against minority groups either in their right to apply for club licenses themselves or in their right to purchase and be served liquor in places of public accommodation.

> The District Court was at pains to point out in its opinion what it considered to be the "pervasive" nature of the regulation of private clubs by the Pennsylvania Liquor Control Board. However detailed this type of regulation may be in some particulars, it cannot be said to in any way foster or encourage racial discrimination. Nor can it be said to make the State in any realistic sense a partner or even a joint venturer in the club's enterprise. The limited effect of the prohibition against obtaining additional club licenses when the maximum number of retail licenses allotted to a municipality has been issued, when considered together with the availability of liquor from hotel, restaurant, and retail licensees, falls far short of conferring upon club licensees a monopoly in the dispensing of liquor in any given municipality . . . . We therefore hold that . . . the operation of the regulatory scheme enforced by

the Pennsylvania Liquor Control Board does not sufficiently implicate the State in the discriminatory guest policies of Moose Lodge to make the latter "state action" within the ambit of the Equal Protection Clause.

Id. at 175–77.

EXERCISE 6:

1.　Using the quantity and quality of contacts approach, describe both axes of private-state interaction.

2.　What is the Court's holding?

3.　Did the Supreme Court fairly distinguish *Burton*?

———————

Moose Lodge was followed by numerous cases where the Supreme Court ruled against claims of state action. *E.g., Flagg Bros., Inc. v. Brooks*, 436 U.S. 149 (1978); *Rendell-Baker v. Kohn*, 457 U.S. 830 (1982); *Blum v. Yaretsky*, 457 U.S. 991 (1982). However, in some later cases, the Court found state action. *E.g., Edmonson v. Leesville Concrete Co.*, 500 U.S. 614, 621–22 (1991); *Georgia v. McCollum*, 505 U.S. 42, 51 (1992). These differing results have created tension in the case law.

Recently, the Supreme Court created more uncertainty in this area with *Brentwood Academy v. Tennessee Secondary School Athletic Ass'n*, 531 U.S. 288 (2001). There, a private school challenged the actions of a purportedly private association that coordinated secondary school athletics in Tennessee. The Court's opinion, like others in this area, was heavily fact intensive. Justice Souter, writing for the Court, also utilized a new label to describe the relationship between the Association and Tennessee, "entwinement":

> What is fairly attributable [to a state] is a matter of normative judgment, and the criteria lack rigid simplicity. From the range of circumstances that could point toward the State behind an individual face, no one fact can function as a necessary condition across the board for finding state action; nor is any set of circumstances absolutely sufficient, for there may be some countervailing reason against attributing activity to the government.

> The nominally private character of the Association is overborne by the pervasive entwinement of public institutions and public officials in its composition and workings, and there is no substantial reason to claim unfairness in applying constitutional standards to it.

> The Association is not an organization of natural persons acting on their own, but of schools, and of public schools to the extent of 84% of the total. Under the Association's bylaws, each member school is represented by its principal or a faculty member, who has a vote in selecting members of the governing legislative council and board of control from eligible principals, assistant principals, and superintendents.

Interscholastic athletics obviously play an integral part in the public education of Tennessee, where nearly every public high school spends money on competitions among schools. Since a pickup system of interscholastic games would not do, these public teams need some mechanism to produce rules and regulate competition. The mechanism is an organization overwhelmingly composed of public school officials who select representatives (all of them public officials at the time in question here), who in turn adopt and enforce the rules that make the system work. Thus, by giving these jobs to the Association, the 290 public schools of Tennessee belonging to it can sensibly be seen as exercising their own authority to meet their own responsibilities. Unsurprisingly, then, the record indicates that half the council or board meetings documented here were held during official school hours, and that public schools have largely provided for the Association's financial support. A small portion of the Association's revenue comes from membership dues paid by the schools, and the principal part from gate receipts at tournaments among the member schools. The Association exercises the authority of the predominantly public schools to charge for admission to their games; the Association does not receive this money from the schools, but enjoys the schools' moneymaking capacity as its own.

In sum, . . . the Association is an organization of public schools represented by their officials acting in their official capacity to provide an integral element of secondary public schooling. There would be no recognizable Association, legal or tangible, without the public school officials, who do not merely control but overwhelmingly perform all but the purely ministerial acts by which the Association exists and functions in practical terms. Only the 16% minority of private school memberships prevents this entwinement of the Association and the public school system from being total and their identities totally indistinguishable.

To complement the entwinement of public school officials with the Association from the bottom up, the State of Tennessee has provided for entwinement from top down. State [Education] Board members are assigned ex officio to serve as members of the board of control and legislative council, and the Association's ministerial employees are treated as state employees to the extent of being eligible for membership in the state retirement system.

The close relationship is confirmed by the Association's enforcement of rules and regulations reviewed and approved by the State Board (including the recruiting Rule challenged by Brentwood), and by the State Board's willingness to allow students to satisfy its physical education requirement by taking part in interscholastic athletics sponsored by the Association.

The entwinement down from the State Board is therefore unmistakable, just as the entwinement up from the member public schools is overwhelming. Entwinement will support a conclusion that an ostensibly private organization ought to be charged with a public character and judged by constitutional standards; entwinement to the degree shown here requires it.

Id. at 295–303.

EXERCISE 7:

1.   Using the quantity and quality of contacts approach, describe both axes of private-state interaction.

2.   What is the Court's holding?

3.   Is *Brentwood Academy* consistent with *Moose Lodge*? With *Burton*?

Chapter 2

THE PRIVILEGES OR IMMUNITIES CLAUSE

A. INTRODUCTION

The Privileges or Immunities Clause states: "No State shall make or enforce any law which shall abridge the privileges or immunities of citizens of the United States." U.S. CONST. amend. XIV, § 1. Despite its central role in the vision of the Fourteenth Amendment's Framers, the Privileges or Immunities Clause plays almost no role today in American constitutional law.

EXERCISE 1:

Apply the first four forms of argument to the Privileges or Immunities Clause.

1.   Looking at the Privileges or Immunities Clause itself, the text of the remainder of Section 1 of the Fourteenth Amendment, and the text of the Privileges and Immunities Clause in Article IV, what do you learn about the Clause's meaning?

2.   Looking at the Constitution's structure, and particularly at the Thirteenth and Fifteenth Amendments, what do you learn about the Privileges or Immunities Clause's meaning?

3.   Reviewing evidence of the Fourteenth Amendment's original meaning, what does it tell you about that meaning?

4.   Do the materials following adoption of the Fourteenth Amendment offer any insight into the Privileges or Immunities Clause's meaning?

The Privileges or Immunities Clause's story is relatively easy to tell. The Framers of the Fourteenth Amendment intended the Clause to serve as the primary vehicle to protect newly freed black Americans by applying the Bill of Rights[1] against the states.[2] However, the Supreme Court shortly thereafter so narrowly interpreted the Clause in *The Slaughter-House Cases*, 83 U.S. 36 (1872), that it has since had almost no practical legal effect. The irony to the Privileges or Immunities Clause's story is that it went from being the most important provision in the Fourteenth Amendment, to its least important.

---

[1] Many scholars believe the Privileges or Immunities Clause was also the intended vehicle to apply unenumerated rights against the states. *E.g.*, RANDY E. BARNETT, RESTORING THE LOST CONSTITUTION: THE PRESUMPTION OF LIBERTY 201 (2004).

[2] This process, labeled "incorporation," is covered in Part C of **Chapter 3**.

As you read the materials below, some of the issues to consider include:

What did the Clause's Framers and Ratifiers intend the Clause to do?

What were the privileges and immunities, as understood in 1868?

Was the Supreme Court faithful to the Privileges or Immunities Clause in *The Slaughter-House Cases*?

What does the Clause mean today?

Should the Supreme Court overrule *The Slaughter-House Cases*?

B. ORIGINAL MEANING OF THE PRIVILEGES OR IMMUNITIES CLAUSE

The original meaning of the Privileges or Immunities Clause, like that of other parts of Section 1 of the Fourteenth Amendment, has been subject to continuing scholarly scrutiny. The scholarly consensus is that the Clause incorporated the Bill of Rights against the states.[3] There are also noteworthy arguments by some scholars that the Clause also protected unenumerated rights, in addition to those listed in the Bill of Rights.[4]

The story of the meaning of the Privileges or Immunities Clause of the Fourteenth Amendment begins with the Supreme Court's decision in *Dred Scott v. Sandford*.[5] There, Chief Justice Taney, for the majority, found that African-Americans, whether in bondage or freemen, were not entitled to the privileges and immunities protected by Article IV, § 2 of the Constitution,[6] because they were not — and could never be — citizens of the United States.[7] Ironically, the Chief Justice argued that, if African-Americans were or could be citizens, then the Constitution would protect their privileges and immunities, including the right to move freely among the states, the liberty to speak freely in public, and the rights to assemble, to bear arms, and to seek redress in the courts.[8] According to Chief Justice Taney, this unpalatable result showed the fallacy of Scott's claim to citizenship.[9] As a result, the Court held that Scott, an African-American suing for his freedom, was not eligible to bring his case to federal court.[10]

---

[3] BARNETT, *supra*, at 66; AKHIL REED AMAR, THE BILL OF RIGHTS: CREATION AND RECONSTRUCTION 181–87 (1998).

[4] BARNETT, *supra*, at 201.

[5] Dred Scott v. Sandford, 60 U.S. (19 How.) 393 (1856).

[6] U.S. CONST. art. IV, § 2 ("The Citizens of each State shall be entitled to all Privileges and Immunities of Citizens of the several States.").

[7] *Dred Scott*, 60 U.S. (19 How.), at 405–07, 409, 411.

[8] *Id.* at 417.

[9] *Id.*

[10] The South praised the decision, exclaiming that the decision was the "supreme law of the land," and that "opposition to southern opinion upon this subject is now opposition to the Constitution." JAMES M. MCPHERSON, ORDEAL BY FIRE 111–12 (3d ed. 2001). Northern and Southern Democrats also seized on the implications of the decision, threatening to charge their Republican counterparts with treason against the

Nine years later, and after four years of the bloodiest war in American history, Congress passed and the states ratified the Thirteenth Amendment.[11] The Amendment abolished slavery and freed over four million people. The Reconstruction Republicans, who controlled Congress and proposed the Amendment, believed that it restored African-Americans to United States citizenship with its accompanying privileges and immunities that the *Dred Scott* Court had denied.

As time passed, however, and Southern Democrats began to regain their political hold in the former Confederacy, life for the ex-slaves began to resemble their lives before the Amendment.[12] Newly-freed black Americans' freedom was undermined by the Southern States' enactment of "black codes."[13] These laws impeded the freedom of black southerners to such an extent that the result was, effectively, a return to slavery.[14] Without explicit protection for the rights of citizens, the freedom protected by the Thirteenth Amendment was, as a practical matter, meaningless. The condition of the freedmen became a central issue facing the Thirty-Ninth Congress. As recounted by Republican congressman William Winden:

> The great struggle through which we are passing is of a two-fold character — it is a war of principles as well as of material forces. The latter is ended and our triumph is complete; but the conflict of principles still rages with increased vigor.[15]

The black codes infuriated the Republicans who viewed mistreatment of freedmen as an affront to the victory for freedom that the Union had secured.[16] Members of Congress continuously referred to the codes during their debates, noting that some states went so far that the result was a revival of slavery itself.[17] Congressman Thomas D. Eliot, a Republican from Massachusetts, cited such a law enacted in Opelousas, Louisiana:

> . . . no negroe or freedmen shall be allowed to come within the limits of the town of Opelousas without special permission from his employer, specifying the object of his visit, and the time necessary for the accomplishment of the same . . . .

Constitution if they defied the Court's ruling. *Id.* at 113. The decision deepened the developing crisis between the North and the South. *Id.* at 114.

[11] U.S. Const. amend. XIII ("Neither slavery nor involuntary servitude . . . shall exist within the United States.").

[12] McPherson, *supra* note, at 542–53.

[13] *Id.* at 552; David Herbert Donald et. al, The Civil War and Reconstruction 526 (2001).

[14] The South's black codes generally excluded blacks from juries, prohibited interracial marriage, required segregation, criminalized "vagrancy" (i.e., unemployment), and inflicted harsher punishments for blacks than for whites guilty of similar crimes. McPherson, *supra*, at 552; Donald, *supra*, at 526–27. Many of the codes forced ex-slaves to work for meager wages that were often forfeited if the ex-slave left the plantation before the end of the season. Donald, *supra*, at 527. In South Carolina, for example, blacks were forbidden to pursue any occupation other than farmer or servant, unless they paid an annual tax. *Id.* In Mississippi, blacks were required to produce written evidence that they were employed. *Id.*

[15] Cong. Globe, 39th Cong., 1st Sess. 3166 (June 14, 1866) (statement of Rep. William Windom).

[16] McPherson, *supra*, at 552.

[17] *Id.*

. . . every negro or freedman who shall be found on the streets of Opelousas after ten o'clock at night without a written pass or permit from his employer shall be imprisoned and compelled to work five days on the public streets, or pay a fine . . . .

No negro or freedman shall be permitted to rent or keep a house within the limits of the town under any circumstances. . . .[18]

Similar statutes in South Carolina, Mississippi, Tennessee, and Virginia were cited by congressional members during the debate.[19] Ignatius L. Donnely, a Republican from Minnesota, said of freed slaves, "he is worse off than before."[20]

In response to the black codes and the lack of protection for black citizens, in 1866 the Senate adopted Senate Resolution 61, "to protect all persons in the United States in their civil rights and furnish the means of their vindication."[21] This became the famous Civil Rights Act of 1866.[22]

Supporters of the Civil Rights Act argued that these civil rights were contained in and guaranteed by the Privileges and Immunities Clause in Article IV, § 2, of the Constitution. Therefore, the Act's passage would simply be an affirmation of the effects of the Thirteenth Amendment:

Th[e Thirteenth] amendment declared that all persons in the United States should be free. This measure is intended to give effect to that declaration and secure to all persons within the United States practical freedom.[23]

In other words, the privileges and immunities of Article IV, § 2, were guaranteed to all free people of the United States; the Thirteenth Amendment freed all slaves; therefore, as free people, the ex-slaves were constitutionally entitled to those same privileges and immunities. However, in the *Dred Scott* decision, the Supreme Court had held that these rights were restricted to individuals with the status of citizenship. As a result, because the Thirteenth Amendment had not granted citizenship to the ex-slaves, their freedom remained unprotected.

With their proposal to protect citizenship of the freedmen through the Civil Rights Act, Republican members of Congress acknowledged the shortcomings of the Thirteenth Amendment. Although the Thirteenth Amendment had abolished slavery, the Amendment's "general principles" were admittedly insufficient to allow the freedmen the "means of availing themselves of their benefits."[24] However, Senator Trumbull argued that Section 2 of the Thirteenth Amendment did grant Congress the power to

---

[18] CONG. GLOBE, 39th Cong., 1st Sess. 516 (Jan. 30, 1866) (statement of Rep. Thomas D. Eliot).

[19] *See id.* at 39 (Dec. 13, 1865) (statement of Senator Henry Wilson) (citing a Louisiana proposal); *id.* at 3170 (June 14, 1866) (statement of Rep. Ignatius L. Donnelly) (citing the South Carolina, Mississippi, Tennessee, and Virginia codes).

[20] *Id.* at 588 (Feb. 1, 1866) (statement of Rep. Ignatius L. Donnelly).

[21] *Id.* at 474 (Jan. 29, 1866) (statement of Senator Lyman Trumbull).

[22] Civil Rights Act of 1866, 14 Stat. 27 (1866).

[23] CONG. GLOBE, 39th Cong., 1st Sess. 474 (Jan. 4, 1866) (statement of Senator Lyman Trumbull).

[24] *Id.*

define those benefits, in part by granting citizenship, as well as to void state-sponsored black codes:

> Then, under the constitutional amendment which we have now adopted . . . which authorizes Congress by appropriate legislation to carry this provision into effect, I hold that we have a right to pass any law which, in our judgment, is deemed appropriate, and which will accomplish the end in view, secure freedom to all people in the United States. The various State laws to which I have referred — and there are many others — although they do not make a man an absolute slave, they deprive him of the rights of a freeman. . . . A law that does not allow a colored person to hold property, does not allow him to teach, does not allow him to preach, is certainly a law in violation of the rights of a freeman, and being so may properly be declared void.[25]

Through protecting the freedmen's citizenship, the Civil Rights Act gave "practical meaning"[26] to the Amendment by overturning the "pestilent" doctrines of the *Dred Scott* decision.[27] As citizens, the freedmen would have the "privileges and immunities" that were described by Chief Justice Taney as guaranteed to all citizens in Article IV, § 2, of the Constitution.[28]

Drafters of the Civil Rights Act of 1866 argued that "privileges and immunities" were personal in nature, and so were "fundamental," and "natural." Many members of Congress cited Justice Bushrod Washington's 1823 opinion in *Corfield v. Coryell*[29] as defining the privileges and immunities protected by Article IV, § 2.[30] In his opinion, Justice Washington wrote that privileges and immunities were:

> the enjoyment of life and liberty, with the right to acquire and possess property of every kind; and to pursue happiness and safety. . . . The right of a citizen of one State to pass through, or to reside in any other State for purposes of trade, agriculture, professional pursuits or otherwise; to claim the benefit of the writ of habeas corpus; to institute and maintain actions of any kind in the courts of the State; to take, hold, and dispose of property, either real or personal, and an exemption from higher taxes or impositions than are paid by other citizens of the State.[31]

---

[25] *Id.*

[26] *Id.*

[27] *Id.* at 1116 (Mar. 1, 1866) (statement of Rep. James F. Wilson).

[28] *Id.* at 474 (Jan. 4, 1866) (statement of Senator Lyman Trumbull); *see also id.* at 1115 (Mar. 1, 1866) (statement of Rep. James F. Wilson) ("This provision [the citizenship clause of the Civil Rights Act] is simply declaratory of what the law now is."); *id.* at 1760 (Apr. 4, 1866) (statement of Senator Lyman Trumbull) ("This bill . . . simply declares that in civil rights there shall be an equality among all classes of citizens . . . [of] the great fundamental rights belonging under the Constitution (Art. IV, Sec. II).").

[29] *Corfield v. Coryell*, 6 F. Cas. 546 (C.C.E.D. Pa. 1823) (No. 3,230).

[30] *See, e.g.*, CONG. GLOBE, 39th Cong., 1st Sess. 2765 (May 23, 1866) (statement of Senator Jacob Howard) ("[I]t would be a curious question to solve what are the privileges and immunities of citizens of each of the States. . . . But we may gather some intimation . . . [b]y referring to a case adjudged many years ago in one of the circuit courts of the United States by Judge Washington.").

[31] *Corfield*, 6 F. Cas. at 551–52; *see also* David R. Upham, Corfield v. Coryell *and the Privileges and*

Blackstone's Commentaries was also regularly cited by congressional members as an authoritative source for determining the nature of civil rights. Blackstone stated that civil rights included:

> the right of personal security consisting in a person's legal and uninterrupted enjoyment of his life, his limbs; the personal liberty of individuals . . . consisting in the power of locomotion, of changing situations or moving one's person to whatsoever place one's own inclination may direct, without imprisonment, or restraint, unless by due course of law; the free use, enjoyment, and disposal of real and personal property, without any control or diminution, save only by the laws of the land.[32]

In general, congressmen supporting the Civil Rights Act considered fundamental rights to include personal security, such as the protection provided by the courts and law enforcement; freedom of movement within a state, as well as from state to state; and, ownership and disposition of real or personal property. This is largely consistent with the language of Section 1 of the Civil Rights Act itself:

> That there shall be no discrimination in civil rights or immunities . . . on account of race . . . but that inhabitants of every race . . . shall have the same right to make and enforce contracts, to sue, be parties, and give evidence, to inherit, purchase, lease, sell, hold and convey real and personal property, and to full and equal benefit of all laws and proceedings for the security of person and property, and shall be subject to like punishment . . . and no other.[33]

However, some members, mostly Democrats, opposed the passage of the Civil Rights Act claiming that the Act was unconstitutional. These members argued that, even if Congress were able to grant citizenship to the freedmen, Article IV, § 2's Privileges and Immunities Clause still would not apply to the ex-slaves in the manner in which the authors of the Civil Rights Act intended. Article IV, § 2, they argued, simply afforded the protection of a *State's* privileges and immunities to out-of-state citizens. In other words, it was the State that defined the privileges and immunities of its citizens, and these privileges and immunities were simply extended to out-of-state citizens traveling within the State's borders. As Senator Samuel Marshall, a Democrat from Illinois declared, "Congress has the power to enforce what? The abolition of slavery. This is not denied. . . . But Congress has acquired not a particle of additional power."[34]

Immunities of American Citizenship, 83 Tex. L. Rev. 1483, 1484 (2004-05) (stating that Justice Washington's pronouncement was "the legal authority to which the congressional framers most frequently appealed in describing the constitutional privileges of citizenship").

The "elective franchise" was also mentioned by Justice Washington; however, Senator Trumbull remarked that "this Judge goes further than the bill under consideration," which is consistent with the opinion of many, though not all, members that the right to vote was not a "fundamental" right, but rather a "political" right. Cong. Globe, 39th Cong., 1st Sess. 475 (Jan. 29, 1866) (statement of Senator Lyman Trumbull).

[32] I Sir William Blackstone, Commentaries on the Laws of England *130–31 (1769).

[33] Civil Rights Act of 1866, 14 Stat. 27 (1866).

[34] Cong. Globe, 39th Cong., 1st Sess. 627 (Feb. 3, 1866) (statement of Senator Samuel Marshall).

Democratic Senator Garrett Davis of Kentucky put forth an argument based on the principles of federalism. Davis pointed out that the Constitution vested Congress with power only over matters concerning foreign nations, the Indian Tribes, and issues that may arise *between or among* the individual States. By applying to citizens of the "several states," Article IV, § 2, was in harmony with those principles, principles that were "in conflict with the bill under consideration":

> Now, Mr. President, what is the power that is vested in Congress on the subject of this bill? 'The citizens of each State shall be entitled to all privileges and immunities of citizens in the several States.' If the Senate would act legitimately upon this subject, its action must be confined to such matters as concern the citizens of different States. It has no power whatever to act in relation to the matters of this bill so far as those matters concern the citizens of a single State . . . . The clause of the Constitution which I have read does not refer to people in their condition. It refers to the citizens of each State being entitled to all privileges and immunities of citizens in the several States. When does this principle of the Constitution apply? Only when a citizen of one State goes to another State. . . . [Trumbull] proposes now to apply his bill to every citizen of the United States. . . . Now, I say that the bill constitutionally can have no such application. . . .[35]

Davis' argument was persuasive for two reasons. First, the Constitution did not appear to grant Congress the power to define the privileges and immunities of citizens. Davis and others argued that such a power was reserved to the states under their police powers; only when an out-of-state citizen was denied the protections of the state they were in, did the Constitution allow Congress to act. Second, the Constitution did not grant Congress the power to enforce privileges and immunities, regardless of what precisely those were. States, Davis argued, defined citizen's rights and the manner of their application. The Thirteenth Amendment had indeed freed the slaves but, beyond that, Congress was without the Constitutional power to define or enforce civil rights. The drafters of the Fourteenth Amendment endeavored to address both obstacles.

In response to the arguments of the opponents of the Civil Rights Act, Congress proposed an Amendment to the Constitution. First, the Amendment protected the Privileges or Immunities of citizens *of the United States*, as opposed to the citizens *of* or *within* a State. These privileges or immunities were understood by Congress to include not only those fundamental rights espoused by supporters of the Civil Rights Act, but were expanded to also include the first Eight Amendments to the Constitution. Second, Section 5 explicitly granted Congress the power to "enforce" the Privileges or Immunities Clause.

A resolution was adopted by the Senate recommending that the Joint Committee on Reconstruction consider amending the Constitution. The stated purpose of the resolution was: "to declare with greater certainty the power of Congress to enforce and determine by appropriate legislation all the guaranties contained in that instrument."[36] Representative John Bingham, a Republican from Ohio and a member of the

---

[35] *Id.* at 595 (Jan. 4, 1866) (statement of Senator Garrett Davis).

[36] *Id.* at 566 (Feb. 1, 1866) (statement of Senator Gatz Brown).

Committee, was instrumental in the creation and development of what would become the Fourteenth Amendment.

On December 6, 1865, Bingham proposed adding the Fourteenth Amendment to the Constitution to provide Congress with the power that opponents of the Civil Rights Act claimed that Congress did not then have.[37] He explained:

> I propose, with the help of this Congress and of the American people, that hereafter there shall not be any disregard of that essential guarantee of your Constitution (Art. IV, Sec. II) in any State of the Union. And how? By simply adding an amendment to the Constitution to operate on all the States of this Union alike, giving to Congress the power to pass all laws necessary and proper to secure to all persons — which includes every citizen of every State — their equal personal rights. . . . That is precisely what is proposed to be accomplished.[38]

On February 3, 1866, the Committee voted to accept Bingham's initial draft to amend the Constitution. In response to opponents of the Civil Rights Act, Bingham's draft stated (in pertinent part):

> The Congress shall have the power to make all laws which shall be necessary and proper to secure to the citizens of each state all privileges *and* immunities of citizens in the several states.[39]

First, Bingham addressed the states rights argument of the opponents of the Civil Rights Act by distinguishing between breadth of the grant of privileges and immunities in Article IV and in his proposal. The privileges and immunities protected by his proposal, Bingham explained, were to be granted to citizens "of the United States in, not of, the several States."[40] Thus, the federal government, and not the state governments, would define the privileges or immunities of national citizenship.

Second, Bingham began to broaden the definition of privileges and immunities championed by supporters of the Civil Rights Act by mentioning the rights enumerated in the Bill of Rights.[41] However, because the language of his proposal tracked the Privileges and Immunities Clause nearly exactly, some of Bingham's supporters believed that the language of his proposal would have the same — limited — effect as that of Article IV.[42] In other words, the proposal would come up against the same federalism arguments facing the Civil Rights Act. As a result, Bingham withdrew the first version of his draft, and Congress resumed debate over the Civil Rights Act.[43]

---

[37] *Id.* at 14 (Dec. 6, 1865) (statement of Rep. John Bingham) ("[A]ll necessary and proper laws to secure to all persons in every State of the Union equal protection in their rights of life, liberty, and property.").

[38] *Id.* at 158 (Jan. 9, 1866) (statement of Rep. John Bingham).

[39] *Id.* at 1033–34 (Feb. 26, 1866); BENJAMIN B. KENDRICK, JOURNAL OF THE JOINT COMMITTEE OF FIFTEEN ON RECONSTRUCTION: 39TH CONGRESS, 1865–67, at 60 (1914).

[40] CONG. GLOBE, 39th Cong., 1st Sess. 158 (Jan. 9, 1866) (statement of Rep. John Bingham).

[41] *Id.* at 1034 (Jan. 9, 1866) (statement of Rep. John Bingham).

[42] *Id.* at 1090 (Feb. 28, 1866) (statement of Rep. Giles Hotchkiss).

[43] *Id.* at 1095.

The second draft of Bingham's proposal more pointedly addressed the concerns of his colleagues: "No State shall make or enforce any law which shall abridge the privileges or immunities of citizens of the United States."[44] This language expressly bound the states and more clearly protected the citizens *of* the United States, rather than the citizens *in the several States*. Additionally, the second version, Bingham would later explain, expressly included "all the limitations for personal protection of every article and section of the Constitution."[45] These changes helped to eventually enable the passage of the Fourteenth Amendment.

It was well understood by members of the Thirty-Ninth Congress that the Bill of Rights was incorporated into the Privileges or Immunities Clause of the Fourteenth Amendment. A primary goal of the Civil Rights Act, and so too the proposed Fourteenth Amendment, was to afford Congress the power to strike down the black codes. Many of the provisions of the Bill of Rights were directly affected by the black codes. For instance, black Americans were not permitted to bear arms; they were regularly searched and their property seized without a judicial warrant; they were denied access to the courts and to trials by jury, and; their freedom to assemble and practice their religion was limited.

Furthermore, as a result of southern paranoia, these restrictions on liberty applied to many white citizens as well. Abolitionists and southern citizens who were sympathetic to the Union cause were discouraged from assembling, the Southern press was tightly controlled, and citizens were routinely searched and their property seized if their actions were suspicious. Bingham stated that the amendment was necessary not only for people of "African descent," but also:

> to protect the hundreds of thousands of loyal white citizens of the United States whose property, by State legislation, has been wrested from them under confiscation, and protect them also against banishment. It is to apply to . . . States . . . that have in their constitutions and laws to-day provisions in direct violation of every principle of our Constitution.[46]

The "privileges or immunities" in the first section of the proposed amendment, Senator Howard stated, was to empower Congress to end the states' interference with the Bill of Rights: "The great object of the first section of this amendment is, therefore, to restrain the power of the states and compel them at all times to respect these great fundamental guarantees."[47] Below, we will review the Supreme Court's hostile reception to the Privileges or Immunities Clause which, to this day, has precluded the Clause from achieving its purpose.

---

[44] KENDRICK, *supra*, at 87.

[45] CONG. GLOBE, 39th Cong., 2d Sess. 811 (Jan. 28, 1867) (statement of Rep. John Bingham). Some members cited only the first Eight Amendments; others simply referred to the Bill of Rights; some members even later referred to the Fourteenth Amendment as a "bill of rights." *Id.* at 1055.

[46] *Id.* at 1065 (Feb. 27, 1867) (statement of Rep. John Bingham).

[47] GLOBE, 39th Cong., 1st Sess. 2766 (May 23, 1866) (statement of Senator Jacob Howard).

C. THE SHORT-LIVED PRIVILEGES OR IMMUNITIES CLAUSE

Four years after the Fourteenth Amendment's ratification, the Supreme Court first heard a case involving the Privileges or Immunities Clause. The Supreme Court and scholars nearly universally agree that the *Slaughter-House Cases* prevented the Clause from having operative legal effect.

THE SLAUGHTER-HOUSE CASES: THE BUTCHERS' BENEVOLENT ASSOCIATION OF NEW ORLEANS v. THE CRESCENT CITY LIVE-STOCK LANDING AND SLAUGHTER-HOUSE COMPANY
83 U.S. (16 Wall.) 36 (1872)

MR. JUSTICE MILLER, delivered the opinion of the court.

[I]

These cases are brought here by writs of error to the Supreme Court of the State of Louisiana. They arise out of the efforts of the butchers of New Orleans to resist the Crescent City Live-Stock Landing and Slaughter-House Company in the exercise of certain powers conferred by the charter which created it, and which was granted by the legislature of that State.

[T]hese cases were argued in January, 1872. At that hearing one of the justices was absent, and it was found, on consultation, that there was a diversity of views among those who were present. Impressed with the gravity of the questions raised in the argument, the court under these circumstances ordered that the cases be placed on the calendar and reargued before a full bench. This argument was had early in February last.

The statute thus assailed as unconstitutional was passed March 8th, 1869, and is entitled 'An act to protect the health of the city of New Orleans, to locate the stock-landings and slaughter-houses, and to incorporate the Crescent City Live-Stock Landing and Slaughter-House Company.' It declares that the company shall have the sole and exclusive privilege of conducting and carrying on the live-stock landing and slaughter-house business. Section five makes it the duty of the company to permit any person to slaughter animals in their slaughter-houses under a heavy penalty for each refusal.

The power here exercised by the legislature of Louisiana is, in its essential nature, one which has been, up to the present period in the constitutional history of this country, always conceded to belong to the States. It may, therefore, be considered as established, that the authority of the legislature of Louisiana to pass the present statute is ample, unless some restraint in the exercise of that power be found in the amendments to the Constitution of the United States.

[II]

The plaintiffs in error allege that the statute is a violation of the Constitution of the United States in these several particulars: That it creates an involuntary servitude forbidden by the thirteenth article of amendment; That it abridges the privileges and immunities of citizens of the United States; That it denies to the plaintiffs the equal protection of the laws; and, That it deprives them of their property without due process of law; contrary to the provisions of the first section of the fourteenth article of amendment. This court is thus called upon for the first time to give construction to these articles.

We do not conceal from ourselves the great responsibility which this duty devolves upon us. No questions so far-reaching and pervading in their consequences, so profoundly interesting to the people of this country, and so important in their bearing upon the relations of the United States, and of the several States to each other and to the citizens of the States and of the United States, have been before this court during the official life of any of its present members. We have given every opportunity for a full hearing at the bar; we have discussed it freely and compared views among ourselves; we have taken ample time for careful deliberation, and we now propose to announce the judgments which we have formed in the construction of those articles.

Within the last eight years three articles of amendment of vast importance have been added by the voice of the people to that now venerable instrument. The most cursory glance at these articles discloses a unity of purpose, when taken in connection with the history of the times, which cannot fail to have an important bearing on any question of doubt concerning their true meaning. Nor can such doubts, when any reasonably exist, be safely and rationally solved without a reference to that history; for in it is found the occasion and the necessity for recurring again to the great source of power in this country, the people of the States, for additional guarantees of human rights; additional powers to the Federal government; additional restraints upon those of the States. Fortunately that history is fresh within the memory of us all, and its leading features, as they bear upon the matter before us, free from doubt.

The process of restoring to their proper relations with the Federal government and with the other States those which had sided with the rebellion, undertaken under the proclamation of President Johnson in 1865, and before the assembling of Congress, developed the fact that, notwithstanding the formal recognition by those States of the abolition of slavery, the condition of the slave race would, without further protection of the Federal government, be almost as bad as it was before. Among the first acts of legislation adopted by several of the States in the legislative bodies which claimed to be in their normal relations with the Federal government, were laws which imposed upon the colored race onerous disabilities and burdens, and curtailed their rights in the pursuit of life, liberty, and property to such an extent that their freedom was of little value, while they had lost the protection which they had received from their former owners from motives both of interest and humanity.

These circumstances, forced upon the statesmen who had conducted the Federal government in safety through the crisis of the rebellion, and who supposed that by the thirteenth article of amendment they had secured the result of their labors, the conviction that something more was necessary in the way of constitutional protection to the unfortunate race who had suffered so much. They accordingly passed through Congress the fourteenth amendment.

A few years' experience satisfied the thoughtful men who had been the authors of the other two amendments that, notwithstanding the restraints of those articles on the States, and the laws passed under the additional powers granted to Congress, these were inadequate for the protection of life, liberty, and property, without which freedom to the slave was no boon. They were in all those States denied the right of suffrage. The laws were administered by the white man alone. It was urged that a race of men distinctively marked as was the negro, living in the midst of another and dominant race, could never be fully secured in their person and their property without the right of suffrage. Hence the fifteenth amendment. The negro having, by the fourteenth amendment, been declared to be a citizen of the United States, is thus made a voter in every State of the Union.

We repeat, then, in the light of this recapitulation of events, almost too recent to be called history, but which are familiar to us all; and on the most casual examination of the language of these amendments, no one can fail to be impressed with the one pervading purpose found in them all, lying at the foundation of each, and without which none of them would have been even suggested; we mean the freedom of the slave race, the security and firm establishment of that freedom, and the protection of the newly-made freeman and citizen from the oppressions of those who had formerly exercised unlimited dominion over him. It is true that only the fifteenth amendment, in terms, mentions the negro by speaking of his color and his slavery. But it is just as true that each of the other articles was addressed to the grievances of that race, and designed to remedy them as the fifteenth.

[III]
[A]

The first section of the fourteenth article opens with a definition of citizenship-not only citizenship of the United States, but citizenship of the States. No such definition was previously found in the Constitution, nor had any attempt been made to define it by act of Congress. [I]t had been held by this court, in the celebrated Dred Scott case, only a few years before the outbreak of the civil war, that a man of African descent, whether a slave or not, was not and could not be a citizen of a State or of the United States. This decision, while it met the condemnation of some of the ablest statesmen and constitutional lawyers of the country, had never been overruled; and if it was to be accepted as a constitutional limitation of the right of citizenship, then all the negro race who had recently been made freemen, were still, not only not citizens, but were incapable of becoming so by anything short of an amendment to the Constitution.

To remove this difficulty primarily, and to establish a clear and comprehensive definition of citizenship which should declare what should constitute citizenship of the United States, and also citizenship of a State, the first clause of the first section was framed.

The first observation we have to make on this clause is, that it puts at rest both the questions which we stated to have been the subject of differences of opinion. It declares that persons may be citizens of the United States without regard to their citizenship of a particular State, and it overturns the Dred Scott decision by making *all persons* born within the United States and subject to its jurisdiction citizens of the United States. That its main purpose was to establish the citizenship of the negro can admit of no doubt.

[B]

The next observation is more important in view of the arguments of counsel in the present case. It is, that the distinction between citizenship of the United States and citizenship of a State is clearly recognized and established. Not only may a man be a citizen of the United States without being a citizen of a State, but an important element is necessary to convert the former into the latter. He must reside within the State to make him a citizen of it, but it is only necessary that he should be born or naturalized in the United States to be a citizen of the Union.

It is quite clear, then, that there is a citizenship of the United States, and a citizenship of a State, which are distinct from each other, and which depend upon different characteristics or circumstances in the individual.

[C]

We think this distinction and its explicit recognition in this amendment of great weight in this argument, because the next paragraph of this same section, which is the one mainly relied on by the plaintiffs in error, speaks only of privileges and immunities of citizens of the United States, and does not speak of those of citizens of the several States. The argument, however, in favor of the plaintiffs rests wholly on the assumption that the citizenship is the same, and the privileges and immunities guaranteed by the clause are the same.

The language is, 'No State shall make or enforce any law which shall abridge the privileges or immunities of citizens of *the United States.*' It is a little remarkable, if this clause was intended as a protection to the citizen of a State against the legislative power of his own State, that the word citizen of the State should be left out when it is so carefully used, and used in contradistinction to citizens of the United States, in the very sentence which precedes it. It is too clear for argument that the change in phraseology was adopted understandingly and with a purpose.

If, then, there is a difference between the privileges and immunities belonging to a citizen of the United States as such, and those belonging to the citizen of the State as such the latter must rest for their security and protection where they have heretofore rested; for they are not embraced by this paragraph of the amendment.

[D]

The first occurrence of the words 'privileges and immunities' in our constitutional history, is to be found in the fourth of the articles of the old Confederation. In the

Constitution of the United States, which superseded the Articles of Confederation, the corresponding provision is found in section two of the fourth article, in the following words: 'The citizens of each State shall be entitled to all the privileges and immunities of citizens of the several States.'

There can be but little question that the purpose of both these provisions is the same, and that the privileges and immunities intended are the same in each. Fortunately we are not without judicial construction of this clause of the Constitution. The first and the leading case on the subject is that of *Corfield* v. *Coryell*, decided by Mr. Justice Washington in the Circuit Court for the District of Pennsylvania in 1823. [6 Fed. Cas. 546 (No. 3,230) (C.C.E.D. Pa. 1823)].

'The inquiry,' he says, 'is, what are the privileges and immunities of citizens of the several States? We feel no hesitation in confining these expressions to those privileges and immunities which are *fundamental;* which belong of right to the citizens of all free governments, and which have at all times been enjoyed by citizens of the several States which compose this Union, from the time of their becoming free, independent, and sovereign. What these fundamental principles are, it would be more tedious than difficult to enumerate. They may all, however, be comprehended under the following general heads: protection by the government, with the right to acquire and possess property of every kind, and to pursue and obtain happiness and safety, subject, nevertheless, to such restraints as the government may prescribe for the general good of the whole.'

The constitutional provision there alluded to did not create those rights, which it called privileges and immunities of citizens of the States. It threw around them in that clause no security for the citizen of the State in which they were claimed or exercised. Nor did it profess to control the power of the State governments over the rights of its own citizens.

Its sole purpose was to declare to the several States, that whatever those rights, as you grant or establish them to your own citizens, or as you limit or qualify, or impose restrictions on their exercise, the same, neither more nor less, shall be the measure of the rights of citizens of other States within your jurisdiction.

[E]

It would be the vainest show of learning to attempt to prove by citations of authority, that up to the adoption of the recent amendments, no claim or pretence was set up that those rights depended on the Federal government for their existence or protection, beyond the very few express limitations which the Federal Constitution imposed upon the States-such, for instance, as the prohibition against ex post facto laws, bills of attainder, and laws impairing the obligation of contracts. But with the exception of these and a few other restrictions, the entire domain of the privileges and immunities of citizens of the States, as above defined, lay within the constitutional and legislative power of the States, and without that of the Federal government. Was it the purpose of the fourteenth amendment, by the simple declaration that no State should make or enforce any law which shall abridge the privileges and immunities of *citizens of the United States*, to transfer the security and protection of all the civil rights which we have mentioned, from the States to the Federal government? And where it is declared that Congress shall have the power to enforce that article, was it intended to bring within the power of Congress the entire domain of civil rights heretofore belonging exclusively to the States?

All this and more must follow, if the proposition of the plaintiffs in error be sound. For not only are these rights subject to the control of Congress whenever in its discretion any of them are supposed to be abridged by State legislation, but that body may also pass laws in advance, limiting and restricting the exercise of legislative power by the States, in their most ordinary and usual functions, as in its judgment it may think proper on all such subjects. And still further, such a construction would constitute this court a perpetual censor upon all legislation of the States, on the civil rights of their own citizens, with authority to nullify such as it did not approve as consistent with those rights, as they existed at the time of the adoption of this amendment. The argument we admit is not always the most conclusive which is drawn from the consequences urged against the adoption of a particular construction of an instrument. But when, as in the case before us, these consequences are so serious, so far-reaching and pervading, so great a departure from the structure and spirit of our institutions; when the effect is to fetter and degrade the State governments by subjecting them to the control of Congress, in the exercise of powers heretofore universally conceded to them of the most ordinary and fundamental character; when in fact it radically changes the whole theory of the relations of the State and Federal governments to each other and of both these governments to the people; the argument has a force that is irresistible, in the absence of language which expresses such a purpose too clearly to admit of doubt. We are convinced that no such results were intended by the Congress which proposed these amendments, nor by the legislatures of the States which ratified them.

[F]

Having shown that the privileges and immunities relied on in the argument are those which belong to citizens of the States as such, and that they are left to the State governments for security and protection, and not by this article placed under the special care of the Federal government, we may hold ourselves excused from defining the privileges and immunities of citizens of the United States which no State can abridge, until some case involving those privileges may make it necessary to do so.

But lest it should be said that no such privileges and immunities are to be found if those we have been considering are excluded, we venture to suggest some which own their existence to the Federal government, its National character, its Constitution, or its laws. One of these is the right of the citizen of this great country 'to come to the seat of government to assert any claim he may have upon that government. He has the right of free access to its seaports, through which all operations of foreign commerce are conducted, to the subtreasuries, land offices, and courts of justice in the several States.'

Another privilege of a citizen of the United States is to demand the care and protection of the Federal government over his life, liberty, and property when on the high seas or within the jurisdiction of a foreign government. The right to peaceably assemble and petition for redress of grievances, the privilege of the writ of *habeas corpus*, are rights of the citizen guaranteed by the Federal Constitution. The right to use the navigable waters of the United States, however they may penetrate the territory of the several States, all rights secured to our citizens by treaties with foreign nations, are dependent upon citizenship of the United States, and not citizenship of a State. One of these privileges is conferred by the very article under consideration. It is that a citizen of the United States can, of his own volition, become a citizen of any State of the Union by a *bonâ fide* residence therein, with the same rights as other citizens of that State. To these may be added the rights secured by the thirteenth and fifteenth articles of amendment, and by the other clause of the fourteenth.

But it is useless to pursue this branch of the inquiry, since we are of opinion that the rights claimed by these plaintiffs in error, if they have any existence, are not privileges and immunities of citizens of the United States within the meaning of the clause of the fourteenth amendment under consideration.

[IV]

In the early history of the organization of the government, its statesmen seem to have divided on the line which should separate the powers of the National government from those of the State governments, and though this line has never been very well defined in public opinion, such a division has continued from that day to this.

The adoption of the first eleven amendments to the Constitution so soon after the original instrument was accepted, shows a prevailing sense of danger at that time from the Federal power. It was then discovered that the true danger to the perpetuity of the Union was in the capacity of the State organizations to combine and concentrate all the powers of the State, and of contiguous States, for a determined resistance to the General Government.

But, however pervading this sentiment, and however it may have contributed to the adoption of the amendments we have been considering, we do not see in those amendments any purpose to destroy the main features of the general system. Under the pressure of all the excited feeling growing out of the war, our statesmen have still believed that the existence of the State with powers for domestic and local government was essential to the perfect working of our complex form of government, though they have thought proper to impose additional limitations on the States, and to confer additional power on that of the Nation.

But whatever fluctuations may be seen in the history of public opinion on this subject during the period of our national existence, we think it will be found that this court, so far as its functions required, has always held with a steady and an even hand the balance between State and Federal power, and we trust that such may continue to be the history of its relation to that subject so long as it shall have duties to perform which demand of it a construction of the Constitution, or of any of its parts.

The judgments of the Supreme Court of Louisiana in these cases are

AFFIRMED.

MR. JUSTICE FIELD, dissenting:

[I]

The provisions of the fourteenth amendment, cover, in my judgment, the case before us, and inhibit any legislation which confers special and exclusive privileges like these under consideration. The amendment was adopted to obviate objections which had been raised and pressed with great force to the validity of the Civil Rights Act, and to place the common rights of American citizens under the protection of the National government.

[II]

The first clause of this amendment determines who are citizens of the United States, and how their citizenship is created. In the Dred Scott case this subject of citizenship of the United States was fully and elaborately discussed. The Chief Justice, in that case, and a majority of the court with him, held that the words 'people of the United States' and 'citizens' were synonymous terms; and that the descendants of persons brought to this country and sold as slaves were not, and could not be citizens within the meaning of the Constitution.

The first clause of the fourteenth amendment changes this whole subject, and removes it from the region of discussion and doubt. It recognizes in express terms citizens of the United States, and it makes their citizenship dependent upon the place of their birth, or the fact of their adoption, and not upon the constitution or laws of any State or the condition of their ancestry. A citizen of a State is now only a citizen of the United States residing in that State. The fundamental rights, privileges, and immunities which belong to him as a free man and a free citizen, now belong to him as a citizen of the United States, and are not dependent upon his citizenship of any State.

The amendment does not attempt to confer any new privileges or immunities upon citizens, or to enumerate or define those already existing. It assumes that there are such privileges and immunities which belong of right to citizens as such, and ordains that they shall not be abridged by State legislation. If this inhibition has no reference to privileges and immunities of this character, but only refers, as held by the majority of the court in their opinion, to such privileges and immunities as were before its adoption specially designated in the Constitution or necessarily implied as belonging to citizens of the United States, it was a vain and idle enactment, which accomplished nothing, and most unnecessarily excited Congress and the people on its passage. With privileges and immunities thus designated or implied no State could ever have interfered by its laws, and no new constitutional provision was required to inhibit such interference. The supremacy of the Constitution and the laws of the United States always controlled any State legislation of that character. But if the amendment refers to the natural and inalienable rights which belong to all citizens, the inhibition has a profound significance and consequence.

[III]
[A]

What, then, are the privileges and immunities which are secured against abridgment by State legislation? In the first section of the Civil Rights Act Congress has given its interpretation to these terms, or at least has stated some of the rights which, in its judgment, these terms include. That act, it is true, was passed before the fourteenth amendment, but the amendment was adopted to obviate objections to the act, or, speaking more accurately, I should say, to obviate objections to legislation of a similar character, extending the protection of the National government over the common rights of all citizens of the United States.

The terms, privileges and immunities, are not new in the amendment; they were in the Constitution before the amendment was adopted. They are found in the second section of the fourth article, and they have been the subject of frequent consideration in judicial decisions. In *Corfield* v. *Coryell*, Mr. Justice Washington said he had 'no hesitation in confining these expressions to those privileges and immunities which were, in their nature, fundamental; which belong of right to citizens of all free governments.' This appears to me to be a sound construction of the clause in question. The privileges and immunities designated are those *which of right belong to the citizens of all free governments*. Clearly among these must be placed the right to pursue a lawful employment in a lawful manner, without other restraint than such as equally affects all persons. In the discussions in Congress upon the passage of the Civil Rights Act repeated reference was made to this language of Mr. Justice Washington.

[B]

What the [privileges and immunities] clause did for the protection of the citizens of one State against hostile and discriminating legislation of other States, the fourteenth amendment does for the protection of every citizen of the United States against hostile and discriminating legislation against him in favor of others, whether they reside in the same or in different States. If under the fourth article of the Constitution equality of privileges and immunities is secured between citizens of different States, under the fourteenth amendment the same equality is secured between citizens of the United States.

It will not be pretended that under the fourth article of the Constitution any State could create a monopoly in any known trade or manufacture in favor of her own citizens which would exclude an equal participation in the trade or manufacture monopolized by citizens of other States. The non-resident citizens could claim equality of privilege under the provisions of the fourth article with the citizens of the State exercising the monopoly as well as with others, and thus, as respects them, the monopoly would cease.

Now, [t]he privileges and immunities of citizens of the United States is secured against abridgment in any form by any State. The fourteenth amendment places them under the guardianship of the National authority. All monopolies in any known trade or manufacture are an invasion of these privileges, for they encroach upon the liberty of citizens to acquire property and pursue happiness. That amendment was intended to give practical effect to the declaration of 1776 of inalienable rights, rights which are the gift of the Creator, which the law does not confer, but only recognizes.

[C]

The State may prescribe such regulations for every pursuit and calling of life as will promote the public health, secure the good order and advance the general prosperity of society, but when once prescribed, the pursuit or calling must be free to be followed by every citizen who is within the conditions designated, and will conform to the regulations. This is the fundamental idea upon which our institutions rest, and unless adhered to in the legislation of the country our government will be a republic only in name. That only is a free government, in the American sense of the term, under which the inalienable right of every citizen to pursue his happiness is unrestrained, except by just, equal, and impartial laws.

[IV]

I am authorized by the CHIEF JUSTICE, MR. JUSTICE SWAYNE, and MR. JUSTICE BRADLEY, to state that they concur with me in this dissenting opinion.

MR. JUSTICE BRADLEY, also dissenting:

[I]

It is contended that this prohibition abridges the privileges and immunities of citizens of the United States; and whether it does so or not is the simple question in this case. And the solution of this question depends upon the solution of two other questions, to wit:

First. Is it one of the rights and privileges of a citizen of the United States to pursue such civil employment as he may choose to adopt, subject to such reasonable regulations as may be prescribed by law? Secondly. Is a monopoly, or exclusive right, given to one person to the exclusion of all others, to keep slaughter-houses, a reasonable regulation of that employment which the legislature has a right to impose?

[I]
[A]

The first of these questions is one of vast importance, and lies at the very foundations of our government. The question is now settled by the fourteenth amendment itself, that citizenship of the United States is the primary citizenship in this country; and that State citizenship is secondary and derivative, depending upon citizenship of the United States and the citizen's place of residence. A citizen of the United States has a perfect constitutional right to go to and reside in any State he chooses, and to claim citizenship therein, and an equality of rights with every other citizen; and the whole power of the nation is pledged to sustain him in that right. Citizenship of the United States ought to be, and, according to the Constitution, is, a sure and undoubted title to equal rights in any and every States in this Union, subject to such regulations as the legislature may rightfully prescribe.

[W]hat, in general, are the privileges and immunities of a citizen of the United States? [I]n my judgment, the right of any citizen to follow whatever lawful employment he chooses to adopt (submitting himself to all lawful regulations) is one of his most valuable rights, and one which the legislature of a State cannot invade, whether restrained by its own constitution or not.

The right of a State to regulate the conduct of its citizens is undoubtedly a very broad and extensive one, and not to be lightly restricted. But there are certain fundamental rights which this right of regulation cannot infringe. It may prescribe the manner of their exercise, but it cannot subvert the rights themselves.

[T]he individual citizen, as a necessity, must be left free to adopt such calling, profession, or trade as may seem to him most conducive to that end. Without this right he cannot be a freeman. This right to choose one's calling is an essential part of that liberty which it is the object of government to protect; and a calling, when chosen, is a man's property and right.

On this point the often-quoted language of Mr. Justice Washington, in *Corfield* v. *Coryell*, is very instructive. It is pertinent to observe that both the clause of the Constitution referred to, and Justice Washington in his comment on it, speak of the privileges and immunities of citizens *in* a State; not of citizens *of* a State. It is the privileges and immunities of citizens, that is, of citizens as such, that are to be accorded to citizens of other States when they are found in any State.

[B]

The keeping of a slaughter-house is part of, and incidental to, the trade of a butcher-one of the ordinary occupations of human life. To compel a butcher, or rather all the butchers of a large city and an extensive district, to slaughter their cattle in another person's slaughter-house and pay him a toll therefor, is such a restriction upon the trade as materially to interfere with its prosecution. It has none of the qualities of a police regulation. If it were really a police regulation, it would undoubtedly be within the power of the legislature. That portion of the act which requires all slaughter-houses to be located below the city, and to be subject to inspection, is clearly a police regulation. That portion which allows no one but the favored company to build, own, or have slaughter-houses is not a police regulation. It is one of those arbitrary and unjust laws made in the interest of a few scheming individuals.

[III]
[A]

Lastly: Can the Federal courts administer relief to citizens of the United States whose privileges and immunities have been abridged by a State? Of this I entertain no doubt. Prior to the fourteenth amendment this could not be done, except in a few instances, for the want of the requisite authority.

As the great mass of citizens of the United States were also citizens of individual

States, many of their general privileges and immunities would be the same in the one capacity as in the other. Having this double citizenship, and the great body of municipal laws intended for the protection of person and property being the laws of the State, and no provision being made, and no machinery provided by the Constitution, except in a few specified cases, for any interference by the General Government between a State and its citizens, the protection of the citizen in the enjoyment of his fundamental privileges and immunities (except where a citizen of one State went into another State) was largely left to State laws and State courts, where they will still continue to be left unless actually invaded by the unconstitutional acts or delinquency of the State governments themselves.

Admitting, therefore, that formerly the States were not prohibited from infringing any of the fundamental privileges and immunities of citizens of the United States, except in a few specified cases, that cannot be said now, since the adoption of the fourteenth amendment. In my judgment, it was the intention of the people of this country in adopting that amendment to provide National security against violation by the States of the fundamental rights of the citizen.

If my views are correct with regard to what are the privileges and immunities of citizens, it follows conclusively that any law which establishes a sheer monopoly, depriving a large class of citizens of the privilege of pursuing a lawful employment, does abridge the privileges of those citizens.

[B]

But great fears are expressed that this construction of the amendment will lead to enactments by Congress interfering with the internal affairs of the States, and establishing therein civil and criminal codes of law for the government of the citizens, and thus abolishing the State governments in everything but name.

In my judgment no such practical inconveniences would arise. Very little, if any, legislation on the part of Congress would be required to carry the amendment into effect. Like the prohibition against passing a law impairing the obligation of a contract, it would execute itself. The point would be regularly raised, in a suit at law, and settled by final reference to the Federal court. As the privileges and immunities protected are only those fundamental ones which belong to every citizen, they would soon become so far defined as to cause but a slight accumulation of business in the Federal courts. Besides, the recognized existence of the law would prevent its frequent violation. But even if the business of the National courts should be increased, Congress could easily supply the remedy by increasing their number and efficiency. The great question is, What is the true construction of the amendment? When once we find that, we shall find the means of giving it effect. The argument from inconvenience ought not to have a very controlling influence in questions of this sort. The National will and National interest are of far greater importance.

In my opinion the judgment of the Supreme Court of Louisiana ought to be reversed.

Mr. Justice Swayne, dissenting: [Opinion omitted.]

EXERCISE 2:

1. What "privilege" or "immunity" did the plaintiffs allege the state denied them?

2. What are the "privileges or immunities" protected by the Clause under the Supreme Court's interpretation?

3. Explain the Supreme Court's textual argument that the Privileges or Immunities Clause only protected the privileges or immunities of *national* citizenship from state infringement.

4. Explain the Supreme Court's use of history to guide its interpretation of the Clause. How did the majority describe the Clause's history, and how did that history impact its interpretation of the Clause?

5. The Supreme Court stated that one of the purposes of the Fourteenth Amendment was to eliminate the Black Codes enacted after the Civil War by recalcitrant southern states. Is this fact in tension with the Supreme Court's ultimate interpretation of the Privileges or Immunities Clause?

6. What role did the principle of federalism play in the Court's opinion? Justice Bradley responded to the majority's federalism-based claims. What was his response? Was it persuasive?

7. Was it appropriate for the majority to rely on the principle of federalism since it is not explicitly stated in the Constitution?

8. The majority pointed to the devastating effect on federalism if it adopted the plaintiffs' relatively broad interpretation of the Clause. But, what about the bad effects of the majority's own interpretation? What are those potential bad effects?

9. Re-read, carefully, Justice Miller's quotation of Article IV's Privileges and Immunities Clause and compare it to the Constitution. *See* Richard L. Arynes, *Constructing the Law of Freedom: Justice Miller, the Fourteenth Amendment, and the* Slaughter-House Cases, 70 Chi.-Kent L. Rev. 627, 646–48 (1994) (arguing that Justice Miller intentionally misquoted the Clause). Construct an argument that Justice Miller's *mis*quotation of the Clause enabled his (mis)interpretation of the Privileges or Immunities Clause.

10. At the end of its opinion, the Supreme Court stated that it "held with a steady and an even hand the balance between State and Federal power." This vision of the Supreme Court as the neutral arbiter of the federal-state balance has been, and continues to be prominent in the Court's case law. For instance, in a recent line of cases, discussed in **Chapter 4**, of Volume 4, the Court explicitly cast itself in the role of arbiter of the federal-state balance. *See also United States v. Morrison*, 529 U.S. 598, 618 n.8 (2000) ("[T]he Constitution's separation of federal power and the creation of the Judicial Branch indicate that disputes regarding the extent of congressional power are largely subject to judicial review.").

11.   The Supreme Court noted that it was interpreting the Reconstruction Amendments, which had been adopted shortly before, and that the Justices were therefore familiar with the Amendment. Is that fact an aid or hindrance to constitutional interpretation?

12.   Justice Bradley, in dissent, argued that one of the privileges protected by the Clause was the privilege to choose one's profession. Justice Bradley did not, however, view this as an absolute privilege. How did he determine, then, whether a regulation of a privilege violated that privilege?

13.   The Supreme Court's narrow interpretation of the Privileges or Immunities Clause was of-a-piece with its limited interpretations of the Reconstruction Amendments more generally during this period. For example, in 1883, the Court decided *The Civil Rights Cases*, 109 U.S. 3 (1883), discussed in **Chapter 1**, which held that the Fourteenth Amendment's restrictions only applied to state action. This interpretation narrowed Congress' ability to directly regulate individual actions and thereby preserved a space for state regulation. Though this "state action doctrine" is a deeply entrenched component of constitutional law, it is criticized as improperly narrowing the Constitution's scope.

14.   The Supreme Court's narrow interpretation of the Clause has been subject to withering criticism, both on and off the bench. *See, e.g., Saenz v. Roe*, 526 U.S. 489, 522, n.1, 527 (1999) (Thomas, J., dissenting) (arguing that scholars agree "that the Clause does not mean what the Court said it meant in 1873"); Akhil Reed Amar, *Substance and Method in the Year 2000*, 28 PEPP. L. REV. 601, 631 n.178 (2001) ("Virtually no serious modern scholar-left, right, and center-thinks that this is a plausible reading of the Amendment."). If these critics are right, should the Supreme Court reverse *The Slaughter-House Cases*? If these critics are wrong, but nearly everyone believes they are correct, should the Supreme Court reverse *The Slaughter-House Cases*?

D.   CONTINUED DORMANCY OF THE PRIVILEGES OR IMMUNITIES CLAUSE

The Slaughter-Houses Cases entombed the Privileges or Immunities Clause in stare decisis. On two occasions, the Supreme Court seemed poised to reinvigorate the Clause. In 1999, the Supreme Court decided *Saenz v. Roe*, 526 U.S. 489 (1999).[48] The Court faced a constitutional challenge to a California law that limited state welfare benefits of residents who had resided in California for less than twelve months to the amount the newly-arrived residents would have received at their state of most-recent residency. In a complicated opinion, written by Justice Stevens, the Court ruled that the statute violated the constitutional right of travel protected, in part, by the Privileges or Immunities Clause. *Id.* at 502–07. The Court found that the residency limitation unconstitutionally burdened the right to travel. Despite the Court's use of the Clause, no subsequent case has followed *Saenz's* ambiguous lead.

---

[48] The Supreme Court relied on the Clause on one other occasion, but that case was overruled shortly thereafter. Colgate v. Harvey, 296 U.S. 404 (1935), *overruled by* Madden v. Kentucky, 309 U.S. 83 (1940).

After *Saenz*, scholars and litigants speculated that the Supreme Court may be open to reviving the Privileges or Immunities Clause. A test case for this view arrived in *McDonald v. Chicago*, 130 S. Ct. 3020 (2010), where the Court was asked to incorporate the Second Amendment against the states via the Privileges or Immunities Clause. Doing so would have required overrule or limiting *The Slaughter-House Cases*. The portion of *McDonald* addressing this question is reprinted below.

McDONALD v. CITY OF CHICAGO
130 S. Ct. 3020 (2010)

JUSTICE ALITO announced the judgment of the Court and delivered the opinion of the Court with respect to Parts I, II-A, II-B, II-D, III-A, and III-B, in which THE CHIEF JUSTICE, JUSTICE SCALIA, JUSTICE KENNEDY, and JUSTICE THOMAS join, and an opinion with respect to Parts II-C, IV, and V, in which THE CHIEF JUSTICE, JUSTICE SCALIA, and JUSTICE KENNEDY join.

Two years ago, in *District of Columbia v. Heller*, 554 U.S. 570 (2008), we held that the Second Amendment protects the right to keep and bear arms for the purpose of self-defense, and we struck down a District of Columbia law that banned the possession of handguns in the home. The city of Chicago (City) and the village of Oak Park, a Chicago suburb, have laws that are similar to the District of Columbia's, but Chicago and Oak Park argue that their laws are constitutional because the Second Amendment has no application to the States.

II
A

Petitioners' primary submission is that this right is among the "privileges or immunities of citizens of the United States" and that the narrow interpretation of the Privileges or Immunities Clause adopted in the *Slaughter-House Cases*, [83 U.S. (16 Wall.) 36 (1873),] should now be rejected.

B

Four years after the adoption of the Fourteenth Amendment, this Court was asked to interpret the Amendment's reference to "the privileges or immunities of citizens of the United States." Justice Samuel Miller's opinion for the Court concluded that the Privileges or Immunities Clause protects only those rights "which owe their existence to the Federal government, its National character, its Constitution, or its laws."

In drawing a sharp distinction between the rights of federal and state citizenship, the Court relied on two principal arguments. First, the Court emphasized that the Fourteenth Amendment's Privileges or Immunities Clause spoke of "the privileges or immunities of *citizens of the United States*," and the Court contrasted this phrasing with the wording in the first sentence of the Fourteenth Amendment and in the Privileges and Immunities Clause of Article IV, both of which refer to *state* citizenship. Second, the Court stated that a contrary reading would "radically chang[e] the whole theory of the relations of the State and Federal governments to each other and of both these governments to the people," and the Court refused to conclude that such a change had been made "in the absence of language which expresses such a purpose too clearly to admit of doubt." Finding the phrase "privileges or immunities of citizens of the United States" lacking by this high standard, the Court reasoned that the phrase must mean something more limited.

Today, many legal scholars dispute the correctness of the narrow *Slaughter-House* interpretation.

C

Petitioners argue that we should hold that the right to keep and bear arms is one of the "privileges or immunities of citizens of the United States." In petitioners' view, the Privileges or Immunities Clause protects all of the rights set out in the Bill of Rights, as well as some others, but petitioners are unable to identify the Clause's full scope, Tr. of Oral Arg. 5-6, 8-11. Nor is there any consensus on that question among the scholars who agree that the *Slaughter-House Cases'* interpretation is flawed. See *Saenz* [*v. Roe*, 526 U.S. 489,] 522, n. 1 (THOMAS, J., dissenting).

We see no need to reconsider that interpretation here. For many decades, the question of the rights protected by the Fourteenth Amendment against state infringement has been analyzed under the Due Process Clause of that Amendment and not under the Privileges or Immunities Clause. We therefore decline to disturb the *Slaughter-House* holding.

EXERCISE 3:

1. What effect does *McDonald* have on the viability of the Privileges or Immunities Clause?

2. Did the Court persuade you that it need not revisit *Slaughter-House*?

3. *McDonald* is reprinted in more detail in **Chapter 3**, where it includes the Supreme Court's most-recent discussion of the Incorporation Doctrine.

Chapter 3

THE DUE PROCESS CLAUSE

A. INTRODUCTION

The Due Process Clause of the Fourteenth Amendment states: "[N]or shall any State deprive any person of life, liberty, or property, without due process of law." U.S. CONST. amend. XIV, § 1. The Clause serves three primary functions. First, it is the vehicle by which the Supreme Court "incorporates" the Bill of Rights against the states. Second, the Supreme Court interprets the Clause as a source of unenumerated constitutional rights. Third, the Clause prescribes the procedures government must utilize to take away a person's life, liberty, or property. **Chapter 3** considers the first two functions.

EXERCISE 1:

Apply the first four forms of argument to the Due Process Clause.

1.   Looking at the Due Process Clause itself, the text of the rest of the Fourteenth Amendment, and the Fifth Amendment, what do you learn about the Due Process Clause's meaning?

2.   Looking at the Constitution's structure, and particularly at the Reconstruction Amendments, what do you learn about the Due Process Clause's meaning?

3.   Reviewing evidence of the Due Process Clause's original meaning, what does it tell you about that meaning?

4.   Do the materials following adoption of the Fourteenth Amendment offer any insight into the Due Process Clause's meaning?

The Due Process Clause of the Fourteenth[1] Amendment, since its ratification, has been and remains a focus of American constitutional law. It is also one of the most contentious areas of constitutional law.

Chapter 3 is divided into two main components, which reflect two of the Due Process Clause's primary functions. Part C reviews the process labeled "incorpora-

---

[1] The Supreme Court, with a few minor exceptions, interprets the Due Process Clauses of the Fourteenth and Fifth Amendments identically. For the two most important exceptions, see Williams v. Florida, 399 U.S. 78 (1970) (holding that the Sixth Amendment does not require states to employ twelve-person juries in criminal trials); Apodaca v. Oregon, 406 U.S. 404 (1972) (ruling that the Sixth Amendment does not require states to utilize unanimous jury verdicts in criminal cases).

tion." This is the case law in which the Supreme Court ruled that the original Bill of Rights applied to the states via the Fourteenth Amendment's Due Process Clause. Over the course of several decades, in the early to mid-twentieth century, the Court employed the Due Process Clause for incorporation, after the near-demise of the Privileges or Immunities Clause in *The Slaughter-House Cases*, 83 U.S. (16 Wall.) 36 (1872), discussed in **Chapter 2**.

Parts D and F cover the Supreme Court's utilization of the Due Process Clause as a source of *un*enumerated rights. Known as "substantive due process," the Court's jurisprudence in this area is conventionally divided into two eras: "classical" substantive due process and "modern" substantive due process. We will review both periods because modern doctrine builds on, in reaction to, and in the shadow of what occurred during the classical period. The key pivot point in substantive due process doctrine was, as in so many areas of constitutional law, the New Deal, which we cover briefly in Section E.

As you read the materials below, some of the issues to consider include:

Is incorporation of the Bill of Rights against the states a faithful reading of the Due Process Clause?

What test does the Supreme Court utilize to determine whether a right is incorporated?

Is incorporation of the Bill of Rights against the states a good idea?

Is substantive due process faithful to the Due Process Clause?

What analysis(es) does the Supreme Court utilize to determine if an unenumerated right is constitutionally protected from state interference under its substantive due process doctrine? Which is the best?

What rights has the Supreme Court ruled are protected under substantive due process? Should all of these be protected? What additional rights, if any, should also be protected?

What analysis does the Supreme Court use to evaluate restrictions on "fundamental" rights? On other rights?

In what ways are incorporation and substantive due process distinct? Similar?

In what ways, if any, are classical and modern substantive due process distinct? For example, are their modes of analysis different? Is one, or are both or neither, legitimate?

Assuming that you believe that at least some of the rights protected by substantive due process are normatively attractive, can you still criticize the doctrine as illegitimate? If so, how?

B. ORIGINAL MEANING OF THE DUE PROCESS CLAUSE

The original meaning of the Due Process Clause of the Fourteenth Amendment (and the Fifth Amendment, to a lesser degree) is deeply contested,[2] and the scholarly consensus on that meaning has altered dramatically over time.[3] This brief review of the Clauses' original meaning focuses on whether, and to what extent, they ensured more than *process*: whether they also protected unenumerated constitutional rights. This summary concludes that, while it is relatively clear that the Fifth Amendment's Due Process Clause did not possess a substantive component, it is also relatively clear that the Fourteenth Amendment's Due Process Clause possessed a limited substantive component.[4]

The history of the Fifth Amendment's Due Process Clause suggests that it protected only process. The Clause was part of the original Bill of Rights introduced by James Madison to assuage Anti-Federalist fears that the new federal government would be too powerful. There was little discussion of the Due Process Clause in the First Congress and state ratification conventions,[5] which indicates that the Clause was uncontroversial in a way that a vaguely worded substantive provision would not have been.[6]

---

[2] *See* JOHN HART ELY, DEMOCRACY AND DISTRUST: A THEORY OF JUDICIAL REVIEW 18 (1980) (stating famously that substantive due process "is a contradiction in terms — sort of like 'green pastel redness' ").

[3] The conventional view — that the Due Process Clauses did not have a substantive component — originated in the Progressive Era and was part of a broader challenge to the Supreme Court's jurisprudence at that time. *E.g.*, EDWARD CORWIN, COURT OVER CONSTITUTION 107 (1938); 2 LOUIS B. BOUDIN, GOVERNMENT BY JUDICIARY? 374–96 (1932); *see also* Ryan C. Williams, *The One and Only Substantive Due Process Clause*, 120 YALE L.J. 408, 413–14 (2010) (describing the scholarly back-and-forth); *id.* at 460 (stating that Corwin's scholarship was the leading progressive critique of *Lochner*-era substantive due process).

For a selection of varying views among more recent scholarship see RAOUL BERGER, GOVERNMENT BY JUDICIARY: THE TRANSFORMATION OF THE FOURTEENTH AMENDMENT 222 (2d ed. 1997) (concluding that the Due Process Clauses "*did not mean*, in either 1789 or 1866 . . . judicial power to override legislation on substantive or policy grounds"); ROBERT H. BORK, THE TEMPTING OF AMERICA: THE POLITICAL SEDUCTION OF THE LAW 31 (1990) (criticizing substantive due process as a "sham"); MICHAEL KENT CURTIS, NO STATE SHALL ABRIDGE: THE FOURTEENTH AMENDMENT AND THE BILL OF RIGHTS 6–9 (1986) ("The [Fourteenth A]mendment declared an anti-slavery constitutional interpretation."); Christopher Wolfe, *The Original Meaning of the Due Process Clause* 228, *in* THE BILL OF RIGHTS: ORIGINAL MEANING AND CURRENT UNDERSTANDING (Eugene W. Hickok, Jr., ed., 1991) (concluding that the Fifth Amendment's Due Process Clause proscribes "acts that deprive people of life, personal liberty, or property without according them the procedures guaranteed by the standing (common and state) law."); MELVIN I. UROFSKY, A MARCH OF LIBERTY: A CONSTITUTIONAL HISTORY OF THE UNITED STATES 496–502 (1988) (arguing that substantive due process arose in the late-nineteenth century); Williams, *supra*, at 415 (concluding that, while the Fifth Amendment's Due Process Clause did not have a substantive component, the Fourteenth Amendment's Due Process Clause had a limited substantive component).

[4] *See, e.g.*, John Harrison, *Substantive Due Process and the Constitutional Text*, 83 Va. L. Rev. 493, 553 (1997) ("While this way of thinking [substantive due process] probably was a novelty . . . in 1791, by 1868 the situation had changed.").

[5] Ely, *supra*, at 325; *see also* Williams, *supra*, at 445 ("The drafting and ratification history of the Fifth Amendment is notoriously sparse.").

[6] Wolfe, *supra*, at 220.

The Clause itself explicitly requires only "process" before the government takes a person's life, liberty, or property.[7] Furthermore, it is nested among other procedural provisions, such as the Fourth Amendment's restrictions on searches and seizures and the Sixth Amendment's regulation of criminal procedure.[8]

The Due Process Clause, during the Founding and today, was traced to *Magna Charta*'s Clause 39,[9] in which King John promised not to imprison, dispossess, banish, or destroy freemen "except by the . . . law of the land."[10] This "law of the land" clause was replaced in 1354 with the words "due process of law,"[11] which later English jurists[12] and, following them, American colonists[13] along with the Framers and Ratifiers,[14] equated with "law of the land."[15] Although not free from doubt,[16] due process during this period probably applied to a particular facet of judicial proceedings.[17]

This limited reading of due process was confirmed by two of the most influential English jurists: Sir Edward Coke and Sir William Blackstone. Coke was the most prominent seventeenth century English jurist. He stated in his *Institutes of the Lawes of England* that "law of the land" was equivalent to "due proces[s] of Law," and that they meant existing common law procedures.[18] Likewise Blackstone, the most prominent eighteenth century jurist, in his famous and influential, *Commentaries on the Laws of England*, described "due process" as one part of proper criminal procedure.[19]

---

[7] U.S. CONST. amend. V; *see also* Harrison, *supra*, at 494 ("[T]he whole idea that the Due Process Clauses have anything to do with the substance of legislation, as opposed to procedures that are used by the government, is subject to the standard objection that because 'process' means procedure, substantive due process is not just an error but a contradiction in terms.").

[8] Wolfe, *supra*, at 217–20.

[9] *See* James W. Ely, Jr., *The Oxymoron Reconsidered: Myth and Reality in the Origins of Substantive Due Process*, 16 CONST. COMMENT 315, 320 (1999) ("Scholars agree that the federal and state due process clauses are derived from the Magna Carta.").

[10] *Magna Charta* 94, *in* THE AMERICAN REPUBLIC: PRIMARY SOURCES (Bruce Frohnen, ed., 2002).

[11] *See* 27 Edw. 3, c. 3 (1354) (Eng.) ("[N]o Man of what Estate or Condition that he be, shall be put out of Land or Tenement, nor taken, nor imprisoned, nor disinherited, nor put to Death, without being brought to Answer by due Process of the Law."); Ely, *supra*, at 320.

[12] *See* 2 EDWARD COKE, INSTITUTES OF THE LAWES OF ENGLAND 50 (Garland ed., 1979) (1797) (stating that the "true sense and exposition of" "by the Law of the Land" is "without due process of law"); *see also id.* at 46 (similar).

[13] Ely, *supra*, at 322.

[14] *Id.* at 321.

[15] *But see* Keith Jurow, *Untimely Thoughts: A Reconsideration of the Origins of Due Process of Law*, 19 AM. J. LEGAL HIST. 265 (1975) (arguing that the phrases were not equivalent).

[16] *See* Ely, *supra*, at 321 (arguing that Sir Edward Coke's description of due process included a substantive component).

[17] Jurow, *supra*, at 267–68.

[18] 2 EDWARD COKE, INSTITUTES OF THE LAWES OF ENGLAND 50 (Lawbook Exchange, Ltd. 2002) (1642).

[19] 4 WILLIAM BLACKSTONE, COMMENTARIES ON THE LAWS OF ENGLAND *318; *see also* 1 *id.* at *133–*34.

This relatively narrow reading is bolstered by a number of relatively contemporary sources. For example, in a debate before the New York general assembly in 1787, Alexander Hamilton defined "due process": "The words 'due process' have a precise technical import, and they are only applicable to the process and proceedings of the courts of justice."[20] Joseph Story, in his influential *Commentaries on the Constitution*, echoed other commentators of the era,[21] stating that the Due Process Clause "in effect affirms the right of trial according to the process of proceedings of the common law."[22] The other, limited, evidence that exists also tends to support this reading.[23]

While most of the evidence suggests that the Fifth Amendment Due Process Clause did not have a substantive component, there is some evidence to the contrary. Stretching back to the eighteenth century, some state courts more broadly interpreted their state due process clauses (or their equivalents).[24] One of the earliest examples is *University of North Carolina v. Foy*, decided in 1804, where a North Carolina state court ruled that the statutory rescission of a previous land grant to the university violated the state constitution because it attempted transfer of property from one party to another without judicial process.[25] Such legislative action lacked, these courts found, the requisite generality and were hence arbitrary.[26]

Given the weight of the evidence, however, the scholarly consensus,[27] though not without dissent,[28] is that the Fifth Amendment Due Process Clause's original meaning did not include a substantive component. For instance, only two states courts utilized a limited substantive due process interpretation prior to 1821, and only one more state court joined them prior to 1838.[29]

---

[20] 4 The Papers of Alexander Hamilton 35–36 (Harold C. Syrett ed., 1962).

[21] *See* Williams, *supra*, at 452–54 (surveying this literature).

[22] 3 Joseph Story, Commentaries on the Constitution of the United States 661 (1833); *see also* 4 James Kent, Commentaries on American Law 10 (1827) (citing Coke's formulation of due process).

[23] *See* First Continental Congress, *Declarations and Resolves* (Oct. 14, 1774), *in* Documents of American History 83 (Henry Steele Commager ed., 7th ed., 1963) ("[T]he respective colonies are entitled to . . . the privilege of being tried by their peers . . . according to the due course of law."); *see also* Williams, *supra*, at 435–45 (surveying American history prior to 1791 and concluding that it supported a procedure-only interpretation of due process).

[24] *See* Williams, *supra*, at 447–48 (describing these cases); *see also* Harrison, *supra*, at 504–10 (tying this evolving jurisprudential articulation of due process to various plausible interpretations of the Clause's text).

[25] University of North Carolina v. Foy, 5 N.C. 58 (1805); *see also* Taylor v. Porter, 4 Hill 140 (N.Y. 1843) (holding that a legislature may not cause the transfer of property from an individual without utilizing judicial process); *compare* Bank of Columbia v. Okely, 17 U.S. (4 Wheat.) 235, 244 (1819) (stating that due process protects "the individual from the arbitrary exercise of the powers of government").

[26] Ely, *supra*, at 336; *see also* Wolfe, *supra*, at 224 (describing this line of cases). Even though cases like *Foy* articulated substantive limits on the legislature, those limits, unlike the Supreme Court's modern substantive due process cases, relatively narrowly pertain to process: the permissible judicial processes by which government can take property or other rights.

[27] *See* Williams, *supra*, at 415 (concluding that, while the Fifth Amendment's Due Process Clause did not have a substantive component, the Fourteenth Amendment's Due Process Clause had a limited substantive component).

[28] *See* Robert E. Riggs, *Substantive Due Process in 1791*, 1990 Wis. L. Rev. 941, 999 (concluding that the Fifth Amendment's Due Process Clause "had substantive as well as procedural content in 1791").

[29] *See* Williams, *supra*, at 461–63 (describing this evolution).

As the nineteenth century progressed, more and more state courts utilized a limited form of substantive due process.[30] State courts used two common analyses to do so.[31] First, they would focus on the word "law" and, after concluding that a challenged governmental action did not constitute "law," hold that it violated due process. In these cases, the courts interpreted their due process clauses to prevent state legislatures from transferring property from one party to another without using *judicial* procedures.[32] Such "laws" did not have the generality requisite for legislation, so courts treated them as judicial appropriations which due process mandated had to proceed via judicial proceedings. Though this was an expansion beyond the purely procedural conception of due process, it was still limited, in its substantive component, to prescribing processes.

The second limited form of substantive due process that arose in the antebellum era interpreted due process to prevent the legislature from taking "vested rights." A vested right was an interest in property or an activity that was lawful when started. Legislatures could not eliminate or take such vested rights. For instance, the most famous and influential antebellum case was the 1856 New York case of *Wynehamer v. New York*.[33] The New York Court of Appeals overturned a conviction under the state's prohibition statute. The court ruled that the state's due process clause meant "that where rights are acquired by the citizen under the existing law, there is no power in any branch of the government to take them away."[34] Since the defendant had lawfully possessed alcoholic beverages prior to passage of the statute, he had a vested right to continue to do so.

Cases like *Wynehamer* represented a broadening from earlier cases like *Foy* because they expanded the substantive limits imposed by substantive due process beyond limits on the extent to which a legislature could modify procedures.[35] These later cases protected rights to such a degree that a legislature could not limit them regardless of the procedures used. These cases set the legal background against which the Reconstruction Congress drafted and debated the Fourteenth Amendment's Due Process Clause.[36]

The first Supreme Court opinion to discuss the meaning of due process, albeit in dicta, was not until the 1852 decision of *Bloomer v. McQuewan*.[37] Chief Justice Taney appeared to articulate the vested rights version of substantive due process when he noted that "a special act of Congress, passed afterwards, depriving the appellees of the right to use [the patented articles], certainly could not be regarded as due process of law."[38]

---

[30] *Id.* at 416.

[31] *Id.* at 416, 424–25.

[32] Ely, *supra*, at 330–33.

[33] Wynehamer v. New York, 13 N.Y. 378 (1856).

[34] *Id.* at 393.

[35] Ely, *supra*, at 338–41.

[36] *Id.* at 345.

[37] Bloomer v. McQuewan, 55 U.S. (14 How.) 539 (1852).

[38] *Id.* at 553. This lack of recourse, until 1852, by plaintiffs to a possible "substantive" component of the

The second Supreme Court interpretation and application of the Due Process Clause occurred three years later in *Murray's Lessee v. Hoboken Land Improvement Co.*[39] There, the Court, after describing the origins of the Due Process Clause in the *Magna Charta*, interpreted the Clause to require that deprivations of life, liberty, or property occur according to "[t]hose settled usages and modes of proceeding existing in the common and statute law of England."[40] To support its reasoning, the Court cited to five state court cases in which the respective courts interpreted their state constitutional provisions in a substantive manner.[41]

One of the precipitating causes of the Civil War, *Dred Scott v. Sanford,*[42] was the first Supreme Court case to actually utilize a substantive due process rationale.[43] Infamously, the *Dred Scott* Court struck down the Missouri Compromise of 1820 based on a substantive reading of the Due Process Clause.[44] Chief Justice Taney held that Congress could not, consistent with the Fifth Amendment, "deprive[] a citizen of the United States of his . . . property, merely because he . . . brought his property into a [a free state or territory]."[45]

Prior to the Civil War, many abolitionists argued that the Due Process Clause outlawed slavery because, among other reasons, slaves had not been deprived of their liberty through proper judicial proceedings.[46] This view was contrary to the broad consensus at the time of the Framing and Ratification, and is therefore not significant evidence on the Fifth Amendment's meaning. However, it is evidence in favor of a substantive view of the Fourteenth Amendment's Due Process Clause because a faction of the Republicans, who controlled the Reconstruction Congress and who where themselves abolitionists,[47] drafted the Fourteenth Amendment.[48] The outstanding significant question is to what extent, if any, did the abolitionists' pre-Civil War — substantive — conception of due process reflect or influence their colleagues in Congress and the rest of America? Most evidence suggests that the abolitionists focused their energy on the Privileges or Immunities Clause's substantive protections and that, in any event, they did not have sufficient influence in Congress to show that

---

Clause is evidence that the Clause was widely understood to have no substantive component. *See* Wolfe, *supra*, at 226 (making this point).

[39] Murray's Lessee v. Hoboken Land Improvement Co., 59 U.S. (18 How.) 272 (1855).

[40] *Id.* at 277.

[41] *Id.* at 280.

[42] Dred Scott v. Sanford, 60 U.S. (19 How.) 393 (1856).

[43] *See* Harrison, *supra*, at 513 (describing *Dred Scott* as an example of "vested rights due process"); *see also* Ely, *supra*, at 317–18 (criticizing the claim that *Dred Scott* was the "fountainhead of substantive due process" because that claim ignores use of the doctrine in "antebellum state and federal courts").

[44] *Dred Scott*, 60 U.S. (19 How.) at 450.

[45] *Id.*

[46] *See, e.g.,* ALVAN STEWART, A CONSTITUTIONAL ARGUMENT ON THE SUBJECT OF SLAVERY (1837).

[47] *See Republican Party Platform of 1856* at 27, *in* NATIONAL PARTY PLATFORMS: 1840–1972 (Donald Bruce Johnson & Kirk H. Porter, eds., 5th ed. 1975) (arguing that the Due Process Clause forbid slavery in national territories).

[48] Williams, *supra*, at 416.

their substantive conception of the Due Process Clause was Congress' conception.[49]

As a result of these developments, by the time of Reconstruction and debate on the Fourteenth Amendment, there was likely a consensus that the concept of due process — at least in the context of states, though, not necessarily, the federal government — incorporated a limited substantive aspect. This substantive component of due process included a prohibition on legislatures eliminating vested property rights and on non-general legislation.[50]

During the congressional debates over the proposed Fourteenth Amendment, the bulk of the debate centered on the Privileges or Immunities Clause. We saw in **Chapter 2** that the Fourteenth Amendment's Framers understood the Privileges or Immunities Clause as the vehicle to incorporate the Bill of Rights against the states. Little debate occurred over the Due Process Clause,[51] it occurred relatively late[52] and, what debate there was suggests that the participants understood the Clause to mean what it meant in then-existing federal and state case law.

The most pointed discussion of the Due Process Clause occurred when Congressman Andrew Rogers, a Democrat from New Jersey, asked: "I only wish to know what you mean by 'due process of law.' "[53] John Bingham, the Republican drafter of the Fourteenth Amendment, answered: "I reply to the gentleman, the courts have settled that long ago, and the gentleman can go and read their decisions."[54] Bingham then appeared to utilize the general-law form of substantive due process when he stated that due process meant "law in its highest sense . . . and which is impartial, equal, exact justice."[55]

What little evidence there is from the congressional debates suggests that the participants understood the Clause as reflecting the legal consensus at the time, developed in state and, to a lesser degree, federal courts. According to this consensus, the Due Process Clause had two limited substantive components: (1) a generality requirement; and (2) a prohibition on the deprivation of vested rights. Evidence from the immediate post-ratification period also seems to support this conclusion.[56]

---

[49] MICHAEL L. BENEDICT, A COMPROMISE OF PRINCIPLE 27 (1975).

[50] Harrison, *supra*, at 553–54.

[51] *See* Williams, *supra*, at 477–83 (reviewing the sparse legislative record).

[52] BERGER, *supra*, at 229.

[53] CONG. GLOBE, 39th Cong., 1st Sess. 1089 (Feb. 28, 1866) (Representative Andrew Rogers).

[54] *Id.* (Representative John Bingham); *see also id.* 1294 (Mar. 9, 1866) (Representative James Wilson) (suggesting a substantive due process conception of the Fifth Amendment's Due Process Clause to support the 1866 Civil Rights Act). However, it appears that Congressman Wilson's view was either not widespread in Congress or perceived as insufficiently widespread because the Republicans introduced the Fourteenth Amendment as a means to cure any constitutional infirmities with the 1866 Civil Rights Act.

[55] *Id.* at 1094 (Feb. 28, 1866) (Representative John Bingham).

[56] *See* Williams, *supra*, at 484–94 (surveying this evidence).

C. THE INCORPORATION DOCTRINE

The Incorporation Doctrine is a key function of the Due Process Clause. The Doctrine holds that (most of) the Bill of Rights applies to the states.

The Incorporation Doctrine was at the heart of intense controversy from the 1920s to the 1960s. The controversy had a number of facets: first, whether the Bill of Rights applied to the states; second, whether the Due Process Clause was the vehicle to make that happen; third, whether the Due Process Clause incorporated some or all of the Bill of Rights; fourth, if the Due Process Clause incorporated only some of the Bill of Rights, what test should the Supreme Court utilize to make that determination; and, fifth, are the rights incorporated against the states identical to the rights as applied to the federal government?

The background to the Incorporation Doctrine has two major components. The first is the Supreme Court case of *Barron v. Baltimore*, 32 U.S. (7 Pet.) 243 (1833), reprinted below, where the Supreme Court ruled that the Bill of Rights only restricted the federal government. The second component is the goal of the Reconstruction Republicans, inherited from the antebellum abolitionist movement, to apply federal constitutional restrictions to the states to prohibit slavery and protect newly freed black Americans.

BARRON v. THE MAYOR AND CITY COUNCIL OF BALTIMORE
32 U.S. (7 Pet.) 243 (1833)

[Barron sued the City of Baltimore for damage caused by the city to his property when it caused his wharf to become silted in.]

MARSHALL, C.J., delivered the opinion of the court.

The plaintiff in error contends, that [the City's act] comes within that clause in the fifth amendment to the constitution, which inhibits the taking of private property for public use, without just compensation. He insists, that this amendment being in favor of the liberty of the citizen, ought to be so construed as to restrain the legislative power of a state, as well as that of the United States. If this proposition be untrue, the court can take no jurisdiction of the cause.

The question thus presented is, we think, of great importance, but not of much difficulty. The constitution was ordained and established by the people of the United States for themselves, for their own government, and not for the government of the individual states. Each state established a constitution for itself, and in that constitution, provided such limitations and restrictions on the powers of its particular government, as its judgment dictated. The people of the United States framed such a government for the United States as they supposed best adapted to their situation and best calculated to promote their interests. The powers they conferred on this government were to be exercised by itself; and the limitations on power, if expressed in general terms, are naturally, and, we think, necessarily, applicable to the government created by the instrument. They are limitations of power granted in the instrument itself; not of distinct governments, framed by different persons and for different purposes.

If these propositions be correct, the fifth amendment must be understood as restraining the power of the general government, not as applicable to the states. In their several constitutions, they have imposed such restrictions on their respective governments, as their own wisdom suggested; such as they deemed most proper for themselves. It is a subject on which they judge exclusively, and with which others interfere no further than they are supposed to have a common interest.

The counsel for the plaintiff relies on the inhibitions contained in the tenth section of the first article. We think, that section affords a strong, if not a conclusive, argument in support of the opinion already indicated by the court.

The preceding section contains restrictions which are obviously intended for the exclusive purpose of restraining the exercise of power by the departments of the general government. Some of them use language applicable only to congress; others are expressed in general terms. The third clause, for example, declares, that 'no bill of attainder or *ex post facto* law shall be passed.' No language can be more general; yet the demonstration is complete, that it applies solely to the government of the United States. In addition to the general arguments furnished by the instrument itself, some of which have been already suggested, the succeeding section, the avowed purpose of which is to restrain state legislation, contains in terms the very prohibition. It declares, that 'no state shall pass any bill of attainder or *ex post facto* law.' This provision, then, of the ninth section, however comprehensive its language, contains no restriction on state legislation.

The ninth section having enumerated, in the nature of a bill of rights, the limitations intended to be imposed on the powers of the general government, the tenth proceeds to enumerate those which were to operate on the state legislatures. These restrictions are brought together in the same section, and are by express words applied to the states. 'No state shall enter into any treaty,' &c. Perceiving, that in a constitution framed by the people of the United States, for the government of all, no limitation of the action of government on the people would apply to the state government, unless expressed in terms, the restrictions contained in the tenth section are in direct words so applied to the states.

It is worthy of remark, too, that these inhibitions generally restrain state legislation on subjects intrusted to the general government, or in which the people of all the states feel an interest. A state is forbidden to enter into any treaty, alliance or confederation. If these compacts are with foreign nations, they interfere with the treaty-making power, which is conferred entirely on the general government; if with each other, for political purposes, they can scarcely fail to interfere with the general purpose and intent of the constitution. In these alone, were the whole people concerned. The question of their application to states is not left to construction. It is averred in positive words.

If the original constitution, in the ninth and tenth sections of the first article, draws this plain and marked line of discrimination between the limitations it imposes on the powers of the general government, and on those of the state; if, in every inhibition intended to act on state power, words are employed, which directly express that intent; some strong reason must be assigned for departing from this safe and judicious course, in framing the amendments, before that departure can be assumed.

We search in vain for that reason. Had the people of the several states, or any of them, required changes in their constitutions; had they required additional safeguards to liberty from the apprehended encroachments of their particular governments; the remedy was in their own hands, and could have been applied by themselves. The unwieldy and cumbrous machinery of procuring a recommendation from two-thirds of congress, and the assent of three-fourths of their sister states, could never have occurred to any human being, as a mode of doing that which might be effected by the state itself. Had the framers of these amendments intended them to be limitations on the powers of the state governments, they would have imitated the framers of the original constitution, and have expressed that intention. Had congress engaged in the extraordinary occupation of improving the constitutions of the several states, by affording the people additional protection from the exercise of power by their own governments, in matters which concerned themselves alone, they would have declared this purpose in plain and intelligible language.

But it is universally understood, it is a part of the history of the day, that the great revolution which established the constitution of the United States, was not effected without immense opposition. Serious fears were extensively entertained, that those powers which the patriot statesmen, who then watched over the interests of our country, deemed essential to union, and to the attainment of those unvaluable objects for which union was sought, might be exercised in a manner dangerous to liberty. In almost every convention by which the constitution was adopted, amendments to guard against the abuse of power were recommended. These amendments demanded security against the apprehended encroachments of the general government not against those of the local governments.

In compliance with a sentiment thus generally expressed, to quiet fears thus extensively entertained, amendments were proposed by the required majority in congress, and adopted by the states. These amendments contain no expression indicating an intention to apply them to the state governments.

We are of opinion, that the provision in the fifth amendment to the constitution, declaring that private property shall not be taken for public use, without just compensation, is intended solely as a limitation on the exercise of power by the government of the United States, and is not applicable to the legislation of the states. This court, therefore, has no jurisdiction of the cause, and it is dismissed.

EXERCISE 2:

1.   What is Chief Justice Marshall's argument based on Article I, §§ 9, 10?

2.   The Court backs up its conclusion that the Bill of Rights is inapplicable to states with a claim grounded in political theory, based on who ratified the federal Constitution. Explain the Court's reasoning.

3.   The Supreme Court further bolstered its conclusion by resort to history. What were the historical contexts of both the original Constitution and the Bill of Rights,

according to the Court, and how did they support the Court's conclusion?

4. The *Barron* Court relied on a robust conception of federalism, one where the states were largely free to order their affairs. Is this an attractive understanding of federalism?

Because of *Barron*, there was a general consensus in the Reconstruction Congress that, even if — as many congressional Republicans argued[57] — *Barron* was wrongly decided, it was prudent to pass a constitutional amendment to ensure the applicability of the Bill of Rights to the states. The Reconstruction Republicans feared that a future Democrat-controlled Congress or the Supreme Court might undermine the gains made during the Civil War and Reconstruction. A constitutional amendment would guarantee that the Supreme Court applied the Bill of Rights to the states despite *Barron*, and prevent later congressional meddling with rights secured during Reconstruction.

Today, most scholars agree that the Framers of the Fourteenth Amendment expected the Privileges or Immunities Clause to apply the Bill of Rights to the states. AKHIL REED AMAR, THE BILL OF RIGHTS: CREATION AND RECONSTRUCTION 181–87 (1998). As recounted above in **Chapter 2**, however, *The Slaughter-House Cases* eliminated that possibility. This set up a dynamic of the temptation to use the Fourteenth Amendment to rein in state injustice coupled with the disappointed original purpose of the Amendment.

Slowly, the Supreme Court moved toward incorporating the Bill of Rights. The first explicit recognition by the Court of the possibility of incorporation via the Due Process Clause occurred in 1908. *Twining v. New Jersey*, 211 U.S. 78, 99 (1908). During this same period, the Supreme Court moved toward explicit recognition of substantive due process (unenumerated rights). For example, in *Allgeyer v. Louisiana*, 165 U.S. 578 (1897), the Court held that the Due Process Clause protected the unenumerated right to contract. The first instance of incorporation occurred in 1925, in *Gitlow v. New York*, 268 U.S. 652 (1925), where the Supreme Court ruled that the states were bound by the Free Speech Clause.

Two main theories of incorporation competed for the Court's allegiance during this period: selective v. total incorporation. Proponents of selective incorporation argued that the Due Process Clause applied some, but not all of the Bill of Rights to the states. Proponents offered different standards to determine which of the Bill of Rights' provisions the Clause would incorporate.

Total incorporation was most famously championed by Justice Black. Justice Black argued that the Fourteenth Amendment's Framers intended the Amendment to apply all of the Bill of Rights against the states. *E.g.*, *Adamson v. California*, 332 U.S. 46, 68–92 (1947) (Black, J., dissenting).

---

[57] Michael Kent Curtis, *The Fourteenth Amendment: Recalling What the Court Forgot*, 56 DRAKE L. REV. 911, 926–27 (2008).

The debates between these two camps consumed many pages in the U.S. Reports but, by the 1960s, the debate became moot. Though utilizing the theory of selective incorporation, the Supreme Court nearly reached the result of total incorporation because all but a handful of the provisions in the Bill of Rights were incorporated against the states.

The most recent case to discuss the Incorporation Doctrine is *McDonald v. Chicago*, a portion of which is reprinted below. *McDonald* describes the history and current status of incorporation.

McDONALD v. CITY OF CHICAGO
130 S. Ct. 3020 (2010)

JUSTICE ALITO announced the judgment of the Court and delivered the opinion of the Court with respect to Parts I, II-A, II-B, II-D, III-A, and III-B, in which THE CHIEF JUSTICE, JUSTICE SCALIA, JUSTICE KENNEDY, and JUSTICE THOMAS join, and an opinion with respect to Parts II-C, IV, and V, in which THE CHIEF JUSTICE, JUSTICE SCALIA, and JUSTICE KENNEDY join.

Two years ago, in *District of Columbia v. Heller*, 554 U.S. 570 (2008), we held that the Second Amendment protects the right to keep and bear arms for the purpose of self-defense, and we struck down a District of Columbia law that banned the possession of handguns in the home. The city of Chicago (City) and the village of Oak Park have laws that are similar to the District of Columbia's, but Chicago and Oak Park argue that their laws are constitutional because the Second Amendment has no application to the States. Applying the standard that is well established in our case law, we hold that the Second Amendment right is fully applicable to the States.

II

B

[The Supreme Court refused to revive the Privileges or Immunities Clause and held instead that the Clause did not protect the right to keep and bear arms from state interference. This portion of the opinion appears in **Chapter 2**. The Court went on to discuss incorporation of the Second Amendment via the Due Process Clause.]

Three years after the decision in the *Slaughter-House Cases*, the Court decided [*United States v.*] *Cruikshank*[, 92 U.S. (2 Otto) 542 (1875)]. In that case, the Court wrote that the right of bearing arms for a lawful purpose "is not a right granted by the Constitution" and is not "in any manner dependent upon that instrument for its existence. The second amendment," the Court continued, "declares that it shall not be infringed; but this . . . means no more than that it shall not be infringed by Congress." "Our later decisions in *Presser v. Illinois*, 116 U.S. 252, 265 (1886), and *Miller v. Texas*, 153 U.S. 535, 538 (1894), reaffirmed that the Second Amendment applies only to the Federal Government."

C

[T]his Court's decisions in *Cruikshank, Presser*, and *Miller* do not preclude us from considering whether the Due Process Clause of the Fourteenth Amendment makes the Second Amendment right binding on the States. As explained more fully below, *Cruikshank, Presser*, and *Miller* all preceded the era in which the Court began the process of "selective incorporation" under the Due Process Clause, and we have never previously addressed the question whether the right to keep and bear arms applies to the States under that theory.

D
1

In the late 19th century, the Court began to consider whether the Due Process Clause prohibits the States from infringing rights set out in the Bill of Rights. Five features of the approach taken during the ensuing era should be noted.

First, the Court viewed the due process question as entirely separate from the question whether a right was a privilege or immunity of national citizenship. Second, the Court explained that the only rights protected against state infringement by the Due Process Clause were those rights "of such a nature that they are included in the conception of due process of law." While it was "possible that some of the personal rights safeguarded by the first eight Amendments against National action [might] also be safeguarded against state action," the Court stated, this was "not because those rights are enumerated in the first eight Amendments." *See Twining* [*v. New Jersey*, 211 U.S. 78,] 99 [(1908)].

The Court used different formulations in describing the boundaries of due process. For example, in *Twining*, the Court referred to "immutable principles of justice which inhere in the very idea of free government which no member of the Union may disregard." And in *Palko*, the Court famously said that due process protects those rights that are "the very essence of a scheme of ordered liberty" and essential to "a fair and enlightened system of justice." *Palko v. Connecticut*, 302 U.S. [319], 325 [(1937)].

Third, in some cases decided during this era the Court "can be seen as having asked, when inquiring into whether some particular procedural safeguard was required of a State, if a civilized system could be imagined that would not accord the particular protection." *Duncan v. Louisiana*, 391 U.S. 145, 149, n. 14, (1968).

Fourth, the Court during this era was not hesitant to hold that a right set out in the Bill of Rights failed to meet the test for inclusion within the protection of the Due Process Clause. Finally, even when a right set out in the Bill of Rights was held to fall within the conception of due process, the protection or remedies afforded against state infringement sometimes differed from the protection or remedies provided against abridgment by the Federal Government.

2

An alternative theory regarding the relationship between the Bill of Rights and § 1 of the Fourteenth Amendment was championed by Justice Black. This theory held that § 1 of the Fourteenth Amendment totally incorporated all of the provisions of the Bill of Rights. As Justice Black noted, the chief congressional proponents of the Fourteenth Amendment espoused the view that the Amendment made the Bill of Rights applicable to the States and, in so doing, overruled this Court's decision in *Barron [v. Baltimore*, 32 U.S. (7 Pet.) 243 (1833)]. Nonetheless, the Court never has embraced Justice Black's "total incorporation" theory.

3

While Justice Black's theory was never adopted, the Court eventually moved in that direction by initiating what has been called a process of "selective incorporation," *i.e.*, the Court began to hold that the Due Process Clause fully incorporates particular rights contained in the first eight Amendments.

The decisions during this time abandoned three of the previously noted characteristics of the earlier period. The Court made it clear that the governing standard is not whether *any* "civilized system [can] be imagined that would not accord the particular protection." *Duncan*, 391 U.S., at 149, n. 14. Instead, the Court inquired whether a particular Bill of Rights guarantee is fundamental to *our* scheme of ordered liberty and system of justice.

The Court also shed any reluctance to hold that rights guaranteed by the Bill of Rights met the requirements for protection under the Due Process Clause. The Court eventually incorporated almost all of the provisions of the Bill of Rights. Only a handful of the Bill of Rights protections remain unincorporated.[13]

Finally, the Court decisively held that incorporated Bill of Rights protections "are all to be enforced against the States under the Fourteenth Amendment according to the same standards that protect those personal rights against federal encroachment."[14]

III

With this framework in mind, we now turn directly to the question whether the Second Amendment right to keep and bear arms is incorporated in the concept of due process. In answering that question, as just explained, we must decide whether the right to keep and bear arms is fundamental to *our* scheme of ordered liberty, *Duncan*,

---

[13] In addition to the right to keep and bear arms, and the Sixth Amendment right to a unanimous jury verdict, the only rights not fully incorporated are (1) the Third Amendment's protection against quartering of soldiers; (2) the Fifth Amendment's grand jury indictment requirement; (3) the Seventh Amendment right to a jury trial in civil cases; and (4) the Eighth Amendment's prohibition on excessive fines.

[14] There is one exception to this general rule. The Court has held that although the Sixth Amendment right to trial by jury requires a unanimous jury verdict in federal criminal trials, it does not require a unanimous jury verdict in state criminal trials.

391 U.S., at 149, or as we have said in a related context, whether this right is "deeply rooted in this Nation's history and tradition," *Washington v. Glucksberg*, 521 U.S. 702, 721 (1997).

A

Our decision in *Heller* points unmistakably to the answer. Self-defense is a basic right, recognized by many legal systems from ancient times to the present day, and in *Heller*, we held that individual self-defense is "the *central component*" of the Second Amendment right.

Heller makes it clear that this right is "deeply rooted in this Nation's history and tradition." *Heller* explored the right's origins, noting that the 1689 English Bill of Rights explicitly protected a right to keep arms for self-defense, and that by 1765, Blackstone was able to assert that the right to keep and bear arms was "one of the fundamental rights of Englishmen." Blackstone's assessment was shared by the American colonists. As we noted in *Heller*, King George III's attempt to disarm the colonists in the 1760's and 1770's "provoked polemical reactions by Americans invoking their rights as Englishmen to keep arms."

The right to keep and bear arms was considered no less fundamental by those who drafted and ratified the Bill of Rights. "During the 1788 ratification debates, the fear that the federal government would disarm the people in order to impose rule through a standing army or select militia was pervasive in Antifederalist rhetoric." Federalists responded, not by arguing that the right was insufficiently important to warrant protection but by contending that the right was adequately protected by the Constitution's assignment of only limited powers to the Federal Government. [C]f. The Federalist No. 46, p. 296 (C. Rossiter ed. 1961) (J. Madison). Thus, Antifederalists and Federalists alike agreed that the right to bear arms was fundamental to the newly formed system of government. This is surely powerful evidence that the right was regarded as fundamental in the sense relevant here.

This understanding persisted in the years immediately following the ratification of the Bill of Rights. In addition to the four States that had adopted Second Amendment analogues before ratification, nine more States adopted state constitutional provisions protecting an individual right to keep and bear arms between 1789 and 1820. Founding-era legal commentators confirmed the importance of the right to early Americans. St. George Tucker, for example, described the right to keep and bear arms as "the true palladium of liberty" and explained that prohibitions on the right would place liberty "on the brink of destruction." 1 Blackstone's Commentaries, Editor's App. 300 (S. Tucker ed. 1803).

B
1

By the 1850's, the perceived threat that had prompted the inclusion of the Second Amendment in the Bill of Rights — the fear that the National Government would disarm the universal militia — had largely faded as a popular concern, but the right to keep and bear arms was highly valued for purposes of self-defense. Abolitionist authors wrote in support of the right. And when attempts were made to disarm "Free-Soilers" in "Bloody Kansas," Senator Charles Sumner, who later played a leading role in the adoption of the Fourteenth Amendment, proclaimed that "[n]ever was [the rifle] more needed in just self-defense than now in Kansas."

After the Civil War, many of the over 180,000 African Americans who served in the Union Army returned to the States of the old Confederacy, where systematic efforts were made to disarm them and other blacks. The laws of some States prohibited African Americans from possessing firearms.

Throughout the South, armed parties, often consisting of ex-Confederate soldiers serving in the state militias, forcibly took firearms from newly freed slaves. In the first session of the 39th Congress, Senator Wilson told his colleagues: "In Mississippi rebel State forces, men who were in the rebel armies, are traversing the State, visiting the freedmen, disarming them, perpetrating murders and outrages upon them; and the same things are done in other sections of the country." 39th Cong. Globe 40 (1865). The Report of the Joint Committee on Reconstruction — which was widely reprinted in the press and distributed by Members of the 39th Congress to their constituents shortly after Congress approved the Fourteenth Amendment — contained numerous examples of such abuses. As Senator Wilson put it during the debate on a failed proposal to disband Southern militias: "There is one unbroken chain of testimony from all people that are loyal to this country, that the greatest outrages are perpetrated by armed men who go up and down the country searching houses, disarming people, committing outrages of every kind and description." 39th Cong. Globe 915 (1866).

[T]he 39th Congress concluded that legislative action was necessary. Its efforts to safeguard the right to keep and bear arms demonstrate that the right was still recognized to be fundamental. The most explicit evidence of Congress' aim appears in § 14 of the Freedmen's Bureau Act of 1866, which explicitly guaranteed that "all the citizens," black and white, would have "the constitutional right to bear arms." 14 Stat. 176–177 [(1866)]. The Civil Rights Act of 1866, 14 Stat. 27, which was considered at the same time as the Freedmen's Bureau Act, similarly sought to protect the right of all citizens to keep and bear arms.

Congress, however, ultimately deemed these legislative remedies insufficient. Southern resistance, Presidential vetoes, and this Court's pre-Civil-War precedent persuaded Congress that a constitutional amendment was necessary to provide full protection for the rights of blacks. Today, it is generally accepted that the Fourteenth Amendment was understood to provide a constitutional basis for protecting the rights set out in the Civil Rights Act of 1866.

In debating the Fourteenth Amendment, the 39th Congress referred to the right to keep and bear arms as a fundamental right deserving of protection. Senator Samuel Pomeroy described three "indispensable" "safeguards of liberty under our form of Government." 39th Cong. Globe 1182. One of these, he said, was the right to keep and bear arms:

> "Every man . . . should have the right to bear arms for the defense of himself and family and his homestead. And if the cabin door of the freedman is broken open and the intruder enters for purposes as vile as were known to slavery,

then should a well-loaded musket be in the hand of the occupant to send the polluted wretch to another world, where his wretchedness will forever remain complete."

The right to keep and bear arms was also widely protected by state constitutions at the time when the Fourteenth Amendment was ratified. In 1868, 22 of the 37 States in the Union had state constitutional provisions explicitly protecting the right to keep and bear arms. See Calabresi & Agudo, Individual Rights Under State Constitutions when the Fourteenth Amendment was Ratified in 1868: What Rights Are Deeply Rooted in American History and Tradition? 87 Texas L. Rev. 7, 50 (2008).

In sum, it is clear that the Framers and ratifiers of the Fourteenth Amendment counted the right to keep and bear arms among those fundamental rights necessary to our system of ordered liberty.

. . . .

In *Heller*, we held that the Second Amendment protects the right to possess a handgun in the home for the purpose of self-defense. [A] provision of the Bill of Rights that protects a right that is fundamental from an American perspective applies equally to the Federal Government and the States. We therefore hold that the Due Process Clause of the Fourteenth Amendment incorporates the Second Amendment right recognized in *Heller*. The judgment of the Court of Appeals is reversed, and the case is remanded for further proceedings.

It is so ordered.

JUSTICE SCALIA, concurring.

I join the Court's opinion. Despite my misgivings about Substantive Due Process as an original matter, I have acquiesced in the Court's incorporation of certain guarantees in the Bill of Rights "because it is both long established and narrowly limited." This case does not require me to reconsider that view, since straightforward application of settled doctrine suffices to decide it.

JUSTICE THOMAS, concurring in part and concurring in the judgment.

I agree with the Court that the Fourteenth Amendment makes the right to keep and bear arms set forth in the Second Amendment "fully applicable to the States." I write separately because I believe there is a more straightforward path to this conclusion, one that is more faithful to the Fourteenth Amendment's text and history.

I cannot agree that [the right to keep and bear arms] is enforceable against the States through a clause that speaks only to "process." Instead, the right to keep and bear arms is a privilege of American citizenship that applies to the States through the Fourteenth Amendment's Privileges or Immunities Clause.

JUSTICE STEVENS, dissenting. [Opinion omitted.]

JUSTICE BREYER, with whom JUSTICE GINSBURG and JUSTICE SOTOMAYOR join, dissenting.

I can find nothing in the Second Amendment's text, history, or underlying rationale that could warrant characterizing it as "fundamental" insofar as it seeks to protect the keeping and bearing of arms for private self-defense purposes. Nor can I find any justification for interpreting the Constitution as transferring ultimate regulatory authority over the private uses of firearms from democratically elected legislatures to courts or from the States to the Federal Government. I therefore conclude that the Fourteenth Amendment does not "incorporate" the Second Amendment's right "to keep and bear Arms." And I consequently dissent.

EXERCISE 3:

1.   The *McDonald* Court described the primary standards that the Court utilized over the years to determine whether a provision of the Bill of Rights was incorporated via the Due Process Clause. Constructing a continuum, which standard is most and which is least capacious? Which standard does the Due Process Clause itself require? Which is the best?

2.   In recounting the history of incorporation, the Supreme Court noted that it occasionally held that the provisions of the Bill of Rights applied differently to the states and federal government. Why might the Court have done this? Though the Supreme Court today rejects that approach, what arguments support and detract from this approach.

3.   Which theory of incorporation, selective or total, is most faithful to the Constitution? Which is best?

4.   What evidence did the majority rely on to show that the right to keep and bear arms for purposes of self-defense is "fundamental to *our* scheme of ordered liberty"? Are you persuaded?

5.   Why did Justice Scalia concur? Should he, as an originalist, have joined Justice Thomas' opinion, or should Justice Thomas have joined his?

6.   Justice Breyer rejected incorporation, in part, because it removed authority from local and state governments. Is that a factor the Court should take into consideration in its incorporation analysis?

D.   "CLASSIC" SUBSTANTIVE DUE PROCESS

In addition to incorporation, the Due Process Clause of the Fourteenth Amendment and, usually parasitically, the Fifth Amendment's Due Process Clause, has been the focus of a related doctrinal development commonly known as "substantive due process." Substantive due process is related to incorporation in many ways: both doctrines apply legal restrictions to the state and federal governments, and both arose around the same time in the Court's case law.

The major difference between the two doctrines is the content of the restrictions. Incorporation deals with the provisions in the Bill of Rights, while substantive due process focuses on *un*enumerated restrictions. This facet of substantive due process, coupled with many of the Supreme Court's contentious uses of the doctrine, have made the doctrine controversial up to the present day, in a way that incorporation is not.

Substantive due process doctrine evolved significantly, and in complex ways, over the twentieth century. In this section, we will cover the doctrine's initial formulation, beginning in the late-nineteenth century. This conception of substantive due process flourished prior to the New Deal. It is frequently labeled — usually pejoratively — the *Lochner* Era, after *Lochner v. New York*, 198 U.S. 45 (1905), reprinted below. Additional labels for this era are "liberty of contract," and "economic substantive due process," because of the Supreme Court's focus on preserving the ability of individuals to enter into contracts without unreasonable state interference.

The Supreme Court tentatively waded into the waters of substantive due process in a series of late-nineteenth century cases, beginning with *Loan Ass'n v. Topeka*, 87 U.S. (20 Wall.) 655, 662–63 (1874), where the Court struck down a local law based on an unenumerated restriction on governmental taxing power. Over the next two decades, the Supreme Court intimated that the Due Process Clause limited state regulation of business relationships. *Munn v. Illinois*, 94 U.S. 113 (1877); *Railroad Comm'n Cases*, 116 U.S. 307 (1886); *Mugler v. Kansas*, 123 U.S. 623 (1887). This line of cases culminated in *Allgeyer v. Louisiana*, 165 U.S. 578 (1897), where the Court struck down a Louisiana law because it violated the unenumerated right to contract protected by the Due Process Clause.

Recall from Volumes 3 and 4 that, during this same period, the Supreme Court utilized a relatively restrictive interpretation of the Commerce Clause, *see United States v. E.C. Knight Co.*, 156 U.S. 1, 12 (1895) (ruling that the Commerce Clause did not authorize Congress to regulate manufacturing, which occurred before and was distinct from commerce), along with a relatively robust interpretation of the Tenth Amendment's limits. *See Hammer v. Dagenhart*, 247 U.S. 251, 274, 276 (1918) (ruling that attempted congressional regulation of child labor violated the Tenth Amendment). This multi-doctrine limit on the scope of governmental power was subject to intense criticism in the legal academy and political world up to the New Deal. Eventually, the Supreme Court modified broad swaths of its case law, and this change in the content of substantive due process we will review below in Part E.

As you read *Lochner*, articulate what level of scrutiny the Supreme Court used when it evaluated New York's challenged law. Keep this in mind as we discuss modern substantive due process.

LOCHNER v. NEW YORK
198 U.S. 45 (1905)

MR. JUSTICE PECKHAM, delivered the opinion of the court:

[I]

The indictment charges that the plaintiff in error violated the labor law of the state of New York, in that he wrongfully and unlawfully required and permitted an employee working for him to work more than sixty hours in one week. It is not an act merely fixing the number of hours which shall constitute a legal day's work, but an absolute prohibition upon the employer permitting, under any circumstances, more than ten hours' work to be done in his establishment. The employee may desire to earn the extra money which would arise from his working more than the prescribed time, but this statute forbids the employer from permitting the employee to earn it.

[II]
[A]

The statute necessarily interferes with the right of contract between the employer and employees, concerning the number of hours in which the latter may labor in the bakery of the employer. The general right to make a contract in relation to his business is part of the liberty of the individual protected by the 14th Amendment of the Federal Constitution. *Allgeyer v. Louisiana*, 165 U. S. 578 [(1897)]. Under that provision no state can deprive any person of life, liberty, or property without due process of law. The right to purchase or to sell labor is part of the liberty protected by this amendment.

[B]

There are, however, certain powers, existing in the sovereignty of each state in the Union, somewhat vaguely termed police powers, the exact description and limitation of which have not been attempted by the courts. Those powers, broadly stated, and without, at present, any attempt at a more specific limitation, relate to the safety, health, morals, and general welfare of the public. Both property and liberty are held on such reasonable conditions as may be imposed by the governing power of the state in the exercise of those powers, and with such conditions the 14th Amendment was not designed to interfere.

The state, therefore, has power to prevent the individual from making certain kinds of contracts, and in regard to them the Federal Constitution offers no protection. If the contract be one which the state, in the legitimate exercise of its police power, has the right to prohibit, it is not prevented from prohibiting it by the 14th Amendment. Contracts in violation of a statute, either of the Federal or state government, or a contract to let one's property for immoral purposes, or to do any other unlawful act, could obtain no protection from the Federal Constitution, as coming under the liberty of person or of free contract.

This court has recognized the existence and upheld the exercise of the police powers of the states in many cases which might fairly be considered as border ones, and it has, in the course of its determination of questions regarding the asserted invalidity of such statutes, on the ground of their violation of the rights secured by the Federal Constitution, been guided by rules of a very liberal nature, the application of which has resulted, in numerous instances, in upholding the validity of state statutes thus assailed. Among the later cases where the state law has been upheld by this court is that of *Holden v. Hardy*, 169 U. S. 366 [(1898)]. A provision in the act of the legislature of Utah was there under consideration, the act limiting the employment of workmen in all underground mines or workings, to eight hours per day, It also limited the hours of labor in smelting and other institutions for the reduction or refining of ores or metals to eight hours per day. The act was held to be a valid exercise of the police powers of the state. It was held that the kind of employment, mining, smelting, etc., and the character of the employees in such kinds of labor, were such as to make it reasonable and proper for the state to interfere to prevent the employees from being constrained by the rules laid down by the proprietors in regard to labor.

The latest case decided by this court, involving the police power, is that of *Jacobson v. Massachusetts*, 197 U. S. 11 [(1905)], decided at this term It related to compulsory vaccination, and the law was held valid as a proper exercise of the police powers with reference to the public health. It was stated in the opinion that it was a case 'of an adult who, for aught that appears, was himself in perfect health and a fit subject of vaccination, and yet, while remaining in the community, refused to obey the statute and the regulation, adopted in execution of its provisions, for the protection of the public health and the public safety, confessedly endangered by the presence of a dangerous disease.'

[C]

It must, of course, be conceded that there is a limit to the valid exercise of the police power by the state. Otherwise the 14th Amendment would have no efficacy and the legislatures of the states would have unbounded power, and it would be enough to say that any piece of legislation was enacted to conserve the morals, the health, or the safety of the people; such legislation would be valid, no matter how absolutely without foundation the claim might be. The claim of the police power would be a mere pretext. In every case that comes before this court, therefore, where legislation of this character is concerned, and where the protection of the Federal Constitution is sought, the question necessarily arises: Is this a fair, reasonable, and appropriate exercise of the police power of the state, or is it an unreasonable, unnecessary, and arbitrary interference with the right of the individual to his personal liberty, or to enter into those contracts in relation to labor which may seem to him appropriate or necessary for the support of himself and his family? Of course the liberty of contract relating to labor includes both parties to it. The one has as much right to purchase as the other to sell labor.

[III]

This is not a question of substituting the judgment of the court for that of the legislature. If the act be within the power of the state it is valid, although the judgment of the court might be totally opposed to the enactment of such a law. But the question would still remain: Is it within the police power of the state? and that question must be answered by the court.

[A]

The question whether this act is valid as a labor law, pure and simple, may be dismissed in a few words. There is no reasonable ground for interfering with the liberty of person or the right of free contract, by determining the hours of labor, in the occupation of a baker. There is no contention that bakers as a class are not equal in intelligence and capacity to men in other trades or manual occupations, or that they are not able to assert their rights and care for themselves without the protecting arm of the state, interfering with their independence of judgment and of action. They are in no sense wards of the state. Viewed in the light of a purely labor law, with no reference whatever to the question of health, we think that a law like the one before us involves neither the safety, the morals, nor the welfare, of the public, and that the interest of the public is not in the slightest degree affected by such an act. The law must be upheld, if at all, as a law pertaining to the health of the individual engaged in the occupation of a baker. Clean and wholesome bread does not depend upon whether the baker works but ten hours per day or only sixty hours a week. The limitation of the hours of labor does not come within the police power on that ground.

[B]

We think the limit of the police power has been reached and passed in this case. There is, in our judgment, no reasonable foundation for holding this to be necessary or appropriate as a health law to safeguard the public health, or the health of the individuals who are following the trade of a baker.

We think that there can be no fair doubt that the trade of a baker, in and of itself, is not an unhealthy one to that degree which would authorize the legislature to interfere with the right to labor, and with the right of free contract on the part of the individual, either as employer or employee. In looking through statistics regarding all trades and occupations, it may be true that the trade of a baker does not appear to be as healthy as some other trades, and is also vastly more healthy than still others. [B]ut we think there are none which might not come under the power of the legislature to supervise and control the hours of working therein, if the mere fact that the occupation is not absolutely and perfectly healthy is to confer that right upon the legislative department of the government. It might be safely affirmed that almost all occupations more or less affect the health. There must be more than the mere fact of the possible existence of some small amount of unhealthiness to warrant legislative interference with liberty. It is unfortunately true that labor, even in any department, may possibly carry with it the seeds of unhealthiness. But are we all, on that account, at the mercy of legislative majorities? A printer, a tinsmith, a locksmith, a carpenter, a cabinetmaker, a dry goods clerk, a bank's, a lawyer's, or a physician's clerk, or a clerk in almost any kind of business, would all come under the power of the legislature, on this assumption. No trade, no occupation, no mode of earning one's living, could escape this all-pervading power, and the acts of the legislature in limiting the hours of labor in all employments would be valid, although such limitation might seriously cripple the ability of the laborer to support himself and his family.

[C]

All that [New York] could properly do has been done by it with regard to the conduct of bakeries, as provided for in the other sections of the act. These several sections provide for the inspection of the premises where the bakery is carried on, with regard to furnishing proper wash rooms and watercloses, apart from the bake room, also with regard to providing proper drainage, plumbing, and painting; the sections, in addition, provide for the height of the ceiling, the cementing or tiling of floors, where necessary in the opinion of the factory inspector, and for other things of that nature. These various sections may be wise and valid regulations, and they certainly go to the full extent of providing for the cleanliness and the healthiness, so far as possible, of the quarters in which bakeries are to be conducted. Adding to all these requirements a prohibition to enter into any contract of labor in a bakery for more than a certain number of hours a week is, in our judgment, so wholly beside the matter of a proper, reasonable, and fair provision as to run counter to that liberty of person and of free contract provided for in the Federal Constitution.

[D]

It was further urged on the argument that restricting the hours of labor in the case of bakers was valid because it tended to cleanliness on the part of the workers, as a man was more apt to be cleanly when not overworked, and if cleanly then his 'output' was also more likely to be so. In our judgment it is not possible in fact to discover the connection between the number of hours a baker may work in the bakery and the healthful quality of the bread made by the workman. The connection, if any exist, is too shadowy and thin to build any argument for the interference of the legislature. If the man works ten hours a day it is all right, but if ten and a half or eleven his health is in danger and his bread may be unhealthy, and, therefore, he shall not be permitted to do it. This, we think, is unreasonable and entirely arbitrary. When assertions such as we have adverted to become necessary in order to give, if possible, a plausible foundation for the contention that the law is a 'health law,' it gives rise to at least a suspicion that there was some other motive dominating the legislature than the purpose to subserve the public health or welfare.

[IV]

This interference on the part of the legislatures of the several states with the ordinary trades and occupations of the people seems to be on the increase. It is impossible for us to shut our eyes to the fact that many of the laws of this character, while passed under what is claimed to be the police power for the purpose of protecting the public health or welfare, are, in reality, passed from other motives. We are justified in saying so when, from the character of the law and the subject upon which it legislates, it is apparent that the public health or welfare bears but the most remote relation to the law.

It seems to us that the real object and purpose [of this law] were simply to regulate the hours of labor between the master and his employees in a private business, not dangerous in any degree to morals, or in any real and substantial degree to the health of the employees. Under such circumstances the freedom of master and employee to contract with each other in relation to their employment, and in defining the same, cannot be prohibited or interfered with, without violating the Federal Constitution.

Reversed.

MR. JUSTICE HOLMES dissenting:

This case is decided upon an economic theory which a large part of the country does not entertain. If it were a question whether I agreed with that theory, I should desire to study it further and long before making up my mind. But I do not conceive that to be my duty, because I strongly believe that my agreement or disagreement has nothing to do with the right of a majority to embody their opinions in law. It is settled by various decisions of this court that state constitutions and state laws may regulate life in many ways which we as legislators might think as injudicious, or if you like as tyrannical, as this, and which, equally with this, interfere with the liberty to contract. Sunday laws and usury laws are ancient examples. A more modern one is the prohibition of lotteries. The liberty of the citizen to do as he likes so long as he does not interfere with the liberty of others to do the same, which has been a shibboleth for some well-known writers, is interfered with by school laws, by the Post office, by every state or municipal institution which takes his money for purposes thought desirable, whether he likes it or not. The 14th Amendment does not enact Mr. Herbert Spencer's Social Statics. The other day we sustained the Massachusetts vaccination law. United States and state statutes and decisions cutting down the liberty to contract by way of combination are familiar to this court. The decision sustaining an eight-hour law for miners is still recent. Some of these laws embody convictions or prejudices which judges are likely to share. Some may not. But a Constitution is not intended to embody a particular economic theory, whether of paternalism and the organic relation of the citizen to the state or of *laissez faire*. It is made for people of fundamentally differing views, and the accident of our finding certain opinions natural and familiar, or novel, and even shocking, ought not to conclude our judgment upon the question whether statutes embodying them conflict with the Constitution of the United States.

General propositions do not decide concrete cases. The decision will depend on a judgment or intuition more subtle than any articulate major premise. But I think that the proposition just stated, if it is accepted, will carry us far toward the end. Every opinion tends to become a law. I think that the word 'liberty,' in the 14th Amendment, is perverted when it is held to prevent the natural outcome of a dominant opinion, unless it can be said that a rational and fair man necessarily would admit that the statute proposed would infringe fundamental principles as they have been understood by the traditions of our people and our law. It does not need research to show that no such sweeping condemnation can be passed upon the statute before us. A reasonable man might think it a proper measure on the score of health. Men whom I certainly could not pronounce unreasonable would uphold it as a first instalment of a general regulation of the hours of work.

MR. JUSTICE HARLAN (with whom MR. JUSTICE WHITE and MR. JUSTICE DAY concurred) dissenting:

While this court has not attempted to mark the precise boundaries of what is called the police power of the state, the existence of the power has been uniformly recognized, equally by the Federal and State courts. [A]ssuming, as according to settled law we may assume, that such liberty of contract is subject to such regulations as the state may reasonably prescribe for the common good and the well-being of society, what are the conditions under which the judiciary may declare such regulations to be in excess of legislative authority and void? In *Jacobson v. Massachusetts*, 197 U. S. 11 [(1905)], we said that the power of the courts to review legislative action in respect of a matter affecting the general welfare exists *only* 'when that which the legislature has done comes within the rule that, if a statute purporting to have been enacted to protect the public health, the public morals, or the public safety has no real or substantial relation to those objects, or is, beyond all question, a plain, palpable invasion of rights secured by the fundamental law.' If there be doubt as to the validity of the statute, that doubt must therefore be resolved in favor of its validity, and the courts must keep their hands off, leaving the legislature to meet the responsibility for unwise legislation. In other words, when the validity of a statute is questioned, the burden of proof, so to speak, is upon those who assert it to be unconstitutional.

Let these principles be applied to the present case. It is plain that this statute was enacted in order to protect the physical well-being of those who work in bakery and confectionery establishments. It may be that the statute had its origin, in part, in the belief that employers and employees in such establishments were not upon an equal footing, and that the necessities of the latter often compelled them to submit to such exactions as unduly taxed their strength. Be this as it may, the statute must be taken as expressing the belief of the people of New York that, as a general rule, and in the case of the average man, labor in excess of sixty hours during a week in such establishments may endanger the health of those who thus labor.

I find it impossible, in view of common experience, to say that there is here no real or substantial relation between the means employed by the state and the end sought to be accomplished by its legislation. Therefore I submit that this court will transcend its functions if it assumes to annul the statute of New York. It must be remembered that this statute does not apply to all kinds of business. It applies only to work in bakery and confectionery establishments, in which, as all know, the air constantly breathed by workmen is not as pure and healthful as that to be found in some other establishments or out of doors. We also judicially know that the number of hours that should constitute a day's labor in particular occupations involving the physical strength and safety of workmen has been the subject of enactments by Congress and by nearly all of the states.

I do not stop to consider whether any particular view of this economic question presents the sounder theory. It is enough for the determination of this case, and it is enough for this court to know, that the question is one about which there is room for debate and for an honest difference of opinion.

We are not to presume that the state of New York has acted in bad faith. Nor can we assume that its legislature acted without due deliberation, or that it did not determine this question upon the fullest attainable information and for the common good. Let the state alone in the management of its purely domestic affairs, so long as it does not appear beyond all question that it has violated the Federal Constitution. This view necessarily results from the principle that the health and safety of the people of a state are primarily for the state to guard and protect.

EXERCISE 4:

1. What is the "police power"? It is not listed in the Constitution's text; from where did it derive its role in the analysis of constitutional questions? What is its role? Is that role proper?

2. The *Lochner* Court described the legal landscape as consisting of a balance between, on the one hand, the individual freedom protected by the Due Process Clause, and, on the other hand, the authority of state governments to regulate pursuant to its "police power." Is that an accurate picture of the relationship between constitutional rights and governmental authority?

3. What is the right to contract, and what is its source? (Keep in mind the right to contact when we discuss modern substantive due process, below.)

4. What analysis did the Court use to distinguish between proper and improper exercises of state police power? In *Lochner*, what was the state's purported end? Did the Court accept the state's judgment?

5. In modern terms, where, in the three-tiered standards of scrutiny, did the majority's analysis fall? What about Justices Holmes and Harlan?

6. One of the criticisms of the right to contract is that it failed to take into account the economic realities of employment relationships. Critics argued that the Supreme Court protected an employee's right to contract for employment even though, given many employees' wage-taker status in the job market, the employees had no bargaining power and hence no ability to use their freedom to contract. Is that a cogent criticism? How does that criticism affect the scope and/or existence of the right to contract?

7. Relatedly, does the Court's mode of analysis open it up to the criticism that the Court is imposing its preferred policy judgments under the guise of constitutional adjudication? Explain this view.

8. Similarly, is the majority protecting the interests of business and capital at the expense of the working class? What evidence supports that view? If it is true, what follows?

9. Critics frequently contended that the *Lochner* Court's use of substantive due process was unprincipled because its cases were inconsistent. Is *Lochner* consistent

with *Holden* and *Jacobson*, discussed in the decision? If the decisions were inconsistent, is that because of the mode of analysis, or because of the majority's strong policy preferences, or something else?

10. The *Lochner* Court argued that, if it accepted New York's justification of the challenged law, there would be no limit to state regulatory authority. What was the majority's argument? Is it persuasive?

11. The Supreme Court asked rhetorically: "But are we all, on that account, at the mercy of legislative majorities?" The Court assumed that the answer is no; is that right?

12. Justice Holmes charged that the majority was reading its own economic policy views into the Constitution. Is that true? What evidence supports that claim? If it is true, why is that bad?

13. There is a long-standing debate over whether the Constitution does, or does not — as Justice Holmes claimed — "embody a particular economic theory." In the early twentieth century, many progressives argued that the Constitution in fact did embody a preference for private economic ordering, and used that claim as a point of criticism of the Constitution. The most famous example of this is CHARLES A. BEARD, AN ECONOMIC INTERPRETATION OF THE CONSTITUTION OF THE UNITED STATES (1913). *See also* FORREST MCDONALD, WE THE PEOPLE: THE ECONOMIC ORIGINS OF THE CONSTITUTION (1958) (challenging Beard's thesis and arguing that the economic interests involved in the Framing and Ratification of the Constitution were multifarious). Reviewing the Constitution's text and historical background, does the Constitution "embody a particular economic theory"? If so, is that bad?

14. Justice Holmes' dissent has frequently been cited over the years as an argument against "judicial activism." Articulate Justice Holmes' argument for a limited judiciary. Is it persuasive? Was the *Lochner* majority an activist court, on this understanding?

15. Relatedly, why might Americans *not* want an independent judiciary "standing up to" the majority when the majority limits fundamental rights?

16. Did Justice Holmes reject substantive due process? Whose conception of substantive due process — the majority's or Justice Holmes' — is more attractive?

17. Justice Holmes famously stated: "General propositions do not decide concrete cases." Many later scholars identified this as an early articulation of one of Legal Realism's core tenets: that judges frequently have discretion when applying the law. Apply that claim to the *Lochner* majority. Is it a sound criticism? If so, what follows?

18. During the late-nineteenth and early-twentieth centuries, there was rapid industrialization and urbanization. Many states and the federal government responded by passing legislation to ameliorate perceived ill-effects of these phenomena. The dissenting justices utilized the argument of "institutional competence." They claimed that legislative bodies were better equipped to evaluate this new legislation. Explain the ways a legislature may be more institutionally competent. Do likewise with the judiciary. On which side do you fall?

19. The majority and Justice Harlan disagreed on whether it was reasonable for New York to regulate bakers' hours. Who had the better of the argument? Was New York reasonably pursuing protecting the health, safety, or morals of bakers, or perhaps the general public?

20. Relatedly, Justice Harlan argued in his dissent that "[w]e are not to presume that the state of New York has acted in bad faith. Nor can we assume that its legislature acted without due deliberation." Should the Court follow Justice Harlan's admonition? Keep Justice Harlan's statement in mind when we review *Carolene Products Co. v. United States*, 323 U.S. 18 (1944), below.

21. The majority criticized New York's choice of a ten-hour workday as arbitrary: "If the man works ten hours a day it is all right, but if ten and a half or eleven his health is in danger and his bread may be unhealthy, and, therefore, he shall not be permitted to do it. This, we think, is unreasonable and entirely arbitrary." What would have satisfied the *Lochner* majority? Does not the choice of a legal rule, to some degree and on the margins, always result in arbitrariness? The classic example of this is limiting driving licenses to sixteen year olds. Some fifteen year olds are competent to drive, while some sixteen year olds are not. Yet, states *must* draw a line.

The *Lochner* era continued, under withering criticism by the 1930s, until 1937. During this time, the Supreme Court struck down many laws dealing with economic and social regulation. For example, the Court struck down a federal minimum wage law for women and children in the District of Columbia in *Adkins v. Children's Hospital*, 261 U.S. 525 (1923). There is no consensus on the extent to which the Supreme Court during this period was exceptionally "activist." Many scholars have argued that the *Lochner* Court was no more prone to strike down legislation than other periods in the Court's history, and that other eras, such as the Warren Court, were even more "activist."

One of the interesting developments during this period was the Brandeis Brief, named after the famous brief authored by Louis Brandeis in *Muller v. Oregon*, 208 U.S. 412 (1908). The state statute at issue in *Muller* was a maximum work hours law directed solely toward women. *Id.* at 416. Brandeis crafted a brief defending the statute that contained empirical evidence of the harmful effects of long work hours on women, with very little traditional legal argumentation. The *Muller* Court explicitly relied on Brandeis' brief to distinguish *Lochner* and hold that the Oregon statute was a proper exercise of Oregon's police power. *Id.* at 419. This technique was later utilized frequently to try to persuade the Court to uphold challenged statutes. It was also of-a-piece with the nascent Legal Realism movement. *See, e.g.,* Roscoe Pound, *The Scope and Purpose of Sociological Jurisprudence*, 25 HARV. L. REV. 489, 512–13 (1912) ("The main problem to which sociological jurists are addressing themselves today is to enable and to compel law-making, and also interpretation and application of legal rules, to take more account, and more intelligent account, of the social facts upon which law must proceed and to which it is to be applied.").

In 1937, the Supreme Court overruled *Adkins* and repudiated the *Lochner* era in *West Coast Hotel Co. v. Parrish*, 300 U.S. 379 (1937), reprinted below.

WEST COAST HOTEL CO. v. PARRISH
300 U.S. 379 (1937)

MR. CHIEF JUSTICE HUGHES delivered the opinion of the Court.

[I]

This case presents the question of the constitutional validity of the minimum wage law of the state of Washington. The act, entitled 'Minimum Wages for Women,' authorizes the fixing of minimum wages for women and minors.

The appellant conducts a hotel. The appellee Elsie Parrish was employed as a chambermaid and brought this suit to recover the difference between the wages paid her and the minimum wage fixed pursuant to the state law. The appellant challenged the act as repugnant to the due process clause of the Fourteenth Amendment. The appellant relies upon the decision of this Court in *Adkins v. Children's Hospital*, 261 U.S. 525 [(1922)], which held invalid the District of Columbia Minimum Wage Act which was attacked under the due process clause of the Fifth Amendment.

[II]

We think that the question [whether to overrule *Adkins*] is necessarily presented here. The importance of the question, in which many states having similar laws are concerned, the close division by which the decision in the *Adkins* Case was reached, and the economic conditions which have supervened, and in the light of which the reasonableness of the exercise of the protective power of the state must be considered, make it not only appropriate, but we think imperative, that in deciding the present case the subject should receive fresh consideration.

[A]

The principle which must control our decision is not in doubt. In each case the violation alleged by those attacking minimum wage regulation for women is deprivation of freedom of contract. What is this freedom? The Constitution does not speak of freedom of contract. It speaks of liberty and prohibits the deprivation of liberty without due process of law. In prohibiting that deprivation, the Constitution does not recognize an absolute and uncontrollable liberty. Liberty in each of its phases has its history and connotation. But the liberty safeguarded is liberty in a social organization which requires the protection of law against the evils which menace the health, safety, morals, and welfare of the people. Liberty under the Constitution is thus necessarily subject to the restraints of due process, and regulation which is reasonable in relation to its subject and is adopted in the interests of the community is due process.

[B]

This essential limitation of liberty in general governs freedom of contract in particular. This power under the Constitution to restrict freedom of contract has had many illustrations. That it may be exercised in the public interest with respect to contracts between employer and employee is undeniable. In dealing with the relation of employer and employed, the Legislature has necessarily a wide field of discretion in order that there may be suitable protection of health and safety, and that peace and good order may be promoted through regulations designed to insure wholesome conditions of work and freedom from oppression.

The point that has been strongly stressed that adult employees should be deemed competent to make their own contracts was decisively met nearly forty years ago in *Holden v. Hardy*, 169 U.S. 366 [(1898)], where we pointed out the inequality in the footing of the parties. We said:

> 'The legislature has also recognized the fact, which the experience of legislators in many states has corroborated, that the proprietors of these establishments and their operatives do not stand upon an equality, and that their interests are, to a certain extent, conflicting. The former naturally desire to obtain as much labor as possible from their employees, while the latter are often induced by the fear of discharge to conform to regulations which their judgment, fairly exercised, would pronounce to be detrimental to their health or strength.'

It is manifest that this established principle is peculiarly applicable in relation to the employment of women in whose protection the state has a special interest. That phase of the subject received elaborate consideration in *Muller v. Oregon*[, 208 U.S. 412] (1908), where the constitutional authority of the state to limit the working hours of women was sustained. We emphasized the consideration that 'woman's physical structure and the performance of maternal functions place her at a disadvantage in the struggle for subsistence' and that her physical well being 'becomes an object of public interest and care in order to preserve the strength and vigor of the race.'

[C]

[An] array of precedents and the principles they applied were thought by the dissenting Justices in the *Adkins* Case to demand that the minimum wage statute be sustained. The validity of the distinction made by the Court between a minimum wage and a maximum of hours in limiting liberty of contract was especially challenged. That challenge persists and is without any satisfactory answer.

We think that the decision in the *Adkins* Case was a departure from the true application of the principles governing the regulation by the state of the relation of employer and employed. Those principles have been reenforced by our subsequent decisions.

With full recognition of the earnestness and vigor which characterize the prevailing opinion in the *Adkins* Case, we find it impossible to reconcile that ruling with these well-considered declarations. What can be closer to the public interest than the health of women and their protection from unscrupulous and overreaching employers? And if the protection of women is a legitimate end of the exercise of state power, how can it be said that the requirement of the payment of a minimum wage fairly fixed in order to meet the very necessities of existence is not an admissible means to that end? The Legislature of the state was clearly entitled to consider the situation of women in employment, the fact that they are in the class receiving the least pay, that their bargaining power is relatively weak, and that they are the ready victims of those who would take advantage of their necessitous circumstances. The adoption of similar requirements by many states evidences a deepseated conviction both as to the presence of the evil and as to the means adapted to check it. Legislative response to that conviction cannot be regarded as arbitrary or capricious and that is all we have to decide. Even if the wisdom of the policy be regarded as debatable and its effects uncertain, still the Legislature is entitled to its judgment.

[D]

There is an additional and compelling consideration which recent economic experience has brought into a strong light. The exploitation of a class of workers who are in an unequal position with respect to bargaining power and are thus relatively defenseless against the denial of a living wage is not only detrimental to their health and well being, but casts a direct burden for their support upon the community. What these workers lose in wages the taxpayers are called upon to pay. The bare cost of living must be met. We may take judicial notice of the unparalleled demands for relief which arose during the recent period of depression and still continue to an alarming extent. While in the instant case no factual brief has been presented, there is no reason to doubt that the state of Washington has encountered the same social problem that is present elsewhere. The community is not bound to provide what is in effect a subsidy for unconscionable employers. The community may direct its law-making power to correct the abuse which springs from their selfish disregard of the public interest.

[E]

The argument that the legislation in question constitutes an arbitrary discrimination, because it does not extend to men, is unavailing. This Court has frequently held that the legislative authority, acting within its proper field, is not bound to extend its regulation to all cases which it might possibly reach. This familiar principle has repeatedly been applied to legislation which singles out women, and particular classes of women, in the exercise of the state's protective power. Their relative need in the presence of the evil, no less than the existence of the evil itself, is a matter for the legislative judgment.

[III]

Our conclusion is that the case of *Adkins v. Children's Hospital*, should be, and it is, overruled. The judgment of the Supreme Court of the state of Washington is affirmed.

Affirmed.

Mr. Justice Sutherland.

Mr. Justice Van Devanter, Mr. Justice McReynolds, Mr. Justice Butler, and I think the judgment of the court below should be reversed.

[I]

Under our form of government, where the written Constitution, by its own terms, is the supreme law, some agency, of necessity, must have the power to say the final word as to the validity of a statute assailed as unconstitutional. The Constitution makes it clear that the power has been intrusted to this court.

It has been pointed out many times, as in the *Adkins* Case, that this judicial duty is one of gravity and delicacy; and that rational doubts must be resolved in favor of the constitutionality of the statute. But whose doubts, and by whom resolved? The oath which he takes as a judge is not a composite oath, but an individual one. And in passing upon the validity of a statute, he discharges a duty imposed upon him, which cannot be consummated justly by an automatic acceptance of the views of others which have neither convinced, nor created a reasonable doubt in, his mind. If upon a question so important he thus surrenders his deliberate judgment, he stands forsworn. He cannot subordinate his convictions to that extent and keep faith with his oath or retain his judicial and moral independence.

The check upon the judge is that imposed by his oath of office, by the Constitution, and by his own conscientious and informed convictions. This Court acts as a unit; and the majority therefore, establishes the controlling rule as the decision of the court, binding, so long as it remains unchanged, equally upon those who disagree and upon those who subscribe to it. Otherwise, orderly administration of justice would cease. But it is the right of those in the minority to disagree.

It is urged that the question involved should now receive fresh consideration, among other reasons, because of 'the economic conditions which have supervened'; but the meaning of the Constitution does not change with the ebb and flow of economic events. We frequently are told in more general words that the Constitution must be construed in the light of the present. If by that it is meant that the Constitution is made up of living words that apply to every new condition which they include, the statement is quite true. But to say, if that be intended, that the words of the Constitution mean today what they did not mean when written-that is, that they do not apply to a situation now to which they would have applied then-is to rob that instrument of the essential element which continues it in force as the people have made it until they, and not their official agents, have made it otherwise.

The judicial function is that of interpretation; it does not include the power of amendment under the guise of interpretation. To miss the point of difference between the two is to miss all that the phrase 'supreme law of the land' stands for and to convert what was intended as inescapable and enduring mandates into mere moral reflections.

If the Constitution, intelligently and reasonably construed in the light of these principles, stands in the way of desirable legislation, the blame must rest upon that instrument, and not upon the court for enforcing it according to its terms. The remedy in that situation-and the only true remedy-is to amend the Constitution. Judge Cooley, in the first volume of his [Treatise on the Constitutional Limitations Which Rest upon the Legislative Power of the States in the American Union 124 (8th ed. 1927)], very clearly pointed out that much of the benefit expected from written Constitutions would be lost if their provisions were to be bent to circumstances or modified by public opinion.

The people by their Constitution created three separate, distinct, independent, and coequal departments of government. The governmental structure rests, and was intended to rest, not upon any one or upon any two, but upon all three of these fundamental pillars. [T]he powers of these departments are different and are to be exercised independently. The differences clearly and definitely appear in the Constitution. Each of the departments is an agent of its creator; and one department is not and cannot be the agent of another. Each is answerable to its creator for what it does, and not to another agent. The view, therefore, of the Executive and of Congress that an act is constitutional is persuasive in a high degree; but it is not controlling.

[II]

Coming, then, to a consideration of the Washington statute, it first is to be observed that it is in every substantial respect identical with the statute involved in [*Adkins v. Children's Hospital*, 261 U.S. 525 (1922)]. And if the *Adkins* Case was properly decided, as we who join in this opinion think it was, it necessarily follows that the Washington statute is invalid.

That the clause of the Fourteenth Amendment which forbids a state to deprive any person of life, liberty, or property without due process of law includes freedom of contract is so well settled as to be no longer open to question. Nor reasonably can it be disputed that contracts of employment of labor are included in the rule.

In the *Adkins* Case we said that while there was no such thing as absolute freedom of contract, but that it was subject to a great variety of restraints, nevertheless, freedom of contract was the general rule and restraint the exception; and that the power to abridge that freedom could only be justified by the existence of exceptional circumstances.

The sole basis upon which the question of validity rests is the assumption that the employee is entitled to receive a sum of money sufficient to provide a living for her, keep her in health and preserve her morals. What we said further in that case is equally applicable here:

'The law takes account of the necessities of only one party to the contract. It ignores the necessities of the employer by compelling him to pay not less than a certain sum, not only whether the employee is capable of earning it, but irrespective of the ability of his business to sustain the burden, generously leaving him, of course, the privilege of abandoning his business as an alternative for going on at a loss. To the extent that the sum fixed exceeds the fair value of the services rendered, it amounts to a compulsory exaction from the employer for the support of a partially indigent person,

for whose condition there rests upon him no peculiar responsibility, and therefore, in effect, arbitrarily shifts to his shoulders a burden which, if it belongs to anybody, belongs to society as a whole.'

The Washington statute, like the one for the District of Columbia, fixes minimum wages for adult women. Adult men and their employers are left free to bargain as they please. The common-law rules restricting the power of women to make contracts have, under our system, long since practically disappeared. Women today stand upon a legal and political equality with men. There is no longer any reason why they should be put in different classes in respect of their legal right to make contracts; nor should they be denied, in effect, the right to compete with men for work paying lower wages which men may be willing to accept. And it is an arbitrary exercise of the legislative power to do so.

Difference of sex affords no reasonable ground for making a restriction applicable to the wage contracts of all working women from which like contracts of all working men are left free. Certainly a suggestion that the bargaining ability of the average woman is not equal to that of the average man would lack substance. The ability to make a fair bargain, as every one knows, does not depend upon sex.

EXERCISE 5:

1. Why did the Supreme Court reconsider *Adkins*? Where those reasons sufficient?

2. What analysis did the Supreme Court utilize to evaluate Washington's law?

3. The majority made the economic claim that Washington state would save money because the statute would prevent people from seeking state welfare assistance. Is that claim true? How did the Court know? Are Supreme Court justice adept at making such economic claims?

4. Unlike in *Lochner*, where the Court relied heavily on the freedom of contract of both parties to an employment relationship, here, the Court argued that the employee did not possess a freedom to contract because of potential employers' greater bargaining power. Which of these two perspectives was right?

5. Does a constitutional right to liberty of contract survive *West Coast Hotel*?

6. As noted earlier, one of the frequent criticisms of the Supreme Court during the *Lochner* era was that the Court acted inconsistently. The majority picked up on that criticism and used it to claim that *Adkins* was inconsistent with other cases. Was *Adkins* inconsistent with cases, such as *Muller*, that had upheld maximum hours statutes?

7. If you were the majority, and you believed that the *Lochner* Court's case law was inconsistent at best, and unprincipled at worst, how might you respond? How could you make the Court's approach more principled?

8. The majority characterized Washington as protecting a relatively vulnerable class of employees: women. Although at the time most progressives applauded the Court for upholding the statute, over the years some have suggested that the Court's

reasoning was premised on a belief in women's inferiority. Today, as we will see below, the Supreme Court's modern equal protection jurisprudence would likely strike down the Washington statute for its facial distinction between men and women. Is that change in approach good?

9.   There has been significant scholarly interest in what caused the Court and, in particular, Justice Jackson, to switch his vote in favor of upholding legislation. One of the more popular hypotheses is that Justice Jackson, out of concern for the Supreme Court's institutional viability, changed his voting pattern to one more amenable to the President and Congress. If that is true, did Justice Jackson fulfill his oath?

10.   Justice Sutherland used the first portion of his dissent to defend a view of constitutional interpretation that today is generally known as originalism. Describe the Constitution's meaning under this theory and Justice Sutherland's reasons for following it.

11.   Relatedly, Justice Sutherland sought to preempt claims that he and the other dissenters were activists. What were his arguments? Are they persuasive?

12.   Justice Sutherland cited to and relied on Thomas M. Cooley's famous treatise, *Constitutional Limitations*. THOMAS M. COOLEY, TREATISE ON THE CONSTITUTIONAL LIMITATIONS WHICH REST UPON THE LEGISLATIVE POWER OF THE STATES IN THE AMERICAN UNION (8th ed. 1927). Cooley's treatise was the most influential statement of American constitutional law in the late-nineteenth and early-twentieth centuries. Cooley synthesized many existing trends in American law and his description of that law influenced further development.

<hr />

As we will see in Subsection F, despite the discrediting of *Lochner* and its progeny, some of the *Lochner* Era's substantive due process cases survived *West Coast Hotel Co.* One of the most important is reprinted below.

MEYER v. NEBRASKA
262 U.S. 390 (1923)

MR. JUSTICE McREYNOLDS delivered the opinion of the Court.

Plaintiff in error was tried and convicted in the district court for Hamilton county, Nebraska, under an information which charged that on May 25, 1920, while an instructor in Zion Parochial School he unlawfully taught the subject of reading in the German language. The information is based upon 'An act relating to the teaching of foreign languages in the state of Nebraska,' approved April 9, 1919.

The problem for our determination is whether the statute as construed and applied unreasonably infringes the liberty guaranteed to the plaintiff in error by the Fourteenth Amendment.

While this court has not attempted to define with exactness the liberty thus guaranteed, the term has received much consideration and some of the included things have been definitely stated. Without doubt, it denotes not merely freedom from bodily

restraint but also the right of the individual to contract, to engage in any of the common occupations of life, to acquire useful knowledge, to marry, establish a home and bring up children, to worship God according to the dictates of his own conscience, and generally to enjoy those privileges long recognized at common law as essential to the orderly pursuit of happiness by free men. The established doctrine is that this liberty may not be interfered with, under the guise of protecting the public interest, by legislative action which is arbitrary or without reasonable relation to some purpose within the competency of the state to effect. Determination by the Legislature of what constitutes proper exercise of police power is not final or conclusive but is subject to supervision by the courts.

The American people have always regarded education and acquisition of knowledge as matters of supreme importance which should be diligently promoted. The Ordinance of 1787 declares: 'Religion, morality and knowledge being necessary to good government and the happiness of mankind, schools and the means of education shall forever be encouraged.'

Corresponding to the right of control, it is the natural duty of the parent to give his children education suitable to their station in life; and nearly all the states, including Nebraska, enforce this obligation by compulsory laws. Practically, education of the young is only possible in schools conducted by especially qualified persons who devote themselves thereto. The calling always has been regarded as useful and honorable, essential, indeed, to the public welfare.

Mere knowledge of the German language cannot reasonably be regarded as harmful. Heretofore it has been commonly looked upon as helpful and desirable. Plaintiff in error taught this language in school as part of his occupation. His right thus to teach and the right of parents to engage him so to instruct their children, we think, are within the liberty of the amendment.

The challenged statute forbids the teaching in school of any subject except in English; also the teaching of any other language until the pupil has attained and successfully passed the eighth grade. Evidently the Legislature has attempted materially to interfere with the calling of modern language teachers, with the opportunities of pupils to acquire knowledge, and with the power of parents to control the education of their own.

It is said the purpose of the legislation was to promote civic development by inhibiting training and education of the immature in foreign tongues and ideals before they could learn English and acquire American ideals, and 'that the English language should be and become the mother tongue of all children reared in this state.' It is also affirmed that the foreign born population is very large, that certain communities commonly use foreign words, follow foreign leaders, move in a foreign atmosphere, and that the children are thereby hindered from becoming citizens of the most useful type and the public safety is imperiled.

That the state may do much, go very far, indeed, in order to improve the quality of its citizens, physically, mentally and morally, is clear; but the individual has certain fundamental rights which must be respected. Perhaps it would be highly advantageous if all had ready understanding of our ordinary speech, but this cannot be coerced by methods which conflict with the Constitution-a desirable end cannot be promoted by prohibited means.

For the welfare of his Ideal Commonwealth, Plato suggested a law which should provide: 'That the wives of our guardians are to be common, and their children are to be common, and no parent is to know his own child, nor any child his parent. * * * The proper officers will take the offspring of the good parents to the pen or fold, and there they will deposit them with certain nurses who dwell in a separate quarter.' Although such measures have been deliberately approved by men of great genius their ideas touching the relation between individual and state were wholly different from those upon which our institutions rest.

The desire of the Legislature to foster a homogeneous people with American ideals prepared readily to understand current discussions of civic matters is easy to appreciate. Unfortunate experiences during the late war and aversion toward every character of truculent adversaries were certainly enough to quicken that aspiration. But the means adopted, we think, exceed the limitations upon the power of the state and conflict with rights assured to plaintiff in error. The interference is plain enough and no adequate reason therefor in time of peace and domestic tranquility has been shown.

The power of the state to compel attendance at some school and to make reasonable regulations for all schools, including a requirement that they shall give instructions in English, is not questioned. Nor has challenge been made of the state's power to prescribe a curriculum for institutions which it supports. Those matters are not within the present controversy. No emergency has arisen which renders knowledge by a child of some language other than English so clearly harmful as to justify its inhibition with the consequent infringement of rights long freely enjoyed. We are constrained to conclude that the statute as applied is arbitrary and without reasonable relation to any end within the competency of the state.

Reversed.

MR. JUSTICE HOLMES and MR. JUSTICE SUTHERLAND, dissent.

EXERCISE 6:

1.   The *Meyer* Court's rendition of what is part of the constitutionally protected "liberty" is capacious; what does it *not* include?

2.   What is the source of the Court's interpretation of "liberty"?

3.   Whose rights, and what rights, in particular, were violated by the Nebraska statute, according to the Court?

4.   What analysis did the Supreme Court use to evaluate the law?

5.   According to Nebraska, what purposes did the statute serve? Why did the Court reject the state's argument?

6.   At a number of times in American history, immigration has been high. One such period was in the late-nineteenth and early-twentieth centuries. This period of immigration included a larger percentage of immigrants from Southern Europe who were Roman Catholic, and from Eastern Europe. One of the responses to this change in the make-up of immigrants was concern for maintaining America's cultural identity and a common reaction by states was to require school attendance and, in some cases, limit or prohibit private school attendance.

7.   After reading *Lochner* and *Pierce*, can you see any basis for distinguishing *Meyer* from *Lochner* so that *Meyer* survived *West Coast Hotel*?

A later case that is usually viewed as a companion case to *Meyer* is *Pierce v. Society of Sisters*, 268 U.S. 510 (1925), which followed *Meyer*'s line of reasoning when it struck down an Oregon statute that prohibited nonpublic education. The statute

> unreasonably interferes with the liberty of parents and guardians to direct the upbringing and education of children under their control. As often heretofore pointed out, rights guaranteed by the Constitution may not be abridged by legislation which has no reasonable relation to some purpose within the competency of the State. The fundamental theory of liberty upon which all governments in this Union repose excludes any general power of the State to standardize its children by forcing them to accept instruction from public teachers only. The child is not the mere creature of the State; those who nurture him and direct his destiny have the right, coupled with the high duty, to recognize and prepare him for additional obligations.

Id. at 534–35.

E.   THE NEW DEAL SETTLEMENT

As in so many areas of constitutional law, the New Deal Supreme Court altered the governing constitutional law in dramatic fashion in the substantive due process context. The Supreme Court, in a series of cases, signaled that it was retreating from its *Lochner* Era case law, and replacing it with significant judicial deference to the constitutional judgments of the states and federal government.

However, buried within its doctrinal flight from *Lochner*, the Court issued a promissory note of significant judicial scrutiny in specific areas of law. The Court redeemed that note in the 1960s, creating modern substantive due process doctrine, discussed below in Part F.

As you review the following two Parts, pay particular attention to the reasons the Supreme Court gave for both its abandonment of *Lochner*, and its embrace of modern substantive due process, and the resulting legal doctrine.

The case that best exemplifies the New Deal Court's newly deferential approach is reprinted below:

WILLIAMSON v. LEE OPTICAL OF OKLAHOMA, INC.
348 U.S. 483 (1955)

MR. JUSTICE DOUGLAS delivered the opinion of the Court.

This suit was instituted in the District Court to have an Oklahoma law declared unconstitutional and to enjoin state officials from enforcing it for the reason that it allegedly violated various provisions of the Federal Constitution.

The District Court held unconstitutional portions of the Act. First, it held invalid under the Due Process Clause of the Fourteenth Amendment the portions of s 2 which make it unlawful for any person not a licensed optometrist or ophthalmologist to fit lenses to a face or to duplicate or replace into frames lenses or other optical appliances, except upon written prescriptive authority of an Oklahoma licensed ophthalmologist or optometrist.

An ophthalmologist is a duly licensed physician who specializes in the care of the eyes. An optometrist examines eyes for refractive error, recognizes (but does not treat) diseases of the eye, and fills prescriptions for eyeglasses. The optician is an artisan qualified to grind lenses, fill prescriptions, and fit frames. The effect of s 2 is that no optician can fit old glasses into new frames or supply a lens, whether it be a new lens or one to duplicate a lost or broken lens, without a prescription.

The Oklahoma law may exact a needless, wasteful requirement in many cases. But it is for the legislature, not the courts, to balance the advantages and disadvantages of the new requirement. It appears that in many cases the optician can easily supply the new frames or new lenses without reference to the old written prescription. It also appears that many written prescriptions contain no directive data in regard to fitting spectacles to the face. But in some cases the directions contained in the prescription are essential, if the glasses are to be fitted so as to correct the particular defects of vision or alleviate the eye condition. The legislature might have concluded that the frequency of occasions when a prescription is necessary was sufficient to justify this regulation of the fitting of eyeglasses. Likewise, when it is necessary to duplicate a lens, a written prescription may or may not be necessary. But the legislature might have concluded that one was needed often enough to require one in every case. Or the legislature may have concluded that eye examinations were so critical, not only for correction of vision but also for detection of latent ailments or diseases, that every change in frames and every duplication of a lens should be accompanied by a prescription from a medical expert. To be sure, the present law does not require a new examination of the eyes every time the frames are changed or the lenses duplicated. For if the old prescription is on file with the optician, he can go ahead and make the new fitting or duplicate the lenses. But the law need not be in every respect logically consistent with its aims to be constitutional. It is enough that there is an evil at hand for correction, and that it might be thought that the particular legislative measure was a rational way to correct it.

The day is gone when this Court uses the Due Process Clause of the Fourteenth Amendment to strike down state laws, regulatory of business and industrial conditions, because they may be unwise, improvident, or out of harmony with a particular school of thought. *See West Coast Hotel Co. v. Parrish*, 300 U.S. 379 [(1937)]. We emphasize again what Chief Justice Waite said in *Munn v. State of Illinois*, 94 U.S. [(4 Otto)] 113, 134 [(1876)], "For protection against abuses by legislatures the people must resort to the polls, not to the courts."

Affirmed in part and reversed in part.

MR. JUSTICE HARLAN took no part in the consideration or decision of this case.

EXERCISE 7:

1.   What standard of review did the Supreme Court utilize to review the challenged Oklahoma legislation?

2.   Did the Court require Oklahoma to provide the Court with its actual state interest, or was a hypothetical state interest sufficient? What are the benefits and costs of such an approach?

3.   How tight must the relationship be between the state's ends and the statutory means it used to achieve those ends? Explain how the statute's advancement of the legislature's goal(s) was weak.

4.   Which party — the state or challenger — bore the burden of persuading the Court that the law was or was not rationally related to a legitimate state interest?

5.   Justice Douglas attempted to assuage concerns caused by the Supreme Court's refusal to strictly review economic legislation by suggesting that opticians "must resort to the polls, not to the courts." Construct an argument that this is little comfort to people in the opticians' position.

6.   Having read now, both *Lochner* and *Williamson*, which of the two approaches is most consistent with the Constitution? With judicial institutional competence? With good public policy?

The Supreme Court's dramatic shift, evidenced by *Williamson*, was obliquely justified in the most famous footnote in all of constitutional law.

CAROLENE PRODUCTS CO. v. UNITED STATES
323 U.S. 18 (1938)

MR. JUSTICE STONE delivered the opinion of the Court.

The question for decision is whether the 'Filled Milk Act' of March 4, 1923, which prohibits the shipment in interstate commerce of skimmed milk compounded with any fat or oil other than milk fat, so as to resemble milk or cream infringes the Fifth Amendment. Appellee was indicted in the District Court for Southern Illinois for violation of the act by the shipment in interstate commerce of certain packages of 'Milnut,' a compound of condensed skimmed milk and coconut oil made in imitation or semblance of condensed milk or cream. Appellee complains that the statute deprives it of its property without due process of law, particularly in that the statute purports to make binding and conclusive upon appellee the legislative declaration that appellee's product 'is an adulterated article of food, injurious to the public health, and its sale constitutes a fraud on the public.'

The prohibition of shipment of appellee's product in interstate commerce does not infringe the Fifth Amendment. Twenty years ago this Court, in *Hebe Co. v. Shaw*, 248 U.S. 297 [(1919)], held that a state law which forbids the manufacture and sale of a product assumed to be wholesome and nutritive, made of condensed skimmed milk, compounded with coconut oil, is not forbidden by the Fourteenth Amendment. The power of the Legislature to secure a minimum of particular nutritive elements in a widely used article of food and to protect the public from fraudulent substitutions, was not doubted; and the Court thought that there was ample scope for the legislative judgment that prohibition of the offending article was an appropriate means of preventing injury to the public.

We see no persuasive reason for departing from that ruling here, where the Fifth Amendment is concerned; and since none is suggested, we might rest decision wholly on the presumption of constitutionality. But affirmative evidence also sustains the statute. In twenty years evidence has steadily accumulated of the danger to the public health from the general consumption of foods which have been stripped of elements essential to the maintenance of health. The Filled Milk Act was adopted by Congress after committee hearings, in the course of which eminent scientists and health experts testified.

There is nothing in the Constitution which compels a Legislature, either national or state, to ignore such evidence, nor need it disregard the other evidence which amply supports the conclusions of the Congressional committees that the danger is greatly enhanced where an inferior product, like appellee's, is indistinguishable from a valuable food of almost universal use, thus making fraudulent distribution easy and protection of the consumer difficult.

Here the prohibition of the statute is inoperative unless the product is 'in imitation or semblance of milk, cream, or skimmed milk, whether or not condensed.' Whether in such circumstance the public would be adequately protected by the prohibition of false labels and false branding imposed by the Pure Food and Drugs Act, or whether it was necessary to go farther and prohibit a substitute food product thought to be injurious to health if used as a substitute when the two are not distinguishable, was a matter for the legislative judgment and not that of courts. *South Carolina State Highway Department v. Barnwell Bros. Inc.*, 303 U.S. 177 [(1938)].

Appellee raises no valid objection to the present statute by arguing that its prohibition has not been extended to oleomargarine or other butter substitutes in which vegetable fats or oils are substituted for butter fat. A Legislature may hit at an abuse which it has found, even though it has failed to strike at another.

There is no need to consider [the congressional findings] here as more than a declaration deemed to support and justify the action taken as a constitutional exertion of the legislative power, aiding informed judicial review, as do the reports of legislative committees, by revealing the rationale of the legislation. Even in the absence of such aids, the existence of facts supporting the legislative judgment is to be presumed, for regulatory legislation affecting ordinary commercial transactions is not to be pronounced unconstitutional unless in the light of the facts made known or generally assumed it is of such a character as to preclude the assumption that it rests upon some rational basis within the knowledge and experience of the legislators.[4]

Where the existence of a rational basis for legislation whose constitutionality is attacked depends upon facts beyond the sphere of judicial notice, such facts may properly be made the subject of judicial inquiry, and the constitutionality of a statute predicated upon the existence of a particular state of facts may be challenged by showing to the court that those facts have ceased to exist. Similarly we recognize that the constitutionality of a statute, valid on its face, may be assailed by proof of facts tending to show that the statute as applied to a particular article is without support in reason because the article, although within the prohibited class, is so different from others of the class as to be without the reason for the prohibition, though the effect of such proof depends on the relevant circumstances of each case, as for example the administrative difficulty of excluding the article from the regulated class. But by their very nature such inquiries, where the legislative judgment is drawn in question, must be restricted to the issue whether any state of facts either known or which could reasonably be assumed affords support for it. Here the demurrer challenges the validity of the statute on its face and it is evident from all the considerations presented to Congress, and those of which we may take judicial notice, that the question is at least debatable whether commerce in filled milk should be left unregulated, or in some measure restricted, or wholly prohibited. As that decision was for Congress, neither the finding of a court arrived at by weighing the evidence, nor the verdict of a jury can be substituted for it.

Reversed.

MR. JUSTICE BLACK concurs in the result.

MR. JUSTICE McREYNOLDS thinks that the judgment should be affirmed.

MR. JUSTICE CARDOZO and MR. JUSTICE REED took no part in the consideration or decision of this case.

MR. JUSTICE BUTLER. [Concurrence omitted.]

---

[4] There may be narrower scope for operation of the presumption of constitutionality when legislation appears on its face to be within a specific prohibition of the Constitution, such as those of the first ten Amendments, which are deemed equally specific when held to be embraced within the Fourteenth.

It is unnecessary to consider now whether legislation which restricts those political processes which can ordinarily be expected to bring about repeal of undesirable legislation, is to be subjected to more exacting judicial scrutiny under the general prohibitions of the Fourteenth Amendment than are most other types of legislation.

Nor need we enquire whether similar considerations enter into the review of statutes directed at particular religious, *Pierce v. Society of Sisters*, 268 U.S. 510 [(1925)], or national, *Meyer v. Nebraska*, 262 U.S. 390 [(1923)]; or racial minorities; whether prejudice against discrete and insular minorities may be a special condition, which tends seriously to curtail the operation of those political processes ordinarily to be relied upon to protect minorities, and which may call for a correspondingly more searching judicial inquiry.

EXERCISE 8:

1. What standard of review did the Supreme Court utilize to review the challenged federal legislation?

2. What were the situations identified by the Supreme Court, in Footnote Four, where the presumption of constitutionality will not apply? Are these the only situations, or are there others?

3. What justification did the Court give for not applying the presumption of constitutionality in those situations? What justifications can *you* provide?

4. Does Footnote Four provide a principled basis upon which to reject *Lochner* and, at the same time, justify stricter judicial scrutiny in some categories of cases (especially the modern substantive due process cases, below)? Does it provide an adequate basis?

5. Why did Carolene Products Company's claim not fall into one of the situations identified by Footnote Four?

6. Note that the *Carolene* Court cited *Meyer* as a case involving "national . . . minorities." Today, *Meyer* is typically cited as standing for the right of parents to educate their children. Which characterization is right? Are both?

Beginning in the 1940s, and culminating in the mid-1950s, a school of thought arose built on Footnote Four's claims. This group of legal scholars and judges was called the Legal Process School, and its most prominent members were on the Harvard law faculty. MORTON J. HORWITZ, THE TRANSFORMATION OF AMERICAN LAW: 1870–1960, at 247–68 (1992); Ernest Young, *Institutional Settlement in a Globalizing Judicial System*, 54 DUKE L.J. 1143 (2005). The Legal Process School had a number of basic commitments including: (1) institutional settlement; and (2) reasoned elaboration. Institutional settlement is the idea that primary responsibility for legal actions should be assigned to one governmental institution based on relative institutional competence, and that other branches of government should respect that assignment. Footnote Four, for instance, instructed the Supreme Court to defer to Congress' judgments regarding regulation of interstate commerce. It also suggested that the Court has primary responsibility for protecting individual rights.

Reasoned elaboration is the duty of courts to give reasons for their decisions. Unlike legislatures, which can create law without giving a reason, a court must explain the neutral principles upon which its ruling is based, argued the School's members. In the Footnote Four context, this means that the Supreme Court must explain the basis upon which it will utilize stricter judicial scrutiny in some areas — minority rights, for example — than in others. Legal Process was in part a response to the earlier Legal Realist movement that seemed to say that judges are legislators with robes, and reasoned elaboration was one mechanism to distinguish judges from legislators.

However, the Warren and Burger Court's modern substantive due process juris-prudence, discussed below, undermined the Legal Process School. Legal Process proponents, such as Alexander Bickel in his famous *The Least Dangerous Branch: The*

Supreme Court at the Bar of Politics (1962), worked very hard to show that modern substantive due process was not results-oriented and instead that it was the reasoned elaboration of existing legal materials. In the end, failure to do so in a plausible manner, caused the School's decline.

F. MODERN SUBSTANTIVE DUE PROCESS

1. Introduction

Modern substantive due process has what are called two "tiers" of judicial scrutiny.[58] The first tier continues the New Deal Court's rational basis review. Rational basis review applies as the baseline to all governmental actions. For example, when a state regulates auto manufacturing processes, those regulations are subject to rational basis review. Rational basis review requires the *challenger* to a governmental action to show that the challenged government action is not: (1) rationally related to; (2) a conceivable; (3) legitimate state interest.

The means-ends relationship — "rationally related" — required by rational basis review is lax. The government may choose one of many avenues to advance its goal even if the means it chooses is less effective than another possible means. The government's goal need only be one within the government's traditional police powers: health, safety, and morals. Indeed, the legitimate state interest relied upon by the government in litigation need not be the goal actually sought by the government when it performed the challenged action. Instead, the government's attorney can proffer a "conceivable" governmental interest in defense of a challenged law. A crucial component of rational basis review is significant judicial deference to the government's justifications for a challenged law.

Rational basis review was exemplified in *Williamson v. Lee Optical*, 348 U.S. 483 (1955), reprinted above. There, the Supreme Court credited Oklahoma's claim that the challenged restriction served the legitimate state interest of public health. The Court also ruled for the state even though the restriction was significantly under and over-inclusive.

Building on scattered earlier cases, some reaching back to the then-discredited *Lochner* Era, the Supreme Court also re-created substantive due process doctrine. This case law includes arguably the Court's most controversial pronouncements with cases touching on abortion, homosexual marriage, and suicide.

Consistent with *Carolene Products* Footnote Four, modern substantive due process case law singles-out "fundamental rights" for special judicial solicitude. If a right is deemed "fundamental," then the Supreme Court subjects it to "strict scrutiny." For example, when a government regulates the fundamental right of marriage, that

---

[58] As we will see, the clean description of substantive due process doctrine as encompassing two clearly defined "tiers," though the Supreme Court's official teaching, is likely misleading. *See* Suzanne B. Goldberg, *Equality Without Tiers*, 77 S. Cal. L. Rev. 481, 482 (2004) (noting that the tiers of scrutiny have fragmented in their application). Instead, different contexts, subject matters, and time periods have pushed and pulled particular tiers toward more and less strictness.

regulation is subject to strict scrutiny. Strict scrutiny requires the defending government — the local, state, or federal government — to persuade a court that the challenged governmental action is: (1) "narrowly tailored" to achieve a; (2) "compelling" governmental interest.

Unlike rational basis review, in the context of strict scrutiny, the *government* has the burden of establishing these two elements. Narrow tailoring requires a very tight means-ends relationship between the government's means — the challenged regulation — and the government's goal. Furthermore, the government's goal must be compelling. This means that only the most important interests, such as national security, are sufficiently weighty.

The cases below describe the rise of modern substantive due process doctrine. Pay particular attention to: (1) what activities are — and are not — fundamental rights; and (2) the strict scrutiny mode of analysis used by the Court to evaluate infringements of fundamental rights.

The cases below are reprinted with an eye toward both the particular right in question and the timeline of the Court's decisions. Section 2 begins with the origin of modern substantive due process. Thereafter, the various rights addressed by the Supreme Court are reviewed. Be aware, that this categorization of rights — and indeed, categorizing and labeling at all! — like any in this contentious area, is subject to reasonable criticism. For instance, one could describe the right to sexual autonomy more or less broadly.

2.   Origins of Modern Substantive Due Process

After the New Deal and into the 1950s, the Supreme Court was relatively reluctant to engage in any activity that could reasonably be criticized as a return to "*Lochner*." One sees this reluctance reflected in statements by the Court distinguishing *Lochner*, attempts by the Court to justify its decisions in a manner distinct from *Lochner*, and the halting way the Court moved back into substantive due process. The first case reprinted below is *Griswold v. Connecticut*, 381 U.S. 479 (1965), one of the most important cases in the twentieth century, more for its analysis than its result.

GRISWOLD v. CONNECTICUT
381 U.S. 479 (1965)

MR. JUSTICE DOUGLAS delivered the opinion of the Court.

Appellant Griswold is Executive Director of the Planned Parenthood League of Connecticut. Appellant Buxton is a licensed physician and a professor at the Yale Medical School who served as Medical Director for the League at its Center in New Haven, when appellants were arrested. They gave information, instruction, and medical advice to *married persons* as to the means of preventing conception. They examined the wife and prescribed the best contraceptive device or material for her use.

The statute whose constitutionality is involved in this appeal provides: 'Any person who uses any drug, medicinal article or instrument for the purpose of preventing conception shall be fined not less than fifty dollars or imprisoned not less than sixty days nor more than one year or be both fined and imprisoned.' The appellants were found guilty and fined $100 each, against the claim that the statute as so applied violated the Fourteenth Amendment. The Appellate Division of the Circuit Court affirmed. The Supreme Court of Errors affirmed that judgment.

[W]e are met with a wide range of questions that implicate the Due Process Clause of the Fourteenth Amendment. Overtones of some arguments suggest that *Lochner v. State of New York*, 198 U.S. 45 [(1905)], should be our guide. But we decline that invitation as we did in *West Coast Hotel Co. v. Parrish*, 300 U.S. 379 [(1937)]; *Williamson v. Lee Optical Co.*, 348 U.S. 483 [(1955)]. We do not sit as a super-legislature to determine the wisdom, need, and propriety of laws that touch economic problems, business affairs, or social conditions. This law, however, operates directly on an intimate relation of husband and wife and their physician's role in one aspect of that relation.

The association of people is not mentioned in the Constitution nor in the Bill of Rights. The right to educate a child in a school of the parents' choice — whether public or private or parochial — is also not mentioned. Nor is the right to study any particular subject or any foreign language. Yet the First Amendment has been construed to include certain of those rights.

By *Pierce v. Society of Sisters*, [268 U.S. 510 (1925)], the right to educate one's children as one chooses is made applicable to the States by the force of the First and Fourteenth Amendments. By *Meyer v. State of Nebraska*, [262 U.S. 390 (1923)], the same dignity is given the right to study the German language in a private school. The right of freedom of speech and press includes not only the right to utter or to print, but the right to distribute, the right to receive, the right to read and freedom of inquiry, freedom of thought, and freedom to teach-indeed the freedom of the entire university community. Without those peripheral rights the specific rights would be less secure. And so we reaffirm the principle of the *Pierce* and the *Meyer* cases.

In *NAACP v. State of Alabama*, 357 U.S. 449, 462 [(1958)], we protected the "freedom to associate and privacy in one's associations," noting that freedom of association was a peripheral First Amendment right. In other words, the First Amendment has a penumbra where privacy is protected from governmental intrusion. In like context, we have protected forms of "association" that are not political in the customary sense but pertain to the social, legal, and economic benefit of the members. *NAACP v. Button*, 371 U.S. 415, 430–431 [(1963)].

Those cases involved more than the "right of assembly." The right of "association," like the right of belief (*West Virginia State Board of Education v. Barnette*, 319 U.S. 624 [(1943)]), is more than the right to attend a meeting; it includes the right to express one's attitudes or philosophies by membership in a group or by affiliation with it or by other lawful means. Association in that context is a form of expression of opinion; and while it is not expressly included in the First Amendment its existence is necessary in making the express guarantees fully meaningful.

The foregoing cases suggest that specific guarantees in the Bill of Rights have penumbras, formed by emanations from those guarantees that help give them life and substance. Various guarantees create zones of privacy. The right of association contained in the penumbra of the First Amendment is one, as we have seen. The Third Amendment in its prohibition against the quartering of soldiers "in any house" in time of peace without the consent of the owner is another facet of that privacy. The Fourth Amendment explicitly affirms the "right of the people to be secure in their persons, houses, papers, and effects, against unreasonable searches and seizures." The Fifth Amendment in its Self-Incrimination Clause enables the citizen to create a zone of privacy which government may not force him to surrender to his detriment. The Ninth Amendment provides: "The enumeration in the Constitution, of certain rights, shall not be construed to deny or disparage others retained by the people."

The Fourth and Fifth Amendments [provide] protection against all governmental invasions "of the sanctity of a man's home and the privacies of life." We recently referred in *Mapp v. Ohio*, 367 U.S. 643, 656 [(1961)], to the Fourth Amendment as creating a "right to privacy, no less important than any other right carefully and particularly reserved to the people." *See* [William M.] Beaney, *The Constitutional Right to Privacy*, 1962 Sup. Ct. Rev. 212; [Erwin M.] Griswold, *The Right to be Let Alone*, 55 Nw. U.L. Rev. 216 (1960).

We have had many controversies over these penumbral rights of "privacy and repose." *See, e.g., Skinner v. State of Oklahoma*, 316 U.S. 535, 541 [(1942)]. These cases bear witness that the right of privacy which presses for recognition here is a legitimate one.

The present case, then, concerns a relationship lying within the zone of privacy created by several fundamental constitutional guarantees. And it concerns a law which, in forbidding the use of contraceptives rather than regulating their manufacture or sale, seeks to achieve its goals by means having a maximum destructive impact upon that relationship. Such a law cannot stand in light of the familiar principle, so often applied by this Court, that a "governmental purpose to control or prevent activities constitutionally subject to state regulation may not be achieved by means which sweep unnecessarily broadly and thereby invade the area of protected freedoms." Would we allow the police to search the sacred precincts of marital bedrooms for telltale signs of the use of contraceptives? The very idea is repulsive to the notions of privacy surrounding the marriage relationship.

We deal with a right of privacy older than the Bill of Rights — older than our political parties, older than our school system. Marriage is a coming together for better or for worse, hopefully enduring, and intimate to the degree of being sacred. It is an association that promotes a way of life, not causes; a harmony in living, not political faiths; a bilateral loyalty, not commercial or social projects. Yet it is an association for as noble a purpose as any involved in our prior decisions.

Reversed.

MR. JUSTICE GOLDBERG, whom THE CHIEF JUSTICE and MR. JUSTICE BRENNAN join, concurring.

In reaching the conclusion that the right of marital privacy is protected, as being within the protected penumbra of specific guarantees of the Bill of Rights, the Court refers to the Ninth Amendment. I add these words to emphasize the relevance of that Amendment to the Court's holding.[1]

This Court, in a series of decisions, has held that the Fourteenth Amendment absorbs and applies to the States those specifics of the first eight amendments which express fundamental personal rights. The language and history of the Ninth Amendment reveal that the Framers of the Constitution believed that there are additional fundamental rights, protected from governmental infringement, which exist alongside those fundamental rights specifically mentioned in the first eight constitutional amendments.

The Ninth Amendment reads, "The enumeration in the Constitution, of certain rights, shall not be construed to deny or disparage others retained by the people." The Amendment is almost entirely the work of James Madison. It was introduced in Congress by him and passed the House and Senate with little or no debate and virtually no change in language. It was proffered to quiet expressed fears that a bill of specifically enumerated rights could not be sufficiently broad to cover all essential rights and that the specific mention of certain rights would be interpreted as a denial that others were protected.

In presenting the proposed Amendment, Madison said:

> "It has been objected also against a bill of rights, that, by enumerating particular exceptions to the grant of power, it would disparage those rights which were not placed in that enumeration; and it might follow by implication, that those rights which were not singled out, were intended to be assigned into the hands of the General Government, and were consequently insecure. This is one of the most plausible arguments I have ever heard urged against the admission of a bill of rights into this system; but, I conceive, that it may be guarded against. I have attempted it, as gentlemen may see by turning to the last clause of the fourth resolution [the Ninth Amendment]." I Annals of Congress 439 (Gales and Seaton ed. 1834).

Mr. Justice Story wrote of this argument against a bill of rights and the meaning of the Ninth Amendment:

> "In regard to * * * (a) suggestion, that the affirmance of certain rights might disparage others, or might lead to argumentative implications in favor of other powers, it might be sufficient to say that such a course of reasoning could never be sustained upon any solid basis * * *. But a conclusive answer is, that such an attempt may be interdicted (as it has been) by a positive declaration in such a bill of rights that the enumeration of certain rights shall not be

---

[1] My BROTHER STEWART dissents on the ground that he "can find no * * * general right of privacy in the Bill of Rights, in any other part of the Constitution, or in any case ever before decided by this Court." He would require a more explicit guarantee than the one which the Court derives from several constitutional amendments. This Court, however, has never held that the Bill of Rights protects only those rights that the Constitution specifically mentions by name. To the contrary, this Court, for example, in *Bolling v. Sharpe*, 347 U.S. 497 [(1954)], while recognizing that the Fifth Amendment does not contain the "explicit safeguard" of an equal protection clause, nevertheless derived an equal protection principle from that Amendment's Due Process Clause.

construed to deny or disparage others retained by the people." II [Joseph] Story, Commentaries on the Constitution of the United States 626–627 (5th ed. 1891).

These statements of Madison and Story make clear that the Framers did not intend that the first eight amendments be construed to exhaust the basic and fundamental rights which the Constitution guaranteed to the people.

While this Court has had little occasion to interpret the Ninth Amendment, "[i]t cannot be presumed that any clause in the constitution is intended to be without effect." *Marbury v. Madison*, [5 U.S. (1 Cranch)] 137, 174 [(1803)]. The Ninth Amendment to the Constitution may be regarded by some as a recent discovery and may be forgotten by others, but since 1791 it has been a basic part of the Constitution which we are sworn to uphold. To hold that a right so basic and fundamental and so deeprooted in our society as the right of privacy in marriage may be infringed because that right is not guaranteed in so many words by the first eight amendments to the Constitution is to ignore the Ninth Amendment and to give it no effect whatsoever. Moreover, a judicial construction that this fundamental right is not protected by the Constitution because it is not mentioned in explicit terms by one of the first eight amendments or elsewhere in the Constitution would violate the Ninth Amendment, which specifically states that "[t]he enumeration in the Constitution, of certain rights shall not be construed to deny or disparage others retained by the people."

I do not take the position of my BROTHER BLACK that the entire Bill of Rights is incorporated in the Fourteenth Amendment, and I do not mean to imply that the Ninth Amendment is applied against the States by the Fourteenth. Nor do I mean to state that the Ninth Amendment constitutes an independent source of rights protected from infringement by either the States or the Federal Government. Rather, the Ninth Amendment shows a belief of the Constitution's authors that fundamental rights exist that are not expressly enumerated in the first eight amendments and an intent that the list of rights included there not be deemed exhaustive. As any student of this Court's opinions knows, this Court has held, often unanimously, that the Fifth and Fourteenth Amendments protect certain fundamental personal liberties from abridgment by the Federal Government or the States. The Ninth Amendment simply shows the intent of the Constitution's authors that other fundamental personal rights should not be denied such protection or disparaged in any other way simply because they are not specifically listed in the first eight constitutional amendments. I do not see how this broadens the authority of the Court; rather it serves to support what this Court has been doing in protecting fundamental rights.

Nor am I turning somersaults with history in arguing that the Ninth Amendment is relevant in a case dealing with a State's infringement of a fundamental right. While the Ninth Amendment — and indeed the entire Bill of Rights — originally concerned restrictions upon federal power, the subsequently enacted Fourteenth Amendment prohibits the States as well from abridging fundamental personal liberties. And, the Ninth Amendment, in indicating that not all such liberties are specifically mentioned in the first eight amendments, is surely relevant in showing the existence of other fundamental personal rights, now protected from state, as well as federal, infringement.

In determining which rights are fundamental, judges are not left at large to decide cases in light of their personal and private notions. Rather, they must look to the "traditions and [collective] conscience of our people" to determine whether a principle is "so rooted [there] * * * as to be ranked as fundamental." The inquiry is whether a right involved 'is of such a character that it cannot be denied without violating those "fundamental principles of liberty and justice which lie at the base of all our civil and political institutions" * * *.

I agree fully with the Court that, applying these tests, the right of privacy is a fundamental personal right. The Connecticut statutes here involved deal with a particularly important and sensitive area of privacy-that of the marital relation and the marital home. This Court recognized in *Meyer v. Nebraska*, [262 U.S. 390 (1923)], that the right "to marry, establish a home and bring up children" was an essential part of the liberty guaranteed by the Fourteenth Amendment. In *Pierce v. Society of Sisters*, 268 U.S. 510 [(1925)], the Court held unconstitutional an Oregon Act which forbade parents from sending their children to private schools because such an act "unreasonably interferes with the liberty of parents and guardians to direct the upbringing and education of children under their control."

Although the Constitution does not speak in so many words of the right of privacy in marriage, I cannot believe that it offers these fundamental rights no protection. The fact that no particular provision of the Constitution explicitly forbids the State from disrupting the traditional relation of the family surely does not show that the Government was meant to have the power to do so. Rather, as the Ninth Amendment expressly recognizes, there are fundamental personal rights such as this one, which are protected from abridgment by the Government though not specifically mentioned in the Constitution.

The logic of the dissents would sanction federal or state legislation that seems to me even more plainly unconstitutional than the statute before us. Surely the Government, absent a showing of a compelling subordinating state interest, could not decree that all husbands and wives must be sterilized after two children have been born to them. Yet by their reasoning such an invasion of marital privacy would not be subject to constitutional challenge because, while it might be "silly," no provision of the Constitution specifically prevents the Government from curtailing the marital right to bear children and raise a family. While it may shock some of my Brethren that the Court today holds that the Constitution protects the right of marital privacy, in my view it is far more shocking to believe that the personal liberty guaranteed by the Constitution does not include protection against such totalitarian limitation of family size, which is at complete variance with our constitutional concepts.

In a long series of cases this Court has held that where fundamental personal liberties are involved, they may not be abridged by the States simply on a showing that a regulatory statute has some rational relationship to the effectuation of a proper state purpose. The law must be shown "necessary, and not merely rationally related to, the accomplishment of a permissible state policy."

Although the Connecticut birth-control law obviously encroaches upon a fundamental personal liberty, the State does not show that the law serves any "subordinating [state] interest which is compelling" or that it is "necessary * * * to the accomplishment of a permissible state policy." The State, at most, argues that there is some rational relation between this statute and what is admittedly a legitimate subject of state concern-the discouraging of extra-marital relations. It says that preventing the use of birth-control devices by married persons helps prevent the indulgence by some in such extra-marital relations. The rationality of this justification is dubious, particularly in light of the admitted widespread availability to all persons in the State of Connecticut, unmarried as well as married, of birth-control devices for the prevention of disease, as distinguished from the prevention of conception. But, in any event, it is clear that the state interest in safeguarding marital fidelity can be served by a more discriminately tailored statute. The State of Connecticut does have statutes, the constitutionality of which is beyond doubt, which prohibit adultery and fornication. These statutes demonstrate that means for achieving the same basic purpose of protecting marital fidelity are available to Connecticut without the need to "invade the area of protected freedoms."

Finally, it should be said of the Court's holding today that it in no way interferes with a State's proper regulation of sexual promiscuity or misconduct. As my Brother Harlan so well stated in his dissenting opinion in *Poe v. Ullman*, 367 U.S. [497,] 553 [(1961)].

> "Adultery, homosexuality and the like are sexual intimacies which the State forbids * * * but the intimacy of husband and wife is necessarily an essential and accepted feature of the institution of marriage, an institution which the State not only must allow, but which always and in every age it has fostered and protected."

MR. JUSTICE HARLAN, concurring in the judgment. [opinion omitted]

MR. JUSTICE WHITE, concurring in the judgment. [opinion omitted]

MR. JUSTICE BLACK, with whom MR. JUSTICE STEWART joins, dissenting.

I agree with my BROTHER STEWART'S dissenting opinion. And like him I do not to any extent whatever base my view that this Connecticut law is constitutional on a belief that the law is wise or that its policy is a good one.

The Court talks about a constitutional 'right of privacy' as though there is some constitutional provision or provisions forbidding any law ever to be passed which might abridge the "privacy" of individuals. But there is not. There are, of course, guarantees in certain specific constitutional provisions which are designed in part to protect privacy at certain times and places with respect to certain activities. Such, for example, is the Fourth Amendment's guarantee against "unreasonable searches and seizures." But I think it belittles that Amendment to talk about it as though it protects nothing but "privacy." To treat it that way is to give it a niggardly interpretation, not the kind of liberal reading I think any Bill of Rights provision should be given. The average man would very likely not have his feelings soothed any more by having his property seized openly than by having it seized privately and by stealth. He simply wants his property left alone.

One of the most effective ways of diluting or expanding a constitutionally guaranteed right is to substitute for the crucial word or words of a constitutional guarantee another word or words, more or less flexible and more or less restricted in meaning. This fact is well illustrated by the use of the term "right of privacy" as a comprehensive substitute for the Fourth Amendment's guarantee against "unreasonable searches and seizures." "Privacy" is a broad, abstract and ambiguous concept which can easily be shrunken in meaning but which can also, on the other hand, easily be interpreted as a constitutional ban against many things other than searches and seizures. For these reasons I get nowhere in this case by talk about a constitutional "right or privacy" as an emanation from one or more constitutional provisions. I like my privacy as well as the next one, but I am nevertheless compelled to admit that government has a right to invade it unless prohibited by some specific constitutional provision.

The due process argument which my BROTHERS HARLAN and WHITE adopt here is based, as their opinions indicate, on the premise that this Court is vested with power to invalidate all state laws that it consider to be arbitrary, capricious, unreasonable, or oppressive. If these formulas based on "natural justice," or others which mean the same thing, are to prevail, they require judges to determine what is or is not constitutional on the basis of their own appraisal of what laws are unwise or unnecessary. The power to make such decisions is of course that of a legislative body. Surely it has to be admitted that no provision of the Constitution specifically gives such blanket power to courts to exercise such a supervisory veto over the wisdom and value of legislative policies and to hold unconstitutional those laws which they believe unwise or dangerous. I readily admit that no legislative body, state or national, should pass laws that can justly be given any of the invidious labels invoked as constitutional excuses to strike down state laws. But perhaps it is not too much to say that no legislative body ever does pass laws without believing that they will accomplish a sane, rational, wise and justifiable purpose. I do not believe that we are granted power by the Due Process Clause or any other constitutional provision or provisions to measure constitutionality by our belief that legislation is arbitrary, capricious or unreasonable. Such an appraisal of the wisdom of legislation is an attribute of the power to make laws, not of the power to interpret them. The use by federal courts of such a formula or doctrine or whatnot to veto federal or state laws simply takes away from Congress and States the power to make laws based on their own judgment of fairness and wisdom and transfers that power to this Court for ultimate determination — a power which was specifically denied to federal courts by the convention that framed the Constitution.[6]

Of the cases on which my BROTHERS WHITE and GOLDBERG rely so heavily, undoubtedly the reasoning of two of them supports their result here-as would that of a number of others which they do not bother to name, e.g., *Lochner v. State of New York*, 198 U.S. 45 [(1905)]. The two they do cite and quote from, *Meyer v. State of Nebraska*, 262 U.S. 390 [(1923)], and *Pierce v. Society of Sisters*, 268 U.S. 510 [(1925)],

---

[6] [T]he Constitutional Convention did on at least two occasions reject proposals which would have given the federal judiciary a part in recommending laws or in vetoing as bad or unwise the legislation passed by the Congress.

were both decided in opinions by Mr. Justice McReynolds which elaborated the same natural law due process philosophy found in *Lochner v. New York,* one of the cases on which he relied in *Meyer.* [T]he reasoning stated in *Meyer* and *Pierce* was the same natural law due process philosophy which many later opinions repudiated, and which I cannot accept.

My BROTHER GOLDBERG has adopted the recent discovery that the Ninth Amendment can be used by this Court as authority to strike down all state legislation which this Court thinks violates "fundamental principles of liberty and justice," or is contrary to the "traditions and [collective] conscience of our people." He also states, without proof satisfactory to me, that in making decisions on this basis judges will not consider "their personal and private notions." One may ask how they can avoid considering them. Our Court certainly has no machinery with which to take a Gallup Poll.[13] And the scientific miracles of this age have not yet produced a gadget which the Court can use to determine what traditions are rooted in the "[collective] conscience of our people." Moreover, one would certainly have to look far beyond the language of the Ninth Amendment to find that the Framers vested in this Court any such awesome veto powers over lawmaking, either by the States or by the Congress. Nor does anything in the history of the Amendment offer any support for such a shocking doctrine. The whole history of the adoption of the Constitution and Bill of Rights points the other way, and the very material quoted by my BROTHER GOLDBERG shows that the Ninth Amendment was intended to protect against the idea that "by enumerating particular exceptions to the grant of power" to the Federal Government, "those rights which were not singled out, were intended to be assigned into the hands of the General Government [the United States], and were consequently insecure." That Amendment was passed, not to broaden the powers of this Court or any other department of "the General Government," but, as every student of history knows, to assure the people that the Constitution in all its provisions was intended to limit the Federal Government to the powers granted expressly or by necessary implication. This fact is perhaps responsible for the peculiar phenomenon that for a period of a century and a half no serious suggestion was ever made that the Ninth Amendment, enacted to protect state powers against federal invasion, could be used as a weapon of federal power to prevent state legislatures from passing laws they consider appropriate to govern local affairs. Use of any such broad, unbounded judicial authority would make of this Court's members a day-to-day constitutional convention.

The adoption of such a loose, flexible, uncontrolled standard for holding laws unconstitutional, if ever it is finally achieved, will amount to a great unconstitutional shift of power to the courts which I believe and am constrained to say will be bad for the courts and worse for the country. Subjecting federal and state laws to such an unrestrained and unrestrainable judicial control as to the wisdom of legislative enactments would, I fear, jeopardize the separation of governmental powers that the

---

[13] Of course one cannot be oblivious to the fact that Mr. Gallup has already published the results of a poll which he says show that 46% of the people in this country believe schools should teach about birth control. Washington Post, May 21, 1965, p. 2, col. 1. I can hardly believe, however, that BROTHER GOLDBERG would view 46% of the persons polled as so overwhelming a proportion that this Court may now rely on it to declare that the Connecticut law infringes "fundamental" rights, and overrule the long-standing view of the people of Connecticut expressed through their elected representatives.

Framers set up and at the same time threaten to take away much of the power of. States to govern themselves which the Constitution plainly intended them to have.

I realize that many good and able men have eloquently spoken and written, sometimes in rhapsodical strains, about the duty of this Court to keep the Constitution in tune with the times. The idea is that the Constitution must be changed from time to time and that this Court is charged with a duty to make those changes. For myself, I must with all deference reject that philosophy. The Constitution makers knew the need for change and provided for it. Amendments suggested by the people's elected representatives can be submitted to the people or their selected agents for ratification. And so, I cannot rely on the Due Process Clause or the Ninth Amendment or any mysterious and uncertain natural law concept as a reason for striking down this state law. The Due Process Clause with an "arbitrary and capricious" or "shocking to the conscience" formula was liberally used by this Court to strike down economic legislation in the early decades of this century, threatening, many people thought, the tranquility and stability of the Nation. *See, e.g., Lochner v. State of New York*, 198 U.S. 45 [(1905)]. That formula, based on subjective considerations of "natural justice," is no less dangerous when used to enforce this Court's views about personal rights than those about economic rights. I had thought that we had laid that formula, as a means for striking down state legislation, to rest once and for all in cases like *West Coast Hotel Co. v. Parrish*, 300 U.S. 379 [(1937),] and many other opinions.

The late Judge Learned Hand, after emphasizing his view that judges should not use the due process formula suggested in the concurring opinions today or any other formula like it to invalidate legislation offensive to their "personal preferences,"[22] made the statement, with which I fully agree, that:

> "For myself it would be most irksome to be ruled by a bevy of Platonic Guardians, even if I knew how to choose them, which I assuredly do not."

So far as I am concerned, Connecticut's law as applied here is not forbidden by any provision of the Federal Constitution as that Constitution was written, and I would therefore affirm.

MR. JUSTICE STEWART, whom MR. JUSTICE BLACK joins, dissenting.

Since 1879 Connecticut has had on its books a law which forbids the use of contraceptives by anyone. I think this is an uncommonly silly law. As a practical matter, the law is obviously unenforceable, except in the oblique context of the present case. As a philosophical matter, I believe the use of contraceptives in the relationship of marriage should be left to personal and private choice, based upon each individual's moral, ethical, and religious beliefs. But we are not asked in this case to say whether we think this law is unwise, or even asinine. We are asked to hold that it violates the United States Constitution. And that I cannot do.

---

[22] [Learned] Hand, The Bill of Rights [70] (1958).

EXERCISE 9:

1.   What is the constitutional right articulated by the Supreme Court? What is its scope? Watch how, as later cases are decided, *Griswold*'s meaning is pushed toward a broader reading.

2.   What is(are) the source(s) of the right articulated in *Griswold*?

3.   Is Justice Douglas' (in)famous penumbras and emanations analysis a correct means to interpret the Constitution?

4.   With what level of judicial scrutiny did the Court evaluate the challenged law? Why? Is that the appropriate level?

5.   Did Justice Douglas persuade you that *Griswold* is not *Lochner* reborn, as Justice Black argued?

6.   Justice Douglas argued that the right to privacy is older than political parties and school systems. Is that true? Is that relevant?

7.   *Griswold* was not the first time the Supreme Court faced a constitutional challenge to a ban on artificial contraception. The Court turned back the previous challenges on standing grounds. In *Tileston v. Ullman*, 318 U.S. 44 (1943), for example, the Court ruled that a physician who initiated a declaratory judgment action to challenge Connecticut's statute lacked standing. Later, in *Poe v. Ullman*, 367 U.S. 497 (1961), a divided Court ruled that another challenge was nonjusticiable.

8.   *Griswold* was a test case. The defendants sought prosecution in order to create a justiciable case in which to challenge the constitutionality of Connecticut's statute. Should this affect one's view of *Griswold*?

9.   What arguments did Justice Goldberg use to support his conclusion?

10.   Justice Goldberg's concurrence is famous for its invocation of the Ninth Amendment as a source of authority for the Supreme Court to protect unenumerated constitutional rights. It garnered the signatures of two other justices and, since then, has been a focus of scholarly attention. On the Court, however, the Ninth Amendment has never, as Justice Goldberg advocated, been used in a case as the sole source of unenumerated right.

11.   Justice Goldberg stated: "To hold that a right so basic and fundamental and so deeprooted in our society as the right of privacy in marriage may be infringed because that right is not guaranteed in so many words by the first eight amendments to the Constitution is to ignore the Ninth Amendment and to give it no effect whatsoever." Is that true? What role could the Ninth Amendment have if one disagreed with Justice Goldberg?

12.   What do you make of Justice Black's reference to the lack of usage of the Ninth Amendment until Justice Goldberg's concurrence? For what purpose did Justice Black make that claim, and how could Justice Goldberg account for that delay?

13.   There is a long-standing and complex scholarly debate on what the Ninth Amendment means. Professor Randy Barnett is the most prominent advocate of the claim that the Ninth Amendment is a textual command to courts to protect unenu-

merated natural rights. RANDY E. BARNETT, RESTORING THE LOST CONSTITUTION: THE PRESUMPTION OF LIBERTY 54–68, 235–42 (2005). On the other end of the spectrum, Robert Bork famously argued that the Ninth Amendment was metaphorically covered by an "inkblot." *Nomination of Robert H. Bork to be Associate Justice of the Supreme Court of the United States: Hearings Before the S. Comm. on the Judiciary*, 100th Cong. 224 (1987) (statement of Judge Robert H. Bork). Other scholars take in-between positions. *See, e.g.*, KURT T. LASH, THE LOST HISTORY OF THE NINTH AMENDMENT (2009) (arguing that the Ninth Amendment was a rule of construction for federal power).

14.   Justice Goldberg utilized a common "slippery slope" argument against the dissent. He claimed that the dissent's position would mean that a state could mandate birth control or sterilization after, for instance, a married couple had two children. "While it may shock some of my Brethren that the Court today holds that the Constitution protects the right of marital privacy, in my view it is far more shocking to believe that the personal liberty guaranteed by the Constitution does not include protection against such totalitarian limitation of family size, which is at complete variance with our constitutional concepts." Is that a good argument?

15.   What standard of review did Justice Goldberg employ to analyze the constitutionality of Connecticut's ban on artificial contraception?

16.   In an almost off-hand comment, Justice Goldberg stated: "admittedly a legitimate subject of state concern-the discouraging of extra-marital relations." Keep this statement in mind as we cover the evolution of substantive due process.

17.   Justice Black accused the majority of returning to a discredited "natural law due process philosophy." What is that? Why is it bad? Why can judges not utilize natural law when interpreting and applying the Constitution?

18.   Justice Black claimed that Justice Goldberg's use of the Ninth Amendment opened the door to unrestricted judicial discretion that was inconsistent with the role of the judge. Justice Goldberg responded that, "[i]n determining which rights are fundamental, judges are not left at large to decide cases in light of their personal and private notions." Who had the better of the argument?

19.   Justice Black argued that Justice Goldberg was turning the Ninth Amendment on its head by construing it to authorize the federal courts to limit *state* power, when the Ninth Amendment was originally intended to limit *federal* power. How does Justice Goldberg respond? Who was right?

20.   If, as the majority and concurring opinions argued — and the dissent apparently agreed — the Connecticut statute was so clearly bad, then why did the Court not reject Griswold's claim and suggest that Griswold take up the issue with the state legislature? After all, legislators wish to get re-elected and voting for clearly bad legislation is not the way to do so.

21.   Justice Black conceded that: "There is no single one of the graphic and eloquent strictures and criticisms fired at the policy of this Connecticut law either by the Court's opinion or by those of my concurring Brethren to which I cannot subscribe." If that is true, then how could he find that the statute rationally served a legitimate state interest?

22.   Justice Black stated that "government has a right to invade it [individual freedom] unless prohibited by some specific constitutional provision." Is that true?

23.   Contrary to common belief, the statute at issue in Connecticut had its origin in the late-nineteenth century, primarily Protestant movement to restore and promote public morality. This movement's members saw artificial contraception as one of many related causes of declining public morality. *See, e.g., Bolger v. Youngs Drug Prods. Corp.*, 463 U.S. 60, 70 n.19 (1983) (internal citations and quotations omitted) ("The driving force behind [the Comstock Act] was Anthony Comstock, who . . . was a prominent antivice crusader who believed that 'anything remotely touching upon sex was . . . obscene.' "); Carol Flora Brooks, *The Early History of the Anti-Contraceptive Laws in Massachusetts and Connecticut*, 18 Am. Q. 3, 3 (1966) ("The anti-contraceptive laws were . . . passed as a byproduct of an attempt to give legal support to a widespread attitude about obscenity.").

In some ways, the *Griswold* case was a good vehicle in which to resurrect substantive due process. Most importantly, the underlying issue — legal regulation of the use of artificial birth control by married persons — was minor and most Americans agreed with the case's substantive result. However, the Supreme Court relatively quickly moved into more controversial waters.

Each section below covers one of the doctrinal areas in which the Supreme Court addressed a substantive due process right.

3.   Right to Marriage

Marriage is one of the most long-standing and fundamental institutions in civil society. Many Americans spend a significant part of their life in marriage. This fundamental role of marriage prompted the Supreme Court to rule that marriage is a fundamental right protected within its substantive due process doctrine.

Like other institutions, marriage has changed. *Loving v. Virginia*, below, represents one of those changes.

LOVING v. VIRGINIA
388 U.S. 1 (1967)

MR. CHIEF JUSTICE WARREN delivered the opinion of the Court.

This case presents a constitutional question never addressed by this Court: whether a statutory scheme adopted by the State of Virginia to prevent marriages between persons solely on the basis of racial classifications violates the Equal Protection and Due Process Clauses of the Fourteenth Amendment. For reasons which seem to us to reflect the central meaning of those constitutional commands, we conclude that these statutes cannot stand consistently with the Fourteenth Amendment.

In June 1958, two residents of Virginia, Mildred Jeter, a Negro woman, and Richard Loving, a white man, were married in the District of Columbia pursuant to its laws.

Shortly after their marriage, the Lovings returned to Virginia and established their marital abode in Caroline County. At the October Term, 1958, of the Circuit Court of Caroline County, a grand jury issued an indictment charging the Lovings with violating Virginia's ban on interracial marriages. On January 6, 1959, the Lovings pleaded guilty to the charge and were sentenced to one year in jail; however, the trial judge suspended the sentence for a period of 25 years on the condition that the Lovings leave the State and not return to Virginia together for 25 years. He stated in an opinion that:

> "Almighty God created the races white, black, yellow, malay and red, and he placed them on separate continents. And but for the interference with his arrangement there would be no cause for such marriages. The fact that he separated the races shows that he did not intend for the races to mix."

After their convictions, the Lovings took up residence in the District of Columbia. On November 6, 1963, they filed a motion in the state trial court to vacate the judgment and set aside the sentence on the ground that the statutes which they had violated were repugnant to the Fourteenth Amendment. On January 22, 1965, the state trial judge denied the motion to vacate the sentences, and the Lovings perfected an appeal to the Supreme Court of Appeals of Virginia. The Supreme Court of Appeals upheld the constitutionality of the antimiscegenation statutes and affirmed the convictions. The Lovings appealed this decision.

The two statutes under which appellants were convicted and sentenced are part of a comprehensive statutory scheme aimed at prohibiting and punishing interracial marriages. Virginia is now one of 16 States which prohibit and punish marriages on the basis of racial classifications.[5] Penalties for miscegenation arose as an incident to slavery and have been common in Virginia since the colonial period. The present statutory scheme dates from the adoption of the Racial Integrity Act of 1924, passed during the period of extreme nativism which followed the end of the First World War. The central features of this Act, and current Virginia law, are the absolute prohibition of a "white person" marrying other than another "white person."

In upholding the constitutionality of these provisions in the decision below, the Supreme Court of Appeals of Virginia concluded that the State's legitimate purposes were "to preserve the racial integrity of its citizens," and to prevent "the corruption of blood," "a mongrel breed of citizens," and "the obliteration of racial pride," obviously an endorsement of the doctrine of White Supremacy. The court also reasoned that marriage has traditionally been subject to state regulation without federal intervention, and, consequently, the regulation of marriage should be left to exclusive state control by the Tenth Amendment.

While the state court is no doubt correct in asserting that marriage is a social relation subject to the State's police power, the State does not contend in its argument

---

[5] Virginia and 15 other States outlaw interracial marriage: Alabama, Arkansas, Delaware, Florida, Georgia, Kentucky, Louisiana, Mississippi, Missouri, North Carolina, Oklahoma, South Carolina, Tennessee, Texas, West Virginia. Over the past 15 years, 14 States have repealed laws outlawing interracial marriages: Arizona, California, Colorado, Idaho, Indiana, Maryland, Montana, Nebraska, Nevada, North Dakota, Oregon, South Dakota, Utah, and Wyoming.

before this Court that its powers to regulate marriage are unlimited notwithstanding the commands of the Fourteenth Amendment. Nor could it do so in light of *Meyer v. State of Nebraska*, 262 U.S. 390 (1923), and *Skinner v. State of Oklahoma*, 316 U.S. 535 (1942).

[The Supreme Court ruled that the Equal Protection Clause prohibited state bans on interracial marriage.]

II.

These statutes also deprive the Lovings of liberty without due process of law in violation of the Due Process Clause of the Fourteenth Amendment. The freedom to marry has long been recognized as one of the vital personal rights essential to the orderly pursuit of happiness by free men.

Marriage is one of the "basic civil rights of man," fundamental to our very existence and survival. *Skinner v. State of Oklahoma*, 316 U.S. 535, 541 (1942). To deny this fundamental freedom on so unsupportable a basis as the racial classifications embodied in these statutes, classifications so directly subversive of the principle of equality at the heart of the Fourteenth Amendment, is surely to deprive all the State's citizens of liberty without due process of law. The Fourteenth Amendment requires that the freedom of choice to marry not be restricted by invidious racial discriminations. Under our Constitution, the freedom to marry or not marry, a person of another race resides with the individual and cannot be infringed by the State.

These convictions must be reversed. It is so ordered.

MR. JUSTICE STEWART, concurring. [opinion omitted]

EXERCISE 10:

1.   The *Loving* Court ruled that the freedom to marry is a fundamental right. What standard did the Court use to determine that marriage was fundamental? What evidence did the Court rely on to support its conclusion? What other activities, using this standard, are or should be fundamental constitutional rights?

2.   *Loving's* core holding — that marriage is a fundamental right — is uncontroversial today. However, the scope of that right is subject to great contention. Based on the *Loving* opinion itself, what is the scope of the right? Traditional marriage? Homosexual marriage? Polygamous marriage?

3.   Relatedly, how much "gravitational effect" does *Loving* have on other areas of law? For example, does *Loving* influence whether there is or should be a fundamental right to education?

Over the past twenty years, there has been significant litigation over the scope of the right to marry, and the major point of contention is whether the right applies to homosexual couples. At this point, the Supreme Court has not faced the question of whether the Constitution prohibits traditional marriage and requires homosexual marriage. Below, in subsection F.8, we will review *Lawrence v. Texas*, 539 U.S. 558 (2003). Consider whether *Lawrence* established a constitutional right to same-sex marriage.

4. Right to Family Integrity

The Supreme Court has also ruled that there is a substantive due process right to family integrity. Like the right to marry, the core of the right to familial integrity is relatively uncontroversial; it is the scope of the right over which debate occurs.

MOORE v. CITY OF EAST CLEVELAND
431 U.S. 494 (1977)

MR. JUSTICE POWELL announced the judgment of the Court, and delivered an opinion in which MR. JUSTICE BRENNAN, MR. JUSTICE MARSHALL, and MR. JUSTICE BLACKMUN joined.

East Cleveland's housing ordinance, like many throughout the country, limits occupancy of a dwelling unit to members of a single family. But the ordinance contains an unusual and complicated definitional section that recognizes as a "family" only a few categories of related individuals, § 1341.08.[2] Because her family, living together in her home, fits none of those categories, appellant stands convicted of a criminal offense. The question in this case is whether the ordinance violates the Due Process Clause of the Fourteenth Amendment.

I

Appellant, Mrs. Inez Moore, lives in her East Cleveland home together with her son, Dale Moore Sr., and her two grandsons, Dale, Jr., and John Moore, Jr. The two boys are first cousins rather than brothers; we are told that John came to live with his grandmother and with the elder and younger Dale Moores after his mother's death.

In early 1973, Mrs. Moore received a notice of violation from the city, stating that John was an "illegal occupant" and directing her to comply with the ordinance. When she failed to remove him from her home, the city filed a criminal charge. Mrs. Moore moved to dismiss, claiming that the ordinance was constitutionally invalid on its face. Her motion was overruled, and upon conviction she was sentenced to five days in jail

---

[2] Section 1341.08 (1966) provides:

" 'Family' means a number of individuals related to the nominal head of the household or to the spouse of the nominal head of the household living as a single housekeeping unit in a single dwelling unit, but limited to the following:

"(a) Husband or wife of the nominal head of the household.

"(b) Unmarried children of the nominal head of the household or of the spouse of the nominal head of the household, provided, however, that such unmarried children have no children residing with them.

"(c) Father or mother of the nominal head of the household or of the spouse of the nominal head of the household.

and a $25 fine. The Ohio Court of Appeals affirmed, and the Ohio Supreme Court denied review.

II

The city argues that our decision in *Village of Belle Terre v. Boraas*, 416 U.S. 1 (1974), requires us to sustain the ordinance attacked here. Belle Terre, like East Cleveland, imposed limits on the types of groups that could occupy a single dwelling unit. [W]e sustained the Belle Terre ordinance on the ground that it bore a rational relationship to permissible state objectives.

But one overriding factor sets this case apart from *Belle Terre*. The ordinance there affected only unrelated individuals. It expressly allowed all who were related by "blood, adoption, or marriage" to live together. East Cleveland, in contrast, has chosen to regulate the occupancy of its housing by slicing deeply into the family itself. On its face it selects certain categories of relatives who may live together and declares that others may not. In particular, it makes a crime of a grandmother's choice to live with her grandson in circumstances like those presented here.

When a city undertakes such intrusive regulation of the family, *Belle Terre* [does not] govern[]; the usual judicial deference to the legislature is inappropriate. A host of cases, tracing their lineage to *Meyer v. Nebraska*, 262 U.S. 390, 399–401 (1923), and *Pierce v. Society of Sisters*, 268 U.S. 510, 534–535 (1925), have consistently acknowledged a "private realm of family life which the state cannot enter." See, e. g., *Roe v. Wade*, 410 U.S. 113, 152–153 (1973); *Griswold v. Connecticut*, 381 U.S. 479 (1965); *id.*, at 495–496 (Goldberg, J., concurring); *cf. Loving v. Virginia*, 388 U.S. 1, 12 (1967); *Skinner v. Oklahoma ex rel. Williamson*, 316 U.S. 535, 541 (1942). Of course, the family is not beyond regulation. But when the government intrudes on choices concerning family living arrangements, this Court must examine carefully the importance of the governmental interests advanced and the extent to which they are served by the challenged regulation.

When thus examined, this ordinance cannot survive. The city seeks to justify it as a means of preventing overcrowding, minimizing traffic and parking congestion, and avoiding an undue financial burden on East Cleveland's school system. Although these are legitimate goals, the ordinance before us serves them marginally, at best. For example, the ordinance permits any family consisting only of husband, wife, and unmarried children to live together, even if the family contains a half dozen licensed drivers, each with his or her own car. At the same time it forbids an adult brother and sister to share a household, even if both faithfully use public transportation. The ordinance would permit a grandmother to live with a single dependent son and children, even if his school-age children number a dozen, yet it forces Mrs. Moore to find another dwelling for her grandson John, simply because of the presence of his uncle and cousin in the same household. We need not labor the point. Section 1341.08 has but a tenuous relation to alleviation of the conditions mentioned by the city.

III

The city would distinguish the cases based on *Meyer* and *Pierce*. It points out that none of them "gives grandmothers any fundamental rights with respect to grandsons," and suggests that any constitutional right to live together as a family extends only to the nuclear family. To be sure, these cases did not expressly consider the family relationship presented here. They were immediately concerned with freedom of choice with respect to childbearing, e.g., *Roe v. Wade, Griswold*, or with the rights of parents to the custody and companionship of their own children, or with traditional parental authority in matters of child rearing and education. *Pierce, Meyer*. But unless we close our eyes to the basic reasons why certain rights associated with the family have been accorded shelter under the Fourteenth Amendment's Due Process Clause, we cannot avoid applying the force and rationale of these precedents to the family choice involved in this case.

Substantive due process has at times been a treacherous field for this Court. There are risks when the judicial branch gives enhanced protection to certain substantive liberties without the guidance of the more specific provisions of the Bill of Rights. As the history of the *Lochner* era demonstrates, there is reason for concern lest the only limits to such judicial intervention become the predilections of those who happen at the time to be Members of this Court. That history counsels caution and restraint. But it does not counsel abandonment, nor does it require what the city urges here: cutting off any protection of family rights at the first convenient, if arbitrary boundary of the nuclear family.

Appropriate limits on substantive due process come not from drawing arbitrary lines but rather from careful "respect for the teachings of history [and], solid recognition of the basic values that underlie our society."[10] *Griswold v. Connecticut*, 381 U.S., at 501 (Harlan, J., concurring). See generally *Lochner v. New York*, 198 U.S. 45, 76 (1905) (Holmes, J., dissenting). Our decisions establish that the Constitution protects the sanctity of the family precisely because the institution of the family is deeply rooted in this Nation's history and tradition.

Ours is by no means a tradition limited to respect for the bonds uniting the members of the nuclear family. The tradition of uncles, aunts, cousins, and especially grandparents sharing a household along with parents and children has roots equally venerable and equally deserving of constitutional recognition. Out of choice, necessity, or a sense of family responsibility, it has been common for close relatives to draw together and participate in the duties and the satisfactions of a common home. Decisions concerning child rearing, which *Meyer, Pierce* and other cases have recognized as entitled to constitutional protection, long have been shared with grandparents or other relatives who occupy the same household. Especially in times of adversity, such as the death of a spouse or economic need, the broader family has

---

[10] A similar restraint marks our approach to the questions whether an asserted substantive right is entitled to heightened solicitude under the Equal Protection Clause because it is "explicitly or implicitly guaranteed by the Constitution," *San Antonio Independent School Dist. v. Rodriguez*, 411 U.S. 1, 33–34 (1973), and whether or to what extent a guarantee in the Bill of Rights should be "incorporated" in the Due Process Clause because it is "necessary to an Anglo-American regime of ordered liberty." *Duncan v. Louisiana*, 391 U.S. 145, 149–150 n. 14 (1968).

tended to come together for mutual sustenance and to maintain or rebuild a secure home life. This is apparently what happened here.

[T]he Constitution prevents East Cleveland from standardizing its children and its adults by forcing all to live in certain narrowly defined family patterns.

Reversed.

MR. JUSTICE BRENNAN, with whom MR. JUSTICE MARSHALL joins, concurring. [Opinion omitted.]

MR. CHIEF JUSTICE BURGER, dissenting. [Opinion omitted.]

MR. JUSTICE STEWART, with whom MR. JUSTICE REHNQUIST joins, dissenting.

Although the Court regularly proceeds on the assumption that the Due Process Clause has more than a procedural dimension, we must always bear in mind that the substantive content of the Clause is suggested neither by its language nor by preconstitutional history; that content is nothing more than the accumulated product of judicial interpretation of the Fifth and Fourteenth Amendments. This is not to suggest, at this point, that any of these cases should be overruled, or that the process by which they were decided was illegitimate, or even unacceptable, but only to underline that the Court has no license to invalidate legislation which it thinks merely arbitrary or unreasonable.

That the Court has ample precedent for the creation of new constitutional rights should not lead it to repeat the process at will. The Judiciary, including this Court is the most vulnerable and comes nearest to illegitimacy when it deals with judge-made constitutional law having little or no cognizable roots in the language or even the design of the Constitution. Realizing that the present construction of the Due Process Clause represents a major judicial gloss on its terms, as well as on the anticipation of the Framers, and that much of the underpinning for the broad, substantive application of the Clause disappeared in the conflict between the Executive and the Judiciary in the 1930's and 1940's, the Court should be extremely reluctant to breathe still further substantive content into the Due Process Clause so as to strike down legislation adopted by a State or city to promote its welfare. Whenever the Judiciary does so, it unavoidably pre-empts for itself another part of the governance of the country without express constitutional authority.

EXERCISE 11:

1.   What is the source of the right protected in *Moore*? What test did Justice Powell utilize to articulate the right? Did he correctly apply it?

2.   What is the scope of the right protected by the Supreme Court?

3.   Is *Moore* a faithful application of the cases cited by Justice Powell?

4. Once the Court determined that the right to family integrity was protected by the Constitution, what analysis did it use to determine whether the challenged city regulation violated the Constitution?

5. The majority noted that "the institution of the family is deeply rooted" in American tradition. If that is true, then how do you explain East Cleveland's deviation from the tradition? Or does East Cleveland's ordinance show that the tradition is not deeply rooted? Or that the tradition is narrow?

6. One of the common criticisms lodged against the Supreme Court's substantive due process doctrine is that it invites, or even requires, judicial activism, where the federal judiciary steps beyond its competency and illegitimately strikes down democratically enacted laws. Justice Stewart's dissent voiced this concern. How did Justice Powell respond to that criticism? Was his response adequate?

———

Justice Powell relied on history and tradition to determine the scope of substantive due process: "Our decisions establish that the Constitution protects the sanctity of the family precisely because the institution of the family is deeply rooted in this Nation's history and tradition." This is one of two basic approaches to ascertaining which rights are protected under substantive due process doctrine. The other approach, famously articulated by Justice Cardozo in *Palko v. Connecticut*, 302 U.S. 319, 325 (1937), is to ask whether the right is "implicit in the concept of ordered liberty." Speaking generally, advocates of the history-and-tradition approach believed that it provided greater judicial restraint and tied the Supreme Court's rulings more closely to the popular will than did Justice Cardozo's approach. The Supreme Court has wavered between these approaches over the years and across doctrinal categories.

The justices, in their opinions, have vigorously debated the merits of the two approaches for decades. One of the most pointed debates occurred in *Michael H. v. Gerald D.*, 491 U.S. 110 (1989). There, Justice Scalia argued that substantive due process analysis should and could be "tamed" through use of the history-and-tradition approach, while Justice Brennan claimed that the Court should not use history and tradition and, in any event, that it could not work in principle.

At some points, it appeared that one of the two approaches had garnered a governing Court majority. For example, many scholars suggested that *Washington v. Glucksberg*, 521 U.S. 702, 710–36 (1997), established the dominance of the history-and-tradition approach in determining substantive due process rights. There, the Supreme Court ruled that, because Anglo-American history had consistently and for centuries rejected suicide, there was no constitutional right to assisted suicide. *Id. See, e.g.*, Michael Stokes Paulsen, *Abrogating Stare Decisis by Statute: May Congress Remove the Precedential Effect of Roe and Casey?*, 109 YALE L.J. 1535, 1557 (2000) ("Chief Justice Rehnquist's opinion for the Court . . . establishes important limitations on the enterprise of judicial creation of substantive due process rights . . . saying that any such claimed right must be 'objectively, "deeply rooted in this Nation's history and tradition" ' and 'implicit in the concept of ordered liberty.' Furthermore, such claimed rights must be identified specifically, not with breezy generality; 'careful description' of the claimed right or tradition is what is required, according to the Court in

Glucksberg.' "). *Washington v. Glucksberg* is reprinted in subsection F.9 below.

However, six short years later, the Supreme Court appeared to reverse course in *Lawrence v. Texas*, 539 U.S. 558 (2003), discussed below, in subsection F.8. In *Lawrence*, the Court ruled that there was a substantive due process right to engage in consensual homosexual sex, and to reach that conclusion it explicitly refused to limit itself to the history and tradition approach: "History and tradition are the starting point but not in all cases the ending point of the substantive due process inquiry." *Id.* at 572 (internal quotations and citation omitted).

Today, there is no consensus on and off the Supreme Court on which analysis the Court should utilize to ascertain which unenumerated rights, if any, are protected under substantive due process. As a result, you must know and be able to utilize both approaches.

5. Right to Rear One's Children

Earlier, in Part D, you reviewed *Meyer v. Nebraska*, 262 U.S. 390 (1923), which, along with *Pierce v. Society of Sisters*, 268 U.S. 510 (1925), articulated a substantive due process right of parents to rear their children. Of course, these cases date from the era of classical substantive due process, but they have retained their vitality through the present day. Below is a recent case affirming the right and applying it in a new context.

TROXEL v. GRANVILLE
530 U.S. 57 (2000)

JUSTICE O'CONNOR announced the judgment of the Court and delivered an opinion, in which THE CHIEF JUSTICE, JUSTICE GINSBURG, and JUSTICE BREYER join.

I

Tommie Granville and Brad Troxel shared a relationship that ended in June 1991. The two never married, but they had two daughters, Isabelle and Natalie. Jenifer and Gary Troxel are Brad's parents, and thus the paternal grandparents of Isabelle and Natalie. After Tommie and Brad separated in 1991, Brad lived with his parents and regularly brought his daughters to his parents' home for weekend visitation. Brad committed suicide in May 1993. Although the Troxels at first continued to see Isabelle and Natalie on a regular basis after their son's death, Tommie Granville informed the Troxels in October 1993 that she wished to limit their visitation with her daughters to one short visit per month.

In December 1993, the Troxels commenced the present action by filing, in Washington Superior Court, a petition to obtain visitation rights with Isabelle and Natalie. The Troxels filed their petition under Wash. Rev. Code § 26.10.160(3) (1994). In 1995, the Superior Court entered a visitation decree ordering visitation one weekend per month, one week during the summer, and four hours on both of the petitioning grandparents' birthdays.

II

Because grandparents and other relatives undertake duties of a parental nature in many households, States have sought to ensure the welfare of the children therein by protecting the relationships those children form with such third parties. The States' nonparental visitation statutes are further supported by a recognition, which varies from State to State, that children should have the opportunity to benefit from relationships with statutorily specified persons — for example, their grandparents. The extension of statutory rights in this area to persons other than a child's parents, however, comes with an obvious cost. For example, the State's recognition of an independent third-party interest in a child can place a substantial burden on the traditional parent-child relationship. In this case, we are asked to decide whether § 26.10.160(3), as applied to Tommie Granville and her family, violates the Federal Constitution.

The Fourteenth Amendment provides that no State shall "deprive any person of life, liberty, or property, without due process of law." We have long recognized that the Amendment's Due Process Clause, like its Fifth Amendment counterpart, "guarantees more than fair process." *Washington v. Glucksberg*, 521 U.S. 702, 719 (1997). The Clause also includes a substantive component that "provides heightened protection against government interference with certain fundamental rights and liberty interests." *Id.*, at 720.

The liberty interest at issue in this case — the interest of parents in the care, custody, and control of their children — is perhaps the oldest of the fundamental liberty interests recognized by this Court. More than 75 years ago, in *Meyer v. Nebraska*, 262 U.S. 390, 399, 401 (1923), we held that the "liberty" protected by the Due Process Clause includes the right of parents to "establish a home and bring up children" and "to control the education of their own." Two years later, in *Pierce v. Society of Sisters*, 268 U.S. 510, 534–535 (1925), we again held that the "liberty of parents and guardians" includes the right "to direct the upbringing and education of children under their control." In light of this extensive precedent, it cannot now be doubted that the Due Process Clause of the Fourteenth Amendment protects the fundamental right of parents to make decisions concerning the care, custody, and control of their children.

Section 26.10.160(3), as applied to Granville and her family in this case, unconstitutionally infringes on that fundamental parental right. The Washington nonparental visitation statute is breathtakingly broad. According to the statute's text, *"[a]ny person* may petition the court for visitation rights *at any time,"* and the court may grant such visitation rights whenever "visitation may serve *the best interest of the child."* That language effectively permits any third party seeking visitation to subject any decision by a parent concerning visitation of the parent's children to state-court review. [A] parent's decision that visitation would not be in the child's best interest is accorded no deference.

Turning to the facts of this case, the record reveals that the Superior Court's order was not founded on any special factors that might justify the State's interference with Granville's fundamental right to make decisions concerning the rearing of her two daughters. First, the Troxels did not allege, and no court has found, that Granville was an unfit parent. [S]o long as a parent adequately cares for his or her children (*i.e.*, is fit), there will normally be no reason for the State to inject itself into the private realm of the family to further question the ability of that parent to make the best decisions concerning the rearing of that parent's children.

The problem here is that the Washington Superior Court gave no special weight at all to Granville's determination of her daughters' best interests. More importantly, it appears that the Superior Court applied exactly the opposite presumption. The judge's comments suggest that he presumed the grandparents' request should be granted unless the children would be "impact[ed] adversely."

The court's presumption failed to provide any protection for Granville's fundamental constitutional right to make decisions concerning the rearing of her own daughters. [T]he decision whether such an intergenerational relationship would be beneficial in any specific case is for the parent to make in the first instance. And, if a fit parent's decision of the kind at issue here becomes subject to judicial review, the court must accord at least some special weight to the parent's own determination.

[T]he combination of these factors demonstrates that the visitation order in this case was an unconstitutional infringement on Granville's fundamental right to make decisions concerning the care, custody, and control of her two daughters. [T]his case involves nothing more than a simple disagreement between the Washington Superior Court and Granville concerning her children's best interests. [T]he Due Process Clause does not permit a State to infringe on the fundamental right of parents to make child rearing decisions simply because a state judge believes a "better" decision could be made. Accordingly, we hold that § 26.10.160(3), as applied in this case, is unconstitutional.

Accordingly, the judgment of the Washington Supreme Court is affirmed.

It is so ordered.

JUSTICE SOUTER, concurring in the judgment. [Opinion omitted.]

JUSTICE THOMAS, concurring in the judgment.

I write separately to note that neither party has argued that our substantive due process cases were wrongly decided and that the original understanding of the Due Process Clause precludes judicial enforcement of unenumerated rights under that constitutional provision. As a result, I express no view on the merits of this matter, and I understand the plurality as well to leave the resolution of that issue for another day.*

---

* This case also does not involve a challenge based upon the Privileges and Immunities Clause and thus does not present an opportunity to reevaluate the meaning of that Clause.

JUSTICE STEVENS, dissenting. [Opinion omitted.]

JUSTICE SCALIA, dissenting.

In my view, a right of parents to direct the upbringing of their children is among the "unalienable Rights" with which the Declaration of Independence proclaims "all men . . . are endowed by their Creator." And in my view that right is also among the "othe[r] [rights] retained by the people" which the Ninth Amendment says the Constitution's enumeration of rights "shall not be construed to deny or disparage." The Declaration of Independence, however, is not a legal prescription conferring powers upon the courts; and the Constitution's refusal to "deny or disparage" other rights is far removed from affirming any one of them, and even further removed from authorizing judges to identify what they might be, and to enforce the judges' list against laws duly enacted by the people. Consequently, while I would think it entirely compatible with the commitment to representative democracy set forth in the founding documents to argue, in legislative chambers or in electoral campaigns, that the State has *no power* to interfere with parents' authority over the rearing of their children, I do not believe that the power which the Constitution confers upon me *as a judge* entitles me to deny legal effect to laws that (in my view) infringe upon what is (in my view) that unenumerated right.

Only three holdings of this Court rest in whole or in part upon a substantive constitutional right of parents to direct the upbringing of their children — two of them from an era rich in substantive due process holdings that have since been repudiated. See *Meyer v. Nebraska*, 262 U.S. 390, 399, 401 (1923); *Pierce v. Society of Sisters*, 268 U.S. 510, 534–535 (1925); *Wisconsin v. Yoder*, 406 U.S. 205, 232–233 (1972). Cf. *West Coast Hotel Co. v. Parrish*, 300 U.S. 379 (1937) (overruling *Adkins v. Children's Hospital of D. C.*, 261 U.S. 525 (1923)). The sheer diversity of today's opinions persuades me that the theory of unenumerated parental rights underlying these three cases has small claim to *stare decisis* protection. A legal principle that can be thought to produce such diverse outcomes in the relatively simple case before us here is not a legal principle that has induced substantial reliance. While I would not now overrule those earlier cases, neither would I extend the theory upon which they rested to this new context.

Judicial vindication of "parental rights" under a Constitution that does not even mention them requires not only a judicially crafted definition of parents, but also — unless, as no one believes, the parental rights are to be absolute — judicially approved assessments of "harm to the child" and judicially defined gradations of other persons (grandparents, extended family, adoptive family in an adoption later found to be invalid, long-term guardians, etc.) who may have some claim against the wishes of the parents. If we embrace this unenumerated right, I think it obvious that we will be ushering in a new regime of judicially prescribed, and federally prescribed, family law. I have no reason to believe that federal judges will be better at this than state legislatures; and state legislatures have the great advantages of doing harm in a more circumscribed area, of being able to correct their mistakes in a flash, and of being removable by the people.

For these reasons, I would reverse the judgment below.

JUSTICE KENNEDY, dissenting. [Opinion omitted.]

EXERCISE 12:

1.   Is it legitimate for the Court to rely on *Lochner*-era precedents liker *Meyer* and *Pierce* to support its holding that parents possess a substantive due process right to raise their children? Did the plurality faithfully apply *Meyer* and *Pierce*?

2.   What analysis did the plurality opinion use to determine whether the challenged Washington statute violated the Fourteenth Amendment?

3.   Justice Thomas, one of the most prominent originalist justices, raised two possibilities not addressed by the Court. First, he suggested that substantive due process cases like *Meyer* and *Pierce* should be overruled. Second, he invited a re-evaluation of the Privileges or Immunities Clause. From an originalist and other perspectives, evaluate both possibilities.

4.   Justice Scalia argued that, though the substantive due process precedents upon which the Court relied should not be overruled, the Court should not extend them. From Justice Scalia's perspective, why not overrule *Meyer* and *Pierce*? Why not extend them?

5.   Justice Scalia also argued that the Supreme Court should not rule in Granville's favor because the Court is less institutionally suited to create and apply rules of family law than state legislatures. Explain Justice Scalia's reasoning. Is it persuasive?

6.   Right to Artificial Birth Control

Griswold v. Connecticut ruled that married people have a constitutional right to use artificial birth control. How broad is that right? *Eisenstadt v. Baird* answers that question. It also set the stage for *Roe v. Wade*, 410 U.S. 113 (1973), reprinted below.

EISENSTADT v. BAIRD
405 U.S. 438 (1972)

MR. JUSTICE BRENNAN delivered the opinion of the Court.

Appellee William Baird was convicted at a bench trial in the Massachusetts Superior Court first, for exhibiting contraceptive articles in the course of delivering a lecture on contraception to a group of students at Boston University and, second, for giving a young woman a package of Emko vaginal foam at the close of his address.[1]

Massachusetts General Laws Ann., c. 272, § 21, under which Baird was convicted, provides a maximum five-year term of imprisonment for "whoever . . . gives away . . . any drug, medicine, instrument or article whatever for the prevention of conception,"

---

[1] The Court of Appeals below described the recipient of the foam as "an unmarried adult woman."

except as authorized in § 21A. Under § 21A, "[a] registered physician may administer to or prescribe for any married person drugs or articles intended for the prevention of pregnancy or conception."

The legislative purposes that the statute is meant to serve are not altogether clear. [T]he Supreme Judicial Court noted only the State's interest in protecting the health of its citizens: "[T]he prohibition in § 21," the court declared, "is directly related to" the State's goal of "preventing the distribution of articles designed to prevent conception which may have undesirable, if not dangerous, physical consequences." In a subsequent decision, the court, however, found "a second and more compelling ground for upholding the statute" — namely, to protect morals through "regulating the private sexual lives of single persons." The Court of Appeals, for reasons that will appear, did not consider the promotion of health or the protection of morals through the deterrence of fornication to be the legislative aim. Instead, the court concluded that the statutory goal was to limit contraception in and of itself — a purpose that the court held conflicted "with fundamental human rights" under *Griswold v. Connecticut*, 381 U.S. 479 (1965).

We agree that the goals of deterring premarital sex and regulating the distribution of potentially harmful articles cannot reasonably be regarded as legislative aims of §§ 21 and 21A. And we hold that the statute, viewed as a prohibition on contraception per se, violates the rights of single persons under the Equal Protection Clause of the Fourteenth Amendment.

II

The basic principles governing application of the Equal Protection Clause of the Fourteenth Amendment are familiar. A classification "must be reasonable, not arbitrary, and must rest upon some ground of difference having a fair and substantial relation to the object of the legislation, so that all persons similarly circumstanced shall be treated alike."

The question for our determination in this case is whether there is some ground of difference that rationally explains the different treatment accorded married and unmarried persons under Massachusetts General Laws Ann., c. 272, §§ 21 and 21A.[7] For the reasons that follow, we conclude that no such ground exists.

First. Section 21 stems from Mass. Stat. 1879, c. 159, § 1, which prohibited without exception, distribution of articles intended to be used as contraceptives. [T]he Massachusetts Supreme Judicial Court explained that the law's "plain purpose is to protect purity, to preserve chastity, to encourage continence and self restraint, to defend the sanctity of the home, and thus to engender in the State and nation a virile and virtuous race of men and women." Although the State clearly abandoned that

---

[7] Of course, if we were to conclude that the Massachusetts statute impinges upon fundamental freedoms under Griswold, the statutory classification would have to be not merely rationally related to a valid public purpose but necessary to the achievement of a compelling state interest. E.g., *Loving v. Virginia*, 388 U.S. 1 (1967). But we do not have to address the statute's validity under that test because the law fails to satisfy even the more lenient equal protection standard.

purpose with the enactment of § 21A, at least insofar as the illicit sexual activities of married persons are concerned, the court reiterated [later] that the object of the legislation is to discourage premarital sexual intercourse. Conceding that the State could, consistently with the Equal Protection Clause, regard the problems of extramarital and premarital sexual relations as "[e]vils . . . of different dimensions and proportions, requiring different remedies," *Williamson v. Lee Optical Inc.*, 348 U.S. 483, 489 (1955), we cannot agree that the deterrence of premarital sex may reasonably be regarded as the purpose of the Massachusetts law.

It would be plainly unreasonable to assume that Massachusetts has prescribed pregnancy and the birth of an unwanted child as punishment for fornication, which is a misdemeanor. Aside from the scheme of values that assumption would attribute to the State, it is abundantly clear that the effect of the ban on distribution of contraceptives to unmarried persons has at best a marginal relation to the proffered objective. What Mr. Justice Goldberg said in *Griswold v. Connecticut*, 381 U.S., at 498, (concurring opinion), concerning the effect of Connecticut's prohibition on the use of contraceptives in discouraging extramarital sexual relations, is equally applicable here. "The rationality of this justification is dubious, particularly in light of the admitted widespread availability to all persons in the State of Connecticut, unmarried as well as married, of birth-control devices for the prevention of disease, as distinguished from the prevention of conception." Like Connecticut's laws, §§ 21 and 21A do not at all regulate the distribution of contraceptives when they are to be used to prevent, not pregnancy, but the spread of disease. Nor, in making contraceptives available to married persons without regard to their intended use, does Massachusetts attempt to deter married persons from engaging in illicit sexual relations with unmarried persons. Even on the assumption that the fear of pregnancy operates as a deterrent to fornication, the Massachusetts statute is thus so riddled with exceptions that deterrence of premarital sex cannot reasonably be regarded as its aim.

Moreover, §§ 21 and 21A on their face have a dubious relation to the State's criminal prohibition on fornication. "Fornication is a misdemeanor [in Massachusetts], entailing a thirty dollar fine, or three months in jail. Violation of the present statute is a felony, punishable by five years in prison. We find it hard to believe that the legislature adopted a statute carrying a five-year penalty for its possible, obviously by no means fully effective, deterrence of the commission of a ninety-day misdemeanor." Even conceding the legislature a full measure of discretion in fashioning means to prevent fornication, and recognizing that the State may seek to deter prohibited conduct by punishing more severely those who facilitate than those who actually engage in its commission, we cannot believe that in this instance Massachusetts has chosen to expose the aider and abetter who simply gives away a contraceptive to 20 times the 90-day sentence of the offender himself. The very terms of the State's criminal statutes, coupled with the de minimis effect of §§ 21 and 21A in deterring fornication, thus compel the conclusion that such deterrence cannot reasonably be taken as the purpose of the ban on distribution of contraceptives to unmarried persons.

Second. Section 21A was added to the Massachusetts General Laws by Stat. 1966, c. 265, § 1. The Supreme Judicial Court held that the purpose of the amendment was to serve the health needs of the community by regulating the distribution of potentially harmful articles. It is plain that Massachusetts had no such purpose in mind before the enactment of § 21A. "Consistent with the fact that the statute was contained in a chapter dealing with 'Crimes Against Chastity, Morality, Decency and Good Order,' it was cast only in terms of morals. A physician was forbidden to prescribe contraceptives even when needed for the protection of health." Nor [do we] "believe that the legislature [in enacting § 21A] suddenly reversed its field and developed an interest in health. Rather, it merely made what it thought to be the precise accommodation necessary to escape the *Griswold* ruling."

If health were the rationale of § 21A, the statute would be both discriminatory and overbroad. The Court of Appeals [stated]: "If the prohibition [on distribution to unmarried persons] . . . is to be taken to mean that the same physician who can prescribe for married patients does not have sufficient skill to protect the health of patients who lack a marriage certificate, or who may be currently divorced, it is illogical to the point of irrationality." Furthermore, we must join the Court of Appeals in noting that not all contraceptives are potentially dangerous. As a result, if the Massachusetts statute were a health measure, it would not only invidiously discriminate against the unmarried, but also be overbroad with respect to the married.

Third. If the Massachusetts statute cannot be upheld as a deterrent to fornication or as a health measure, may it, nevertheless, be sustained simply as a prohibition on contraception? We need not and do not, however, decide that important question in this case because, whatever the rights of the individual to access to contraceptives may be, the rights must be the same for the unmarried and the married alike.

If under Griswold the distribution of contraceptives to married persons cannot be prohibited, a ban on distribution to unmarried persons would be equally impermissible. It is true that in Griswold the right of privacy in question inhered in the marital relationship. Yet the marital couple is not an independent entity with a mind and heart of its own, but an association of two individuals each with a separate intellectual and emotional makeup. If the right of privacy means anything, it is the right of the individual, married or single, to be free from unwarranted governmental intrusion into matters so fundamentally affecting a person as the decision whether to bear or beget a child. See also *Skinner v. Oklahoma*, 316 U.S. 535 (1942).

We hold that by providing dissimilar treatment for married and unmarried persons who are similarly situated, Massachusetts General Laws Ann., c. 272, §§ 21 and 21A, violate the Equal Protection Clause. The judgment of the Court of Appeals is affirmed.

Affirmed.

Mr. Justice Powell and Mr. Justice Rehnquist took no part in the consideration or decision of this case.

MR. JUSTICE DOUGLAS, concurring. [opinion omitted]

MR. JUSTICE WHITE, with whom MR. JUSTICE BLACKMUN joins, concurring in the result. [opinion omitted]

MR. CHIEF JUSTICE BURGER, dissenting.

It is revealing, I think, that those portions of the majority opinion[] rejecting the statutory limitation on distributors rely on no particular provision of the Constitution. I see nothing in the Fourteenth Amendment or any other part of the Constitution that even vaguely suggests that these medicinal forms of contraceptives must be available in the open market. I do not challenge *Griswold v. Connecticut*, despite its tenuous moorings to the text of the Constitution, but I cannot view it as controlling authority for this case. By relying in *Griswold* on the present context, the Court has passed beyond the penumbras of the specific guarantees into the uncircumscribed area of personal predilections.

EXERCISE 13:

1. What analysis did the Supreme Court use to evaluate Massachusetts' law? Apply that analysis.

2. The Supreme Court ruled that the Massachusetts legislature's purpose in adopting § 21A in 1966 was to avoid *Griswold v. Connecticut*. How did the Court know that? Was the Court right?

3. Is *Eisenstadt* faithful to *Griswold*? In its reasoning? Its result?

4. After *Eisenstadt*, how broad is the right to artificial birth control?

5. The *Eisenstadt* Court struck down the Massachusetts law for violating the Equal Protection Clause. In the late-1960s and early 1970s, the Supreme Court had yet to fully articulate modern substantive due process doctrine, so many cases reviewed legislation under the Due Process and the Equal Protection Clauses almost interchangeably. Gradually, in the 1970s, the doctrines diverged and solidified. Today, *Eisenstadt* is in the canon of substantive due process cases. We cover the "fundamental rights" aspect of equal protection, which is related to substantive due process, at the end of **Chapter 4**.

7. Right to Abortion

One of the most controversial areas of legal doctrine you will encounter is the Supreme Court's substantive due process right to abortion. The academic scholarship, popular commentary, and political observations on the subject are voluminous. We will review *Roe v. Wade*, 410 U.S. 113 (1973), *Planned Parenthood v. Casey*, 505 U.S. 833 (1992), and a summary of *Gonzales v. Carhart*, 550 U.S. 124 (2007), the three most important cases dealing with abortion. Be aware, however, that there are many cases that the Court has faced, including abortion funding limits and other restrictions short of an outright ban, that we will not cover.

ROE v. WADE
410 U.S. 113 (1973)

MR. JUSTICE BLACKMUN delivered the opinion of the Court.

This Texas federal appeal and its Georgia companion, *Doe v. Bolton*, 410 U.S. 179 [(1973)], present constitutional challenges to state criminal abortion legislation.

We forthwith acknowledge our awareness of the sensitive and emotional nature of the abortion controversy, of the vigorous opposing views, even among physicians, and of the deep and seemingly absolute convictions that the subject inspires. One's philosophy, one's experiences, one's exposure to the raw edges of human existence, one's religious training, one's attitudes toward life and family and their values, and the moral standards one establishes and seeks to observe, are all likely to influence and to color one's thinking and conclusions about abortion. In addition, population growth, pollution, poverty, and racial overtones tend to complicate and not to simplify the problem.

Our task, of course, is to resolve the issue by constitutional measurement, free of emotion and of predilection. We seek earnestly to do this, and, because we do, we have inquired into, and in this opinion place some emphasis upon, medical and medical-legal history and what that history reveals about man's attitudes toward the abortion procedure over the centuries. We bear in mind, too, Mr. Justice Holmes' admonition in his now-vindicated dissent in *Lochner v. New York*, 198 U.S. 45, 76 (1905):

"[The Constitution] is made for people of fundamentally differing views, and the accident of our finding certain opinions natural and familiar, or novel, and even shocking, ought not to conclude our judgment upon the question whether statutes embodying them conflict with the Constitution of the United States."

I

The Texas statutes that concern us here make it a crime to "procure an abortion," except with respect to "an abortion procured or attempted by medical advice for the purpose of saving the life of the mother." Similar statutes are in existence in a majority of the States.[2]

Texas first enacted a criminal abortion statute in 1854. This was soon modified into language that has remained substantially unchanged to the present time.

II

Jane Roe, a single woman who was residing in Dallas County, Texas, instituted this federal action in March 1970 against the District Attorney of the county. She sought

---

[2] [Listing the legal provisions in Arizona, Connecticut, Idaho, Illinois, Indiana, Iowa, Kentucky, Louisiana, Maine, Massachusetts, Michigan, Minnesota, Montana, Nebraska, Nevada, New Hampshire, New Jersey, North Dakota, Ohio, Oklahoma, Pennsylvania, Rhode Island, South Dakota, Tennessee, Utah, Vermont, West Virginia, Wisconsin, and Wyoming.]

a declaratory judgment that the Texas criminal abortion statutes were unconstitutional on their face, and an injunction restraining the defendant from enforcing the statutes.

Roe alleged that she was unmarried and pregnant; that she wished to terminate her pregnancy by an abortion; that she was unable to get a "legal" abortion in Texas because her life did not appear to be threatened by the continuation of her pregnancy; and that she could not afford to travel to another jurisdiction in order to secure a legal abortion under safe conditions. She claimed that the Texas statutes abridged her right of personal privacy, protected by the First, Fourth, Fifth, Ninth, and Fourteenth Amendments.

V

The principal thrust of appellant's attack on the Texas statutes is that they improperly invade a right, said to be possessed by the pregnant woman, to choose to terminate her pregnancy. Appellant would discover this right in the concept of personal "liberty" embodied in the Fourteenth Amendment's Due Process Clause; or in personal marital, familial, and sexual privacy said to be protected by the Bill of Rights or its penumbras, see *Griswold v. Connecticut*, 381 U.S. 479 (1965); *Eisenstadt v. Baird*, 405 U.S. 438 (1972); or among those rights reserved to the people by the Ninth Amendment, *Griswold v. Connecticut*, 381 U.S. at 486 (Goldberg, J., concurring). Before addressing this claim, we feel it desirable briefly to survey the history of abortion, for such insight as that history may afford us, and then to examine the state purposes and interests behind the criminal abortion laws.

VI

It perhaps is not generally appreciated that the restrictive criminal abortion laws in effect in a majority of States today are of relatively recent vintage. Those laws, generally proscribing abortion or its attempt at any time during pregnancy except when necessary to preserve the pregnant woman's life, are not of ancient or even of common-law origin. Instead, they derive from statutory changes effected, for the most part, in the latter half of the 19th century.

1. Ancient attitudes. These are not capable of precise determination. We are told that at the time of the Persian Empire abortifacients were known and that criminal abortions were severely punished. We are also told, however, that abortion was practiced in Greek times as well as in the Roman Era. Greek and Roman law afforded little protection to the unborn. Ancient religion did not bar abortion.

2. The Hippocratic Oath. What then of the famous Oath that has stood so long as the ethical guide of the medical profession and that bears the name of the great Greek (460(?)-377(?) B.C.), who has been described as the Father of Medicine? The Oath varies somewhat according to the particular translation, but in any translation the content is clear: "I will not give to a woman a pessary to produce abortion," or "I will not give to a woman an abortive remedy."

[T]he Oath represents the apex of the development of strict ethical concepts in medicine, and its influence endures to this day. Why did not the authority of Hippocrates dissuade abortion practice in his time and that of Rome? The Oath was not uncontested even in Hippocrates' day; only the Pythagorean school of philosophers frowned upon the related act of suicide. Most Greek thinkers, on the other hand, commended abortion, at least prior to viability. See Plato, Republic, V, 461; Aristotle, Politics, VII, 1335b. For the Pythagoreans, however, the embryo was animate from the moment of conception, and abortion meant destruction of a living being.

But with the end of antiquity a decided change took place. Resistance against suicide and against abortion became common. The Oath came to be popular. The emerging teachings of Christianity were in agreement with the Phthagorean ethic. The Oath "became the nucleus of all medical ethics."

3. The common law. It is undisputed that at common law, abortion performed before "quickening" — the first recognizable movement of the fetus in utero, appearing usually from the 16th to the 18th week of pregnancy — was not an indictable offense. The absence of a common-law crime for pre-quickening abortion appears to have developed from a confluence of earlier philosophical, theological, and civil and canon law concepts of when life begins. These disciplines variously approached the question in terms of the point at which the embryo or fetus became "formed" or recognizably human, or in terms of when a "person" came into being, that is, infused with a "soul" or "animated." A loose consensus evolved in early English law that these events occurred at some point between conception and live birth. There was agreement that prior to this point the fetus was to be regarded as part of the mother, and its destruction, therefore, was not homicide. Due to continued uncertainty about the precise time when animation occurred, [Henry de] Bracton focused upon quickening as the critical point. The significance of quickening was echoed by later common-law scholars and found its way into the received common law in this country.

Whether abortion of a quick fetus was a felony at common law, or even a lesser crime, is still disputed. [T]he later and predominant view, has been that it was, at most, a lesser offense. In a frequently cited passage, [Sir Edward] Coke took the position that abortion of a woman "quick with childe" is "a great misprision, and no murder." [Sir William] Blackstone followed, saying that while abortion after quickening had once been considered manslaughter (though not murder), "modern law" took a less severe view.

4. The English statutory law. * * *

5. The American law. In this country, the law in effect in all but a few States until mid-19th century was the pre-existing English common law. Connecticut, the first State to enact abortion legislation, in 1821 [made abortion a crime for] a woman "quick with child." In 1828, New York enacted legislation that, in two respects, was to serve as a model for early anti-abortion statutes. First, while barring destruction of an unquickend fetus as well as a quick fetus, it made the former only a misdemeanor, but the latter second-degree manslaughter. Second, it incorporated a concept of therapeutic abortion by providing that an abortion was excused if it "shall have been necessary to preserve the life of such mother." By 1840, when Texas had received the common law, only eight American States had statutes dealing with abortion. It was not until after the War Between the States that legislation began generally to replace the

common law. Most of these initial statutes dealt severely with abortion after quickening but were lenient with it before quickening.

Gradually, in the middle and late 19th century the quickening distinction disappeared from the statutory law of most States and the degree of the offense and the penalties were increased. By the end of the 1950's a large majority of the jurisdictions banned abortion, however and whenever performed, unless done to save or preserve the life of the mother. In the past several years, however, a trend toward liberalization of abortion statutes has resulted in adoption, by about one-third of the States, of less stringent laws, most of them patterned after the ALI Model Penal Code.[37]

It is thus apparent that at common law, at the time of the adoption of our Constitution, and throughout the major portion of the 19th century, abortion was viewed with less disfavor than under most American statutes currently in effect. At least with respect to the early stage of pregnancy, and very possibly without such a limitation, the opportunity to make this choice was present in this country well into the 19th century. Even later, the law continued for some time to treat less punitively an abortion procured in early pregnancy.

6. The position of the American Medical Association. The anti-abortion mood prevalent in this country in the late 19th century was shared by the medical profession.

An AMA Committee on Criminal Abortion was appointed in May 1857. It presented its report to the Twelfth Annual Meeting. It deplored abortion and its frequency. In 1871 a long and vivid report was submitted by the Committee on Criminal Abortion. It proffered resolutions, adopted by the Association, recommending, among other things, that it "be unlawful and unprofessional for any physician to induce abortion or premature labor, without the concurrent opinion of at least one respectable consulting physician, and then always with a view to the safety of the child — if that be possible."

Except for periodic condemnation of the criminal abortionist, no further formal AMA action took place until 1967. In that year, the Committee on Human Reproduction urged the adoption of a stated policy of opposition to induced abortion, except when there is "documented medical evidence" of a threat to the health or life of the mother, or that the child "may be born with incapacitating physical deformity or mental deficiency," or that a pregnancy "resulting from legally established statutory or forcible rape or incest may constitute a threat to the mental or physical health of the patient."

On June 25, 1970, the House of Delegates adopted resolutions [which] asserted that abortion is a medical procedure that should be performed by a licensed physician in an accredited hospital only after consultation with two other physicians and in conformity with state law, and that no party to the procedure should be required to violate personally held moral principles.

---

[37] Fourteen States have adopted some form of the ALI statute. [Listing the statutory provisions of Arkansas, California, Colorado, Delaware, Florida, Georgia, Kansas, Maryland, Mississippi, New Mexico, North Carolina, Oregon, South Carolina, and Virginia.] By the end of 1970, four other States had repealed criminal penalties for abortions performed in early pregnancy. [Listing Alaska, Hawaii, New York, and Washington state.]

8. The position of the American Bar Association. At its meeting in February 1972 the ABA House of Delegates approved the Uniform Abortion Act. 58 A.B.A.J. 380 (1972). We set forth the Act in full in the margin.[40]

VII

Three reasons have been advanced to explain historically the enactment of criminal abortion laws in the 19th century and to justify their continued existence. It has been argued occasionally that these laws were the product of a Victorian social concern to discourage illicit sexual conduct. Texas, however, does not advance this justification in the present case.

A second reason is concerned with abortion as a medical procedure. When most criminal abortion laws were first enacted, the procedure was a hazardous one for the woman. This was particularly true prior to the development of antisepsis. Antiseptic techniques were not generally accepted and employed until about the turn of the century. Abortion mortality was high. Even after 1900, and perhaps until as late as the development of antibiotics in the 1940's, standard modern techniques such as dilation and curettage were not nearly so safe as they are today. Thus, it has been argued that a State's real concern in enacting a criminal abortion law was to protect the pregnant woman, that is, to restrain her from submitting to a procedure that placed her life in serious jeopardy.

Modern medical techniques have altered this situation. Appellants and various amici refer to medical data indicating that abortion in early pregnancy, that is, prior to the end of the first trimester, although not without its risk, is now relatively safe. Mortality rates for women undergoing early abortions, where the procedure is legal, appear to be as low as or lower than the rates for normal childbirth. Consequently, any interest of the State in protecting the woman from an inherently hazardous procedure, except when it would be equally dangerous for her to forgo it, has largely disappeared. Of course, important state interests in the areas of health and medical standards do remain. The State has a legitimate interest in seeing to it that abortion, like any other medical procedure, is performed under circumstances that insure maximum safety for the patient. Moreover, the risk to the woman increases as her pregnancy continues. Thus, the State retains a definite interest in protecting the woman's own health and safety when an abortion is proposed at a late stage of pregnancy.

The third reason is the State's interest in protecting prenatal life. Some of the argument for this justification rests on the theory that a new human life is present

---

[40] "UNIFORM ABORTION ACT

"(b) An abortion may be performed in this state only if it is performed:

"(1) by a physician licensed to practice medicine in this state . . . and the abortion is performed in the physician's office or in a medical clinic, or in a hospital; and

"(2) within (20) weeks after the commencement of the pregnancy (or after (20) weeks only if the physician has reasonable cause to believe (i) there is a substantial risk that continuance of the pregnancy would endanger the life of the mother or would gravely impair the physical or mental health of the mother, (ii) that the child would be born with grave physical or mental defect, or (iii) that the pregnancy resulted from rape or incest, or illicit intercourse with a girl under the age of 16 years)."

from the moment of conception. The State's interest and general obligation to protect life then extends, it is argued, to prenatal life. Only when the life of the pregnant mother herself is at stake, balanced against the life she carries within her, should the interest of the embryo or fetus not prevail. Logically, of course, a legitimate state interest in this area need not stand or fall on acceptance of the belief that life begins at conception or at some other point prior to live birth. In assessing the State's interest, recognition may be given to the less rigid claim that as long as at least potential life is involved, the State may assert interests beyond the protection of the pregnant woman alone.

It is with these interests, and the weight to be attached to them, that this case is concerned.

VIII

The Constitution does not explicitly mention any right of privacy. In a line of decisions, however, the Court has recognized that a right of personal privacy, or a guarantee of certain areas or zones of privacy, does exist under the Constitution. In varying contexts, the Court or individual Justices have, indeed, found at least the roots of that right in the First Amendment, in the Fourth and Fifth Amendments, in the penumbras of the Bill of Rights, *Griswold v. Connecticut*, 381 U.S., at 484–485; in the Ninth Amendment, *id.*, at 486 (Goldberg, J., concurring); or in the concept of liberty guaranteed by the first section of the Fourteenth Amendment, see *Meyer v. Nebraska*, 262 U.S. 390, 399 (1923). These decisions make it clear that only personal rights that can be deemed "fundamental" or "implicit in the concept of ordered liberty," are included in this guarantee of personal privacy. They also make it clear that the right has some extension to activities relating to marriage, *Loving v. Virginia*, 388 U.S. 1, 12 (1967); procreation, *Skinner v. Oklahoma*, 316 U.S. 535, 541–542 (1942); contraception, *Eisenstadt v. Baird*, 405 U.S., at 453–454; family relationships, and child rearing and education, *Pierce v. Society of Sisters*, 268 U.S. 510, 535 (1925), *Meyer v. Nebraska*, [262 U.S. 390 (1923)].

This right of privacy, whether it be founded in the Fourteenth Amendment's concept of personal liberty and restrictions upon state action, as we feel it is, or, as the District Court determined, in the Ninth Amendment's reservation of rights to the people, is broad enough to encompass a woman's decision whether or not to terminate her pregnancy. The detriment that the State would impose upon the pregnant woman by denying this choice altogether is apparent. Specific and direct harm medically diagnosable even in early pregnancy may be involved. Maternity, or additional offspring, may force upon the woman a distressful life and future. Psychological harm may be imminent. Mental and physical health may be taxed by child care. There is also the distress, for all concerned, associated with the unwanted child, and there is the problem of bringing a child into a family already unable, psychologically and otherwise, to care for it. In other cases, as in this one, the additional difficulties and continuing stigma of unwed motherhood may be involved. All these are factors the woman and her responsible physician necessarily will consider in consultation.

On the basis of elements such as these, appellant and some amici argue that the woman's right is absolute and that she is entitled to terminate her pregnancy at whatever time, in whatever way, and for whatever reason she alone chooses. With this we do not agree. The Court's decisions recognizing a right of privacy also acknowledge that some state regulation in areas protected by that right is appropriate. As noted above, a State may properly assert important interests in safeguarding health, in maintaining medical standards, and in protecting potential life. At some point in pregnancy, these respective interests become sufficiently compelling to sustain regulation of the factors that govern the abortion decision. The privacy right involved, therefore, cannot be said to be absolute.

We, therefore, conclude that the right of personal privacy includes the abortion decision, but that this right is not unqualified and must be considered against important state interests in regulation. Where certain "fundamental rights" are involved, the Court has held that regulation limiting these rights may be justified only by a "compelling state interest," and that legislative enactments must be narrowly drawn to express only the legitimate state interests at stake. *Griswold v. Connecticut*, 381 U.S., at 485.

IX

A. The appellee and certain amici argue that the fetus is a "person" within the language and meaning of the Fourteenth Amendment. In support of this, they outline at length and in detail the well-known facts of fetal development. If this suggestion of personhood is established, the appellant's case, of course, collapses, for the fetus' right to life would then be guaranteed specifically by the Amendment. On the other hand, the appellee conceded that no case could be cited that holds that a fetus is a person within the meaning of the Fourteenth Amendment.

The Constitution does not define "person" in so many words. Section 1 of the Fourteenth Amendment contains three references to "person." The first, in defining "citizens," speaks of "persons born or naturalized in the United States." The word also appears both in the Due Process Clause and in the Equal Protection Clause. "Person" is used in other places in the Constitution: in the listing of qualifications for Representatives and Senators, Art, I, § 2, cl. 2, and § 3, cl. 3; in the Apportionment Clause, Art. I, § 2, cl. 3; in the Migration and Importation provision, Art. I, § 9, cl. 1; in the Emoulument Clause, Art, I, § 9, cl. 8; in the Elections provisions, Art. II, § 1, cl. 2, and the superseded cl. 3; in the provision outlining qualifications for the office of President, Art. II, § 1, cl. 5; in the Extradition provisions, Art. IV, § 2, cl. 2, and the superseded Fugitive Slave Clause 3; and in the Fifth, Twelfth, and Twenty-second Amendments, as well as in §§ 2 and 3 of the Fourteenth Amendment. But in nearly all these instances, the use of the word is such that it has application only postnatally. None indicates, with any assurance, that it has any possible prenatal application.[54]

---

[54] When Texas urges that a fetus is entitled to Fourteenth Amendment protection as a person, it faces a dilemma. Neither in Texas nor in any other State are all abortions prohibited. Despite broad proscription, an exception always exists. The exception for an abortion procured or attempted by medical advice for the purpose of saving the life of the mother, is typical. But if the fetus is a person who is not to be deprived of life without due process of law, and if the mother's condition is the sole determinant, does not the Texas exception appear to be out of line with the Amendment's command?

All this, together with our observation that throughout the major portion of the 19th century prevailing legal abortion practices were far freer than they are today, persuades us that the word "person," as used in the Fourteenth Amendment, does not include the unborn. This conclusion, however, does not of itself fully answer the contentions raised by Texas, and we pass on to other considerations.

B. The pregnant woman cannot be isolated in her privacy. She carries an embryo and, later, a fetus, if one accepts the medical definitions of the developing young in the human uterus. The situation therefore is inherently different from marital intimacy, or marriage, or procreation, or education, with which Eisenstadt and Griswold, Loving, Skinner and Pierce and Meyer were respectively concerned. As we have intimated above, it is reasonable and appropriate for a State to decide that at some point in time another interest, that of health of the mother or that of potential human life, becomes significantly involved. The woman's privacy is no longer sole and any right of privacy she possesses must be measured accordingly.

Texas urges that, apart from the Fourteenth Amendment, life begins at conception and is present throughout pregnancy, and that, therefore, the State has a compelling interest in protecting that life from and after conception. We need not resolve the difficult question of when life begins. When those trained in the respective disciplines of medicine, philosophy, and theology are unable to arrive at any consensus, the judiciary, at this point in the development of man's knowledge, is not in a position to speculate as to the answer.

It should be sufficient to note briefly the wide divergence of thinking on this most sensitive and difficult question. There has always been strong support for the view that life does not begin until live birth. This was the belief of the Stoics. It appears to be the predominant, though not the unanimous, attitude of the Jewish faith. It may be taken to represent also the position of a large segment of the Protestant community, insofar as that can be ascertained. As we have noted, the common law found greater significance in quickening. Physicians and their scientific colleagues have regarded that event with less interest and have tended to focus either upon conception, upon live birth, or upon the interim point at which the fetus becomes "viable," that is, potentially able to live outside the mother's womb, albeit with artificial aid. Viability is usually placed at about seven months (28 weeks) but may occur earlier, even at 24 weeks. The Aristotelian theory of "mediate animation," that held sway throughout the Middle Ages and the Renaissance in Europe, continued to be official Roman Catholic dogma until the 19th century, despite opposition to this "ensoulment" theory from those in the Church who would recognize the existence of life from the moment of conception. The latter is now, of course, the official belief of the Catholic Church.

In areas other than criminal abortion, the law has been reluctant to endorse any theory that life, as we recognize it, begins before live birth or to accord legal rights to the unborn except in narrowly defined situations and except when the rights are contingent upon live birth. For example, the traditional rule of tort law denied recovery for prenatal injuries even though the child was born alive. That rule has been changed in almost every jurisdiction. In a recent development, some States permit the parents of a stillborn child to maintain an action for wrongful death because of prenatal injuries. Such an action, however, would appear to be one to vindicate the parents' interest and is thus consistent with the view that the fetus, at most, represents only the potentiality of life. Similarly, unborn children have been recognized as acquiring rights or interests by way of inheritance or other devolution of property, and have been represented by guardians ad litem. Perfection of the interests involved, again, has generally been contingent upon live birth. In short, the unborn have never been recognized in the law as persons in the whole sense.

X

In view of all this, we do not agree that, by adopting one theory of life, Texas may override the rights of the pregnant woman that are at stake. We repeat, however, that the State does have an important and legitimate interest in preserving and protecting the health of the pregnant woman, and that it has still another important and legitimate interest in protecting the potentiality of human life. These interests are separate and distinct. Each grows in substantiality as the woman approaches term and, at a point during pregnancy, each becomes "compelling."

With respect to the State's important and legitimate interest in the health of the mother, the "compelling" point, in the light of present medical knowledge, is at approximately the end of the first trimester. This is so because of the now-established medical fact that until the end of the first trimester mortality in abortion may be less than mortality in normal childbirth. It follows that, from and after this point, a State may regulate the abortion procedure to the extent that the regulation reasonably relates to the preservation and protection of maternal health. Examples of permissible state regulation in this area are requirements as to the qualifications of the person who is to perform the abortion; as to the licensure of that person; as to the facility in which the procedure is to be performed, that is, whether it must be a hospital or may be a clinic or some other place of less-than-hospital status; as to the licensing of the facility; and the like.

This means, on the other hand, that, for the period of pregnancy prior to this "compelling" point, the attending physician, in consultation with his patient, is free to determine, without regulation by the State, that, in his medical judgment, the patient's pregnancy should be terminated. If that decision is reached, the judgment may be effectuated by an abortion free of interference by the State.

With respect to the State's important and legitimate interest in potential life, the "compelling" point is at viability. This is so because the fetus then presumably has the capability of meaningful life outside the mother's womb. State regulation protective of fetal life after viability thus has both logical and biological justifications. If the State is interested in protecting fetal life after viability, it may go so far as to proscribe abortion during that period, except when it is necessary to preserve the life or health of the mother.

Measured against these standards, Art. 1196 of the Texas Penal Code sweeps too broadly. The statute makes no distinction between abortions performed early in pregnancy and those performed later, and it limits to a single reason, "saving" the mother's life, the legal justification for the procedure. The statute, therefore, cannot survive the constitutional attack made upon it here.

XI

To summarize and to repeat:

1. A state criminal abortion statute, that excepts from criminality only a life-saving procedure on behalf of the mother, without regard to pregnancy stage and without recognition of the other interests involved, is violative of the Due Process Clause of the Fourteenth Amendment.

(a) For the stage prior to approximately the end of the first trimester, the abortion decision and its effectuation must be left to the medical judgment of the pregnant woman's attending physician.

(b) For the stage subsequent to approximately the end of the first trimester, the State, in promoting its interest in the health of the mother, may, if it chooses, regulate the abortion procedure in ways that are reasonably related to maternal health.

(c) For the stage subsequent to viability, the State in promoting its interest in the potentiality of human life may, if it chooses, regulate, and even proscribe, abortion except where it is necessary, in appropriate medical judgment, for the preservation of the life or health of the mother.

This holding, we feel, is consistent with the relative weights of the respective interests involved, with the lessons and examples of medical and legal history, with the lenity of the common law, and with the demands of the profound problems of the present day.

XII

The judgment of the District Court is affirmed.

It is so ordered.

MR. CHIEF JUSTICE BURGER, concurring. [Opinion omitted.]

MR. JUSTICE DOUGLAS, concurring. [Opinion omitted.]

MR. JUSTICE STEWART, concurring. [Opinion omitted.]

MR. JUSTICE WHITE, with whom MR. JUSTICE REHNQUIST joins, dissenting.

With all due respect, I dissent. I find nothing in the language or history of the Constitution to support the Court's judgments. The Court simply fashions and announces a new constitutional right for pregnant women and, with scarcely any reason or authority for its action, invests that right with sufficient substance to override most existing state abortion statutes. The upshot is that the people and the legislatures of the 50 States are constitutionally disentitled to weigh the relative importance of the continued existence and development of the fetus, on the one hand, against a spectrum of possible impacts on the mother, on the other hand.

In a sensitive area such as this, involving as it does issues over which reasonable men may easily and heatedly differ, I cannot accept the Court's exercise of its clear power of choice by interposing a constitutional barrier to state efforts to protect human life and by investing women and doctors with the constitutionally protected right to exterminate it. This issue, for the most part, should be left with the people and to the political processes the people have devised to govern their affairs.

MR. JUSTICE REHNQUIST, dissenting.

I have difficulty in concluding, as the Court does, that the right of "privacy" is involved in this case. Texas, by the statute here challenged, bars the performance of a medical abortion by a licensed physician on a plaintiff such as Roe. A transaction resulting in an operation such as this is not "private" in the ordinary usage of that word.

If the Court means by the term "privacy" no more than that the claim of a person to be free from unwanted state regulation of consensual transactions may be a form of "liberty" protected by the Fourteenth Amendment, there is no doubt that similar claims have been upheld in our earlier decisions on the basis of that liberty. I agree that the "liberty," against deprivation of which without due process the Fourteenth Amendment protects, embraces more than the rights found in the Bill of Rights. But that liberty is not guaranteed absolutely against deprivation, only against deprivation without due process of law. The test traditionally applied in the area of social and economic legislation is whether or not a law such as that challenged has a rational relation to a valid state objective. *Williamson v. Lee Optical Inc.*, 348 U.S. 483, 491 (1955). The Due Process Clause of the Fourteenth Amendment undoubtedly does place a limit, albeit a broad one, on legislative power to enact laws such as this. If the Texas statute were to prohibit an abortion even where the mother's life is in jeopardy, I have little doubt that such a statute would lack a rational relation to a valid state objective under the test stated in Williamson. But the Court's sweeping invalidation of any restrictions on abortion during the first trimester is impossible to justify under that standard, and the conscious weighing of competing factors that the Court's opinion apparently substitutes for the established test is far more appropriate to a legislative judgment than to a judicial one.

While the Court's opinion quotes from the dissent of Mr. Justice Holmes in *Lochner v. New York*, 198 U.S. 45, 74 (1905), the result it reaches is more closely attuned to the majority opinion of Mr. Justice Peckham in that case. As in *Lochner* and similar cases applying substantive due process standards to economic and social welfare legislation, the adoption of the compelling state interest standard will inevitably require this Court to examine the legislative policies and pass on the wisdom of these policies in the very process of deciding whether a particular state interest put forward may or may not be "compelling." The decision here to break pregnancy into three distinct terms and to outline the permissible restrictions the State may impose in each one, for example, partakes more of judicial legislation than it does of a determination of the intent of the drafters of the Fourteenth Amendment.

The fact that a majority of the States reflecting, after all the majority sentiment in those States, have had restrictions on abortions for at least a century is a strong indication, it seems to me, that the asserted right to an abortion is not "so rooted in the traditions and conscience of our people as to be ranked as fundamental." Even today, when society's views on abortion are changing, the very existence of the debate is evidence that the "right" to an abortion is not so universally accepted as the appellant would have us believe.

To reach its result, the Court necessarily has had to find within the Scope of the Fourteenth Amendment a right that was apparently completely unknown to the drafters of the Amendment. By the time of the adoption of the Fourteenth Amendment in 1868, there were at least 36 laws enacted by state or territorial legislatures limiting abortion. While many States have amended or updated their laws, 21 of the laws on the books in 1868 remain in effect today. Indeed, the Texas statute struck down today was first enacted in 1857. There apparently was no question concerning the validity of this provision or of any of the other state statutes when the Fourteenth Amendment was adopted. The only conclusion possible from this history is that the drafters did not intend to have the Fourteenth Amendment withdraw from the States the power to legislate with respect to this matter.

For all of the foregoing reasons, I respectfully dissent.

EXERCISE 14:

1.   What is *Roe*'s holding?

2.   What is the legal source of that holding? The Constitution? History? Precedent? Something else?

3.   One of the criticisms frequently leveled at the majority opinion is that it reads like legislation, not a judicial ruling. Is that true? Is that bad?

4.   What state interests did the Court say were legitimate goals for states to pursue?

5.   What level of scrutiny did the Court employ? Why did it employ that level? What level of scrutiny would Justice Rehnquist have used? Why? Which was more appropriate?

6.   Justice Blackmun concluded that human fetuses are not constitutionally protected persons, within the meaning of the Fourteenth Amendment. What arguments established that claim? Are the arguments used by Justice Blackman to establish that proposition consistent with the argument he used to establish a constitutionally protected right to abortion?

7.   Was *Roe* faithful to *Griswold* and/or *Eisenstadt*?

8.   What role did the majority opinion's historical survey play in the Court's constitutional analysis?

9.   Justice Blackmun's recounting of the history of abortion has been subject to withering criticism. The most thorough critique of *Roe*'s history of abortion regulation is JOSEPH W. DELLAPENNA, DISPELLING THE MYTHS OF ABORTION HISTORY (2006).

10.   One of the key axes in the *Roe* opinion is viability. What arguments did the Court use to justify that line? Are those arguments persuasive?

11.   Another key move made by the *Roe* Court was concluding that an unborn human is "potential life" and therefore not an independent, constitutional-rights bearing being. What arguments did the Court use to support that claim? Is it accurate?

12.   The Supreme Court's ruling depended on numerous factual predicates. For example, the Court stated that abortion is safer than childbirth during the beginning period of pregnancy. What if those predicates have changed or, if later it was discovered that the predicates were not true in 1973? Does that undermine the ruling?

13.   Justice Blackmun noted, at the end of his opinion, that his ruling is "consistent with . . . the demands of the profound problems of the present day." What did he have in mind?

14.   Justice White's concurrence pointed to the fact that the majority's ruling conflicted with the laws in nearly all fifty states. Should the majority have taken into account that fact when it interpreted the Fourteenth Amendment?

15.   Justice White also argued that, given the deeply contested nature of abortion, "[t]his issue, for the most part, should be left with the people and to the political processes the people have devised to govern their affairs." Was Justice White correct?

16.   Justice Rehnquist called *Roe* a modern *Lochner*, and the majority emphatically disclaimed the *Lochner* label in the beginning of its opinion. Is that criticism accurate? If so, what follows?

17.   The Supreme Court articulated a relatively permissive abortion regime, by international standards. Most other countries restrict the reasons for which a woman can procure an abortion and the period during pregnancy when abortion is permissible. Should this fact have impacted the Court?

18.   *Roe* set off a firestorm of scholarly activity. There have been two broad categories of responses. One response has been to argue that *Roe* was right, but not for the reasons given by the Court. For example, Professor Jed Rubenfeld criticized *Roe*'s analysis and then offered a substitute rationale in JED RUBENFELD, FREEDOM AND TIME: A THEORY OF CONSTITUTIONAL SELF-GOVERNMENT (2001). The other has been to criticize the reasoning and result in *Roe*. For instance, Christopher Wolfe argued that *Roe* was the most significant modern manifestation of illegitimate "judge-made law." CHRISTOPHER WOLFE, THE RISE OF MODERN JUDICIAL REVIEW: FROM CONSTITUTIONAL INTERPRETATION TO JUDGE-MADE LAW (2d ed. 1994).

19.   In a companion case, *Doe v. Bolton*, 410 U.S. 179 (1973), the Supreme Court explained the breadth of the health and life exception noted in *Roe*. The *Doe* Court ruled that the health and life exception encompasses "all factors — physical, emotional, psychological, familial, and the woman's age — relevant to the well-being of the patient," *id.* at 192, and that a "physician's 'best clinical judgment that an abortion is necessary' . . . [is] sufficient." *Id.* at 199.

20.   Ironically, Norma McCorvey, *Roe*'s Jane Roe, later became a pro-life activist and, in 2003, moved the District Court for the Northern District of Texas for relief

from judgment. *McCorvey v. Hill*, 2003 U.S. Dist. LEXIS 12986 (N.D. Tex. June 19, 2003). The district court denied McCorvey's motion because it was not timely filed. *Id.* at *1.

For nearly twenty years after *Roe*, numerous state and federal laws were passed that restricted abortion and which were challenged. Initially, the Supreme Court struck down a significant number of these restrictions based on a broad reading of *Roe*. Beginning in the mid-1980s, however, it appeared that a majority of the Supreme Court was sympathetic to limiting or even overruling *Roe*. *Planned Parenthood v. Casey*, 505 U.S. 833 (1992), was the test case where a bare majority narrowed, but ultimately upheld *Roe*.

PLANNED PARENTHOOD OF SOUTHEASTERN PENNSYLVANIA v. CASEY
505 U.S. 833 (1992)

JUSTICE O'CONNOR, JUSTICE KENNEDY, and JUSTICE SOUTER announced the judgment of the Court and delivered the opinion of the Court with respect to Parts I, II, III, V-A, V-C, and VI, an opinion with respect to Part V-E, in which JUSTICE STEVENS joins, and an opinion with respect to Parts IV, V-B, and V-D.

I

Liberty finds no refuge in a jurisprudence of doubt. Yet 19 years after our holding that the Constitution protects a woman's right to terminate her pregnancy in its early stages, *Roe v. Wade*, 410 U.S. 113 (1973), that definition of liberty is still questioned. Joining the respondents as *amicus curiae*, the United States, as it has done in five other cases in the last decade, again asks us to overrule *Roe*.

At issue in these cases are five provisions of the Pennsylvania Abortion Control Act of 1982. The Act requires that a woman seeking an abortion give her informed consent prior to the abortion procedure, and specifies that she be provided with certain information at least 24 hours before the abortion is performed. For a minor to obtain an abortion, the Act requires the informed consent of one of her parents, but provides for a judicial bypass option if the minor does not wish to or cannot obtain a parent's consent. Another provision of the Act requires that, unless certain exceptions apply, a married woman seeking an abortion must sign a statement indicating that she has notified her husband of her intended abortion. The Act exempts compliance with these three requirements in the event of a "medical emergency." In addition to the above provisions regulating the performance of abortions, the Act imposes certain reporting requirements on facilities that provide abortion services.

Before any of these provisions took effect, the petitioners, who are five abortion clinics and one physician representing himself as well as a class of physicians who provide abortion services, brought this suit seeking declaratory and injunctive relief. The District Court held all the provisions at issue here unconstitutional. The Court of

Appeals for the Third Circuit affirmed in part and reversed in part, upholding all of the regulations except for the husband notification requirement.

[A]t oral argument in this Court, the attorney for the parties challenging the statute took the position that none of the enactments can be upheld without overruling *Roe v. Wade*. We disagree with that analysis; but we acknowledge that our decisions after *Roe* cast doubt upon the meaning and reach of its holding. Further, THE CHIEF JUSTICE admits that he would overrule the central holding of *Roe* and adopt the rational relationship test as the sole criterion of constitutionality. State and federal courts as well as legislatures throughout the Union must have guidance as they seek to address this subject in conformance with the Constitution. Given these premises, we find it imperative to review once more the principles that define the rights of the woman and the legitimate authority of the State respecting the termination of pregnancies by abortion procedures.

After considering the fundamental constitutional questions resolved by *Roe*, principles of institutional integrity, and the rule of *stare decisis*, we are led to conclude this: the essential holding of *Roe v. Wade* should be retained and once again reaffirmed.

It must be stated at the outset and with clarity that *Roe*'s essential holding, the holding we reaffirm, has three parts. First is a recognition of the right of the woman to choose to have an abortion before viability and to obtain it without undue interference from the State. Before viability, the State's interests are not strong enough to support a prohibition of abortion or the imposition of a substantial obstacle to the woman's effective right to elect the procedure. Second is a confirmation of the State's power to restrict abortions after fetal viability, if the law contains exceptions for pregnancies which endanger the woman's life or health. And third is the principle that the State has legitimate interests from the outset of the pregnancy in protecting the health of the woman and the life of the fetus that may become a child. These principles do not contradict one another; and we adhere to each.

II

Constitutional protection of the woman's decision to terminate her pregnancy derives from the Due Process Clause of the Fourteenth Amendment. It declares that no State shall "deprive any person of life, liberty, or property, without due process of law." The controlling word in the cases before us is "liberty." Although a literal reading of the Clause might suggest that it governs only the procedures by which a State may deprive persons of liberty, for at least 105 years, since *Mugler v. Kansas*, 123 U.S. 623, 660–661 (1887), the Clause has been understood to contain a substantive component as well.

The most familiar of the substantive liberties protected by the Fourteenth Amendment are those recognized by the Bill of Rights. We have held that the Due Process Clause of the Fourteenth Amendment incorporates most of the Bill of Rights against the States. See, *e.g.*, *Duncan v. Louisiana*, 391 U.S. 145, 147–148 (1968). It is tempting, as a means of curbing the discretion of federal judges, to suppose that liberty encompasses no more than those rights already guaranteed to the individual against federal interference by the express provisions of the first eight Amendments to the Constitution. See *Adamson v. California*, 332 U.S. 46, 68–92 (1947) (Black, J., dissenting). But of course this Court has never accepted that view.

It is also tempting, for the same reason, to suppose that the Due Process Clause protects only those practices, defined at the most specific level, that were protected against government interference by other rules of law when the Fourteenth Amendment was ratified. See *Michael H. v. Gerald D.*, 491 U.S. 110, 127–128, n. 6 (1989) (opinion of Scalia, J.). But such a view would be inconsistent with our law. It is a promise of the Constitution that there is a realm of personal liberty which the government may not enter. We have vindicated this principle before. Marriage is mentioned nowhere in the Bill of Rights and interracial marriage was illegal in most States in the 19th century, but the Court was no doubt correct in finding it to be an aspect of liberty protected against state interference by the substantive component of the Due Process Clause in *Loving v. Virginia*, 388 U.S. 1, 12 (1967). Similar examples may be found in *Griswold v. Connecticut*, 381 U.S. 479, 481–482 (1965); in *Pierce v. Society of Sisters*, 268 U.S. 510, 534–535 (1925); and in *Meyer v. Nebraska*, 262 U.S. 390, 399–403 (1923).

Neither the Bill of Rights nor the specific practices of States at the time of the adoption of the Fourteenth Amendment marks the outer limits of the substantive sphere of liberty which the Fourteenth Amendment protects. See U.S. Const., Amdt. 9. In *Griswold*, we held that the Constitution does not permit a State to forbid a married couple to use contraceptives. That same freedom was later guaranteed, under the Equal Protection Clause, for unmarried couples. See *Eisenstadt v. Baird*, 405 U.S. 438 (1972). It is settled now, as it was when the Court heard arguments in *Roe v. Wade*, that the Constitution places limits on a State's right to interfere with a person's most basic decisions about family and parenthood, see *Moore v. East Cleveland*, 431 U.S. 494 (1977); *Eisenstadt v. Baird; Loving v. Virginia; Griswold v. Connecticut; Skinner v. Oklahoma*, 316 U.S. 535 (1942); *Pierce v. Society of Sisters; Meyer v. Nebraska.*

The inescapable fact is that adjudication of substantive due process claims may call upon the Court in interpreting the Constitution to exercise that same capacity which by tradition courts always have exercised: reasoned judgment. Its boundaries are not susceptible of expression as a simple rule. That does not mean we are free to invalidate state policy choices with which we disagree; yet neither does it permit us to shrink from the duties of our office.

Men and women of good conscience can disagree, and we suppose some always shall disagree, about the profound moral and spiritual implications of terminating a pregnancy, even in its earliest stage. Some of us as individuals find abortion offensive to our most basic principles of morality, but that cannot control our decision. Our obligation is to define the liberty of all, not to mandate our own moral code. The underlying constitutional issue is whether the State can resolve these philosophic questions in such a definitive way that a woman lacks all choice in the matter.

It is conventional constitutional doctrine that where reasonable people disagree the government can adopt one position or the other. See, *e.g.*, *Williamson v. Lee Optical of Okla., Inc.*, 348 U.S. 483 (1955). That theorem, however, assumes a state of affairs in which the choice does not intrude upon a protected liberty.

Our law affords constitutional protection to personal decisions relating to marriage, procreation, contraception, family relationships, child rearing, and education. Our precedents "have respected the private realm of family life which the state cannot enter." These matters, involving the most intimate and personal choices a person may make in a lifetime, choices central to personal dignity and autonomy, are central to the liberty protected by the Fourteenth Amendment. At the heart of liberty is the right to define one's own concept of existence, of meaning, of the universe, and of the mystery of human life. Beliefs about these matters could not define the attributes of personhood were they formed under compulsion of the State.

These considerations begin our analysis of the woman's interest in terminating her pregnancy but cannot end it, for this reason: though the abortion decision may originate within the zone of conscience and belief, it is more than a philosophic exercise. Abortion is a unique act. It is an act fraught with consequences for others: for the woman who must live with the implications of her decision; for the persons who perform and assist in the procedure; for the spouse, family, and society which must confront the knowledge that these procedures exist, procedures some deem nothing short of an act of violence against innocent human life; and, depending on one's beliefs, for the life or potential life that is aborted. Though abortion is conduct, it does not follow that the State is entitled to proscribe it in all instances. That is because the liberty of the woman is at stake in a sense unique to the human condition and so unique to the law. The mother who carries a child to full term is subject to anxieties, to physical constraints, to pain that only she must bear. That these sacrifices have from the beginning of the human race been endured by woman with a pride that ennobles her in the eyes of others and gives to the infant a bond of love cannot alone be grounds for the State to insist she make the sacrifice. Her suffering is too intimate and personal for the State to insist, without more, upon its own vision of the woman's role, however dominant that vision has been in the course of our history and our culture. The destiny of the woman must be shaped to a large extent on her own conception of her spiritual imperatives and her place in society.

It should be recognized, moreover, that in some critical respects the abortion decision is of the same character as the decision to use contraception, to which *Griswold v. Connecticut*, and *Eisenstadt v. Baird*, afford constitutional protection. We have no doubt as to the correctness of those decisions. They support the reasoning in *Roe* relating to the woman's liberty because they involve personal decisions concerning not only the meaning of procreation but also human responsibility and respect for it. As with abortion, reasonable people will have differences of opinion about these matters. These are intimate views with infinite variations, and their deep, personal character underlay our decisions in *Griswold, Eisenstadt*. The same concerns are present when the woman confronts the reality that, perhaps despite her attempts to avoid it, she has become pregnant.

While we appreciate the weight of the arguments made on behalf of the State in the cases before us, arguments which in their ultimate formulation conclude that *Roe* should be overruled, the reservations any of us may have in reaffirming the central holding of *Roe* are outweighed by the explication of individual liberty we have given combined with the force of *stare decisis*. We turn now to that doctrine.

III

A

The obligation to follow precedent begins with necessity, and a contrary necessity marks its outer limit. With Cardozo, we recognize that no judicial system could do society's work if it eyed each issue afresh in every case that raised it. See B[enjamin] Cardozo, The Nature of the Judicial Process 149 (1921). Indeed, the very concept of the rule of law underlying our own Constitution requires such continuity over time that a respect for precedent is, by definition, indispensable. At the other extreme, a different necessity would make itself felt if a prior judicial ruling should come to be seen so clearly as error that its enforcement was for that very reason doomed.

Even when the decision to overrule a prior case is not, as in the rare, latter instance, virtually foreordained, it is common wisdom that the rule of *stare decisis* is not an "inexorable command," and certainly it is not such in every constitutional case. Rather, when this Court reexamines a prior holding, its judgment is customarily informed by a series of prudential and pragmatic considerations designed to test the consistency of overruling a prior decision with the ideal of the rule of law, and to gauge the respective costs of reaffirming and overruling a prior case. Thus, for example, we may ask whether the rule has proven to be intolerable simply in defying practical workability, whether the rule is subject to a kind of reliance that would lend a special hardship to the consequences of overruling and add inequity to the cost of repudiation, whether related principles of law have so far developed as to have left the old rule no more than a remnant of abandoned doctrine, or whether facts have so changed, or come to be seen so differently, as to have robbed the old rule of significant application or justification.

1

Although *Roe* has engendered opposition, it has in no sense proven "unworkable," representing as it does a simple limitation beyond which a state law is unenforceable. While *Roe* has, of course, required judicial assessment of state laws affecting the exercise of the choice guaranteed against government infringement, and although the need for such review will remain as a consequence of today's decision, the required determinations fall within judicial competence.

2

The inquiry into reliance counts the cost of a rule's repudiation as it would fall on those who have relied reasonably on the rule's continued application. Abortion is customarily chosen as an unplanned response to the consequence of unplanned activity or to the failure of conventional birth control, and except on the assumption that no intercourse would have occurred but for *Roe*'s holding, such behavior may appear to justify no reliance claim. This argument would be premised on the hypothesis that reproductive planning could take virtually immediate account of any sudden restoration of state authority to ban abortions.

To eliminate the issue of reliance that easily, however, one would need to limit cognizable reliance to specific instances of sexual activity. But to do this would be simply to refuse to face the fact that for two decades of economic and social developments, people have organized intimate relationships and made choices that define their views of themselves and their places in society, in reliance on the availability of abortion in the event that contraception should fail. The ability of women to participate equally in the economic and social life of the Nation has been facilitated by their ability to control their reproductive lives.

3

No evolution of legal principle has left *Roe*'s doctrinal footings weaker than they were in 1973. The *Roe* Court itself placed its holding in the succession of cases most prominently exemplified by *Griswold v. Connecticut*, 381 U.S. 479 (1965). When it is so seen, *Roe* is clearly in no jeopardy, since subsequent constitutional developments have neither disturbed, nor do they threaten to diminish, the scope of recognized protection accorded to the liberty relating to intimate relationships, the family, and decisions about whether or not to beget or bear a child. See, *e.g.*, *Moore v. East Cleveland*, 431 U.S. 494 (1977).

4

We have seen how time has overtaken some of *Roe*'s factual assumptions: advances in maternal health care allow for abortions safe to the mother later in pregnancy than was true in 1973, and advances in neonatal care have advanced viability to a point somewhat earlier. But these facts go only to the scheme of time limits on the realization of competing interests, and the divergences from the factual premises of 1973 have no bearing on the validity of *Roe*'s central holding, that viability marks the earliest point at which the State's interest in fetal life is constitutionally adequate to justify a legislative ban on nontherapeutic abortions. The soundness or unsoundness of that constitutional judgment in no sense turns on whether viability occurs at approximately 28 weeks, as was usual at the time of *Roe*, at 23 to 24 weeks, as it sometimes does today.

5

The sum of the precedential enquiry to this point shows *Roe*'s underpinnings unweakened in any way affecting its central holding. Within the bounds of normal *stare decisis* analysis, then, and subject to the considerations on which it customarily turns, the stronger argument is for affirming *Roe*'s central holding, with whatever degree of personal reluctance any of us may have, not for overruling it.

C

Our analysis would not be complete, however, without explaining why overruling *Roe*'s central holding would seriously weaken the Court's capacity to exercise the judicial power and to function as the Supreme Court of a Nation dedicated to the rule of law.

The root of American governmental power is revealed most clearly in the instance of the power conferred by the Constitution upon the Judiciary of the United States and specifically upon this Court. As Americans of each succeeding generation are rightly told, the Court cannot buy support for its decisions by spending money and, except to a minor degree, it cannot independently coerce obedience to its decrees. The Court's power lies, rather, in its legitimacy, a product of substance and perception that shows itself in the people's acceptance of the Judiciary as fit to determine what the Nation's law means and to declare what it demands.

The underlying substance of this legitimacy is of course the warrant for the Court's decisions in the Constitution and the lesser sources of legal principle on which the Court draws. That substance is expressed in the Court's opinions, and our contemporary understanding is such that a decision without principled justification would be no judicial act at all. The Court must take care to speak and act in ways that allow people to accept its decisions on the terms the Court claims for them, as grounded truly in principle, not as compromises with social and political pressures having, as such, no bearing on the principled choices that the Court is obliged to make.

The need for principled action to be perceived as such is implicated to some degree whenever this [C]ourt overrules a prior case. This is not to say, of course, that this Court cannot give a perfectly satisfactory explanation in most cases. People understand that some of the Constitution's language is hard to fathom and that the Court's Justices are sometimes able to perceive significant facts or to understand principles of law that eluded their predecessors and that justify departures from existing decisions.

In two circumstances, however, the Court would almost certainly fail to receive the benefit of the doubt in overruling prior cases. There is, first, a point beyond which frequent overruling would overtax the country's belief in the Court's good faith. Despite the variety of reasons that may inform and justify a decision to overrule, we cannot forget that such a decision is usually perceived (and perceived correctly) as, at the least, a statement that a prior decision was wrong. There is a limit to the amount of error that can plausibly be imputed to prior Courts. If that limit should be exceeded, disturbance of prior rulings would be taken as evidence that justifiable reexamination of principle had given way to drives for particular results in the short term.

That first circumstance can be described as hypothetical; the second is to the point here and now. Where, in the performance of its judicial duties, the Court decides a case in such a way as to resolve the sort of intensely divisive controversy reflected in *Roe* and those rare, comparable cases, its decision has a dimension that the resolution of the normal case does not carry. It is the dimension present whenever the Court's interpretation of the Constitution calls the contending sides of a national controversy to end their national division by accepting a common mandate rooted in the Constitution.

The Court is not asked to do this very often, having thus addressed the Nation only twice in our lifetime, in the decisions of *Brown* and *Roe*. But when the Court does act in this way, its decision requires an equally rare precedential force to counter the inevitable efforts to overturn it and to thwart its implementation. [O]nly the most convincing justification under accepted standards of precedent could suffice to demonstrate that a later decision overruling the first was anything but a surrender to political pressure, and an unjustified repudiation of the principle on which the Court staked its authority in the first instance. So to overrule under fire in the absence of the most compelling reason to reexamine a watershed decision would subvert the Court's legitimacy beyond any serious question.

Some cost will be paid by anyone who approves or implements a constitutional decision where it is unpopular, or who refuses to work to undermine the decision or to force its reversal. An extra price will be paid by those who themselves disapprove of the decision's results when viewed outside of constitutional terms, but who neverthe-less struggle to accept it, because they respect the rule of law. To all those who will be so tested by following, the Court implicitly undertakes to remain steadfast, lest in the end a price be paid for nothing. The promise of constancy, once given, binds its maker for as long as the power to stand by the decision survives and the understanding of the issue has not changed so fundamentally as to render the commitment obsolete. A willing breach of it would be nothing less than a breach of faith, and no Court that broke its faith with the people could sensibly expect credit for principle in the decision by which it did that.

Like the character of an individual, the legitimacy of the Court must be earned over time. So, indeed, must be the character of a Nation of people who aspire to live according to the rule of law. Their belief in themselves as such a people is not readily separable from their understanding of the Court invested with the authority to decide their constitutional cases and speak before all others for their constitutional ideals. If the Court's legitimacy should be undermined, then, so would the country be in its very ability to see itself through its constitutional ideals.

The Court's duty in the present cases is clear. In 1973, it confronted the already-divisive issue of governmental power to limit personal choice to undergo abortion, for which it provided a new resolution based on the due process guaranteed by the Fourteenth Amendment. Whether or not a new social consensus is developing on that issue, its divisiveness is no less today than in 1973, and pressure to overrule the decision, like pressure to retain it, has grown only more intense. A decision to overrule *Roe*'s essential holding under the existing circumstances would address error, if error there was, at the cost of both profound and unnecessary damage to the Court's legitimacy, and to the Nation's commitment to the rule of law. It is therefore imperative to adhere to the essence of *Roe*'s original decision, and we do so today.

IV

That brings us, of course, to the point where much criticism has been directed at *Roe*, a criticism that always inheres when the Court draws a specific rule from what in the Constitution is but a general standard. We conclude the line should be drawn at viability. We adhere to this principle for two reasons. First, as we have said, is the doctrine of *stare decisis*.

The second reason is that the concept of viability is the time at which there is a realistic possibility of maintaining and nourishing a life outside the womb, so that the independent existence of the second life can in reason and all fairness be the object of state protection that now overrides the rights of the woman. Consistent with other constitutional norms, legislatures may draw lines which appear arbitrary without the necessity of offering a justification. But courts may not. We must justify the lines we draw. And there is no line other than viability which is more workable. The viability line also has, as a practical matter, an element of fairness. In some broad sense it might be said that a woman who fails to act before viability has consented to the State's intervention on behalf of the developing child.

On the other side of the equation is the interest of the State in the protection of potential life. The *Roe* Court recognized the State's "important and legitimate interest in protecting the potentiality of human life." We do not need to say whether each of us, had we been Members of the Court when the valuation of the state interest came before it as an original matter, would have concluded, as the *Roe* Court did, that its weight is insufficient to justify a ban on abortions prior to viability even when it is subject to certain exceptions. The matter is not before us in the first instance, and coming as it does after nearly 20 years of litigation in *Roe*'s wake we are satisfied that the immediate question is not the soundness of *Roe*'s resolution of the issue, but the precedential force that must be accorded to its holding. And we have concluded that the essential holding of *Roe* should be reaffirmed. Yet it must be remembered that *Roe v. Wade* speaks with clarity in establishing not only the woman's liberty but also the State's "important and legitimate interest in potential life."

Roe established a trimester framework to govern abortion regulations. A framework of this rigidity was unnecessary. Though the woman has a right to choose to terminate or continue her pregnancy before viability, it does not at all follow that the State is prohibited from taking steps to ensure that this choice is thoughtful and informed. Even in the earliest stages of pregnancy, the State may enact rules and regulations designed to encourage her to know that there are philosophic and social arguments of great weight that can be brought to bear in favor of continuing the pregnancy to full term and that there are procedures and institutions to allow adoption of unwanted children as well as a certain degree of state assistance if the mother chooses to raise the child herself. It follows that States are free to enact laws to provide a reasonable framework for a woman to make a decision that has such profound and lasting meaning.

The trimester framework suffers from these basic flaws: in its formulation it misconceives the nature of the pregnant woman's interest; and in practice it under-values the State's interest in potential life, as recognized in *Roe*. As our jurisprudence relating to all liberties save perhaps abortion has recognized, not every law which makes a right more difficult to exercise is, *ipso facto*, an infringement of that right. An example clarifies the point. We have held that not every ballot access limitation amounts to an infringement of the right to vote. Rather, the States are granted substantial flexibility in establishing the framework within which voters choose the candidates for whom they wish to vote.

The abortion right is similar. Numerous forms of state regulation might have the incidental effect of increasing the cost or decreasing the availability of medical care, whether for abortion or any other medical procedure. The fact that a law which serves a valid purpose, one not designed to strike at the right itself, has the incidental effect of making it more difficult or more expensive to procure an abortion cannot be enough to invalidate it. Only where state regulation imposes an undue burden on a woman's ability to make this decision does the power of the State reach into the heart of the liberty protected by the Due Process Clause.

Not all governmental intrusion is of necessity unwarranted; and that brings us to the other basic flaw in the trimester framework: even in *Roe*'s terms, in practice it undervalues the State's interest in the potential life within the woman. *Roe v. Wade* was express in its recognition of the State's "important and legitimate interest[s] in preserving and protecting the health of the pregnant woman [and] in protecting the potentiality of human life." The trimester framework, however, does not fulfill *Roe*'s own promise that the State has an interest in protecting fetal life or potential life. *Roe* began the contradiction by using the trimester framework to forbid any regulation of abortion designed to advance that interest before viability. In our view, the undue burden standard is the appropriate means of reconciling the State's interest with the woman's constitutionally protected liberty.

Because we set forth a standard of general application to which we intend to adhere, it is important to clarify what is meant by an undue burden. A finding of an undue burden is a shorthand for the conclusion that a state regulation has the purpose or effect of placing a substantial obstacle in the path of a woman seeking an abortion of a nonviable fetus. A statute with this purpose is invalid because the means chosen by the State to further the interest in potential life must be calculated to inform the woman's free choice, not hinder it. And a statute which, while furthering the interest in potential life or some other valid state interest, has the effect of placing a substantial obstacle in the path of a woman's choice cannot be considered a permissible means of serving its legitimate ends.

Some guiding principles should emerge. What is at stake is the woman's right to make the ultimate decision, not a right to be insulated from all others in doing so. Regulations which do no more than create a structural mechanism by which the State, or the parent or guardian of a minor, may express profound respect for the life of the unborn are permitted, if they are not a substantial obstacle to the woman's exercise of the right to choose. Unless it has that effect on her right of choice, a state measure designed to persuade her to choose childbirth over abortion will be upheld if reasonably related to that goal. Regulations designed to foster the health of a woman seeking an abortion are valid if they do not constitute an undue burden.

We give this summary:

(a) To protect the central right recognized by *Roe v. Wade* while at the same time accommodating the State's profound interest in potential life, we will employ the undue burden analysis as explained in this opinion. An undue burden exists, and therefore a provision of law is invalid, if its purpose or effect is to place a substantial obstacle in the path of a woman seeking an abortion before the fetus attains viability.

(b) We reject the rigid trimester framework of *Roe v. Wade.* To promote the State's profound interest in potential life, throughout pregnancy the State may take measures to ensure that the woman's choice is informed, and measures designed to advance this interest will not be invalidated as long as their purpose is to persuade the woman to choose childbirth over abortion. These measures must not be an undue burden on the right.

(c) As with any medical procedure, the State may enact regulations to further the health or safety of a woman seeking an abortion. Unnecessary health regulations that have the purpose or effect of presenting a substantial obstacle to a woman seeking an abortion impose an undue burden on the right.

(d) Our adoption of the undue burden analysis does not disturb the central holding of *Roe v. Wade,* and we reaffirm that holding. Regardless of whether exceptions are made for particular circumstances, a State may not prohibit any woman from making the ultimate decision to terminate her pregnancy before viability.

(e) We also reaffirm *Roe*'s holding that "subsequent to viability, the State in promoting its interest in the potentiality of human life may, if it chooses, regulate, and even proscribe, abortion except where it is necessary, in appropriate medical judgment, for the preservation of the life or health of the mother."

V

We now consider the separate statutory sections at issue.

A

[The Court upheld Pennsylvania's medical emergency exception that permitted abortions when the mother faced "significant health risks."]

B

[The Court next upheld] the informed consent requirement[, which provided that, e]xcept in a medical emergency, at least 24 hours before performing an abortion, a physician inform the woman of the nature of the procedure, the health risks of the abortion and of childbirth, and the "probable gestational age of the unborn child."

C

[The Court struck down] Section 3209 of Pennsylvania's abortion law [which] provides, except in cases of medical emergency, that no physician shall perform an abortion on a married woman without receiving a signed statement from the woman that she has notified her spouse that she is about to undergo an abortion.

D

[The Court next upheld] the parental consent provision[, which provided that, e]xcept in a medical emergency, an unemancipated young woman under 18 may not obtain an abortion unless she and one of her parents (or guardian) provides informed consent as defined above. If neither a parent nor a guardian provides consent, a court may authorize the performance of an abortion upon a determination that the young woman is mature and capable of giving informed consent and has in fact given her informed consent, or that an abortion would be in her best interests.

E

For each abortion performed, a report must be filed. We think that all the provisions at issue here, except that relating to spousal notice, are constitutional.

It is so ordered.

JUSTICE STEVENS, concurring in part and dissenting in part. [Opinion omitted.]

JUSTICE BLACKMUN, concurring in part, concurring in the judgment in part, and dissenting in part.

I join Parts I, II, III, V-A, V-C, and VI of the joint opinion of JUSTICES O'CONNOR, KENNEDY, and SOUTER.

Three years ago, in *Webster v. Reproductive Health Services*, 492 U.S. 490 (1989), four Members of this Court appeared poised to "cas[t] into darkness the hopes and visions of every woman in this country" who had come to believe that the Constitution guaranteed her the right to reproductive choice. All that remained between the promise of *Roe* and the darkness of the plurality was a single, flickering flame. But now, just when so many expected the darkness to fall, the flame has grown bright.

I do not underestimate the significance of today's joint opinion. Yet I remain steadfast in my belief that the right to reproductive choice is entitled to full protection. And I fear for the darkness as four Justices anxiously await the single vote necessary to extinguish the light.

I

Make no mistake, the joint opinion of JUSTICES O'CONNOR, KENNEDY, and SOUTER is an act of personal courage and constitutional principle. A fervent view of individual liberty and the force of *stare decisis* have led the Court to this conclusion.

IV

In one sense, the Court's approach is worlds apart from that of THE CHIEF JUSTICE and JUSTICE SCALIA. And yet, in another sense, the distance between the two approaches is short — the distance is but a single vote. I am 83 years old. I cannot remain on this Court forever, and when I do step down, the confirmation process for my successor may well focus on the issue before us today. That, I regret, may be exactly where the choice between the two worlds will be made.

CHIEF JUSTICE REHNQUIST, with whom JUSTICE WHITE, JUSTICE SCALIA, and JUSTICE THOMAS join, concurring in the judgment in part and dissenting in part.

The joint opinion, following its newly minted variation on *stare decisis*, retains the outer shell of *Roe v. Wade*, 410 U.S. 113 (1973), but beats a wholesale retreat from the substance of that case. We believe that *Roe* was wrongly decided, and that it can and should be overruled consistently with our traditional approach to *stare decisis* in constitutional cases. We would uphold the challenged provisions of the Pennsylvania statute in their entirety.

I

In construing the phrase "liberty" incorporated in the Due Process Clause of the Fourteenth Amendment, we have recognized that its meaning extends beyond freedom from physical restraint. In *Pierce v. Society of Sisters*, 268 U.S. 510 (1925), we held that it included a parent's right to send a child to private school; in *Meyer v. Nebraska*, 262 U.S. 390 (1923), we held that it included a right to teach a foreign language in a parochial school. Building on these cases, we have held that the term "liberty" includes a right to marry, *Loving v. Virginia*, 388 U.S. 1 (1967); a right to procreate, *Skinner v. Oklahoma ex rel. Williamson*, 316 U.S. 535 (1942); and a right to use contraceptives, *Griswold v. Connecticut*, 381 U.S. 479 (1965); *Eisenstadt v. Baird*, 405 U.S. 438 (1972). But a reading of these opinions makes clear that they do not endorse any all-encompassing "right of privacy."

We are now of the view that, in terming th[e] right [to abortion] fundamental, the Court in *Roe* read the earlier opinions upon which it based its decision much too broadly. Unlike marriage, procreation, and contraception, abortion "involves the purposeful termination of a potential life." The abortion decision must therefore "be recognized as *sui generis*, different in kind from the others that the Court has protected under the rubric of personal or family privacy and autonomy."

Nor do the historical traditions of the American people support the view that the right to terminate one's pregnancy is "fundamental." The common law which we inherited from England made abortion after "quickening" an offense. At the time of the adoption of the Fourteenth Amendment, statutory prohibitions or restrictions on abortion were commonplace; in 1868, at least 28 of the then-37 States and 8 Territories had statutes banning or limiting abortion.

We think, therefore, both in view of this history and of our decided cases dealing with substantive liberty under the Due Process Clause, that the Court was mistaken in *Roe* when it classified a woman's decision to terminate her pregnancy as a "fundamental right."

II

In our view, authentic principles of *stare decisis* do not require that any portion of the reasoning in *Roe* be kept intact. Erroneous decisions in such constitutional cases are uniquely durable, because correction through legislative action, save for constitutional amendment, is impossible. It is therefore our duty to reconsider constitutional interpretations that "depar[t] from a proper understanding" of the Constitution.

The joint opinion discusses several *stare decisis* factors which, it asserts, point toward retaining a portion of *Roe*. Two of these factors are that the main "factual underpinning" of *Roe* has remained the same, and that its doctrinal foundation is no weaker now than it was in 1973. But this is only to say that the same facts which gave rise to *Roe* will continue to give rise to similar cases. It is not a reason, in and of itself, why those cases must be decided in the same incorrect manner as was the first case to deal with the question.

The joint opinion also points to the reliance interests involved in this context. But, as the joint opinion apparently agrees, any traditional notion of reliance is not applicable here. The joint opinion thus turns to what can only be described as an unconventional — and unconvincing — notion of reliance, a view based on the surmise that the availability of abortion since *Roe* has led to "two decades of economic and social developments" that would be undercut if the error of *Roe* were recognized. The joint opinion's assertion of this fact is undeveloped and totally conclusory. Surely it is dubious to suggest that women have reached their "places in society" in reliance upon *Roe*, rather than as a result of their determination to obtain higher education and compete with men in the job market, and of society's increasing recognition of their ability to fill positions that were previously thought to be reserved only for men.

Apparently realizing that conventional *stare decisis* principles do not support its position, the joint opinion advances a belief that retaining a portion of *Roe* is necessary to protect the "legitimacy" of this Court. This is a truly novel principle, one which is contrary to both the Court's historical practice and to the Court's traditional willingness to tolerate criticism of its opinions. Under this principle, when the Court has ruled on a divisive issue, it is apparently prevented from overruling that decision for the sole reason that it was incorrect, *unless opposition to the original decision has died away.*

The end result of the joint opinion's paeans of praise for legitimacy is the enunciation of a brand new standard for evaluating state regulation of a woman's right to abortion — the "undue burden" standard. The "undue burden" standard is created largely out of whole cloth by the authors of the joint opinion. [T]his standard is based even more on a judge's subjective determinations than was the trimester framework. Because the undue burden standard is plucked from nowhere, the question of what is a "substantial obstacle" to abortion will undoubtedly engender a variety of conflicting views.

A woman's interest in having an abortion is a form of liberty protected by the Due Process Clause, but States may regulate abortion procedures in ways rationally related to a legitimate state interest. *Williamson v. Lee Optical of Oklahoma, Inc.*, 348 U.S. 483, 491 (1955).

JUSTICE SCALIA, with whom THE CHIEF JUSTICE, JUSTICE WHITE, and JUSTICE THOMAS join, concurring in the judgment in part and dissenting in part.

The States may, if they wish, permit abortion on demand, but the Constitution does not *require* them to do so. The permissibility of abortion, and the limitations upon it, are to be resolved like most important questions in our democracy: by citizens trying to persuade one another and then voting.

That is, quite simply, the issue in these cases: not whether the power of a woman to abort her unborn child is a "liberty" in the absolute sense; or even whether it is a liberty of great importance to many women. Of course it is both. The issue is whether it is a liberty protected by the Constitution of the United States. I am sure it is not. I reach that conclusion not because of anything so exalted as my views concerning the "concept of existence, of meaning, of the universe, and of the mystery of human life." Rather, I reach it for the same reason I reach the conclusion that bigamy is not constitutionally protected — because of two simple facts: (1) the Constitution says absolutely nothing about it, and (2) the longstanding traditions of American society have permitted it to be legally proscribed.[1]

I must respond to a few of the more outrageous arguments in today's opinion, which it is beyond human nature to leave unanswered. I shall discuss each of them under a quotation from the Court's opinion to which they pertain.

"The inescapable fact is that adjudication of substantive due process claims may call upon the Court in interpreting the Constitution to exercise that same capacity which by tradition courts always have exercised: reasoned judgment."

Assuming that the question before us is to be resolved at such a level of philosophical abstraction, in such isolation from the traditions of American society, as by simply applying "reasoned judgment," I do not see how that could possibly have produced the answer the Court arrived at in *Roe v. Wade*, 410 U.S. 113 (1973). But "reasoned judgment" does not begin by begging the question, as *Roe* and subsequent cases unquestionably did by assuming that what the State is protecting is the mere "potentiality of human life." The whole argument of abortion opponents is that what the Court calls the fetus and what others call the unborn child *is a human life*. Thus, whatever answer *Roe* came up with is bound to be wrong, unless it is correct that the human fetus is in some critical sense merely potentially human. There is of course no way to determine that as a legal matter; it is in fact a value judgment. Some societies have considered newborn children not yet human, or the incompetent elderly no longer so.

The emptiness of the "reasoned judgment" that produced *Roe* is displayed in plain view by the fact that, after more than 19 years of effort by some of the brightest (and most determined) legal minds in the country, after more than 10 cases upholding abortion rights in this Court, and after dozens upon dozens of *amicus* briefs submitted in these and other cases, the best the Court can do to explain how it is that the word "liberty" *must* be thought to include the right to destroy human fetuses is to rattle off a collection of adjectives that simply decorate a value judgment and conceal a political

---

[1] The Court's suggestion that adherence to tradition would require us to uphold laws against interracial marriage is entirely wrong. Any tradition in that case was contradicted *by a text* — an Equal Protection Clause that explicitly establishes racial equality as a constitutional value. See *Loving v. Virginia*, 388 U.S. 1, 9 (1967). The enterprise launched in *Roe v. Wade*, 410 U.S. 113 (1973), by contrast, sought to *establish* — in the teeth of a clear, contrary tradition — a value found nowhere in the constitutional text.

choice. But it is obvious to anyone applying "reasoned judgment" that the same adjectives can be applied to many forms of conduct that this Court has held are *not* entitled to constitutional protection — because, like abortion, they are forms of conduct that have long been criminalized in American society. Those adjectives might be applied, for example, to homosexual sodomy, polygamy, adult incest, and suicide, all of which are equally "intimate" and "deep[ly] personal" decisions involving "personal autonomy and bodily integrity," and all of which can constitutionally be proscribed because it is our unquestionable constitutional tradition that they are proscribable.

"Where, in the performance of its judicial duties, the Court decides a case in such a way as to resolve the sort of intensely divisive controversy reflected in *Roe* . . . , its decision has a dimension that the resolution of the normal case does not carry. It is the dimension present whenever the Court's interpretation of the Constitution calls the contending sides of a national controversy to end their national division by accepting a common mandate rooted in the Constitution."

The Court's description of the place of *Roe* in the social history of the United States is unrecognizable. Not only did *Roe* not, as the Court suggests, *resolve* the deeply divisive issue of abortion; it did more than anything else to nourish it, by elevating it to the national level where it is infinitely more difficult to resolve. National politics were not plagued by abortion protests, national abortion lobbying, or abortion marches on Congress before *Roe v. Wade* was decided. Profound disagreement existed among our citizens over the issue but that disagreement was being worked out at the state level. As with many other issues, the division of sentiment within each State was not as closely balanced as it was among the population of the Nation as a whole, meaning not only that more people would be satisfied with the results of state-by-state resolution, but also that those results would be more stable.

Pre-*Roe*, moreover, political compromise was possible. *Roe*'s mandate for abortion on demand destroyed the compromises of the past, rendered compromise impossible for the future, and required the entire issue to be resolved uniformly, at the national level.

[T]o portray *Roe* as the statesmanlike "settlement" of a divisive issue, is nothing less than Orwellian. *Roe* fanned into life an issue that has inflamed our national politics in general, and has obscured with its smoke the selection of Justices to this Court in particular, ever since. And by keeping us in the abortion-umpiring business, it is the perpetuation of that disruption, rather than of any *Pax Roeana*, that the Court's new majority decrees.

"[T]o overrule under fire . . . would subvert the Court's legitimacy . . .

". . . To all those who will be . . . tested by following, the Court implicitly undertakes to remain steadfast . . .

"[The American people's] belief in themselves as . . . a people [who aspire to live according to the rule of law] is not readily separable from their understanding of the Court invested with the authority to decide their constitutional cases and speak before all others for their constitutional ideals."

The Imperial Judiciary lives. It is instructive to compare this Nietzschean vision of us unelected, life-tenured judges with the somewhat more modest role envisioned for these lawyers by the Founders.

"The judiciary . . . has . . . no direction either of the strength or of the wealth of the society, and can take no active resolution whatever. It may truly be said to have neither Force nor Will, but merely judgment . . ." The Federalist No. 78.

"[T]he candid citizen must confess that if the policy of the Government upon vital questions affecting the whole people is to be irrevocably fixed by decisions of the Supreme Court, . . . the people will have ceased to be their own rulers, having to that extent practically resigned their Government into the hands of that eminent tribunal." A. Lincoln, First Inaugural Address (Mar. 4, 1861).

I cannot agree with, indeed I am appalled by, the Court's suggestion that the decision whether to stand by an erroneous constitutional decision must be strongly influenced — *against* overruling, no less — by the substantial and continuing public opposition the decision has generated. The Court's judgment that any other course would "subvert the Court's legitimacy" must be another consequence of reading the error-filled history book that described the deeply divided country brought together by *Roe.* In my history-book, the Court was covered with dishonor and deprived of legitimacy by *Dred Scott v. Sandford,* [60 U.S. (]19 How.[)] 393 (1857), an erroneous (and widely opposed) opinion that it did not abandon.

But whether it would "subvert the Court's legitimacy" or not, the notion that we would decide a case differently from the way we otherwise would have in order to show that we can stand firm against public disapproval is frightening. It is a bad enough idea, even in the head of someone like me, who believes that the text of the Constitution, and our traditions, say what they say and there is no fiddling with them. But when it is in the mind of a Court that believes the Constitution has an evolving meaning, that the Ninth Amendment's reference to "othe [r]" rights is not a disclaimer, but a charter for action, and that the function of this Court is to "speak before all others for [the people's] constitutional ideals" unrestrained by meaningful text or tradition — then the notion that the Court must adhere to a decision for as long as the decision faces "great opposition" and the Court is "under fire" acquires a character of almost czarist arrogance. We are offended by these marchers who descend upon us, every year on the anniversary of *Roe,* to protest our saying that the Constitution requires what our society has never thought the Constitution requires. These people who refuse to be "tested by following" must be taught a lesson. We have no Cossacks, but at least we can stubbornly refuse to abandon an erroneous opinion that we might otherwise change — to show how little they intimidate us.

What makes all this relevant to the bothersome application of "political pressure" against the Court are the twin facts that the American people love democracy and the American people are not fools. As long as this Court thought (and the people thought) that we Justices were doing essentially lawyers' work up here — reading text and discerning our society's traditional understanding of that text — the public pretty much left us alone. Texts and traditions are facts to study, not convictions to demonstrate about. But if in reality our process of constitutional adjudication consists primarily of making *value judgments*, then a free and intelligent people's attitude towards us can be expected to be (*ought* to be) quite different. The people know that their value judgments are quite as good as those taught in any law school — maybe better. If, indeed, the "liberties" protected by the Constitution are, as the Court says, undefined and unbounded, then the people *should* demonstrate, to protest that we do not implement *their* values instead of *ours*. Not only that, but confirmation hearings for new Justices *should* deteriorate into question-and-answer sessions in which Senators go through a list of their constituents' most favored and most disfavored alleged constitutional rights, and seek the nominee's commitment to support or oppose them. JUSTICE BLACKMUN not only regards this prospect with equanimity, he solicits it.

. . . .

There is a poignant aspect to today's opinion. Its length, and what might be called its epic tone, suggest that its authors believe they are bringing to an end a troublesome era in the history of our Nation and of our Court. There comes vividly to mind a portrait by Emanuel Leutze that hangs in the Harvard Law School: Roger Brooke Taney, painted in 1859, the 82d year of his life, the 24th of his Chief Justiceship, the second after his opinion in *Dred Scott*. He is all in black, sitting in a shadowed red armchair, left hand resting upon a pad of paper in his lap, right hand hanging limply, almost lifelessly, beside the inner arm of the chair. He sits facing the viewer and staring straight out. There seems to be on his face, and in his deep-set eyes, an expression of profound sadness and disillusionment. Perhaps he always looked that way, even when dwelling upon the happiest of thoughts. But those of us who know how the lustre of his great Chief Justiceship came to be eclipsed by *Dred Scott* cannot help believing that he had that case burning on his mind. I expect that two years earlier he, too, had thought himself "call[ing] the contending sides of national controversy to end their national division by accepting a common mandate rooted in the Constitution."

We should get out of this area, where we have no right to be, and where we do neither ourselves nor the country any good by remaining.

EXERCISE 15:

1. What was *Casey*'s holding?

2. What was the legal source of that holding? The Constitution? History? Precedent? Something else?

3. In what ways did *Casey* change, and in what ways did it adhere to *Roe*?

4. What state interests did the Court say were legitimate goals for states to pursue?

5. The Supreme Court shifted the timeline for state regulation; what was the new timeline and what justifications did the Court give for the shift?

6. What justifications did the plurality give for utilizing viability as the point at which state regulatory authority changed and increased? Are those justifications persuasive? What other line might the Court have drawn? Would that have been a better line?

7.   What level of scrutiny did the Court employ? Why did it employ that level? What would be wrong with following Chief Justice Rehnquist's conclusion that abortion regulations should be subject to rational basis review? Why not utilize strict scrutiny?

8.   The plurality articulated the undue burden standard. What is that? When does it apply? Did the plurality correctly apply it?

9.   The plurality's discussion of stare decisis was the most extensive modern discussion by the Court. It is also the most controversial. What analysis did the plurality utilize in light of stare decisis? What relative weight did each factor have? Are those the correct factors? Did the plurality correctly apply the factors?

10.   Where does the Court's obligation to follow precedent come from? The Constitution? If so, where in the Constitution? Someplace else?

11.   Justice O'Connor claimed that stare decisis was essential to the rule of law. Explain why that may be true. What are some contrary arguments?

12.   The plurality suggested that risk to the Supreme Court's authority was a factor in upholding *Roe* because it would "weaken the Court's capacity to exercise the judicial power and to function as the Supreme Court of a Nation dedicated to the rule of law." Is that a legitimate reason to refrain from overruling an incorrect decision? If a legitimate reason, did it apply in *Casey*?

13.   The plurality contended that "to overrule under fire in the absence of the most compelling reason to reexamine a watershed decision would subvert the Court's legitimacy beyond any serious question." Is that true? Would the harm caused by overruling be greater than the harm caused by following an incorrect decision? How would the Court know? Is Justice Scalia correct that *Roe* has actually caused *greater* divisiveness over the issue of abortion? Relatedly, does that mean that the Court could or should overrule a controversial decision once opposition has abated?

14.   The plurality stated that ready access to abortion has facilitated women's equality. What evidence would one use to support that claim? Is the claim true?

15.   The plurality stated that, in *Roe*, the "Court's interpretation of the Constitution calls the contending sides of a national controversy to end their national division by accepting a common mandate rooted in the Constitution." Has that happened? Was it likely to happen? Is that the Court's role? Is Justice Scalia correct to compare *Roe* to *Dred Scott*?

16.   One of the major currents in constitutional theory today is called Popular Constitutionalism. The core thesis of this school of thought is that the Supreme Court does and should interpret the Constitution to reflect popular interpretations. LARRY D. KRAMER, THE PEOPLE THEMSELVES: POPULAR CONSTITUTIONALISM AND JUDICIAL REVIEW (2004). On this understanding, for instance, the Court was right to broaden the Commerce Clause's interpretation to fit the New Deal popular constitutional movement. Following this line of thinking, which way does Popular Constitutionalism cut in the context of abortion?

17. Justice Blackmun bemoaned the possibility that the "confirmation process for [his] successor" would hinge on whether the nominee would follow the Supreme Court's abortion precedents. Why is that bad, in Justice Blackmun's view? What did Justice Scalia argue in response?

18. Did the plurality effectively respond to the charge that substantive due process licensed judges to act beyond their legal authority? How?

19. Relatedly, Justice Scalia argued that the plurality's substantive due process analysis was the cause of much of the divisiveness surrounding and subsequent to *Roe*. Is that true? What evidence is there for that claim?

20. One of Justice Scalia's central criticisms of the *Casey* majority is that the majority is imposing its own "value" judgment on American society. He differentiates that from his approach to constitutional interpretation which is "lawyer's work" of "reading text and discerning our society's traditional understanding of that text." Is there such a dichotomy? Does it support Justice Scalia's position?

21. One of the most controversial aspects of the *Casey* plurality opinion is the so-called "sweet mystery of life" passage: "At the heart of liberty is the right to define one's own concept of existence, of meaning, of the universe, and of the mystery of human life. Beliefs about these matters could not define the attributes of personhood were they formed under compulsion of the State." Articulate substantive criticisms of the passage's claim; also criticize its breadth: what laws that restrict individual autonomy can stand in light of the passage?

22. In response to the dissenters' claim that substantive due process is inconsistent with the Constitution, the plurality pointed to the numerous, deeply entrenched, and widely respected precedents, such as *Loving v. Virginia*, that, it claimed, protected unenumerated constitutional rights. The plurality argued that the dissenters' approach would require overruling such decisions and therefore was an unattractive approach. Who had the better of the argument?

23. The plurality noted that the United States had argued before the Court in six cases since *Roe* that the Court should overrule *Roe*. Should that matter?

24. Justice O'Connor, for the plurality, stated that "[s]ome of us as individuals find abortion offensive to our most basic principles of morality, but that cannot control our decision." Is that true? Why?

25. The *Casey* plurality opinion is one of the rare situations where a non-majority opinion is the controlling opinion. How is that possible, since the opinion did not speak for a majority of the Court and hence, not the Court?

Following *Casey*, many states and the federal government introduced restrictions on abortion. These included waiting periods, informed consent requirements, parental notice and consent prescriptions, and regulations of abortion providers as medical professionals. One of the most popular post-*Casey* restrictions was a ban on partial-birth abortion. In *Stenberg v. Carhart*, 530 U.S. 914 (2000), the Supreme Court struck down Nebraska's ban on partial-birth abortion. The five-to-four majority opinion held that Nebraska's ban was unconstitutional because it lacked a life and health exception and because the ban's broad language applied to numerous types of abortion, not just partial-birth abortion, and hence constituted an undue burden under *Casey. Id.* at 930.

After *Stenberg*, the U.S. Congress passed and the President signed the federal Partial-Birth Abortion Ban Act of 2003, 117 Stat. 1201 (2003), *codified at* 18 U.S.C.A. § 1531. The Supreme Court evaluated the constitutionality of the Ban in *Gonzales v. Carhart*, 550 U.S. 124 (2007). The Act proscribed "partial-birth abortion," which is when a physician "deliberately and intentionally vaginally delivers a living fetus until, in the case of a head-first presentation, the entire fetal head is outside the body of the mother, or, in the case of breech presentation, any part of the fetal trunk past the navel is outside the body of the mother . . . and performs the overt act, other than completion of delivery, that kills the partially delivered living fetus." 18 U.S.C.A. § 1531(b)(1). The Act contained a narrow health exception that exempted abortions that are "necessary to save the life of a mother whose life is endangered by a physical disorder, physical illness, or physical injury." *Id.* § 1531(a).

Justice Kennedy, in an opinion notable for its graphic detail[59] and choice of language,[60] wrote for a five-justice majority[61] and upheld the Act. Adhering to *Casey*, the Court ruled that the Act did not have the purpose or effect of creating an "undue burden" on the right to abortion. *Gonzales*, 550 U.S. at 157–67. The Court found that the Act's purposes included expressing "respect for the dignity of human life" and protecting the integrity of the medical profession. *Id.* at 157–60. Then, the Court deferred to Congress' judgment that the Act did not have the effect of an undue burden because of the medical uncertainty surrounding whether, if ever, partial-birth abortion was necessary. *Id.* at 160–67.

There remains significant debate on whether *Gonzales* is consistent with *Casey*, much less *Carhart*, and whether *Gonzales* represents a possible change in the Court's approach to abortion regulations.

8.   Right to Sexual Autonomy

Griswold, Eisenstadt, and *Roe* all involved discrete facets of sexual autonomy. How broad is the substantive due process right to sexual autonomy? *Lawrence v. Texas*, 539 U.S. 558 (2003), expanded the right to include consensual homosexual sexual relations. *Lawrence*, however, was decided against the background of intense debate over the

---

[59] *See, e.g., Gonzales*, 550 U.S. at 139 (citation and internal quotations omitted) ("Dr. Haskell went in with forceps and grabbed the baby's legs and pulled them down into the birth canal. Then he delivered the baby's body and the arms — everything but the head. The doctor kept the head right inside the uterus. . . . The baby's little fingers were clasping and unclasping, and his little feet were kicking. Then the doctor stuck the scissors in the back of his head, and the baby's arms jerked out, like a startle reaction, like a flinch, like a baby does when he thinks he is going to fall. . . . The doctor opened up the scissors, stuck a high-powered suction tube into the opening, and sucked the baby's brains out. Now the baby went completely limp. . . . He cut the umbilical cord and delivered the placenta. He threw the baby in a pan, along with the placenta and the instruments he had just used.").

[60] *See, e.g., id.* at 159 ("Respect for human life finds an ultimate expression in the bond of love the mother has for her child.").

[61] Justice O'Connor retired and was replaced by Justice Alito in 2006.

scope of substantive due process generally and the place of homosexual sex within that doctrine in particular.

The first of what was to become a trilogy of cases culminating in *Lawrence* was *Bowers v. Hardwick*, 478 U.S. 186 (1986). Hardwick sued challenging the constitutionality of Georgia's sodomy statute. He argued that the statute violated the Due Process Clause, as interpreted by the Supreme Court in *Griswold*, *Eisenstadt*, *Roe*, and related substantive due process cases. *Id.* at 189. The *Bowers* Court first ruled that its precedent did not "confer a right of privacy that extends to homosexual sodomy," and that instead it protected discrete areas of liberty, such as the right to procreate. *Id.* at 190.

Second, the *Bowers* Court used both the history and tradition, and the *Palko* tests, to conclude that the Due Process Clause did not protect "a fundamental right to engage in homosexual sodomy." *Id.* at 192. Instead, Georgia's proscription of sodomy was a rational means of preserving the majority of Georgians' conclusion that homosexual sexual acts were immoral. *Id.* at 196.

Romer v. Evans, 517 U.S. 620 (1996), decided ten years later and discussed more fully in **Chapter 4**, marked a shift in the Supreme Court's jurisprudence. A number of local governments in Colorado had passed laws adding sexual orientation to their antidiscrimination laws' lists of protected classifications. *Id.* at 623–24. In response, voters in Colorado passed a state constitutional amendment that prohibited any political subdivision of the state from protecting sexual orientation in its antidiscrimination laws. *Id.* at 624.

The *Romer* Court ruled that the challenged Colorado constitutional amendment violated the Equal Protection Clause because it was irrational. *Id.* at 632. The law was irrational both because its purpose was "a bare . . . desire to harm a politically unpopular group," *id.* at 634–35 (internal quotations omitted), and because it restricted more activity than was necessary to achieve any legitimate state interests. *Id.* at 631–34.

Oddly, the *Romer* majority did not distinguish *Bowers*, which seemed to support Colorado. *See id.* at 640–43 (Scalia, J., dissenting) (questioning why the *Romer* Court did not address *Bowers*). This gap was explained in *Lawrence v. Texas*, reprinted below.

LAWRENCE v. TEXAS
539 U.S. 558 (2003)

Justice Kennedy delivered the opinion of the Court.

I

The question before the Court is the validity of a Texas statute making it a crime for two persons of the same sex to engage in certain intimate sexual conduct.

In Houston, Texas, officers of the Harris County Police Department were dispatched to a private residence in response to a reported weapons disturbance. They entered an apartment where one of the petitioners, John Geddes Lawrence, resided. The officers observed Lawrence and another man engaging in a sexual act. The two petitioners were arrested, held in custody overnight, and charged and convicted before a Justice of the Peace.

The complaints described their crime as "deviate sexual intercourse, namely anal sex, with a member of the same sex (man)." The applicable state law is Tex. Penal Code Ann. § 21.06(a) (2003).

The petitioners challenged the statute as a violation of the Equal Protection Clause of the Fourteenth Amendment. Those contentions were rejected.

The Court of Appeals for the Texas Fourteenth District considered the petitioners' federal constitutional arguments under both the Equal Protection and Due Process Clauses of the Fourteenth Amendment. [T]he court rejected the constitutional arguments and affirmed the convictions. The majority opinion indicates that the Court of Appeals considered our decision in *Bowers v. Hardwick*, 478 U.S. 186 (1986), to be controlling on the federal due process aspect of the case.

The petitioners were adults at the time of the alleged offense. Their conduct was private and consensual.

II

We conclude the case should be resolved by determining whether the petitioners were free as adults to engage in the private conduct in the exercise of their liberty under the Due Process Clause of the Fourteenth Amendment to the Constitution. For this inquiry we deem it necessary to reconsider the Court's holding in *Bowers*.

There are broad statements of the substantive reach of liberty under the Due Process Clause in earlier cases, including *Pierce v. Society of Sisters*, 268 U.S. 510 (1925), and *Meyer v. Nebraska*, 262 U.S. 390 (1923); but the most pertinent beginning point is our decision in *Griswold v. Connecticut*, 381 U.S. 479 (1965). In *Griswold* the Court described the protected interest as a right to privacy and placed emphasis on the marriage relation and the protected space of the marital bedroom. In *Eisenstadt v. Baird*, 405 U.S. 438 (1972), the Court invalidated a law prohibiting the distribution of contraceptives to unmarried persons. The opinions in *Griswold* and *Eisenstadt* were part of the background for the decision in *Roe v. Wade*, 410 U.S. 113 (1973). *Roe* recognized the right of a woman to make certain fundamental decisions affecting her destiny.

This was the state of the law with respect to some of the most relevant cases when the Court considered *Bowers v. Hardwick*. The Court began its substantive discussion in *Bowers* as follows: "The issue presented is whether the Federal Constitution confers a fundamental right upon homosexuals to engage in sodomy and hence invalidates the laws of the many States that still make such conduct illegal and have done so for a very long time." That statement, we now conclude, discloses the Court's own failure to appreciate the extent of the liberty at stake. To say that the issue in *Bowers* was simply the right to engage in certain sexual conduct demeans the claim the individual put forward, just as it would demean a married couple were it to be said marriage is simply about the right to have sexual intercourse. The laws involved in *Bowers* and here are, to be sure, statutes that purport to do no more than prohibit a particular sexual act. Their penalties and purposes, though, have more far-reaching consequences, touching upon the most private human conduct, sexual behavior, and in the most private of places, the home. The statutes do seek to control a personal relationship that, whether or not entitled to formal recognition in the law, is within the liberty of persons to choose without being punished as criminals.

It suffices for us to acknowledge that adults may choose to enter upon this relationship in the confines of their homes and their own private lives and still retain their dignity as free persons. When sexuality finds overt expression in intimate conduct with another person, the conduct can be but one element in a personal bond that is more enduring. The liberty protected by the Constitution allows homosexual persons the right to make this choice.

Having misapprehended the claim of liberty there presented to it, the *Bowers* Court said: "Proscriptions against that conduct have ancient roots." In academic writings, and in many of the scholarly *amicus* briefs filed to assist the Court in this case, there are fundamental criticisms of the historical premises relied upon by the majority and concurring opinions in *Bowers*. We need not enter this debate in the attempt to reach a definitive historical judgment, but the following considerations counsel against adopting the definitive conclusions upon which *Bowers* placed such reliance.

At the outset it should be noted that there is no longstanding history in this country of laws directed at homosexual conduct as a distinct matter. Beginning in colonial times there were prohibitions of sodomy derived from the English criminal laws passed in the first instance by the Reformation Parliament of 1533. The English prohibition was understood to include relations between men and women as well as relations between men and men. See, *e.g., King v. Wiseman,* 92 Eng. Rep. 774, 775 (K.B.1718) (interpreting "mankind" in Act of 1533 as including women and girls). Nineteenth-century commentators similarly read American sodomy, buggery, and crime-against-nature statutes as criminalizing certain relations between men and women and between men and men. See, *e.g.,* 2 J[oel Prentiss] Bishop, Criminal Law § 1028 (1858); 2 J[oseph] Chitty, Criminal Law 47–50 (5th Am. ed. 1847). Thus early American sodomy laws were not directed at homosexuals as such but instead sought to prohibit nonprocreative sexual activity more generally. This does not suggest approval of homosexual conduct.

Laws prohibiting sodomy do not seem to have been enforced against consenting adults acting in private. A substantial number of sodomy prosecutions and convictions for which there are surviving records were for predatory acts against those who could not or did not consent, as in the case of a minor or the victim of an assault. As to these, one purpose for the prohibitions was to ensure there would be no lack of coverage if a predator committed a sexual assault that did not constitute rape as defined by the criminal law. In all events that infrequency makes it difficult to say that society approved of a rigorous and systematic punishment of the consensual acts committed in private and by adults. The longstanding criminal prohibition of homosexual sodomy upon which the *Bowers* decision placed such reliance is as consistent with a general condemnation of nonprocreative sex as it is with an established tradition of prosecuting acts because of their homosexual character.

Despite the absence of prosecutions, there may have been periods in which there was public criticism of homosexuals as such and an insistence that the criminal laws be enforced to discourage their practices. But far from possessing "ancient roots," American laws targeting same-sex couples did not develop until the last third of the 20th century. It was not until the 1970's that any State singled out same-sex relations for criminal prosecution, and only nine States have done so. Over the course of the last decades, States with same-sex prohibitions have moved toward abolishing them.

In summary, the historical grounds relied upon in *Bowers* are more complex than the majority opinion and the concurring opinion by Chief Justice Burger indicate. Their historical premises are not without doubt and, at the very least, are overstated.

It must be acknowledged, of course, that the Court in *Bowers* was making the broader point that for centuries there have been powerful voices to condemn homosexual conduct as immoral. The condemnation has been shaped by religious beliefs, conceptions of right and acceptable behavior, and respect for the traditional family. These considerations do not answer the question before us, however. The issue is whether the majority may use the power of the State to enforce these views on the whole society through operation of the criminal law. "Our obligation is to define the liberty of all, not to mandate our own moral code." *Planned Parenthood of Southeastern Pa. v. Casey*, 505 U.S. 833, 850 (1992).

In all events we think that our laws and traditions in the past half century are of most relevance here. These references show an emerging awareness that liberty gives substantial protection to adult persons in deciding how to conduct their private lives in matters pertaining to sex. "[H]istory and tradition are the starting point but not in all cases the ending point of the substantive due process inquiry." *County of Sacramento v. Lewis*, 523 U.S. 833, 857 (1998) (KENNEDY, J., concurring).

This emerging recognition should have been apparent when *Bowers* was decided. In 1955 the American Law Institute promulgated the Model Penal Code and made clear that it did not recommend or provide for "criminal penalties for consensual sexual relations conducted in private." ALI, Model Penal Code § 213.2, Comment 2, p. 372 (1980). In 1961 Illinois changed its laws to conform to the Model Penal Code. Other States soon followed.

The sweeping references [in] Chief Justice Burger['s concurrence] to the history of Western civilization and to Judeo-Christian moral and ethical standards did not take account of other authorities pointing in an opposite direction. A committee advising the British Parliament recommended in 1957 repeal of laws punishing homosexual conduct. The Wolfenden Report: Report of the Committee on Homosexual Offenses and Prostitution (1963). Parliament enacted the substance of those recommendations 10 years later. Of even more importance, almost five years before *Bowers* was decided the European Court of Human Rights considered a case with parallels to *Bowers* and to today's case. The court held that the laws proscribing the conduct were invalid under the European Convention on Human Rights. *Dudgeon v. United Kingdom*, 45 Eur. Ct. H.R. (1981) & ¶ 52.

In our own constitutional system the deficiencies in *Bowers* became even more apparent in the years following its announcement. The 25 States with laws prohibiting the relevant conduct referenced in the *Bowers* decision are reduced now to 13, of which 4 enforce their laws only against homosexual conduct. In those States where sodomy is still proscribed, whether for same-sex or heterosexual conduct, there is a pattern of nonenforcement with respect to consenting adults acting in private.

Two principal cases decided after *Bowers* cast its holding into even more doubt. In *Planned Parenthood of Southeastern Pa. v. Casey*, 505 U.S. 833 (1992), the [Court] again confirmed that our laws and tradition afford constitutional protection to personal decisions relating to marriage, procreation, contraception, family relationships, child rearing, and education. In explaining the respect the Constitution demands for the autonomy of the person in making these choices, we stated as follows: "At the heart of liberty is the right to define one's own concept of existence, of meaning, of the universe, and of the mystery of human life. Beliefs about these matters could not define the attributes of personhood were they formed under compulsion of the State." Persons in a homosexual relationship may seek autonomy for these purposes, just as heterosexual persons do. The decision in *Bowers* would deny them this right.

The second post-*Bowers* case of principal relevance is *Romer v. Evans*, 517 U.S. 620 (1996). We concluded that the [challenged] provision was "born of animosity toward the class of persons affected" and further that it had no rational relation to a legitimate governmental purpose.

As an alternative argument in this case, counsel for the petitioners and some *amici* contend that *Romer* provides the basis for declaring the Texas statute invalid under the Equal Protection Clause. That is a tenable argument, but we conclude the instant case requires us to address whether *Bowers* itself has continuing validity. Were we to hold the statute invalid under the Equal Protection Clause some might question whether a prohibition would be valid if drawn differently, say, to prohibit the conduct both between same-sex and different-sex participants.

If protected conduct is made criminal and the law which does so remains unexamined for its substantive validity, its stigma might remain even if it were not enforceable as drawn for equal protection reasons. When homosexual conduct is made criminal by the law of the State, that declaration in and of itself is an invitation to subject homosexual persons to discrimination both in the public and in the private spheres. The central holding of *Bowers* has been brought in question by this case, and it should be addressed. Its continuance as precedent demeans the lives of homosexual persons.

The foundations of *Bowers* have sustained serious erosion from our recent decisions in *Casey* and *Romer.* When our precedent has been thus weakened, criticism from other sources is of greater significance. In the United States criticism of *Bowers* has been substantial and continuing, disapproving of its reasoning in all respects, not just as to its historical assumptions. See, *e.g.*, C[harles] Fried, Order and Law: Arguing the Reagan Revolution — A Firsthand Account 81–84 (1991); R[ichard] Posner, Sex and Reason 341–350 (1992). The courts of five different States have declined to follow it in interpreting provisions in their own state constitutions parallel to the Due Process Clause of the Fourteenth Amendment. To the extent *Bowers* relied on values we share with a wider civilization, it should be noted that the reasoning and holding in *Bowers* have been rejected elsewhere. The European Court of Human Rights has not followed *Bowers*.

The doctrine of *stare decisis* is essential to the respect accorded to the judgments of the Court and to the stability of the law. It is not, however, an inexorable command. In *Casey* we noted that when a court is asked to overrule a precedent recognizing a constitutional liberty interest, individual or societal reliance on the existence of that liberty cautions with particular strength against reversing course. The holding in *Bowers*, however, has not induced detrimental reliance comparable to some instances where recognized individual rights are involved. *Bowers* itself causes uncertainty, for the precedents before and after its issuance contradict its central holding.

Bowers was not correct when it was decided, and it is not correct today. It ought not to remain binding precedent. *Bowers v. Hardwick* should be and now is overruled.

The present case does not involve minors. It does not involve persons who might be injured or coerced or who are situated in relationships where consent might not easily be refused. It does not involve public conduct or prostitution. It does not involve whether the government must give formal recognition to any relationship that homosexual persons seek to enter. The case does involve two adults who, with full and mutual consent from each other, engaged in sexual practices common to a homosexual lifestyle. The petitioners are entitled to respect for their private lives. The State cannot demean their existence or control their destiny by making their private sexual conduct a crime. The Texas statute furthers no legitimate state interest which can justify its intrusion into the personal and private life of the individual.

Had those who drew and ratified the Due Process Clauses of the Fifth Amendment or the Fourteenth Amendment known the components of liberty in its manifold possibilities, they might have been more specific. They did not presume to have this insight. They knew times can blind us to certain truths and later generations can see that laws once thought necessary and proper in fact serve only to oppress. As the Constitution endures, persons in every generation can invoke its principles in their own search for greater freedom.

The judgment of the Court of Appeals for the Texas Fourteenth District is reversed, and the case is remanded for further proceedings not inconsistent with this opinion.

It is so ordered.

Justice O'CONNOR, concurring in the judgment.

The Court today overrules *Bowers v. Hardwick*, 478 U.S. 186 (1986). I joined *Bowers*, and do not join the Court in overruling it. Nevertheless, I agree with the Court that Texas' statute banning same-sex sodomy is unconstitutional. Rather than relying on the substantive component of the Fourteenth Amendment's Due Process Clause, as the Court does, I base my conclusion on the Fourteenth Amendment's Equal Protection Clause.

This case raises a different issue than *Bowers:* whether, under the Equal Protection Clause, moral disapproval is a legitimate state interest to justify by itself a statute that bans homosexual sodomy, but not heterosexual sodomy. It is not. Moral disapproval of this group, like a bare desire to harm the group, is an interest that is insufficient to satisfy rational basis review under the Equal Protection Clause. See, *e.g., Department of Agriculture v. Moreno*, 413 U.S. [528], 534 [(1973)]; *Romer v. Evans*, 517 U.S. [620], 634–635 [(1996)].

That this law as applied to private, consensual conduct is unconstitutional under the Equal Protection Clause does not mean that other laws distinguishing between heterosexuals and homosexuals would similarly fail under rational basis review. Texas cannot assert any legitimate state interest here, such as national security or preserving the traditional institution of marriage. Unlike the moral disapproval of same-sex relations — the asserted state interest in this case — other reasons exist to promote the institution of marriage beyond mere moral disapproval of an excluded group.

JUSTICE SCALIA, with whom THE CHIEF JUSTICE and JUSTICE THOMAS join, dissenting.

I

I begin with the Court's surprising readiness to reconsider a decision rendered a mere 17 years ago in *Bowers v. Hardwick*[, 478 U.S. 186 (1986)]. I do not myself believe in rigid adherence to *stare decisis* in constitutional cases; but I do believe that we should be consistent rather than manipulative in invoking the doctrine. Today's opinions in support of reversal do not bother to distinguish — or indeed, even bother to mention — the paean to *stare decisis* coauthored by three Members of today's majority in *Planned Parenthood v. Casey*[, 505 U.S. 833, 844 (1992)]. There, when *stare decisis* meant preservation of judicially invented abortion rights, the widespread criticism of *Roe* [*v. Wade*, 410 U.S. 113 (1973),] was strong reason to *reaffirm* it. Today, however, the widespread opposition to *Bowers*, is offered as a reason in favor of *overruling* it.

Today's approach to *stare decisis* invites us to overrule an erroneously decided precedent *if*: (1) its foundations have been "ero[ded]" by subsequent decisions; (2) it has been subject to "substantial and continuing" criticism; and (3) it has not induced "individual or societal reliance" that counsels against overturning. The problem is that *Roe* itself — which today's majority surely has no disposition to overrule — satisfies these conditions to at least the same degree as *Bowers*.

(1) I do not quarrel with the Court's claim that *Romer v. Evans*, 517 U.S. 620 (1996), "eroded" the "foundations" of *Bowers*' rational-basis holding. But *Roe* and *Casey* have been equally "eroded" by *Washington v. Glucksberg*, 521 U.S. 702, 721 (1997), which held that *only* fundamental rights which are " 'deeply rooted in this Nation's history and tradition' " qualify for anything other than rational-basis scrutiny under the doctrine of "substantive due process." *Roe* and *Casey*, of course, subjected the restriction of abortion to heightened scrutiny without even attempting to establish that the freedom to abort *was* rooted in this Nation's tradition.

(2) *Bowers*, the Court says, has been subject to "substantial and continuing [criticism], disapproving of its reasoning in all respects, not just as to its historical

assumptions." Exactly what those nonhistorical criticisms are, and whether the Court even agrees with them, are left unsaid, although the Court does cite two books. Of course, *Roe* too (and by extension *Casey*) had been (and still is) subject to unrelenting criticism, including criticism from the two commentators cited by the Court today. See Fried, *supra*, at 75 ("*Roe* was a prime example of twisted judging"); Posner, *supra*, at 337 ("[The Court's] opinion in *Roe* fails to measure up to professional expectations regarding judicial opinions").

(3) That leaves, to distinguish the rock-solid, unamendable disposition of *Roe* from the readily overrulable *Bowers*, only the third factor. "[T]here has been," the Court says, "no individual or societal reliance on *Bowers* of the sort that could counsel against overturning its holding . . ." It seems to me that the "societal reliance" on the principles confirmed in *Bowers* and discarded today has been overwhelming. Countless judicial decisions and legislative enactments have relied on the ancient proposition that a governing majority's belief that certain sexual behavior is "immoral and unaccept-able" constitutes a rational basis for regulation. State laws against bigamy, same-sex marriage, adult incest, prostitution, masturbation, adultery, fornication, bestiality, and obscenity are likewise sustainable only in light of *Bowers'* validation of laws based on moral choices. The impossibility of distinguishing homosexuality from other traditional "morals" offenses is precisely why *Bowers* rejected the rational-basis challenge.

What a massive disruption of the current social order, therefore, the overruling of *Bowers* entails. Not so the overruling of *Roe*, which would simply have restored the regime that existed for centuries before 1973, in which the permissibility of, and restrictions upon, abortion were determined legislatively State by State.

To tell the truth, it does not surprise me, and should surprise no one, that the Court has chosen today to revise the standards of *stare decisis* set forth in *Casey*. It has thereby exposed *Casey's* extraordinary deference to precedent for the result-oriented expedient that it is.

II

Having decided that it need not adhere to *stare decisis*, the Court still must establish that *Bowers* was wrongly decided and that the Texas statute is unconstitu-tional.

Texas Penal Code Ann. § 21.06(a) (2003) undoubtedly imposes constraints on liberty. So do laws prohibiting prostitution, recreational use of heroin, and, for that matter, working more than 60 hours per week in a bakery. But there is no right to "liberty" under the Due Process Clause, though today's opinion repeatedly makes that claim. The Fourteenth Amendment *expressly allows* States to deprive their citizens of "liberty," *so long as "due process of law" is provided.*

Our opinions applying the doctrine known as "substantive due process" hold that the Due Process Clause prohibits States from infringing *fundamental* liberty inter-ests, unless the infringement is narrowly tailored to serve a compelling state interest. *Washington v. Glucksberg*, 521 U.S., at 721. We have held repeatedly, in cases the Court today does not overrule, that *only* fundamental rights qualify for this so-called "heightened scrutiny" protection — that is, rights which are " 'deeply rooted in this

Nation's history and tradition.' " *Ibid.* See also *Michael H. v. Gerald D.*, 491 U.S. 110, 122 (1989) ("[W]e have insisted not merely that the interest denominated as a 'liberty' be 'fundamental' . . . but also that it be an interest traditionally protected by our society"); *Moore v. East Cleveland*, 431 U.S. 494, 503 (1977); *Meyer v. Nebraska*, 262 U.S. 390, 399 (1923) (Fourteenth Amendment protects "those privileges *long recognized at common law* as essential to the orderly pursuit of happiness by free men"). All other liberty interests may be abridged or abrogated pursuant to a validly enacted state law if that law is rationally related to a legitimate state interest.

Bowers held, first, that criminal prohibitions of homosexual sodomy are not subject to heightened scrutiny because they do not implicate a "fundamental right" under the Due Process Clause. The Court today does not overrule this holding. Not once does it describe homosexual sodomy as a "fundamental right," nor does it subject the Texas statute to strict scrutiny. Instead, the Court concludes that the application of Texas's statute to petitioners' conduct fails the rational-basis test, and overrules *Bowers'* holding to the contrary.

I shall address that rational-basis holding presently. First, however, I address some aspersions that the Court casts upon *Bowers'* conclusion that homosexual sodomy is not a "fundamental right."

III

After discussing the history of antisodomy laws, the Court proclaims that, "it should be noted that there is no longstanding history in this country of laws directed at homosexual conduct as a distinct matter." This observation in no way casts into doubt the "definitive [historical] conclusio[n]," on which *Bowers* relied: that our Nation has a longstanding history of laws prohibiting *sodomy in general* — regardless of whether it was performed by same-sex or opposite-sex couples:

> "Proscriptions against that conduct have ancient roots. *Sodomy* was a criminal offense at common law and was forbidden by the laws of the original 13 States when they ratified the Bill of Rights. In 1868, when the Fourteenth Amendment was ratified, all but 5 of the 37 States in the Union had *criminal sodomy laws*. In fact, until 1961, all 50 States outlawed *sodomy*, and today, 24 States and the District of Columbia continue to provide criminal penalties for *sodomy* performed in private and between consenting adults."

Whether homosexual sodomy was prohibited by a law targeted at same-sex sexual relations or by a more general law prohibiting both homosexual and heterosexual sodomy, the only relevant point is that it *was* criminalized — which suffices to establish that homosexual sodomy is not a right "deeply rooted in our Nation's history and tradition."

Next the Court makes the claim, again unsupported by any citations, that "[l]aws prohibiting sodomy do not seem to have been enforced against consenting adults acting in private." The key qualifier here is "acting in private" — since the Court admits that sodomy laws *were* enforced against consenting adults. There are 203 prosecutions for consensual, adult homosexual sodomy reported in the West Reporting system and official state reporters from the years 1880–1995. See W. Eskridge,

Gaylaw: Challenging the Apartheid of the Closet 375 (1999). *Bowers'* conclusion that homosexual sodomy is not a fundamental right "deeply rooted in this Nation's history and tradition" is utterly unassailable.

Realizing that fact, the Court instead says: "[W]e think that our laws and traditions in the past half century are of most relevance here. These references show *an emerging awareness* that liberty gives substantial protection to adult persons in deciding how to conduct their private lives *in matters pertaining to sex.*" Apart from the fact that such an "emerging awareness" does not establish a "fundamental right," the statement is factually false. States continue to prosecute all sorts of crimes by adults "in matters pertaining to sex": prostitution, adult incest, adultery, obscenity, and child pornography. Sodomy laws, too, have been enforced "in the past half century," in which there have been 134 reported cases involving prosecutions for consensual, adult, homosexual sodomy.

In any event, an "emerging awareness" is by definition not "deeply rooted in this Nation's history and tradition[s]." Constitutional entitlements do not spring into existence because some States choose to lessen or eliminate criminal sanctions on certain behavior. Much less do they spring into existence, as the Court seems to believe, because *foreign nations* decriminalize conduct. The *Bowers* majority opinion rejected the claimed right to sodomy on the ground that such a right was not " 'deeply rooted in *this Nation's* history and tradition.' " The Court's discussion of these foreign views (ignoring, of course, the many countries that have retained criminal prohibitions on sodomy) is therefore meaningless dicta.

IV

I turn now to the ground on which the Court squarely rests its holding: the contention that there is no rational basis for the law here under attack. This proposition is so out of accord with our jurisprudence — indeed, with the jurisprudence of *any* society we know — that it requires little discussion.

The Texas statute undeniably seeks to further the belief of its citizens that certain forms of sexual behavior are "immoral and unacceptable," — the same interest furthered by criminal laws against fornication, bigamy, adultery, adult incest, bestiality, and obscenity. *Bowers* held that this *was* a legitimate state interest. The Court today reaches the opposite conclusion. This effectively decrees the end of all morals legislation. If, as the Court asserts, the promotion of majoritarian sexual morality is not even a *legitimate* state interest, none of the above-mentioned laws can survive rational-basis review.

V

Finally, I turn to petitioners' equal-protection challenge. This reasoning leaves on pretty shaky grounds state laws limiting marriage to opposite-sex couples. Justice O'Connor seeks to preserve them by the conclusory statement that "preserving the traditional institution of marriage" is a legitimate state interest. But "preserving the traditional institution of marriage" is just a kinder way of describing the State's *moral disapproval* of same-sex couples. Texas's interest in § 21.06 could be recast in similarly euphemistic terms: "preserving the traditional sexual mores of our society."

* * *

Today's opinion is the product of a Court, which is the product of a law-profession culture, that has largely signed on to the so-called homosexual agenda, by which I mean the agenda promoted by some homosexual activists directed at eliminating the moral opprobrium that has traditionally attached to homosexual conduct.

One of the most revealing statements in today's opinion is the Court's grim warning that the criminalization of homosexual conduct is "an invitation to subject homosexual persons to discrimination both in the public and in the private spheres." It is clear from this that the Court has taken sides in the culture war, departing from its role of assuring, as neutral observer, that the democratic rules of engagement are observed. Many Americans do not want persons who openly engage in homosexual conduct as partners in their business, as scoutmasters for their children, as teachers in their children's schools, or as boarders in their home. They view this as protecting themselves and their families from a lifestyle that they believe to be immoral and destructive. The Court views it as "discrimination." So imbued is the Court with the law profession's anti-anti-homosexual culture, that it is seemingly unaware that the attitudes of that culture are not obviously "mainstream"; that in most States what the Court calls "discrimination" against those who engage in homosexual acts is perfectly legal; that proposals to ban such "discrimination" under Title VII have repeatedly been rejected by Congress, see Employment Non-Discrimination Act of 1994, S. 2238, 103d Cong., 2d Sess. (1994); Civil Rights Amendments, H.R. 5452, 94th Cong., 1st Sess. (1975); that in some cases such "discrimination" is *mandated* by federal statute, see 10 U.S.C. § 654(b)(1) (mandating discharge from the Armed Forces of any service member who engages in or intends to engage in homosexual acts); and that in some cases such "discrimination" is a constitutional right, see *Boy Scouts of America v. Dale*, 530 U.S. 640 (2000).

Let me be clear that I have nothing against homosexuals, or any other group, promoting their agenda through normal democratic means. Social perceptions of sexual and other morality change over time, and every group has the right to persuade its fellow citizens that its view of such matters is the best. But persuading one's fellow citizens is one thing, and imposing one's views in absence of democratic majority will is something else. What Texas has chosen to do is well within the range of traditional democratic action, and its hand should not be stayed through the invention of a brand-new "constitutional right" by a Court that is impatient of democratic change. It is indeed true that "later generations can see that laws once thought necessary and proper in fact serve only to oppress"; and when that happens, later generations can repeal those laws. But it is the premise of our system that those judgments are to be made by the people, and not imposed by a governing caste that knows best.

One of the benefits of leaving regulation of this matter to the people rather than to the courts is that the people, unlike judges, need not carry things to their logical conclusion. The people may feel that their disapprobation of homosexual conduct is strong enough to disallow homosexual marriage, but not strong enough to criminalize private homosexual acts — and may legislate accordingly. The Court today pretends that it possesses a similar freedom of action, so that we need not fear judicial imposition of homosexual marriage, as has recently occurred in Canada. See *Halpern v. Toronto*, 65 O.R. (3d) 161, 2003 Ont. Rep. LEXIS 153 (Ontario Ct. App.). At the end of its opinion — after having laid waste the foundations of our rational-basis jurisprudence — the Court says that the present case "does not involve whether the government must give formal recognition to any relationship that homosexual persons seek to enter." Do not believe it. Today's opinion dismantles the structure of constitutional law that has permitted a distinction to be made between heterosexual and homosexual unions, insofar as formal recognition in marriage is concerned. If moral disapprobation of homosexual conduct is "no legitimate state interest" for purposes of proscribing that conduct; and if, as the Court coos (casting aside all pretense of neutrality), "[w]hen sexuality finds overt expression in intimate conduct with another person, the conduct can be but one element in a personal bond that is more enduring"; what justification could there possibly be for denying the benefits of marriage to homosexual couples exercising "[t]he liberty protected by the Constitution"? This case "does not involve" the issue of homosexual marriage only if one entertains the belief that principle and logic have nothing to do with the decisions of this Court. Many will hope that, as the Court comfortingly assures us, this is so.

I dissent.

JUSTICE THOMAS, dissenting. [Opinion omitted.]

EXERCISE 16:

1.   What standard of review did the *Lawrence* Court employ? Strict scrutiny or rational basis? Why did it use that standard?

2.   Why did the challenged Texas law violate the Constitution?

3.   One of Justice Kennedy's arguments was that, historically, prohibitions on sodomy were part of broader prohibitions on nonprocreative sex. Therefore, there was no particular tradition against homosexual sex as *Bowers* indicated. Construct a rebuttal argument.

4.   Relatedly, the history of legal prohibitions on sodomy has been subject to substantial scholarly debate. Two prominent scholarly perspectives are represented by William N. Eskridge, Jr., *A History of Same-Sex Marriage*, 79 VA. L. REV. 1419 (1993) (arguing that same-sex marriage and relationships were relatively widespread across time and cultures), and Peter Lubin & Dwight Duncan, *Follow the Footnote or the Advocate as Historian of Same-Sex Marriage*, 47 CATH. U. L. REV. 1271 (1998) (critiquing Professor Eskridge's historical account).

5.   The Court placed special emphasis on "our laws and traditions in the past half century." Why? How does that fit, if at all, substantive due process analysis?

6.   The *Lawrence* Court and Justice O'Conner's concurrence stated that a majority in a state may not "use the power of the State to enforce [its moral] views on the whole society through operation of the criminal law." Flesh-out that argument. How did Justice Scalia respond in dissent? Who had the better of the argument?

7.   The Supreme Court overruled *Bowers v. Hardwick*. What reasons did it give for

not following stare decisis? Were those reasons sufficient?

8.   Do you agree with Justice Scalia's argument that the majority manipulated the *Casey* stare decisis factors to overrule *Bowers* even though it refused to overrule *Roe*?

9.   Justice Kennedy, writing for the Supreme Court, relied on the recent legal developments in other countries. For example, he referenced the European Court of Human Rights' handling of a similar case. Is that a proper source to rely upon when interpreting the Constitution of the United States? Does your answer depend on the method of constitutional interpretation?

10.   What does *Lawrence* indicate regarding the analysis that the Supreme Court will utilize to determine the scope of substantive due process? In other words, will *Casey* or *Glucksburg* control?

11.   Justice Scalia argued (in a portion of his dissent not reprinted above) that *Lawrence*'s reasoning was a threat to the Rule of Law. He suggested that if the *Casey* "sweet-mystery-of-life passage" "calls into question the government's power to regulate *actions based on* one's self-defined 'concept of existence, etc.,' it is the passage that ate the rule of law." Do you agree? What limits are there to *Lawrence*?

12.   Relatedly, both the majority opinion and Justice O'Connor's concurrence suggested that *Lawrence* did not include a constitutional right to homosexual marriage, while Justice Scalia, in dissent, argued to the contrary. Who had the better of the argument? If one is faithful to *Lawrence*, does that mean there is a constitutional right to homosexual marriage? To polygamy?

13.   Relatedly, after *Lawrence*, there was and remains significant uncertainty on the scope of the right articulated, and lower courts have struggled to determine what other limits on sexual autonomy violate that right. States and the federal government have numerous laws that restrict sexual autonomy in one way or another, such as laws against prostitution, and one could plausibly construe both statements — "substantial protection to adult persons in deciding how to conduct their private lives in matters pertaining to sex" — and the reasoning — "whether the majority may use the power of the State to enforce these views on the whole society through operation of the criminal law" — in *Lawrence* to cast doubt on the constitutionality of such restrictions. *See* Audrey K. Hagedorn, *"Don't Ask, Don't Tell,"* the Supreme Court, *and* Lawrence the *"Laggard,"* 87 IND. L.J. 795, 805–10 (2012) ("Generally courts have erred on the conservative side and held that *Lawrence* does not recognize a fundamental right to private sexual intimacy."). What is the scope of the constitutionally protected right to sexual autonomy after *Lawrence*? Does *Lawrence* spell the end of "morals legislation" as Justice Scalia charged?

14.   Justice Scalia accused the *Lawrence* majority of having "taken sides in the culture war" by imposing its "law-profession" culture on the rest of the country. Are those charges true? What is the evidence? If it is true, so what?

9. Right to Assisted Suicide

One of the most intense public policy debates during the late-1980s and 1990s focused on the ethical and legal facets of euthanasia. As with other hot-button subjects such as abortion, advocates pursued a multi-pronged strategy to broaden access to euthanasia, including legal and political avenues.

In the legal realm, the first major Supreme Court pronouncement was *Cruzan v. Director, Mo. Dep't of Health*, 497 U.S. 261 (1990). There, the Supreme Court ruled that the Due Process Clause protected a right to refuse unwanted medical treatment. *Id.* at 279. Proponents of widespread euthanasia sought to leverage *Cruzan* into a broader substantive due process right to assisted suicide. The Court addressed that claim below.

WASHINGTON v. GLUCKSBERG
521 U.S. 702 (1997)

Chief Justice Rehnquist delivered the opinion of the Court.

The question presented in this case is whether Washington's prohibition against "caus[ing]" or "aid[ing]" a suicide offends the Fourteenth Amendment to the United States Constitution. We hold that it does not.

It has always been a crime to assist a suicide in the State of Washington. In 1854, Washington's first Territorial Legislature outlawed "assisting another in the commission of self-murder." Today, Washington law provides: "A person is guilty of promoting a suicide attempt when he knowingly causes or aids another person to attempt suicide." Wash. Rev. Code § 9A.36.060(1) (1994). "Promoting a suicide attempt" is a felony.

Petitioners in this case are the State of Washington and its Attorney General. Respondents are physicians who practice in Washington. These doctors occasionally treat terminally ill, suffering patients, and declare that they would assist these patients in ending their lives if not for Washington's assisted-suicide ban. In January 1994, respondents, along with three gravely ill, pseudonymous plaintiffs who have since died, sued in the United States District Court, seeking a declaration that Wash. Rev. Code § 9A.36.060(1) (1994) is, on its face, unconstitutional.

The plaintiffs asserted "the existence of a liberty interest protected by the Fourteenth Amendment which extends to a personal choice by a mentally competent, terminally ill adult to commit physician-assisted suicide." Relying primarily on *Planned Parenthood of Southeastern Pa. v. Casey*, 505 U.S. 833 (1992), and *Cruzan v. Director, Mo. Dept. of Health*, 497 U.S. 261 (1990), the District Court agreed and concluded that Washington's assisted-suicide ban is unconstitutional. A panel of the Court of Appeals for the Ninth Circuit reversed. The Ninth Circuit reheard the case en banc, reversed the panel's decision, and affirmed the District Court. Like the District Court, the en banc Court of Appeals emphasized our *Casey* and *Cruzan* decisions. We now reverse.[7]

We begin, as we do in all due process cases, by examining our Nation's history, legal traditions, and practices. See, e.g., *Casey*, at 849–850; *Moore v. East Cleveland*, 431 U.S. 494, 503 (1977) (noting importance of "careful 'respect for the teachings of history' "). In almost every State-indeed, in almost every western democracy-it is a crime to assist a suicide. The States' assisted-suicide bans are not innovations. Rather, they are longstanding expressions of the States' commitment to the protection and preservation of all human life.

More specifically, for over 700 years, the Anglo-American common-law tradition has punished or otherwise disapproved of both suicide and assisting suicide. In the 13th century, Henry de Bracton observed that "[j]ust as a man may commit felony by slaying another so may he do so by slaying himself." 2 Bracton on Laws and Customs of England 423 (f.150) (G. Woodbine ed., S. Thorne transl., 1968). Centuries later, Sir William Blackstone, whose Commentaries on the Laws of England not only provided a definitive summary of the common law but was also a primary legal authority for 18th- and 19th-century American lawyers, referred to suicide as "self-murder." 4 W[illiam] Blackstone, Commentaries *189.

For the most part, the early American Colonies adopted the common-law approach. For example, the legislators of Rhode Island declared, in 1647, that "[s]elf-murder is by all agreed to be the most unnatural, and it is by this present Assembly declared, to be that, wherein he that doth it, kills himself out of a premeditated hatred against his own life or other humor: . . . his goods and chattels are the king's custom; but in case he be an infant, a lunatic, mad or distracted man, he forfeits nothing."

Over time, however, the American Colonies abolished these harsh common-law penalties. William Penn abandoned the criminal-forfeiture sanction in Pennsylvania in 1701, and the other Colonies (and later, the other States) eventually followed this example. [T]he movement away from the common law's harsh sanctions did not represent an acceptance of suicide; rather, this change reflected the growing consensus that it was unfair to punish the suicide's family for his wrongdoing. Nonetheless, although States moved away from Blackstone's treatment of suicide, courts continued to condemn it as a grave public wrong.

That suicide remained a grievous, though nonfelonious, wrong is confirmed by the fact that colonial and early state legislatures and courts did not retreat from prohibiting assisting suicide. This was the well-established common-law view. And the prohibitions against assisting suicide never contained exceptions for those who were near death. Rather, "[t]he life of those to whom life ha[d] become a burden-of those who [were] hopelessly diseased or fatally wounded-nay, even the lives of criminals condemned to death, [were] under the protection of the law, equally as the lives of those who [were] in the full tide of life's enjoyment." *Blackburn v. State*, 23 Ohio St. 146, 163 (1872).

The earliest American statute explicitly to outlaw assisting suicide was enacted in

---

[7] In *Vacco v. Quill*, 521 U.S. 793 (1997), decided today, we hold that New York's assisted-suicide ban does not violate the Equal Protection Clause.

New York in 1828, and many of the new States and Territories followed New York's example. By the time the Fourteenth Amendment was ratified, it was a crime in most States to assist a suicide. In this century, the Model Penal Code also prohibited "aiding" suicide, prompting many States to enact or revise their assisted-suicide bans.

Though deeply rooted, the States' assisted-suicide bans have in recent years been reexamined and, generally, reaffirmed. Because of advances in medicine and technology, Americans today are increasingly likely to die in institutions, from chronic illnesses. Public concern and democratic action are therefore sharply focused on how best to protect dignity and independence at the end of life, with the result that there have been many significant changes in state laws and in the attitudes these laws reflect. At the same time, however, voters and legislators continue for the most part to reaffirm their States' prohibitions on assisting suicide.

The Washington statute at issue in this case was enacted in 1975 as part of a revision of that State's criminal code. Four years later, Washington passed its Natural Death Act, which specifically stated that "[n]othing in this chapter shall be construed to condone, authorize, or approve mercy killing . . ." Natural Death Act, 1979 Wash. Laws, ch. 112, § 8(1). In 1991, Washington voters rejected a ballot initiative which, had it passed, would have permitted a form of physician-assisted suicide. Washington then added a provision to the Natural Death Act expressly excluding physician-assisted suicide.

California voters rejected an assisted-suicide initiative similar to Washington's in 1993. On the other hand, in 1994, voters in Oregon enacted, also through ballot initiative, that State's "Death With Dignity Act," which legalized physician-assisted suicide for competent, terminally ill adults. Since the Oregon vote, many proposals to legalize assisted-suicide have been and continue to be introduced in the States' legislatures, but none has been enacted. Also, on April 30, 1997, President Clinton signed the Federal Assisted Suicide Funding Restriction Act of 1997, which prohibits the use of federal funds in support of physician-assisted suicide. Pub. L. 105-12, 111 Stat. 23 (codified at 42 U.S.C. § 14401 *et seq*).[16]

Thus, the States are currently engaged in serious, thoughtful examinations of physician-assisted suicide and other similar issues. Attitudes toward suicide itself have changed since Bracton, but our laws have consistently condemned, and continue to prohibit, assisting suicide.

II

The Due Process Clause guarantees more than fair process, and the "liberty" it protects includes more than the absence of physical restraint. The Clause also provides

---

[16] Other countries are embroiled in similar debates: The Supreme Court of Canada recently rejected a claim that the Canadian Charter of Rights and Freedoms establishes a fundamental right to assisted suicide; the British House of Lords Select Committee on Medical Ethics refused to recommend any change in Great Britain's assisted-suicide prohibition; New Zealand's Parliament rejected a proposed "Death With Dignity Bill" that would have legalized physician-assisted suicide; and the Northern Territory of Australia legalized assisted suicide and voluntary euthanasia in 1995, however, the Australian Senate voted to overturn the Northern Territory's law.

heightened protection against government interference with certain fundamental rights and liberty interests. *Casey*, 505 U.S., at 851. In a long line of cases, we have held that, in addition to the specific freedoms protected by the Bill of Rights, the "liberty" specially protected by the Due Process Clause includes the rights to marry, *Loving v. Virginia*, 388 U.S. 1 (1967); to have children, *Skinner v. Oklahoma ex rel. Williamson*, 316 U.S. 535 (1942); to direct the education and upbringing of one's children, *Meyer v. Nebraska*, 262 U.S. 390 (1923); *Pierce v. Society of Sisters*, 268 U.S. 510 (1925); to marital privacy, *Griswold v. Connecticut*, 381 U.S. 479 (1965); to use contraception, *Eisenstadt v. Baird*, 405 U.S. 438 (1972); and to abortion, *Casey*. We have also assumed, and strongly suggested, that the Due Process Clause protects the traditional right to refuse unwanted lifesaving medical treatment. *Cruzan*, 497 U.S., at 278–279.

But we "ha[ve] always been reluctant to expand the concept of substantive due process because guideposts for responsible decisionmaking in this unchartered area are scarce and open-ended." By extending constitutional protection to an asserted right or liberty interest, we, to a great extent, place the matter outside the arena of public debate and legislative action. We must therefore "exercise the utmost care whenever we are asked to break new ground in this field," lest the liberty protected by the Due Process Clause be subtly transformed into the policy preferences of the Members of this Court, *Moore*, 431 U.S., at 502.

Our established method of substantive-due-process analysis has two primary features: First, we have regularly observed that the Due Process Clause specially protects those fundamental rights and liberties which are, objectively, "deeply rooted in this Nation's history and tradition," *id.*, at 503, and "implicit in the concept of ordered liberty," such that "neither liberty nor justice would exist if they were sacrificed," *Palko v. Connecticut*, 302 U.S. 319, 325, 326 (1937). Second, we have required in substantive-due-process cases a "careful description" of the asserted fundamental liberty interest. *Cruzan*, at 277–278. Our Nation's history, legal traditions, and practices thus provide the crucial "guideposts for responsible decisionmaking," that direct and restrain our exposition of the Due Process Clause.

In our view, the development of this Court's substantive-due-process jurisprudence has been a process whereby the outlines of the "liberty" specially protected by the Fourteenth Amendment have at least been carefully refined by concrete examples involving fundamental rights found to be deeply rooted in our legal tradition. This approach tends to rein in the subjective elements that are necessarily present in due-process judicial review. In addition, by establishing a threshold requirement-that a challenged state action implicate a fundamental right-before requiring more than a reasonable relation to a legitimate state interest to justify the action, it avoids the need for complex balancing of competing interests in every case.

[T]he question before us is whether the "liberty" specially protected by the Due Process Clause includes a right to commit suicide which itself includes a right to assistance in doing so. Here, as discussed, we are confronted with a consistent and almost universal tradition that has long rejected the asserted right, and continues explicitly to reject it today, even for terminally ill, mentally competent adults. To hold for respondents, we would have to reverse centuries of legal doctrine and practice, and strike down the considered policy choice of almost every State.

Respondents contend, however, that the liberty interest they assert *is* consistent with this Court's substantive-due-process line of cases, if not with this Nation's history and practice. Pointing to *Casey*, respondents read our jurisprudence in this area as reflecting a general tradition of "self-sovereignty," and as teaching that the "liberty" protected by the Due Process Clause includes "basic and intimate exercises of personal autonomy," see *Casey*, 505 U.S., at 847. According to respondents, our liberty jurisprudence, and the broad, individualistic principles it reflects, protects the "liberty of competent, terminally ill adults to make end-of-life decisions free of undue government interference."

[In *Casey*], the Court's opinion concluded that "the essential holding of *Roe v. Wade* [, 410 U.S. 113 (1973),] should be retained and once again reaffirmed." In reaching this conclusion, the opinion discussed in some detail this Court's substantive-due-process tradition of interpreting the Due Process Clause to protect certain fundamental rights and "personal decisions relating to marriage, procreation, contraception, family relationships, child rearing, and education," and noted that many of those rights and liberties "involv[e] the most intimate and personal choices a person may make in a lifetime."

By choosing this language, the Court's opinion in *Casey* described, in a general way and in light of our prior cases, those personal activities and decisions that this Court has identified as so deeply rooted in our history and traditions, or so fundamental to our concept of constitutionally ordered liberty, that they are protected by the Fourteenth Amendment. The opinion moved from the recognition that liberty necessarily includes freedom of conscience and belief about ultimate considerations to the observation that "though the abortion decision may originate within the zone of conscience and belief, it is *more than a philosophic exercise.*" *Casey*, 505 U.S., at 852 (emphasis added). That many of the rights and liberties protected by the Due Process Clause sound in personal autonomy does not warrant the sweeping conclusion that any and all important, intimate, and personal decisions are so protected, *San Antonio Independent School Dist. v. Rodriguez*, 411 U.S. 1, 33–35 (1973), and *Casey* did not suggest otherwise.

The history of the law's treatment of assisted suicide in this country has been and continues to be one of the rejection of nearly all efforts to permit it. That being the case, our decisions lead us to conclude that the asserted "right" to assistance in committing suicide is not a fundamental liberty interest protected by the Due Process Clause. The Constitution also requires, however, that Washington's assisted-suicide ban be rationally related to legitimate government interests. This requirement is unquestionably met here.

First, Washington has an "unqualified interest in the preservation of human life." *Cruzan*, 497 U.S., at 282. The State's prohibition on assisted suicide, like all homicide laws, both reflects and advances its commitment to this interest. Washington rejected [a] sliding-scale approach and, through its assisted-suicide ban, insists that all persons' lives, from beginning to end, regardless of physical or mental condition, are under the full protection of the law.

Relatedly, all admit that suicide is a serious public-health problem, especially among persons in otherwise vulnerable groups. The State has an interest in preventing suicide, and in studying, identifying, and treating its causes. Those who attempt suicide-terminally ill or not-often suffer from depression or other mental disorders. Research indicates, however, that many people who request physician-assisted suicide withdraw that request if their depression and pain are treated. [However,] because depression is difficult to diagnose, physicians and medical professionals often fail to respond adequately to seriously ill patients' needs. Thus, legal physician-assisted suicide could make it more difficult for the State to protect depressed or mentally ill persons, or those who are suffering from untreated pain, from suicidal impulses.

The State also has an interest in protecting the integrity and ethics of the medical profession. [T]he American Medical Association, like many other medical and physicians' groups, has concluded that "[p]hysician-assisted suicide is fundamentally incompatible with the physician's role as healer." American Medical Association, Code of Ethics § 2.211 (1994). And physician-assisted suicide could undermine the trust that is essential to the doctor-patient relationship by blurring the time-honored line between healing and harming.

Next, the State has an interest in protecting vulnerable groups-including the poor, the elderly, and disabled persons-from abuse, neglect, and mistakes. We have recognized the real risk of subtle coercion and undue influence in end-of-life situations. *Cruzan*, 497 U.S., at 281. If physician-assisted suicide were permitted, many might resort to it to spare their families the substantial financial burden of end-of-life health-care costs.

The State's interest here goes beyond protecting the vulnerable from coercion; it extends to protecting disabled and terminally ill people from prejudice, negative and inaccurate stereotypes, and "societal indifference." The State's assisted-suicide ban reflects and reinforces its policy that the lives of terminally ill, disabled, and elderly people must be no less valued than the lives of the young and healthy, and that a seriously disabled person's suicidal impulses should be interpreted and treated the same way as anyone else's.

Finally, the State may fear that permitting assisted suicide will start it down the path to voluntary and perhaps even involuntary euthanasia. If suicide is protected as a matter of constitutional right, it is argued, "every man and woman in the United States must enjoy it." The Court of Appeals' decision, and its expansive reasoning, provide ample support for the State's concerns. The court noted, for example, that the "decision of a duly appointed surrogate decision maker is for all legal purposes the decision of the patient himself," that "in some instances, the patient may be unable to self-administer the drugs and . . . administration by the physician . . . may be the only way the patient may be able to receive them," and that not only physicians, but also family members and loved ones, will inevitably participate in assisting suicide.

This concern is further supported by evidence about the practice of euthanasia in the Netherlands. The Dutch government's own study revealed that in 1990, there were 2,300 cases of voluntary euthanasia, 400 cases of assisted suicide, and more than 1,000 cases of euthanasia without an explicit request. In addition to these latter 1,000 cases, the study found an additional 4,941 cases where physicians administered lethal morphine overdoses without the patients' explicit consent. Washington, like most other States, reasonably ensures against this risk by banning, rather than regulating, assisting suicide.

We need not weigh exactingly the relative strengths of these various interests. They are unquestionably important and legitimate, and Washington's ban on assisted suicide is at least reasonably related to their promotion and protection. We therefore hold that Wash. Rev. Code § 9A.36.060(1) (1994) does not violate the Fourteenth Amendment.

It is so ordered.

JUSTICE O'CONNOR, concurring.[*]

The Court frames the issue in *Washington v. Glucksberg* as whether the Due Process Clause of the Constitution protects a "right to commit suicide which itself includes a right to assistance in doing so," and concludes that our Nation's history, legal traditions, and practices do not support the existence of such a right. I join the Court's opinions because I agree that there is no generalized right to "commit suicide." But respondents urge us to address the narrower question whether a mentally competent person who is experiencing great suffering has a constitutionally cognizable interest in controlling the circumstances of his or her imminent death. I see no need to reach that question in the context of the facial challenges to the New York and Washington laws at issue here. The parties and *amici* agree that in these States a patient who is suffering from a terminal illness and who is experiencing great pain has no legal barriers to obtaining medication, from qualified physicians, to alleviate that suffering, even to the point of causing unconsciousness and hastening death. In this light, even assuming that we would recognize such an interest, I agree that the State's interests in protecting those who are not truly competent or facing imminent death, or those whose decisions to hasten death would not truly be voluntary, are sufficiently weighty to justify a prohibition against physician-assisted suicide.

Every one of us at some point may be affected by our own or a family member's terminal illness. There is no reason to think the democratic process will not strike the proper balance between the interests of terminally ill, mentally competent individuals who would seek to end their suffering and the State's interests in protecting those who might seek to end life mistakenly or under pressure. As the Court recognizes, States are presently undertaking extensive and serious evaluation of physician-assisted suicide and other related issues. In such circumstances, "the . . . challenging task of crafting appropriate procedures for safeguarding . . . liberty interests is entrusted to the 'laboratory' of the States . . . in the first instance."

---

[*] JUSTICE GINSBURG concurs in the Court's judgments substantially for the reasons stated in this opinion. JUSTICE BREYER joins this opinion except insofar as it joins the opinions of the Court.

JUSTICE SOUTER, concurring in the judgment. [Opinion omitted.]

JUSTICE STEVENS, concurring in the judgment. [Opinion omitted]

EXERCISE 17:

1. Why did the majority spend so much time describing the history and current state of legal and social attitudes toward assisted suicide? How did the majority's narrative impact its ruling?

2. The *Glucksberg* Court claimed that there was a thoughtful debate over assisted suicide occurring in the United States and that, therefore, the Court should be reluctant to expand the scope of substantive due process to include such a right. Similarly, Justice O'Connor suggested that the democratic process would lead to an appropriate resolution. Explain the Court's and Justice O'Connor's reasoning and evaluate it. To what other substantive due process rights, identified by the Supreme Court, could or should such reasoning also apply? For example, should states have primary authority over abortion, marriage, and contraception, subject only to rational basis review?

3. Why did the majority describe how most states approached assisted suicide? What is the reason for the majority's note on how foreign nations approached the subject? Are these reasons adequate?

4. Chief Justice Rehnquist's description of the Supreme Court's substantive due process analysis included the following statement: " 'deeply rooted in this Nation's history and tradition' and 'implicit in the concept of ordered liberty,' such that 'neither liberty nor justice would exist if they were sacrificed.' " Are those inquiries the same, or will they sometimes diverge? If so, what should the Court do in those situations?

5. The Court expressed concern with "the subjective elements that are necessarily present in due-process judicial review." Why the concern? Should Supreme Court Justices not exercise judgment? How would they do that?

6. Is the Supreme Court's analysis in *Glucksberg* consistent with *Planned Parenthood v. Casey*? *Lawrence v. Texas*?

7. Ultimately, what test did the Supreme Court utilize to evaluate the challenged Washington statute? Explain the Court's application of that test. Did it appropriately apply that test?

8. After *Washington v. Glucksberg*, is there a constitutional right to commit or assist suicide?

10.   Rights to Education and Welfare

The doctrinal high-point of substantive due process, and the related doctrine of fundamental rights equal protection (covered in **Chapter 4**), was the early 1970s. In the late 1960s and early 1970s, the Supreme Court majority was confidently articulating new fundamental rights and, despite some controversy, the Court delivered consistently progressive results. One of the last major doctrinal hurdles for progressives on and off the Supreme Court was "positive" constitutional rights. Positive rights are entitlements to a benefit or good, such as material subsistence, and are contrasted with "negative" rights, which are zones of freedom from governmental regulation, such as free speech. This distinction has a long philosophical pedigree, especially in the post-Enlightenment West. *See, e.g.*, JOHN LOCKE, THE SECOND TREATISE OF GOVERNMENT § 123 (Peter Laslett ed. 1988) (1698) (describing the end of government as the "Preservation" of "Property"). Nearly all of the Warren and Burger Courts' progressive decisions had involved negative rights.[62]

Jurisprudential movement toward protecting positive constitutional rights occurred in many other areas of the Court's case law. Most famously, in *Goldberg v. Kelly*, 397 U.S. 254 (1970), the Court ruled that welfare benefits constituted "property" under the Due Process Clause so that stopping such benefits required extensive (procedural) due process. Even more important than the Court's holding was its reasoning and language, where the Court described welfare as "not mere charity," but instead an "entitlement." *Id.* at 263–64 n.8. The Court, in these cases, was aided by and relied on scholarship advocating such a move. *See, e.g.*, Charles Reich, *Individual Rights and Social Welfare: The Emerging Legal Issues*, 74 YALE L.J. 1245, 1255–56 (1965) (describing the need for a constitutional entitlement to welfare); *see also* Frank I. Michelman, *Foreword: On Protecting the Poor Through the Fourteenth Amendment*, 83 HARV. L. REV. 7 (1969) (arguing that many of the Supreme Court's late-1960s equal protection cases indicated a "sensitivity" to "minimum welfare" and advocating further moves in the same direction).

The high-water mark passed, however, when the Court turned back claims for positive rights to education and welfare, discussed below.

SAN ANTONIO INDEPENDENT SCHOOL DISTRICT v. RODRIGUEZ
411 U.S. 1 (1973)

MR. JUSTICE POWELL delivered the opinion of the Court.

This suit attacking the Texas system of financing public education was initiated by Mexican-American parents whose children attend the elementary and secondary schools in the Edgewood Independent School District, Texas. They brought a class action on behalf of schoolchildren throughout the State who are members of minority groups or who are poor and reside in school districts having a low property tax base. The complaint was filed in the summer of 1968. In December 1971 the [three judge district court] panel rendered its judgment holding the Texas school finance system

---

[62] The most prominent exception to this statement was in the context of access to courts, discussed in **Chapter 4**. *See Griffin v. Illinois*, 351 U.S. 12 (1956) (ruling that a state had to provide a trial transcript to indigent criminal defendants for their first appeal-as-of-right); *Mayer v. Chicago*, 404 U.S. 189 (1971) (holding that the right to transcripts for a first appeal applied to indigent defendants charged with nonfelony crimes); *Gideon v. Wainwright*, 372 U.S. 335 (1963) (ruling that states must provide indigent criminal defendants with counsel in trials); *Douglas v. California*, 372 U.S. 353 (1963) (ruling that states must provide indigent criminal defendants with counsel in first appeals-as-of-right).

unconstitutional under the Equal Protection Clause of the Fourteenth Amendment.[5] The State appealed. For the reasons stated in this opinion, we reverse the decision of the District Court.

I

The first Texas State Constitution, promulgated upon Texas' entry into the Union in 1845, provided for the establishment of a system of free schools. As early as 1883, the state constitution was amended to provide for the creation of local school districts empowered to levy ad valorem taxes with the consent of local taxpayers. Such local funds as were raised were supplemented by funds distributed to each district from the State's Permanent and Available School Funds. The Permanent School Fund, its predecessor established in 1854, was thereafter endowed with millions of acres of public land set aside to assure a continued source of income for school support. The Available School Fund, which received income from the Permanent School Fund as well as from a state ad valorem property tax and other designated taxes, served as the disbursing arm for most state educational funds throughout the late 1800's and first half of this century. Additionally, in 1918 an increase in state property taxes was used to finance a program providing free textbooks throughout the State.

Until recent times, Texas was a predominantly rural State and its population and property wealth were spread relatively evenly across the State. Sizable differences in the value of assessable property between local school districts became increasingly evident as the State became more industrialized and as rural-to-urban population shifts became more pronounced. These growing disparities in population and taxable property between districts were responsible in part for increasingly notable differences in levels of local expenditure for education.

In due time it became apparent to those concerned with financing public education that contributions from the Available School Fund were not sufficient to ameliorate these disparities. Recognizing th[is] need, the state legislature in the late 1940's undertook a thorough evaluation of public education. In 1947, an 18-member committee was appointed to propose a funding scheme that would guarantee a minimum or basic educational offering to each child and that would help overcome interdistrict disparities in taxable resources. The Committee's efforts led to establishing the Texas Minimum Foundation School Program. Today, this Program accounts for approximately half of the total educational expenditures in Texas.

The Program calls for state and local contributions to a fund earmarked specifically for teacher salaries, operating expenses, and transportation costs. The State, supplying funds from its general revenues, finances approximately 80% of the Program, and the school districts are responsible — as a unit — for providing the remaining 20%. The districts' share, known as the Local Fund Assignment, is apportioned among the school districts under a formula designed to reflect each district's relative taxpaying ability. The district finances its share of the Assignment out of revenues from local

---

[5] The District Court stayed its mandate for two years to provide Texas an opportunity to remedy the inequities found in its financing program.

property taxation. The design of this complex system was an attempt to assure that the Foundation Program would have an equalizing influence on expenditure levels between school districts by placing the heaviest burden on the school districts most capable of paying. Between 1949 and 1967, expenditures increased approximately 500%.

The school district in which appellees reside, the Edgewood Independent School District, has been compared throughout this litigation with the Alamo Heights Independent School District. This comparison between the least and most affluent districts in the San Antonio area serves to illustrate the manner in which the dual system of finance operates and to indicate the extent to which substantial disparities exist despite the State's impressive progress in recent years. Approximately 22,000 students are enrolled in [Edgewood's] 25 elementary and secondary schools. The district is in the core-city sector of San Antonio in a residential neighborhood that has little commercial or industrial property. The residents are predominantly of Mexican-American descent. The average assessed property value per pupil is $5,960 — the lowest in the metropolitan area — and the median family income ($4,686) is also the lowest. At an equalized tax rate of $1.05 per $100 of assessed property — the highest in the metropolitan area — the district contributed $26 to the education of each child for the 1967–1968 school year above its Local Fund Assignment for the Minimum Foundation Program. The Foundation Program contributed $222 per pupil for a state-local total of $248. Federal funds added another $108 for a total of $356 per pupil.

Alamo Heights is the most affluent school district in San Antonio. Its six schools, housing approximately 5,000 students, are situated in a residential community. The school population is predominantly "Anglo." The assessed property value per pupil exceeds $49,000, and the median family income is $8,001. In 1967–1968 the local tax rate of $.85 per $100 of valuation yielded $333 per pupil over and above its contribution to the Foundation Program. Coupled with the $225 provided from that Program, the district was able to supply $558 per student. Supplemented by a $36 per-pupil grant from federal sources, Alamo Heights spent $594 per pupil.

[I]t was these disparities, largely attributable to differences in the amounts of money collected through local property taxation, that led the District Court to conclude that Texas' dual system of public school financing violated the Equal Protection Clause. Finding that wealth is a "suspect" classification and that education is a "fundamental" interest, the court concluded that "(n)ot only are defendants unable to demonstrate compelling state interests . . . they fail even to establish a reasonable basis for these classifications."

Texas virtually concedes that its historically rooted dual system of financing education could not withstanding strict judicial scrutiny. If strict scrutiny [applies], the Texas financing system and its counterpart in virtually every other State will not pass muster. [T]he State defends the system's rationality with vigor and disputes the District Court's finding that it lacks a "reasonable basis."

We must decide, first, whether the Texas system of financing public education operates to the disadvantage of some suspect class or impinges upon a fundamental right explicitly or implicitly protected by the Constitution, thereby requiring strict judicial scrutiny. If so, the judgment of the District Court should be affirmed. If not, the Texas scheme must still be examined to determine whether it rationally furthers some legitimate, articulated state purpose.

II

[F]or the several reasons that follow, we find neither the suspect-classification nor the fundamental-interest analysis persuasive.

A

The wealth discrimination discovered by the District Court in this case, and by several other courts that have recently struck down school-financing laws in other States, is quite unlike any of the forms of wealth discrimination heretofore reviewed by this Court. Rather than focusing on the unique features of the alleged discrimination, the courts in these cases have virtually assumed their findings of a suspect classification through a simplistic process of analysis: since, under the traditional systems of financing public schools, some poorer people receive less expensive educations than other more affluent people, these systems discriminate on the basis of wealth. This approach ignores the hard threshold questions, including whether it makes a difference that the class of disadvantaged "poor" cannot be identified or defined in customary equal protection terms.

However described, it is clear that appellees' suit asks this Court to extend its most exacting scrutiny to review a system that allegedly discriminates against a large, diverse, and amorphous class, unified only by the common factor of residence in districts that happen to have less taxable wealth than other districts. The system of alleged discrimination and the class it defines have none of the traditional indicia of suspectness: the class is not saddled with such disabilities, or subjected to such a history of purposeful unequal treatment, or relegated to such a position of political powerlessness as to command extraordinary protection from the majoritarian political process.

We thus conclude that the Texas system does not operate to the peculiar disadvantage of any suspect class.

B

In *Brown v. Board of Education*, 347 U.S. 483 (1954), a unanimous Court recognized that "education is perhaps the most important function of state and local governments." This theme, expressing an abiding respect for the vital role of education in a free society, may be found in numerous opinions of Justices of this Court writing both before and after *Brown* was decided. *Pierce v. Society of Sisters*, 268 U.S. 510 (1925); *Meyer v. Nebraska*, 262 U.S. 390 (1923).

Nothing this Court holds today in any way detracts from our historic dedication to public education. But the importance of a service performed by the State does not determine whether it must be regarded as fundamental for purposes of examination under the Equal Protection Clause. If the degree of judicial scrutiny of state legislation fluctuated, depending on a majority's view of the importance of the interest affected, we would have gone "far toward making this Court a 'super-legislature.' " We would, indeed, then be assuming a legislative role and one for which the Court lacks both authority and competence.

It is not the province of this Court to create substantive constitutional rights in the name of guaranteeing equal protection of the laws. Thus, the key to discovering whether education is "fundamental" is not to be found in comparisons of the relative societal significance of education as opposed to subsistence or housing. Nor is it to be found by weighing whether education is as important as the right to travel. Rather, the answer lies in assessing whether there is a right to education explicitly or implicitly guaranteed by the Constitution. *Eisenstadt v. Baird*, 405 U.S. 438 (1972); *Skinner v. Oklahoma*, 316 U.S. 535 (1942).

Education, of course, is not among the rights afforded explicit protection under our Federal Constitution. Nor do we find any basis for saying it is implicitly so protected. As we have said, the undisputed importance of education will not alone cause this Court to depart from the usual standard for reviewing a State's social and economic legislation. It is appellees' contention, however, that education is distinguishable from other services and benefits provided by the State because it bears a peculiarly close relationship to other rights and liberties accorded protection under the Constitution. Specifically, they insist that education is itself a fundamental personal right because it is essential to the effective exercise of First Amendment freedoms and to intelligent utilization of the right to vote.

We need not dispute any of these propositions. The Court has long afforded zealous protection against unjustifiable governmental interference with the individual's rights to speak and to vote. Yet we have never presumed to possess either the ability or the authority to guarantee to the citizenry the most effective speech or the most informed electoral choice. That these may be desirable goals of a system of freedom of expression and of a representative form of government is not to be doubted. But they are not values to be implemented by judicial instruction into otherwise legitimate state activities.

Even if it were conceded that some identifiable quantum of education is a constitutionally protected prerequisite to the meaningful exercise of either right, we have no indication that the present levels of educational expenditures in Texas provide an education that falls short. Whatever merit appellees' argument might have if a State's financing system occasioned an absolute denial of educational opportunities to any of its children, that argument provides no basis for finding an interference with fundamental rights where only relative differences in spending levels are involved and where no charge fairly could be made that the system fails to provide each child with an opportunity to acquire the basic minimal skills necessary for the enjoyment of the rights of speech and of full participation in the political process.

Furthermore, the logical limitations on appellees' nexus theory are difficult to perceive. How, for instance, is education to be distinguished from the significant personal interests in the basics of decent food and shelter? Empirical examination might well buttress an assumption that the ill-fed, ill-clothed, and ill-housed are among the most ineffective participants in the political process, and that they derive the least enjoyment from the benefits of the First Amendment.

In one further respect we find this a particularly inappropriate case in which to subject state action to strict judicial scrutiny. Every step leading to the establishment of the system Texas utilizes today was implemented in an effort to extend public education and to improve its quality. Of course, every reform that benefits some more than others may be criticized for what it fails to accomplish. But we think it plain that the thrust of the Texas system is affirmative and reformatory and, therefore, should be scrutinized under judicial principles sensitive to the nature of the State's efforts and to the rights reserved to the States under the Constitution.

C

This case represents far more than a challenge to the manner in which Texas provides for the education of its children. We have here nothing less than a direct attack on the way in which Texas has chosen to raise and disburse state and local tax revenues. We are asked to condemn the State's judgment in conferring on political subdivisions the power to tax local property to supply revenues for local interests. In so doing, appellees would have the Court intrude in an area in which it has traditionally deferred to state legislatures.

Thus, we stand on familiar grounds when we continue to acknowledge that the Justices of this Court lack both the expertise and the familiarity with local problems so necessary to the making of wise decisions with respect to the raising and disposition of public revenues. Yet, we are urged to direct the States either to alter drastically the present system or to throw out the property tax altogether in favor of some other form of taxation. No scheme of taxation has yet been devised which is free of all discriminatory impact. In such a complex arena in which no perfect alternatives exist, the Court does well not to impose too rigorous a standard of scrutiny lest all local fiscal schemes become subjects of criticism under the Equal Protection Clause.

In addition to matters of fiscal policy, this case also involves the most persistent and difficult questions of educational policy, another area in which this Court's lack of specialized knowledge and experience counsels against premature interference with the informed judgments made at the state and local levels. Education presents a myriad of "intractable economic, social, and even philosophical problems." The very complexity of the problems of financing and managing a statewide public school system suggests that "there will be more than one constitutionally permissible method of solving them," and that, within the limits of rationality, "the legislature's efforts to tackle the problems" should be entitled to respect. On even the most basic questions in this area the scholars and educational experts are divided. In such circumstances, the judiciary is well advised to refrain from imposing on the States inflexible constitutional restraints that could circumscribe or handicap the continued research and experimentation so vital to finding even partial solutions to educational problems and to keeping abreast of ever-changing conditions.

It must be remembered, also, that every claim arising under the Equal Protection Clause has implications for the relationship between national and state power under our federal system. Questions of federalism are always inherent in the process of determining whether a State's laws are to be accorded the traditional presumption of constitutionality, or are to be subjected instead to rigorous judicial scrutiny. [I]t would be difficult to imagine a case having a greater potential impact on our federal system than the one now before us, in which we are urged to abrogate systems of financing public education presently in existence in virtually every State.

The foregoing considerations buttress our conclusion that Texas' system of public school finance is an inappropriate candidate for strict judicial scrutiny.

III

The Texas system of school finance is responsive to two [primary] forces. While assuring a basic education for every child in the State, it permits and encourages a large measure of participation in and control of each district's schools at the local level. In an era that has witnessed a consistent trend toward centralization of the functions of government, local sharing of responsibility for public education has survived.

The persistence of attachment to government at the lowest level where education is concerned reflects the depth of commitment of its supporters. In part, local control means the freedom to devote more money to the education of one's children. Equally important, however, is the opportunity it offers for participation in the decisionmaking process that determines how those local tax dollars will be spent. Each locality is free to tailor local programs to local needs. Pluralism also affords some opportunity for experimentation, innovation, and a healthy competition for educational excellence.

Appellees do not question the propriety of Texas' dedication to local control of education. To the contrary, they attack the school-financing system precisely because, in their view, it does not provide the same level of local control and fiscal flexibility in all districts. Appellees suggest that local control could be preserved and promoted under other financing systems that resulted in more equality in education expenditures. While it is no doubt true that reliance on local property taxation for school revenues provides less freedom of choice with respect to expenditures for some districts than for others, the existence of "some inequality" in the manner in which the State's rationale is achieved is not alone a sufficient basis for striking down the entire system. Nor must the financing system fail because, as appellees suggest, other methods of satisfying the State's interest, which occasion "less drastic" disparities in expenditures, might be conceived. Only where state action impinges on the exercise of fundamental constitutional rights or liberties must it be found to have chosen the least restrictive alternative. It is also well to remember that even those districts that have reduced ability to make free decisions with respect to how much they spend on education still retain under the present system a large measure of authority as to how available funds will be allocated. They further enjoy the power to make numerous other decisions with respect to the operation of the schools. The people of Texas may be justified in believing that other systems of school financing, which place more of the financial responsibility in the hands of the State, will result in a comparable lessening of desired local autonomy. That is, they may believe that along with increased control of the purse strings at the state level will go increased control over local policies.

Appellees further urge that the Texas system is unconstitutionally arbitrary because it allows the availability of local taxable resources to turn on "happenstance." But any scheme of local taxation — indeed the very existence of identifiable local governmental units — requires the establishment of jurisdictional boundaries that are inevitably arbitrary. It is equally inevitable that some localities are going to be blessed with more taxable assets than others. Nor is local wealth a static quantity. Changes in the level of taxable wealth within any district may result from any number of events, some of which local residents can and do influence. Moreover, if local taxation for local expenditures were an unconstitutional method of providing for education then it might be an equally impermissible means of providing other necessary services customarily financed largely from local property taxes, including local police and fire protection, public health and hospitals, and public utility facilities of various kinds.

In sum, to the extent that the Texas system of school financing results in unequal expenditures between children who happen to reside in different districts, we cannot say that such disparities are the product of a system that is so irrational as to be invidiously discriminatory. Texas has acknowledged its shortcomings and has persistently endeavored — not without some success — to ameliorate the differences in levels of expenditures without sacrificing the benefits of local participation. One also must remember that the system here challenged is not peculiar to Texas or to any other State. We are unwilling to assume for ourselves a level of wisdom superior to that of legislators, scholars, and educational authorities in 50 States. The constitutional standard under the Equal Protection Clause is whether the challenged state action rationally furthers a legitimate state purpose or interest. We hold that the Texas plan abundantly satisfies this standard.

Reversed.

MR. JUSTICE STEWART, concurring. [Opinion omitted.]

MR. JUSTICE BRENNAN, dissenting. [Opinion omitted.]

MR. JUSTICE WHITE, with whom MR. JUSTICE DOUGLAS and MR. JUSTICE BRENNAN join, dissenting. [Opinion omitted.]

MR. JUSTICE MARSHALL, with whom MR. JUSTICE DOUGLAS concurs, dissenting.

II

A

I cannot accept the majority's labored efforts to demonstrate that fundamental interests, which call for strict scrutiny of the challenged classification, encompass only established rights which we are somehow bound to recognize from the text of the Constitution itself. I would like to know where the Constitution guarantees the right to procreate, *Skinner v. Oklahoma*, 316 U.S. 535, 541 (1942), or the right to vote in state elections, e.g., *Reynolds v. Sims*, 377 U.S. 533 (1964), or the right to an appeal from a criminal conviction, e.g., *Griffin v. Illinois*, 351 U.S. 12 (1956). These are instances in which, due to the importance of the interests at stake, the Court has displayed a strong concern with the existence of discriminatory state treatment.

The majority is, of course, correct when it suggests that the process of determining which interests are fundamental is a difficult one. I certainly do not accept the view that the process need necessarily degenerate into an unprincipled, subjective "picking-and-choosing" between various interests. Although not all fundamental interests are constitutionally guaranteed, the determination of which interests are fundamental should be firmly rooted in the text of the Constitution. The task in every case should be to determine the extent to which constitutionally guaranteed rights are dependent on interests not mentioned in the Constitution. As the nexus between the specific constitutional guarantee and the nonconstitutional interest draws closer, the nonconstitutional interest becomes more fundamental and the degree of judicial scrutiny applied when the interest is infringed on a discriminatory basis must be adjusted accordingly. Thus, it cannot be denied that interests such as procreation, the exercise of the state franchise, and access to criminal appellate processes are not fully guaranteed to the citizen by our Constitution. But these interests have nonetheless been afforded special judicial consideration in the face of discrimination because they are interrelated with constitutional guarantees. Procreation is now understood to be important because of its interaction with the established constitutional right of privacy. The exercise of the state franchise is closely tied to basic civil and political rights inherent in the First Amendment. And access to criminal appellate processes enhances the integrity of the range of rights implicit in the Fourteenth Amendment guarantee of due process of law. Only if we closely protect the related interests from state discrimination do we ultimately ensure the integrity of the constitutional guarantee itself.

B

[T]he fundamental importance of education is amply indicated by the prior decisions of this Court, by the unique status accorded public education by our society, and by the close relationship between education and some of our most basic constitutional values. Undoubtedly, this Court's most famous statement on the subject is that contained in *Brown v. Board of Education*, 347 U.S. [483], 493 [(1954)]. This is clearly borne out by the fact that in 48 of our 50 States the provision of public education is mandated by the state constitution.

Education directly affects the ability of a child to exercise his First Amendment rights, both as a source and as a receiver of information and ideas, whatever interests he may pursue in life. Of particular importance is the relationship between education and the political process.

The factors just considered, including the relationship between education and the social and political interests enshrined within the Constitution, compel us to recognize the fundamentality of education and to scrutinize with appropriate care the bases for state discrimination affecting equality of educational opportunity in Texas' school districts — a conclusion which is only strengthened when we consider the character of the classification in this case.

C

This Court has frequently recognized that discrimination on the basis of wealth may create a classification of a suspect character and thereby call for exacting judicial scrutiny. See, e.g., *Griffin v. Illinois*, 351 U.S. 12 (1956); *Douglas v. California*, 372 U.S. 353 (1963).

[I]t seems to me that discrimination on the basis of group wealth in this case likewise calls for careful judicial scrutiny. First, it must be recognized that while local district wealth may serve other interests, it bears no relationship whatsoever to the interest of Texas schoolchildren in the educational opportunity afforded them by the State of Texas. Discrimination on the basis of group wealth may not, to be sure, reflect the social stigma frequently attached to personal poverty. Nevertheless, insofar as group wealth discrimination involves wealth over which the disadvantaged individual has no significant control, it represents in fact a more serious basis of discrimination than does personal wealth. For such discrimination is no reflection of the individual's characteristics or his abilities.

The disability of the disadvantaged class in this case extends as well into the political processes upon which we ordinarily rely as adequate for the protection and promotion of all interests. Here legislative reallocation of the State's property wealth must be sought in the face of inevitable opposition from significantly advantaged districts that have a strong vested interest in the preservation of the status quo.

Nor can we ignore the extent to which, in contrast to our prior decisions, the State is responsible for the wealth discrimination in this instance. It is the State that has created local school districts, and tied educational funding to the local property tax and thereby to local district wealth.

D

The nature of our inquiry is: We must consider the substantiality of the state interests sought to be served, and we must scrutinize the reasonableness of the means by which the State has sought to advance its interests. Here, both the nature of the interest and the classification dictate close judicial scrutiny.

The only justification offered by appellants to sustain the discrimination in educational opportunity caused by the Texas financing scheme is local educational control. At the outset, I do not question that local control of public education, as an abstract matter, constitutes a very substantial state interest. But I need not now decide how I might ultimately strike the balance were we confronted with a situation where the State's sincere concern for local control inevitably produced educational inequality. For, on this record, it is apparent that the State's purported concern with local control is offered primarily as an excuse rather than as a justification for interdistrict inequality.

In Texas, statewide laws regulate in fact the most minute details of local public education. For example, the State prescribes required courses. All textbooks must be submitted for state approval, and only approved textbooks may be used. The State has established the qualifications necessary for teaching in Texas public schools and the procedures for obtaining certification. The State has even legislated on the length of the school day.

Moreover, even if we accept Texas' general dedication to local control in educational matters, it is difficult to find any evidence of such dedication with respect to fiscal matters. It ignores reality to suggest that the local property tax element of the Texas financing scheme reflects a conscious legislative effort to provide school districts with local fiscal control. If Texas had a system truly dedicated to local fiscal control, one would expect the quality of the educational opportunity provided in each district to vary with the decision of the voters in that district as to the level of sacrifice they wish to make for public education. In fact, the Texas scheme produces precisely the opposite result. Local school districts cannot choose to have the best education in the State by imposing the highest tax rate. Instead, the quality of the educational opportunity offered by any particular district is largely determined by the amount of taxable property located in the district — a factor over which local voters can exercise no control.

In my judgment, the State has selected means wholly inappropriate to secure its purported interest in assuring its school districts local fiscal control.

III

[A]ffirmance of the District Court's decisions would hardly sound the death knell for local control of education. It would mean neither centralized decisionmaking nor federal court intervention in the operation of public schools. In fact, in striking down interdistrict disparities in taxable local wealth, the District Court took the course which is most likely to make true local control over educational decision-making a reality for all Texas school districts.

Nor does the District Court's decision even necessarily eliminate local control of educational funding. The District Court struck down nothing more than the continued interdistrict wealth discrimination inherent in the present property tax. Both central-ized and decentralized plans for educational funding not involving such interdistrict discrimination have been put forward. The choice among these or other alternatives would remain with the State, not with the federal courts.

The Court seeks solace for its action today in the possibility of legislative reform. The Court's suggestions of legislative redress and experimentation will doubtless be of great comfort to the schoolchildren of Texas' disadvantaged districts, but considering the vested interests of wealthy school districts in the preservation of the status quo, they are worth little more. The possibility of legislative action is, in all events, no answer to this Court's duty under the Constitution to eliminate unjustified state discrimination.

I would therefore affirm the judgment of the District Court.

EXERCISE 18:

1. Why did the Supreme Court go into significant detail on the history and structure of Texas' educational funding system?

2. Why did the majority rule that Texas' educational financing system did not impact on a suspect classification? Evaluate the majority's analysis. What alternative analysis did Justice Marshall suggest in dissent? Which is more persuasive?

3. Why did the majority rule that education was not a fundamental right? What alternative analysis did Justice Marshall suggest in dissent? Which is more persuasive?

4. Consequently, what analysis did the Court utilize to evaluate whether Texas' educational funding system violated the Fourteenth Amendment? Explain the Court's analysis: (1) what interest(s) did Texas pursue; and (2) to what extent, if any, were Texas' means over- and under-inclusive?

5. The justices in *San Antonio v. Rodriguez* decided the case in the shadow of *Lochner*. For the majority, ruling that education was a fundamental right would amount to a return to *Lochner*, while, for Justice Marshall, the articulation of unenumerated constitutional rights could be and was a principled endeavor. With whom do you agree, and why?

6. What role did concerns about the Supreme Court's and lower federal courts' institutional competence play in the Court's decision? Is that an appropriate role?

7. What role did federalism play in the Court's decision? Is that an appropriate role?

8. Justice Marshall's equal protection analysis would have concluded that the importance of public education to the full exercise of explicitly protected constitutional rights, such as free speech, makes access to public education a fundamental right. If public education is so important, as Justice Marshall argued, then how would he account for the fact that nearly all states (at the time of *Rodriguez*) utilized a public education funding system that he believed was unconstitutional?

9. The Court noted that the district court had "retained jurisdiction to fashion its own remedial order if the State failed to offer an acceptable plan." Is it appropriate for federal district courts to direct state school financing? Is it effective?

10. Relatedly, the dissenters would have ruled that Texas had to equalize its public school spending. How, in practice, would that have worked? For example, would the federal district court order the Texas legislature to increase or re-allocate income taxes in a particular manner? Did the dissenters adequately respond to the majority's concern regarding the courts' institutional competence to engage in such "structural litigation"?

11. *San Antonio v. Rodriguez*, in addition to representing a turning point for substantive due process, also began the Supreme Court's move away from "structural litigation." Structural litigation is court-directed restructuring of large governmental institutions. Structural litigation began with *Brown II*, where the Supreme Court ordered lower federal courts "to take such proceedings and enter such orders and

decrees consistent with this opinion as are necessary and proper to admit to public schools on a racially nondiscriminatory basis with all deliberate speed." *Brown v. Board of Educ.*, 349 U.S. 294, 301 (1955).

Some Americans, unsatisfied with what they perceived as no or slow progress in reform of many areas of American public life, saw structural litigation before federal courts friendly to their causes as an opportunity. As a result, federal courts began overseeing and restructuring prisons, public school bussing, among other areas. This trend carried over to state courts as well. *See, e.g., Southern Burlington County N.A.A.C.P. v. Township of Mount Laurel*, 336 A.2d 713 (N.J. 1975) (ordering revision of the state's zoning laws). In fact, before and after the Supreme Court's refusal in *San Antonio v. Rodriguez* to find a constitutional right to education, some state supreme courts — including Texas' — ruled that their state constitutions guaranteed such a right. *See, e.g., Edgewood Indep. Sch. Dist. v. Kirby*, 777 S.W.2d 391 (Tex. 1989) (holding that Texas' public school financing system violated the state constitution); *see also Edgewood Indep. Sch. Dist. v. Kirby*, 804 S.W.2d 491 (Tex. 1991) (ruling that the state legislature's attempt to conform Texas' public school funding system to the Texas Supreme Court's prior ruling failed to meet state constitutional standards); *Carrollton-Farmers Branch Indep. Sch. Dist. v. Edgewood Indep. Sch. Dist.*, 826 S.W.2d 489 (Tex. 1992) (same regarding a subsequent legislative effort); *Edgewood Indep. Sch. Dist. v. Meno*, 917 S.W.2d 717 (Tex. 1995) (approving the legislature's third effort).

Over time, many members of the public, elected officials, legal scholars, and judges came to believe that structural litigation was ineffective, or at least less effective than anticipated. For example, the Ohio Supreme Court, in a series of cases, initially ruled that the Ohio Constitution required the state legislature to modify the state's public education funding system in order to reduce reliance on local property taxes. *DeRolph v. State*, 78 Ohio St. 3d 193 (1997). The Court even issued an order to the legislature. *DeRolph v. State*, 93 Ohio St. 3d 309, 325 (2001). After years of legislative intransigence, and repeated appeals to the Court on the same issue, see, e.g., *DeRolph v. State*, 89 Ohio St. 3d 1 (2000) (holding that the Ohio legislature's first attempt to comply with the Court's prior ruling did not meet constitutional standards), the Ohio Supreme Court unceremoniously backed out of public school funding litigation stating: "we now . . . end any further *DeRolph* litigation." *State v. Lewis*, 99 Ohio St. 3d 97, 104 (2003).

Chapter 4

THE EQUAL PROTECTION CLAUSE

A. INTRODUCTION

The Equal Protection Clause of the Fourteenth Amendment states: "nor deny to any person within its jurisdiction the equal protection of the laws." U.S. Const. amend. XIV, § 1.

EXERCISE 1:

Apply the first four forms of argument to the Equal Protection Clause.

1. Looking at the Equal Protection Clause itself, the text of the rest of the Fourteenth Amendment, what do you learn about the Clause's meaning?

2. Looking at the Constitution's structure, and particularly at the Reconstruction Amendments, what do you learn about the Equal Protection Clause's meaning?

3. Reviewing evidence of the Equal Protection Clause's original meaning, what does it tell you about that meaning?

4. Do the materials following adoption of the Fourteenth Amendment offer any insight into the Equal Protection Clause's meaning?

The Equal Protection Clause's fortunes, since its ratification, have ebbed and waned. Today, it is one of the main focuses of American constitutional law.

You will continue to utilize the conceptual tools you learned in **Chapter 3**, such as compelling state interest and fundamental right. **Chapter 4** will also introduce you to another key analytical tool: over-inclusiveness and under-inclusiveness.

Chapter 4 is divided into five parts: Part B reviews the history and original meaning of the Clause; Part C briefly examines the Supreme Court's narrow interpretation of the Clause in the late nineteenth and early twentieth centuries; Part D covers the revival of the Clause that began in *Brown v. Board of Education*, 347 U.S. 483 (1954); and Part E details the Supreme Court's modern Equal Protection Clause case law.

As you read the materials below, some of the issues to consider include:

What classifications and fundamental rights receive heightened Equal Protection Clause scrutiny by the Supreme Court?

How does the Supreme Court determine whether a particular law embodies a suspect classification?

How did the Supreme Court determine that those, and only those, classifications and rights should receive heightened scrutiny?

In what ways does current Equal Protection Clause law fit and diverge from the Clause's original meaning?

How does the Supreme Court evaluate laws that utilize "suspect classifications" or infringe on "fundamental rights"?

B. ORIGINAL MEANING OF THE EQUAL PROTECTION CLAUSE

1. Race in Antebellum America

The Civil War, and the resulting Reconstruction Amendments, were in part caused by and were reactions against one of the seminal cases in American constitutional law, *Dred Scott v. Sandford*, 60 U.S. (19 How.) 393 (1856). *Dred Scott* was a major precipitating cause of the Civil War because it undermined the major prior legislative compromise — the Missouri Compromise — governing slavery, it set the stage for the expansion of slavery into previously free territories and possibly free states, and it made the problem of slavery immune to legislative resolution because of the Supreme Court's purported constitutional pronouncement.

Dred Scott also served as the focus of two of the Fourteenth Amendment's major provisions. The Citizenship Clause, in Section 1, overruled *Dred Scott*'s holding that African-Americans could not be U.S. citizens, by making all persons born (or naturalized) in the United States, American citizens. The Privileges or Immunities Clause, building on the Citizenship Clause, rejected one of *Dred Scott*'s major implications by protecting the privileges or immunities of all American citizens, including black Americans.

We review *Dred Scott* here, in the **Chapter** covering equal protection, because of its pivotal place in the history of race in America. Reprinted below is a portion of Chief Justice Taney's opinion, which was one of a number of opinions — that covered almost 250 pages in the U.S. Reports! — since there was no identified majority opinion and his opinion is generally considered controlling.

Dred Scott, after a failed attempt to sue for freedom in Missouri state court, sued for his and his family's freedom in federal court, under Article III diversity jurisdiction. Scott argued that he became free when his master transported him to a free state, Illinois, and later a free territory, the Wisconsin territory. Defendant John F.A. Sanford (whose name was misspelled in the U.S. Reports), a resident of New York, argued that the federal court lacked jurisdiction because Scott, an African-American, was not and could not be a U.S. citizen. As a result, the primary issue before the Supreme Court was jurisdictional.

DRED SCOTT v. SANDFORD
60 U.S. (19 How.) 393 (1856)

MR. CHIEF JUSTICE TANEY delivered the opinion of the court.

[I]

Can a negro, whose ancestors were imported into this country, and sold as slaves, become a member of the political community formed and brought into existence by the Constitution of the United States, and as such become entitled to all the rights, and privileges, and immunities, guarantied by that instrument to the citizen? One of which rights is the privilege of suing in a court of the United States in the cases specified in the Constitution.

The words "people of the United States" and "citizens" are synonymous terms, and mean the same thing. They both describe the political body who, according to our republican institutions, form the sovereignty, and who hold the power and conduct the Government through their representatives. They are what we familiarly call the "sovereign people," and every citizen is one of this people, and a constituent member of this sovereignty.

The question before us is, whether the class of persons described in the plea in abatement compose a portion of this people? We think they are not. On the contrary, they were at that time considered as a subordinate and inferior class of beings, who had been subjugated by the dominant race, and, whether emancipated or not, yet remained subject to their authority, and had no rights or privileges.

It is not the province of the court to decide upon the justice or injustice, the policy or impolicy, of these laws. The decision of that question belonged to the political or law-making power; to those who formed the sovereignty and framed the Constitution. The duty of the court is, to interpret the instrument they have framed, with the best lights we can obtain on the subject, and to administer it as we find it, according to its true intent and meaning when it was adopted.

It becomes necessary, therefore, to determine who were citizens of the several States when the Constitution was adopted. In the opinion of the court, the legislation and histories of the times, and the language used in the Declaration of Independence, show, that neither the class of persons who had been imported as slaves, nor their descendants, whether they had become free or not, were then acknowledged as a part of the people.

It is difficult at this day to realize the state of public opinion in relation to that unfortunate race, which prevailed in the civilized and enlightened portions of the world at the time of the Declaration of Independence, and when the Constitution of the United States was framed and adopted. They had for more than a century before been regarded as beings of an inferior order, and altogether unfit to associate with the white race, either in social or political relations; and so far inferior, that they had no rights which the white man was bound to respect; and that the negro might justly and lawfully be reduced to slavery for his benefit. He was bought and sold, and treated as an ordinary article of merchandise and traffic, whenever a profit could be made by it.

And in no nation was this opinion more firmly fixed or more uniformly acted upon than by the English Government and English people. The opinion thus entertained and acted upon in England was naturally impressed upon the colonies they founded on this side of the Atlantic. And, accordingly, a negro of the African race was regarded by them as an article of property, and held, and bought and sold as such. [After reviewing a number of state statutes, the Chief Justice stated that these statutes:] show that a perpetual and impassable barrier was intended to be erected between the white race and the one which they had reduced to slavery, and governed as subjects with absolute and despotic power, and which they then looked upon as so far below them in the scale of created beings, that intermarriages between white persons and negroes or mulattoes were regarded as unnatural and immoral, and punished as crimes.

The language of the Declaration of Independence is equally conclusive: "We hold these truths to be self-evident: that all men are created equal . . . ." The general words above quoted would seem to embrace the whole human family, and if they were used in a similar instrument at this day would be so understood. But it is too clear for dispute, that the enslaved African race were not intended to be included; for if the language, as understood in that day, would embrace them, the conduct of the distinguished men who framed the Declaration of Independence would have been utterly and flagrantly inconsistent with the principles they asserted.

Yet the men who framed this declaration were great men — high in literary acquirements — high in their sense of honor, and incapable of asserting principles inconsistent with those on which they were acting. They perfectly understood the meaning of the language they used, and how it would be understood by others; and they knew that it would not in any part of the civilized world be supposed to embrace the negro race. The unhappy black race were separated from the white by indelible marks, and laws long before established, and were never thought of or spoken of except as property.

This state of public opinion had undergone no change when the Constitution was adopted, as is equally evident from its provisions and language. The brief preamble sets forth by whom it was formed, for what purposes, and for whose benefit and protection. It declares that it is formed by the *people* of the United States; that is to say, by those who were members of the different political communities in the several States. It does not define what description of persons are intended to be included under these terms, or who shall be regarded as a citizen and one of the people. It uses them as terms so well understood, that no further description or definition was necessary.

But there are two clauses in the Constitution which point directly and specifically to the negro race as a separate class of persons, and show clearly that they were not regarded as a portion of the people or citizens of the Government then formed. One of these clauses reserves to each of the thirteen States the right to import slaves until the year 1808, if it thinks proper. And by the other provision the States pledge themselves to each other to maintain the right of property of the master, by delivering up to him any slave who may have escaped from his service, and be found within their respective territories.

More especially, it cannot be believed that the large slaveholding States regarded them as included in the word citizens, or would have consented to a Constitution which might compel them to receive them in that character from another State. For if they were so received, and entitled to the privileges and immunities of citizens, it would give to persons of the negro race, who were recognized as citizens in any one State of the Union, the right to enter every other State whenever they pleased, singly or in companies, without pass or passport, and without obstruction, to sojourn there as long as they pleased, to go where they pleased at every hour of the day or night without molestation; and it would give them the full liberty of speech in public and in private upon all subjects upon which its own citizens might speak; to hold public meetings upon political affairs, and to keep and carry arms wherever they went.

To all this mass of proof we have still to add, that Congress has repeatedly legislated upon the same construction of the Constitution that we have given. Three laws will be abundantly sufficient to show this. The first of these acts is the naturalization law, which was passed at the second session of the first Congress, March 26, 1790, and confines the right of becoming citizens "*to aliens being free white persons.*" Another of the early laws of which we have spoken, is the first militia law, which was passed in 1792, at the first session of the second Congress. It directs that every "free able-bodied white male citizen" shall be enrolled in the militia. The third act to which we have alluded is even still more decisive; it was passed as late as 1813, and it provides: "That from and after the termination of the war in which the United States are now engaged with Great Britain, it shall not be lawful to employ, on board of any public or private vessels of the United States, any person or persons except citizens of the United States, *or* persons of color, natives of the United States."

The conduct of the Executive Department of the Government has been in perfect harmony upon this subject with this course of legislation.

No one, we presume, supposes that any change in public opinion or feeling, in relation to this unfortunate race, should induce the court to give to the words of the Constitution a more liberal construction in their favor than they were intended to bear when the instrument was framed and adopted. Such an argument would be altogether inadmissible in any tribunal called on to interpret it. If any of its provisions are deemed unjust, there is a mode prescribed in the instrument itself by which it may be amended; but while it remains unaltered, it must be construed now as it was understood at the time of its adoption. [A]s long as it continues to exist in its present form, it speaks not only in the same words, but with the same meaning and intent with which it spoke when it came from the hands of its framers, and was voted on and adopted by the people of the United States. Any other rule of construction would abrogate the judicial character of this court, and make it the mere reflex of the popular opinion or passion of the day.

And upon a full and careful consideration of the subject, the court is of opinion, that, upon the facts stated in the plea in abatement, Dred Scott was not a citizen of Missouri within the meaning of the Constitution of the United States, and not entitled as such to sue in its courts; and, consequently, that the Circuit Court had no jurisdiction of the case.

[II]

We proceed, therefore, to inquire whether the facts relied on by the plaintiff entitled him to his freedom. Was he, together with his family, free in Missouri by reason of the stay in the territory of the United States hereinbefore mentioned? The act of Congress, upon which the plaintiff relies, declares that slavery and involuntary servitude, except as a punishment for crime, shall be forever prohibited in all that part of the territory ceded by France, under the name of Louisiana, which lies north of thirty-six degrees thirty minutes north latitude, and not included within the limits of Missouri.

* * *

[T]he power of Congress over the person or property of a citizen can never be a mere discretionary power under our Constitution and form of Government. The powers of the Government and the rights and privileges of the citizen are regulated and plainly defined by the Constitution itself. These powers, and others, in relation to rights of person, are, in express and positive terms, denied to the General Government; and the rights of private property have been guarded with equal care. Thus the rights of property are united with the rights of person, and placed on the same ground by the fifth amendment to the Constitution, which provides that no person shall be deprived of life, liberty, and property, without due process of law. And an act of Congress which deprives a citizen of the United States of his liberty or property, merely because he came himself or brought his property into a particular Territory of the United States, and who had committed no offence against the laws, could hardly be dignified with the name of due process of law.

It seems, however, to be supposed, that there is a difference between property in a slave and other property, and that different rules may be applied to it in expounding the Constitution of the United States. Now, the right of property in a slave is distinctly and expressly affirmed in the Constitution. The right to traffic in it, like an ordinary article of merchandise and property, was guarantied to the citizens of the United States, in every State that might desire it, for twenty years. And the Government in express terms is pledged to protect it in all future time, if the slave escapes from his owner.

Upon these considerations, it is the opinion of the court that the act of Congress which prohibited a citizen from holding and owning property of this kind in the territory of the United States north of the line therein mentioned, is not warranted by the Constitution, and is therefore void; and that neither Dred Scott himself, nor any of his family, were made free by being carried into this territory.

EXERCISE 2:

1. What is or are *Dred Scott*'s holding(s)?

2. Explain Chief Justice Taney's reasoning in concluding that black Americans are not United States citizens, within the meaning of Article III.

3. What interpretative methodology did the Chief Justice utilize to arrive at his conclusion?

4.   Critique the Chief Justice's reasoning.

5.   Explain Chief Justice Taney's reasoning in concluding that slaves are property protected by the Fifth Amendment's Due Process Clause.

6.   What interpretative methodology did the Chief Justice utilize to arrive at his conclusion?

7.   Critique the Chief Justice's reasoning.

8.   What was the role of race in antebellum America, as described in Chief Justice Taney's opinion?

9.   What was the role of race in antebellum America, as reflected by Chief Justice Taney's opinion?

10.   There has been and remains significant scholarly criticism of Chief Justice Taney's historical claims, such as his claim that black Americans were not citizens of the United States at the ratification of the Constitution.

11.   Chief Justice Taney was a Jacksonian Democrat, appointed to the Supreme Court by President Jackson, after he served Jackson as Attorney General. Chief Justice Taney was from a Maryland slaveholding family but, ironically, he freed the slaves he inherited upon his father's death.

12.   Historical evidence suggests that the Chief Justice believed that the *Dred Scott* decision would lessen the intense national strife over slavery. Was that a reasonable belief? Should Supreme Court justices rely on that belief as a factor in making their decisions?

Against the background of the role of race both described in and exemplified by *Dred Scott*, the evolution of the Supreme Court's equal protection case law described in this **Chapter** is clearer.

2.   The Equal Protection Clause's Original Meaning

The Equal Protection Clause's original meaning is — relative to the other clauses in Section 1 of the Fourteenth Amendment — challenging to recover, and for two main of reasons. First, unlike both the Privileges or Immunities Clause and the Due Process Clause, the Equal Protection Clause does not have a predecessor text in the original Constitution. Second, unlike the Privileges or Immunities Clause, there was little discussion in the Reconstruction Congress focused on the Equal Protection Clause.

That being said, by examining other sources of evidence — including traditional notions of the role of government at the time of enactment of the Fourteenth Amendment; the customary uses of the language employed by the Framers; and, the congressional debates during and after enactment — it is possible to arrive at the Clause's original meaning with a fair degree of confidence. The original meaning of the Equal Protection Clause is that "protection of the laws" is the duty of state governments to affirmatively protect all persons and their property "from violence and to enforce their rights through the court system."[1] This is known as the "duty-to-protect" or "remedial" interpretation of the Clause.[2]

The first important piece of evidence regarding the Equal Protection Clause's original meaning is the long-standing, pervasive, and influential understanding of government that is labeled "allegiance-for protection."[3] Based on the philosophies of influential theorists like John Locke[4] and jurists such as Sir William Blackstone,[5] the allegiance-for-protection theory states that government has a duty to protect persons within its jurisdiction in exchange for allegiance to the government and its laws.[6] This arrangement is a "social compact" in which (natural) rights are relinquished in exchange for the creation of and protection by a government.[7] For instance, a prominent justification for the American Revolution was that the colonists no longer owed allegiance to the king because the king had ceased protecting them.[8] In 1765, John Adams asked: "Are not protection and allegiance reciprocal? And if we are out of the king's protection, are we not discharged from our allegiance?"[9] The idea of allegiance-for-protection also became a central theme in the Declaration of Independence.[10]

The Declaration of Independence held deep significance for Republicans from the party's inception. The 1856 Republican Party Platform began by resolving that "[t]he maintenance of the principles promulgated in the Declaration of Independence . . . must and shall be preserved."[11] For many Republicans, the Declaration was America's founding document.[12]

The Republican embrace of the Declaration was evident in the debates leading up to the enactment of the Fourteenth Amendment, especially among the more radical

---

[1] Christopher R. Green, *The Original Sense of the (Equal) Protection Clause: Pre-enactment History*, 19 GEO. MASON. U. CIV. RTS. L.J. 1, 1 (2008). Professor Green's scholarship describing the Equal Protection Clause's original meaning is thorough and persuasive. For a contrary view, see Melissa L. Saunders, *Equal Protection, Class Legislation, and Color-Blindness*, 96 MICH. L. REV. 245 (1997).

[2] *See* Green, *supra*, at 3 (using the first of these labels).

[3] *Id.* at 34–43; *see also* ROBERT J. HARRIS, THE QUEST FOR EQUALITY: THE CONSTITUTION, CONGRESS, AND THE SUPREME COURT 32 (1960).

[4] JOHN LOCKE, SECOND TREATISE OF GOVERNMENT § 191 (1698) (Peter Laslett ed. 1988).

[5] 1 SIR WILLIAM BLACKSTONE, COMMENTARIES ON THE LAWS OF ENGLAND *365 (1769).

[6] *See* Green, *supra*, at 34–43 (providing abundant evidence for this).

[7] HARRIS, *supra*, at 2–3, 9.

[8] Green, *supra*, at 34–35.

[9] JOHN ADAMS, THE WORKS OF JOHN ADAMS 162 (1856); *see also* Green, *supra*, at 34.

[10] The Declaration of Independence para. 2 (1776) ("That to secure these rights, governments are instituted among men, deriving their just powers from the consent of the governed."); *see also id.* at para. 25 ("He has abdicated government here, withdrawing his governors, and declaring us out of his protection.").

[11] Republican Party Platform, para. 2 (June 18, 1856).

[12] Jack B. Weinstein, *The Role of Judges in a Government of, by, and for the People: Notes for the Fifty-Eighth Cardozo Lecture*, 30 CARDOZO L. REV. 1, 15 (2008). President Lincoln went so far as to proclaim the Declaration an "apple of gold" surrounded by the "silver frame" of the Constitution. Allen C. Guelzo, *Apple of Gold in a Picture of Silver: The Constitution and Liberty, in* THE LINCOLN ENIGMA, at 86–87 (Gabor Boritt ed., 2001).

sections of the party.[13] Thaddeus Stevens declared that the principles of Section 1 "are all asserted, in some form or other, in our Declaration."[14] The congressional Republicans also explicitly relied on the allegiance-for-protection theory to justify Reconstruction legislation, such as the 1866 Civil Rights Act.[15] The allegiance-for-protection view was so powerful that it was widely accepted that protection of the laws extended even to foreigners. Senator Edgar Cowan observed:

> If a traveler comes here from Ethiopia, from Australia, or from Great Britain, he is entitled, to a certain extent, to the protection of the laws. You cannot murder him with impunity. It is murder to kill him, the same as it is to kill another man. You cannot commit an assault and battery on him, I apprehend. He has a right to the protection of the laws.[16]

The text of the Equal Protection Clause likewise reflects this allegiance-for-protection ideal.[17] The Clause requires allegiance from protected persons by limiting the Clause's sweep to "person[s] within its jurisdiction."[18] Second, it textually mandates protection: "protection of the laws."[19]

This weaving together of the allegiance-for-protection and the Equal Protection Clause's text also fits nicely with the background against which the Clause was drafted. After the Civil War, southern states enacted oppressive laws that came to be known as Black Codes. These Codes denied government protection of certain rights, among them many of the fundamental rights to life, liberty, and property.[20] In addition, during this period, southern state officials either turned a blind eye toward or actively participated in violations of newly-freed black Americans' personal integrity and property. For the Equal Protection Clause's drafters, the Clause helped remedy these depredations by mandating that southern governmental officials actively enforce laws against, for example, murder and theft. In other words, the Clause forced states

---

[13] Green, *supra*, at 38–40.

[14] CONG. GLOBE, 39th Cong., 1st Sess. 2459 (May 8, 1866) (Representative Thaddeus Stevens); *see also* CONG. GLOBE, 39th Cong., 1st Sess. 2961 (June 5, 1866) (statement of Senator Luke Poland) (stating that Section 1 "is the very spirit and inspiration of our system of government, the absolute foundation upon which it was established. It is essentially declared in the Declaration of Independence.").

[15] *E.g.*, CONG. GLOBE, 39th Cong., 1st Sess. 2799 (May 24, 1866) (Senator William M. Stewart); *see also* Green, *supra*, at 38–39 (collecting evidence).

[16] CONG. GLOBE, 39th Cong., 1st Sess. 516 (May 30, 1866) (statement of Senator Edgar Cowan).

In harmony with the allegiance-for-protection theory, by the mid-nineteenth century, protection of the laws was viewed as a discrete right that belonged to individuals. *See* Earl A. Maltz, *The Concept of Equal Protection of the Laws — A Historical Inquiry*, 22 SAN DIEGO L. REV. 499, 507 (1985). For instance, Justice Bushrod Washington, in his recitation of the privileges and immunities contained in Article IV of the Constitution, stated that "protection by the government" was a right protected by the Constitution. *Corfield v. Coryell*, 6 F. Cas. 546, 551 (C.C.E.D. Pa. 1823) (No. 3,230); *see also* Green, *supra*, at 71–72.

[17] *See* Green, *supra*, at 41–42 (making this point).

[18] U.S. CONST. amend. XIV, § 1.

[19] *Id.*

[20] CONG. GLOBE, 39th Cong., 1st Sess. 516 (Jan. 30, 1866) (statement of Rep. Thomas D. Eliot); *see also id.* at 39 (Dec. 13, 1865) (statement of Senator Henry Wilson) (citing a Louisiana proposal); *id.* at 3170 (June 14, 1866) (statement of Rep. Ignatius L. Donnelly) (citing the South Carolina, Mississippi, Tennessee, and Virginia codes).

to live up to their end of the allegiance-for-protection bargain with their black citizens.

The second body of important evidence of the Clause's original meaning is that the Clause's key phrase, "protection of the laws," had acquired, by 1868, a traditional legal meaning: "the enforcement and remedial functions of law."[21] For instance, William Blackstone defined "protection of the law" as the assertion and recovery for violation of rights.[22]

The governmental functions covered by the phrase "protection of the laws" included executive protection of rights to person and property, along with open access to state court systems for redress of rights violations. For instance, if an African American was subject to private violence, such as the theft of his horse, the "protection of the laws" mandated that the state enable the victim to bring suit in state court for the recovery of the horse (or damages). As recounted by Congressman John Beatty:

> Now, certain States have denied to persons within their jurisdiction the equal protection of the laws. The proof on this point is voluminous and unquestionable. It consists of the sworn testimony of ministers of the Gospel who have been scourged because of their political opinions, of humble citizens who have been whipped and wounded for the same reason, of learned judges within whose circuits men were murdered, houses were burned, women were outraged, men were scourged, and officers of the law shot down; and the State made no successful effort to bring the guilty to punishment or afford protection or redress to the outraged and innocent. The State, from lack of power or inclination, practically denied the equal protection of the law to these persons.[23]

As shown by the Black Codes, the denial of the right to protection of the laws could occur as a result of affirmative state action. However, as the Reconstruction Republicans were also aware, state *inaction* could just as easily result in the denial of protection. Abolitionists, which included many Republicans, were regularly subject to mob violence in the South and "sought protection for their own rights of life, liberty, and property."[24] Southern governments were often unsympathetic to victims, and sometimes even encouraged mob violence.[25]

Again, this interpretation fits nicely with the historical background. After the Civil War, both through their action and inaction, southern state executive officials failed to protect ex-slaves' rights and closed the metaphorical courthouse door to their legal claims for redress.

The debates in Congress over Reconstruction legislation provide the third important source of evidence of the Equal Protection Clause's original meaning. Beyond brief allusions and vague descriptions of the principles underlying the Equal Protection Clause, the Clause itself was never clearly addressed during the debates over the

---

[21] Green, *supra*, at 43–69.

[22] BLACKSTONE, *supra*, at *37.

[23] CONG. GLOBE, 42d Cong., 1st Sess. 428 (Apr. 3, 1871) (statement of Rep. John Beatty).

[24] Maltz, *supra*, at 510.

[25] *Id.* at 511.

Fourteenth Amendment,[26] and scholars generally acknowledge that the congressional debates leading up to the enactment of the Fourteenth Amendment provide less-than-clear evidence of the Clause's meaning.[27] Whereas the Privileges or Immunities Clause received a fair amount of discussion during the debates, when the text of the Equal Protection Clause was addressed, members of Congress typically "lumped" it together with other provisions of Section 1.[28]

Nevertheless, there was a direct and informative discussion bearing on the Equal Protection Clause's original meaning in congressional debates over other Reconstruction legislation. Most important is the debate over the Civil Rights Act of 1871.[29] The importance of this debate is bolstered by the fact that many of the Fourteenth Amendment's Framers were congressmen when the federal government was asked to intervene against rampant private acts of violence committed by the Ku Klux Klan.[30] The Klan's acts went unpunished and were frequently aided by southern officials so, in response, Congress enacted the Civil Rights Act of 1871.[31]

The Act forbade private action "impeding, hindering, obstructing, or defeating the due course of justice in any State."[32] This text supports the remedial interpretation of the Clause because it prohibits interference with the execution of a state's laws and remedying rights violations in court.[33]

In the debates leading up to the Act, several proponents voiced their remedial understanding of the Equal Protection Clause. Supporters of the Act denied their opponents' argument that the Equal Protection Clause only applied to state legislative action. Senator Edmunds responded:

---

[26] Green, *supra*, at 16. Some supporters of the theory that the Equal Protection Clause forbids discriminatory classifications in legislation base their argument on Senator Jacob Howard's speech on May 23, 1866. In his speech, Senator Howard declared that: "The last two clauses of the first section of the amendment disable a State from depriving not merely a citizen of the United States, but any person, whoever he may be, of life, liberty, or property without due process of law, or from denying to him the equal protection of the laws of the State. *This abolishes all class legislation in the States*." Cong. Globe, 39th Cong., 1st Sess. 2549 (May 23, 1866) (statement of Senator Jacob Howard) (emphasis added). However, Senator Howard appears to be combining the Due Process and Equal Protection Clauses, and so it is unclear as to which clause he is referring at various points during his speech. For a thorough discussion, *see* Green, *supra*, at 16, 28–31.

[27] Green, *supra*, at 12; *see also* Harris, *supra*, at 35–36, 39–40 (stating that the debates were "ambiguous," and "confusing"); Christopher Wolfe, The Rise of Modern Judicial Review 140 (1986); Akhil Reed Amar, The Bill of Rights: Creation and Reconstruction 182 (1998).

[28] Green, *supra*, at 16; Harris, *supra*, at 35–36; Wolfe, *supra*, at 140.

[29] An Act to Enforce the Provisions of the Fourteenth Amendment to the Constitution of the United States, and for Other Purposes, 17 Stat. 13 (1871).

[30] *See* Christopher R. Green, *The Original Sense of the (Equal) Protection Clause: Subsequent Interpretation and Application*, 19 Geo. Mason. U. Civ. Rts. L.J. 219, 223–52 (2008) (discussing this evidence in detail).

[31] An Act to Enforce the Provisions of the Fourteenth Amendment to the Constitution of the United States, and for Other Purposes, 17 Stat. 13 (1871).

[32] *Id.* at § 2; Green, *supra*, at 225–26.

[33] *See also* An Act to Enforce the Provisions of the Fourteenth Amendment to the Constitution of the United States, and for Other Purposes, 17 Stat. 13, § 3 (1871) (stating that a state's failure or active refusal to protect people's rights is a denial of equal protection).

A Legislature acting directly does not afford to any person the protection of the law; it makes the law under which and through which, being executed by the functionaries appointed by the State for that purpose, citizens receive the protection of the law.[34]

Representative Job E. Stevenson argued that it was the federal government's duty to execute the laws, and not to compel protection through legislation:

Gentlemen contend that this provision will operate only where a State fails to pass equal laws and excludes a class of citizens from protection; but the language is, "equal protection of the laws." The words "the laws" imply existing laws; and the benefit secured is the "protection" of the laws, and this requires their execution. Unexecuted laws are no "protection." And this brings us to this very case: the States have laws providing for equal protection, but they do not, because either they will not or cannot, enforce them equally; and hence a class of citizens have not "the protection of the laws. Union men, white and black, are "denied" the protection of laws.[35]

Senator John Pool summarized the Republicans' position:

The [Equal Protection Clause] relates more particularly to the executive branch of the State governments, and embraces failure to act. It is in these words: "Nor deny to any person within its jurisdiction the equal protection of the laws." The protection of the laws can hardly be denied except by failure to execute them. While the laws are executed their protection is necessarily afforded. Rights conferred by laws as worthless unless the laws be executed. The right to personal liberty or personal security can be protected only by the execution of the laws upon those who violate such rights. A failure to punish the offender is not only to deny to the person injured the protection of the laws, but to deprive him, in effect, of the rights themselves. By the first section of the fourteenth amendment a new right, so far as it depends on express constitutional provision, is conferred upon every citizen: it is the right to the protection of the laws. This is the most valuable of all rights, without which all others are worthless and all right and all liberty but an empty name. To deny this greatest of all rights is expressly prohibited to the States as a breach of that primary duty upon them by the national Constitution. Where any State, by commission or omission, denies this right to the protection of the laws, Congress may, by appropriate legislation, enforce and maintain it. But Congress must deal with individuals, not States. It must punish the offender against the rights of the citizen; for in no other way can protection of the laws be secured and its denial prevented.[36]

---

[34] Cong. Globe, 42d Cong., 1st Sess. 697 (Apr. 14, 1871) (statement of Senator George Franklin Edmunds).

[35] Id. at 300 (Mar. 27, 1871) (statement of Rep. Job E. Stevenson).

[36] Id. at 608 (Apr. 12, 1871) (statement of Senator John Pool).

Just as government could deny protection of the laws through legislation, similar results would occur if government failed or refused to act.[37] The Equal Protection Clause granted all persons the discrete right to protection of the laws; only by requiring the States to execute their laws would *equal* protection be achieved.

The arguments offered in favor of the 1871 Civil Rights Act dovetail with the allegiance-for-protection theory. Republican proponents pointed to southern states' failures — both through action and inaction — as evidence of the states' breach of their duty to protect. For example, Representative John Bingham argued that the federal government's own duty-to-protect allowed it to supplant the state governments where they failed or refused to do their duty.[38]

In sum, based on the evidence discussed above, the Equal Protection Clause's original meaning is that it required states to protect individual bodily integrity and property rights through enforcement of state law and prescribed that state courts must offer redress for violations of personal and property rights.

C. LIMITED APPLICATION

Soon after passage of the Fourteenth Amendment, the Supreme Court had a number of opportunities to interpret the Equal Protection Clause. It did so with progressively more narrowness until, in 1927, Justice Holmes could quip that the Clause was "the usual last resort of constitutional arguments."[39]

The first major Supreme Court case was *Strauder v. West Virginia*, 100 U.S. (10 Otto) 303 (1879), which involved a challenge to a West Virginia law that permitted only white, male citizens, at least twenty-one years old, to serve on juries. Strauder was a black man convicted of murder by an all-white jury composed under the challenged statute. *Id.* at 304.

The Supreme Court ruled that the statute violated the Equal Protection Clause. In a key passage interpreting the Clause, the Court stated:

> What is [equal protection] but declaring that the law in the States shall be the same for the black as for the white; that all persons, whether colored or white, shall stand equal before the laws of the States, and, in regard to the colored race . . . that no discrimination shall be made against them by law because of their color? The words of the amendment . . . contain a necessary implication of a positive immunity, or right, most valuable to the colored race — the right to exemption from unfriendly legislation against them distinctively as colored — exemption from legal discriminations, implying inferiority in civil society, lessening the security of their enjoyment of the rights which others enjoy, and discriminations which are steps towards reducing them to the condition of a subject race.

Id. at 307–08. West Virginia's discrimination in access to the justice system, on the

---

[37] *See also* Green, *supra*, at 231–34 (making this point).

[38] HARRIS, *supra*, at 45.

[39] Buck v. Bell, 274 U.S. 200, 208 (1927).

basis of race, violated the Clause, the Court held. *Id.* at 308–09; *see also id.* at 309 ("It is not easy to comprehend how it can be said that while every white man is entitled to a trial by a jury selected . . . without discrimination against his color, and a negro is not, the latter is equally protected by the law with the former.").

The *Strauder* Court's interpretation of the Equal Protection Clause could be understood fairly capaciously. A similar use of the Clause occurred in *Yick Wo v. Hopkins*, 118 U.S. 356 (1886), where the Supreme Court struck down a San Francisco city ordinance that had prohibited operating laundries in wooden building without a permit. The ordinance's purported goal was to limit the fires frequently caused by wooden laundries. However, the vast majority of wooden laundries were owned by people of Chinese descent and, while all requests for permission by Chinese launderers were denied, nearly all such permits by non-Chinese launderers were granted. *Id.* at 374.

The Supreme Court ruled that discriminatory application of the ordinance caused it to violate the Equal Protection Clause. *Id.* at 373–74. "Though the law itself be fair on its face, and impartial in appearance, yet, if it is applied and administered by public authority with an evil eye and an unequal hand, so as practically to make unjust and illegal discriminations between persons in similar circumstances, material to their rights, the denial of equal justice is still within the prohibition of the constitution." *Id.* at 374.

However, ten years later, the Supreme Court articulated what has become known as the infamous "separate but equal" doctrine, in *Plessy v. Ferguson*, 163 U.S. 537 (1896).

PLESSY v. FERGUSON
163 U.S. 537 (1896)

MR. JUSTICE BROWN delivered the opinion of the court.

This case turns upon the constitutionality of an act of the general assembly of the state of Louisiana, passed in 1890, providing for separate railway carriages for the white and colored races. The information filed in the criminal district court charged, in substance, that Plessy, being a passenger, was assigned by officers of the company to the coach used for the race to which he belonged, but he insisted upon going into a coach used by the race to which he did not belong.

The constitutionality of this act is attacked upon the ground that it conflicts with the fourteenth amendment. The object of the amendment was undoubtedly to enforce the absolute equality of the two races before the law, but, in the nature of things, it could not have been intended to abolish distinctions based upon color, or to enforce social, as distinguished from political, equality, or a commingling of the two races upon terms unsatisfactory to either. Laws permitting, and even requiring, their separation, in places where they are liable to be brought into contact, do not necessarily imply the inferiority of either race to the other, and have been generally, if not universally, recognized as within the competency of the state legislatures in the exercise of their police power. The most common instance of this is connected with the establishment of separate schools for white and colored children, which have been held to be a valid exercise of the legislative power even by courts of states where the political rights of the colored race have been longest and most earnestly enforced.

One of the earliest of these cases is that of *Roberts v. City of Boston*, [59 Mass.] (5 Cush.) 198 [(1849)], in which the supreme judicial court of Massachusetts held that the general school committee of Boston had power to make provision for the instruction of colored children in separate schools established exclusively for them, and to prohibit their attendance upon the other schools. Similar laws have been enacted by congress under its general power of legislation over the District of Columbia, as well as by the legislatures of many of the states. [Listing cases from Ohio, Missouri, New York, Indiana, Louisiana, and Kentucky.]

Laws forbidding the intermarriage of the two races may be said in a technical sense to interfere with the freedom of contract, and yet have been universally recognized as within the police power of the state.

The distinction between laws interfering with the political equality of the negro and those requiring the separation of the two races in schools, theaters, and railway carriages has been frequently drawn by this court. Thus, in *Strauder v. West Virginia*, 100 U. S. [(10 Otto)] 303 [(1879)], it was held that a law of West Virginia limiting to white male persons 21 years of age, and citizens of the state, the right to sit upon juries, was a discrimination which implied a legal inferiority in civil society, which lessened the security of the right of the colored race, and was a step towards reducing them to a condition of servility. Similar statutes for the separation of the two races upon public conveyances were held to be constitutional in [cases from Pennsylvania, Michigan, Illinois, Tennessee, federal admiralty, New York, and Texas].

We think the enforced separation of the races neither abridges the privileges or immunities of the colored man, deprives him of his property without due process of law, nor denies him the equal protection of the laws, within the meaning of the fourteenth amendment.

In this connection, it is also suggested by the learned counsel for the plaintiff in error that the same argument that will justify the state legislature in requiring railways to provide separate accommodations for the two races will also authorize them to require separate cars to be provided for people whose hair is of a certain color, or who are aliens, or who belong to certain nationalities, or to enact laws requiring colored people to walk upon one side of the street, and white people upon the other, or requiring white men's houses to be painted white, and colored men's black, or their vehicles or business signs to be of different colors, upon the theory that one side of the street is as good as the other, or that a house or vehicle of one color is as good as one of another color. The reply to all this is that every exercise of the police power must be reasonable, and extend only to such laws as are enacted in good faith for the promotion of the public good, and not for the annoyance or oppression of a particular class. Thus, in *Yick Wo v. Hopkins*, 118 U. S. 356 (1886), [the municipal ordinance] was held to be a covert attempt on the part of the municipality to make an arbitrary and unjust discrimination against the Chinese race.

We consider the underlying fallacy of the plaintiff's argument to consist in the assumption that the enforced separation of the two races stamps the colored race with a badge of inferiority. If this be so, it is not by reason of anything found in the act, but solely because the colored race chooses to put that construction upon it. The argument necessarily assumes that if, as has been more than once the case, and is not unlikely to be so again, the colored race should become the dominant power in the state legislature, and should enact a law in precisely similar terms, it would thereby relegate the white race to an inferior position. We imagine that the white race, at least, would not acquiesce in this assumption. The argument also assumes that social prejudices may be overcome by legislation, and that equal rights cannot be secured to the negro except by an enforced commingling of the two races. We cannot accept this proposition. If the two races are to meet upon terms of social equality, it must be the result of natural affinities, a mutual appreciation of each other's merits, and a voluntary consent of individuals. Legislation is powerless to eradicate racial instincts, or to abolish distinctions based upon physical differences, and the attempt to do so can only result in accentuating the difficulties of the present situation. If the civil and political rights of both races be equal, one cannot be inferior to the other civilly or politically. If one race be inferior to the other socially, the constitution of the United States cannot put them upon the same plane.

The judgment of the court below is therefore affirmed.

MR. JUSTICE BREWER did not hear the argument or participate in the decision of this case.

MR. JUSTICE HARLAN dissenting.

In respect of civil rights, common to all citizens, the constitution of the United States does not, I think, permit any public authority to know the race of those entitled to be protected in the enjoyment of such rights. Every true man has pride of race, and under appropriate circumstances, when the rights of others, his equals before the law, are not to be affected, it is his privilege to express such pride and to take such action based upon it as to him seems proper. But I deny that any legislative body or judicial tribunal may have regard to the race of citizens when the civil rights of those citizens are involved. Indeed, such legislation as that here in question is inconsistent not only with that equality of rights which pertains to citizenship, national and state, but with the personal liberty enjoyed by every one within the United States.

The thirteenth amendment does not permit the withholding or the deprivation of any right necessarily inhering in freedom. It not only struck down the institution of slavery as previously existing in the United States, but it prevents the imposition of any burdens or disabilities that constitute badges of slavery or servitude. But, that amendment having been found inadequate to the protection of the rights of those who had been in slavery, it was followed by the fourteenth amendment. These two amendments, if enforced according to their true intent and meaning, will protect all the civil rights that pertain to freedom and citizenship. Finally, and to the end that no citizen should be denied, on account of his race, the privilege of participating in the political control of his country, the fifteenth amendment [was adopted].

These notable additions to the fundamental law removed the race line from our governmental systems. It was, consequently, adjudged that a state law that excluded citizens of the colored race from juries, because of their race, was repugnant to the fourteenth amendment. *Strauder v. West Virginia*, 100 U. S. [(10 Otto)] 303 [(1879)].

It was said in argument that the statute of Louisiana does not discriminate against either race, but prescribes a rule applicable alike to white and colored citizens. But this argument does not meet the difficulty. Every one knows that the statute in question had its origin in the purpose, not so much to exclude white persons from railroad cars occupied by blacks, as to exclude colored people from coaches occupied by or assigned to white persons. The thing to accomplish was, under the guise of giving equal accommodation for whites and blacks, to compel the latter to keep to themselves while traveling in railroad passenger coaches. No one would be so wanting in candor as to assert the contrary. The fundamental objection, therefore, to the statute, is that it interferes with the personal freedom of citizens. If a white man and a black man choose to occupy the same public conveyance on a public highway, it is their right to do so; and no government, proceeding alone on grounds of race, can prevent it without infringing the personal liberty of each.

If a state can prescribe, as a rule of civil conduct, that whites and blacks shall not travel as passengers in the same railroad coach, why may it not so regulate the use of the streets of its cities and towns as to compel white citizens to keep on one side of a street, and black citizens to keep on the other? The answer given at the argument to these questions was that regulations of the kind they suggest would be unreasonable, and could not, therefore, stand before the law. Is it meant that the determination of questions of legislative power depends upon the inquiry whether the statute whose validity is questioned is, in the judgment of the courts, a reasonable one, taking all the circumstances into consideration? A statute may be unreasonable merely because a sound public policy forbade its enactment. But I do not understand that the courts have anything to do with the policy or expediency of legislation. There is a dangerous tendency in these latter days to enlarge the functions of the courts, by means of judicial interference with the will of the people as expressed by the legislature. Our institutions have the distinguishing characteristic that the three departments of government are co-ordinate and separate. Each much keep within the limits defined by the constitution. And the courts best discharge their duty by executing the will of the law-making power, constitutionally expressed, leaving the results of legislation to be dealt with by the people through their representatives. [T]he intent of the legislature is to be respected if the particular statute in question is valid, although the courts, looking at the public interests, may conceive the statute to be both unreasonable and impolitic. If the power exists to enact a statute, that ends the matter so far as the courts are concerned.

The white race deems itself to be the dominant race in this country. And so it is, in prestige, in achievements, in education, in wealth, and in power. So, I doubt not, it will continue to be for all time, if it remains true to its great heritage, and holds fast to the principles of constitutional liberty. But in view of the constitution, in the eye of the law, there is in this country no superior, dominant, ruling class of citizens. There is no caste here. Our constitution is color-blind, and neither knows nor tolerates classes among citizens. In respect of civil rights, all citizens are equal before the law. The humblest is the peer of the most powerful. The law regards man as man, and takes no account of his surroundings or of his color when his civil rights as guaranteed by the supreme law of the land are involved.

In my opinion, the judgment this day rendered will, in time, prove to be quite as pernicious as the decision made by this tribunal in the *Dred Scott Case*. The present decision, it may well be apprehended, will not only stimulate aggressions, more or less brutal and irritating, upon the admitted rights of colored citizens, but will encourage the belief that it is possible, by means of state enactments, to defeat the beneficent purposes which the people of the United States had in view when they adopted the recent amendments of the constitution.

The destinies of the two races, in this country, are indissolubly linked together, and the interests of both require that the common government of all shall not permit the seeds of race hate to be planted under the sanction of law. What can more certainly arouse race hate, what more certainly create and perpetuate a feeling of distrust between these races, than state enactments which, in fact, proceed on the ground that colored citizens are so inferior and degraded that they cannot be allowed to sit in public coaches occupied by white citizens? That, as all will admit, is the real meaning of such legislation as was enacted in Louisiana.

For the reason stated, I am constrained to withhold my assent from the opinion and judgment of the majority.

EXERCISE 3:

1.   The majority stated that the Equal Protection Clause's goal "was undoubtedly to enforce the absolute equality of the two races before the law, but, in the nature of things, it could not have been intended to . . . enforce social, as distinguished from political, equality, or a commingling of the two races." Does this distinction articulated by the majority really exist? Does the Equal Protection Clause embody this distinction?

2.   The *Plessy* Court claimed that legally-enforced separation based on race, by itself, did not create racial inferiority. Is that true?

3.   Relatedly, the *Plessy* Court claimed that legally-enforced separation based on race, by itself, did not violate equal protection. We are going to see that the *Brown* Court rejected this claim.

4.   What was the Court's response to Plessy's slippery-slope argument that states would enact outrageous laws that "require separate cars to be provided for people whose hair is of a certain color, or who are aliens, or who belong to certain nationalities, or to enact laws requiring colored people to walk upon one side of the street, and white people upon the other, or requiring white men's houses to be painted white, and colored men's black, or their vehicles or business signs to be of different colors"?

5.   Using today's analytical categories, what standard of review did the Supreme Court employ to evaluate Louisiana's separate-but-equal law?

6.   The majority argued that legally-enforced co-mingling of people — in other words, no separate-but-equal — of different races would not help advance social

equality for black Americans. This argument is a particular manifestation of a broader claim that is more frequently made: law cannot change how people believe and act; instead, culture must first change. Are either or both of these claims true?

7.   Was *Plessy* consistent with the Equal Protection Clause's original meaning?

8.   One of the disputes between the majority and Justice Harlan is over how to characterize the challenged Louisiana law. The majority rejected Justice Harlan's claim that the law was targeted against black Americans. What evidence should one look to in order to ascertain who was right? Who was right?

9.   Which is the better way to characterize Justice Harlan's interpretation of the Equal Protection Clause: (1) It forbids state use of race to harm racial minorities; or (2) It forbids state use of race for whatever reason, purpose, or effect? This is an extremely important question because Justice Harlan's dissent is one of those rare dissenting opinions that later comes to be seen as correct, so current justices appeal to Justice Harlan's dissent to support their respective conclusions. We will see this especially when we cover cases dealing with affirmative action.

10.   Justice Harlan argued that federal courts could not evaluate the "reasonableness" of state use of race because doing so would violate the separation of powers between the three branches of government. Is that true? How, if at all, would Justice Harlan's claim impact modern rational basis review under the Due Process and Equal Protection Clauses?

11.   There is a long-standing scholarly debate over whether the original meaning of the Equal Protection Clause prohibited racially segregated public education. Some of the evidence in favor of the conclusion that the Clause did not prohibit such practices is the existence of racially segregated public schools in the District of Columbia, and in northern states, contemporaneous with the Fourteenth Amendment's adoption. There was also concern expressed during congressional debates on the Fourteenth Amendment that it might be construed to prohibit states from racially segregating aspects of public life, such as schools. We will pick up this question again when discussing *Brown*, below.

12.   Racially segregated public life slowly gained steam as the nineteenth century progressed. By the time the Court decided *Plessy*, in 1896, legal and social practice had clearly moved in the direction of racial segregation (though *Plessy* gave pro-segregation forces a significant boost). One piece of evidence for this is found in the Court's reference to anti-miscegenation statutes to support its conclusion that racially segregated train cars are reasonable. Given this background, could the Supreme Court have ruled, even if it had wanted to, in Plessy's favor?

Following *Plessy*, the Supreme rejected nearly all challenges to state imposed or required racial discrimination. For example, in *Berea College v. Kentucky*, 211 U.S. 45 (1908), the Supreme Court upheld a Kentucky law that prohibited racially integrated education, even in private schools. Berea College had been the only institution of higher education in Kentucky to offer integrated education. *See also Gong Lum v. Rice*, 275 U.S. 78 (1927) (upholding Mississippi's decision to force a resident of Chinese descent to attend the "colored" public school under Mississippi's segregation law).

D.   REVIVAL OF THE EQUAL PROTECTION CLAUSE

1.   Pre-*Brown*

However, beginning with *Missouri ex rel. Gaines v. Canada*, 305 U.S. 337 (1938), the Supreme Court began to enforce the "equal" aspect of separate-but-equal, and struck down discriminatory laws with more frequency. In *Canada*, for instance, Gaines was denied admittance to the University of Missouri's law school. Because Missouri did not have a segregated, blacks-only law school, it offered to send Gaines to an out-of-state law school. Gaines sued to gain admission to the University of Missouri, and the Supreme Court ruled in his favor. The Court, working within the separate-but-equal doctrine, held that Missouri did not offer equal educational opportunities for law school. *Id.* at 345–50.

In *Sweatt v. Painter*, 339 U.S. 629 (1950), the Supreme Court ruled that, because the educational opportunities for black Texans at a recently established law school for blacks were not substantially equal to those of white Texans at the segregated University of Texas law school, the University of Texas must admit Sweatt. The Court explicitly worked within the confines of the separate-but-equal doctrine. *Id.* at 635–36. *See also McLaurin v. Oklahoma State Regents for Higher Education*, 339 U.S. 637 (1950) (ruling that admission to a state university, where the student would be segregated from other students on the basis of race, violated the separate-but-equal doctrine).

Around the same time, the Court also began utilizing other legal doctrines to limit racial discrimination. Most importantly, the Court began to articulate exceptions to the State Action Doctrine, reviewed in **Chapter 1**. For instance, in *Nixon v. Herndon*, 273 U.S. 536 (1927), *Nixon v. Condon*, 286 U.S. 73 (1932), and *Smith v. Allwright*, 321 U.S. 649 (1944), the Supreme Court relied on the nascent Public Functions Exception to rule that Texas' segregated Democratic Party primaries violated the Fourteenth and Fifteenth Amendments. *See also Terry v. Adams*, 345 U.S. 461 (1953) (ruling that the segregated "Jay Bird Democratic Association" primary constituted unconstitutional state action).

2.   *Brown v. Board of Education* (1954)

Brown v. Board of Education, 347 U.S. 483 (1954), is one of the most important Supreme Court cases in American history. First, it directly attacked a deeply entrenched — both legally and socially — institution: Jim Crow racial segregation. Second, *Brown* articulated a new and broader interpretation of the Equal Protection Clause. Third, it subjected the Supreme Court to criticism based on its interpretative methodology.

BROWN v. BOARD OF EDUCATION
347 U.S. 483 (1954)

MR. CHIEF JUSTICE WARREN delivered the opinion of the Court.

These cases come to us from the States of Kansas, South Carolina, Virginia, and Delaware. They are premised on different facts and different local conditions, but a common legal question justifies their consideration together in this consolidated opinion. In each of the cases, minors of the Negro race, through their legal representatives, seek the aid of the courts in obtaining admission to the public schools of their community on a nonsegregated basis. In each instance, they have been denied admission to schools attended by white children under laws requiring or permitting segregation according to race. This segregation was alleged to deprive the plaintiffs of the equal protection of the laws under the Fourteenth Amendment. In each of the cases other than the Delaware case, a three-judge federal district court denied relief to the plaintiffs on the so-called "separate but equal" doctrine announced by this Court in *Plessy v. Ferguson*, 163 U.S. 537 [(1896)].

The plaintiffs contend that segregated public schools are not "equal" and cannot be made "equal," and that hence they are deprived of the equal protection of the laws. Because of the obvious importance of the question presented, the Court took jurisdiction. Argument was heard in the 1952 Term, and reargument was heard this Term on certain questions propounded by the Court.

Reargument was largely devoted to the circumstances surrounding the adoption of the Fourteenth Amendment in 1868. It covered exhaustively consideration of the Amendment in Congress, ratification by the states, then existing practices in racial segregation, and the views of proponents and opponents of the Amendment. This discussion and our own investigation convince us that, although these sources cast some light, it is not enough to resolve the problem with which we are faced. At best, they are inconclusive. The most avid proponents of the post-War Amendments undoubtedly intended them to remove all legal distinctions. Their opponents, just as certainly, were antagonistic to both the letter and the spirit of the Amendments and wished them to have the most limited effect. What others in Congress and the state legislatures had in mind cannot be determined with any degree of certainty.

An additional reason for the inconclusive nature of the Amendment's history, with respect to segregated schools, is the status of public education at that time. In the South, the movement toward free common schools had not yet taken hold. Education of white children was largely in the hands of private groups. Education of Negroes was almost nonexistent. In fact, any education of Negroes was forbidden by law in some states. Today, in contrast, many Negroes have achieved outstanding success in the arts and sciences as well as in the business and professional world. It is true that public school education at the time of the Amendment had advanced further in the North, but the effect of the Amendment on Northern States was generally ignored in the congressional debates. Even in the North, the conditions of public education did not approximate those existing today. As a consequence, it is not surprising that there should be so little in the history of the Fourteenth Amendment relating to its intended effect on public education.

In the first cases in this Court construing the Fourteenth Amendment, decided shortly after its adoption, the Court interpreted it as proscribing all state-imposed discriminations against the Negro race.[5] The doctrine of "separate but equal" did not make its appearance in this court until 1896 in the case of *Plessy v. Ferguson*, involving not education but transportation. American courts have since labored with the doctrine for over half a century. In this Court, there have been six cases involving the "separate but equal" doctrine in the field of public education. In none of these cases was it necessary to re-examine the doctrine to grant relief to the Negro plaintiff.

In the instant cases, that question is directly presented. Here, unlike *Sweatt v. Painter*, [339 U.S. 629 (1950)], there are findings below that the Negro and white schools involved have been equalized, or are being equalized, with respect to buildings, curricula, qualifications and salaries of teachers, and other "tangible" factors. We must look instead to the effect of segregation itself on public education.

In approaching this problem, we cannot turn the clock back to 1868 when the Amendment was adopted, or even to 1896 when *Plessy v. Ferguson* was written. We must consider public education in the light of its full development and its present place in American life throughout the Nation.

Today, education is perhaps the most important function of state and local governments. Compulsory school attendance laws and the great expenditures for education both demonstrate our recognition of the importance of education to our democratic society. It is required in the performance of our most basic public responsibilities. It is the very foundation of good citizenship. Today it is a principal instrument in awakening the child to cultural values, in preparing him for later professional training, and in helping him to adjust normally to his environment. In these days, it is doubtful that any child may reasonably be expected to succeed in life if he is denied the opportunity of an education. Such an opportunity, where the state has undertaken to provide it, is a right which must be made available to all on equal terms.

We come then to the question presented: Does segregation of children in public schools solely on the basis of race deprive the children of the minority group of equal educational opportunities? We believe that it does.

[Intangible] considerations apply with added force to children in grade and high schools. To separate them from others of similar age and qualifications solely because of their race generates a feeling of inferiority as to their status in the community that may affect their hearts and minds in a way unlikely ever to be undone. The effect of this separation on their educational opportunities was well stated by a finding in the Kansas case by a court which nevertheless felt compelled to rule against the Negro plaintiffs:

> "Segregation of white and colored children in public schools has a detrimental effect upon the colored children. The impact is greater when it has the

---

[5] *In re Slaughter-House Cases*, [183 U.S.] 16 Wall. 36, 67–72 [(1872)]; *Strauder v. West Virginia*, 100 U.S. 303, 307–308 [(1880)].

sanction of the law; for the policy of separating the races is usually interpreted as denoting the inferiority of the negro group. A sense of inferiority affects the motivation of a child to learn."

Whatever may have been the extent of psychological knowledge at the time of *Plessy v. Ferguson*, this finding is amply supported by modern authority.[11] Any language in *Plessy v. Ferguson* contrary to this finding is rejected.

We conclude that in the field of public education the doctrine of "separate but equal" has no place. Separate educational facilities are inherently unequal. Therefore, we hold that the plaintiffs and others similarly situated for whom the actions have been brought are, by reason of the segregation complained of, deprived of the equal protection of the laws guaranteed by the Fourteenth Amendment.

Because these are class actions, because of the wide applicability of this decision, and because of the great variety of local conditions, the formulation of decrees in these cases presents problems of considerable complexity. We have now announced that such segregation is a denial of the equal protection of the laws. In order that we may have the full assistance of the parties in formulating decrees, the cases will be restored to the docket, and the parties are requested to present further argument on [what remedial decree(s) the Court should issue.]

It is so ordered.

Cases ordered restored to docket for further argument on question of appropriate decrees.

EXERCISE 4:

1. According to the *Brown* Court, what does the Equal Protection Clause proscribe? What is the scope of *Brown*'s holding?

2. The *Brown* Court claimed that the history of the Equal Protection Clause was indeterminate on the question of racially segregated public education. What arguments did the Court offer to support that claim? Are they persuasive?

3. Assume that the Supreme Court was correct and that the Equal Protection Clause did not have an accessible original meaning. Then, what is the basis of the Supreme Court's authority to strike down the state laws?

4. The rise and modern importance of public education played a major role in the Supreme Court's reasoning. What was that role?

5. The Supreme Court relied on the empirical claim that racially segregated public education harmed African-American children. This claim was and remains controver-

---

[11] K.B. Clark, Effect of Prejudice and Discrimination on Personality Development (Midcentury White House Conference on Children and Youth, 1950); Witmer and Kotinsky, Personality in the Making (1952), c. VI; Deutscher and Chein, *The Psychological Effects of Enforced Segregation: A Survey of Social Science Opinion*, 26 J. Psychol. 259 (1948); Chein, *What are the Psychological Effects of Segregation Under Conditions of Equal Facilities?*, 3 Int. J. Opinion and Attitude Res. 229 (1949); Brameld, Educational Costs, in Discrimination and National Welfare (MacIver, ed., 1949), 44–48; Frazier, The Negro in the United States (1949), 674–681. And see generally Myrdal, An American Dilemma (1944).

sial. Mark G. Yudof, *School Desegregation: Legal Realism, Reasoned Elaboration, and Social Science Research in the Supreme Court*, 42 LAW & CONTEMP. PROBS. 57, 70 (1978). What if, as some critical race scholars have argued, it turns out that, in fact, black children perform better, at least in some circumstances, in racially segregated environments? Would that undermine *Brown*?

6. After re-argument was scheduled on the question of the Equal Protection Clause's history, Alexander Bickel, who was clerking for Justice Frankfurter, prepared a memorandum. (Bickel later published the substance of the memorandum here: Alexander M. Bickel, *The Original Understanding and the Segregation Decision*, 69 HARV. L. REV. 1, 64–65 (1955) (arguing that *Brown* was consistent with the Clause's meaning).)

7. There continues to be a vigorous debate over whether *Brown* or *Plessy* is more faithful to the Equal Protection Clause's original meaning. *See, e.g.*, Alexander M. Bickel, *The Original Understanding and the Segregation Decision*, 69 HARV. L. REV. 1, 64–65 (1955) (the seminal piece of scholarship on this issue). Assuming that *Brown* is inconsistent with the Clause's original meaning, what does that say about originalism? Continuing to follow that assumption, would a Supreme Court justice have violated his oath in *Brown*?

8. After *Brown* was first argued, a majority of the justices were inclined to affirm separate-but-equal. According to Justice Douglas' account, Chief Justice Warren persuaded these justices to vote to strike down separate-but-equal in the context of public education. WILLIAM O. DOUGLAS, THE COURT YEARS 1939–1975: THE AUTOBIOGRAPHY OF WILLIAM O. DOUGLAS 113–15 (1980). Chief Justice Warren was the popular governor of California prior to President Eisenhower's appointment of him to the Supreme Court, and Douglas suggested that the skills he gained from his political background helped secure a unanimous opinion. *Id.*

9. *Brown* was a short opinion for such an important case. One suggested reason for the opinion's brevity was that a longer, more detailed opinion could not command the assent of all the justices. Another proffered reason was that the shorter opinion provided less of a target for the inevitable criticism. *Brown*'s brevity is exacerbated by the per curium opinions issued by the Supreme Court later, which applied *Brown*, in one sentence rulings, to other contexts, such as golf courses and parks. *E.g., Holmes v. City of Atlanta*, 350 U.S. 879 (1955). Did the Supreme Court have an obligation to provide a more thorough justification on these later ruling(s)?

10. Historians who reviewed the history of *Brown* have concluded that the school districts at issue in *Brown* were not, as the Court claimed, substantially equal. Why might the Court have mischaracterized the underlying factual circumstances? Assuming that these historians are correct, was it appropriate for the Court to rule as it did?

11. You studied *Planned Parenthood v. Casey*, 505 U.S. 833 (1992), in **Chapter 3**. There, you saw the Supreme Court provide its most comprehensive statement regarding stare decisis. Using the factors articulated by the Court, apply them to *Plessy* at the time of *Brown*. Should the Court have overruled *Plessy*?

12. In its description of the value of education, the Court stated: "Such an opportunity, where the state has undertaken to provide it, is a right which must be

made available to all on equal terms." Was the Court saying that there is a constitutional right to a public education?

After a re-hearing on what remedy the Supreme Court should impose, the Court issued *Brown-II, Brown v. Board of Educ.*, 349 U.S. 294 (1955). There, the Court ordered that "the cases are remanded to the District Courts to take such proceedings and enter such orders and decrees consistent with this opinion as are necessary and proper to admit to public schools on a racially nondiscriminatory basis with all deliberate speed the parties to these cases." *Id.* at 301. The Court's decision to require desegregation "with all deliberate speed," instead of immediately, was its response to the variety of circumstances facing school districts, the authority of local school districts as primary educators, and the deeply entrenched nature of de jure racial segregation. *Id.* at 299–300.

Brown-II's relatively cautious approach to desegregation has been criticized for a number of reasons. First, it was criticized for failing to remedy the unconstitutional and unjust segregation in as speedy a manner as possible. Second, it was criticized as beyond the Court's equitable authority to order a remedy that required long-term, intrusive oversight by federal courts of state institutions.

The immediate reaction to the Court's announcement in *Brown* was mixed. In the popular realm, the reaction by the segregation-establishment in the South was very hostile, including violence. In the academic realm, though most legal academics supported *Brown*'s result, many criticized what they saw as a results-oriented decision lacking in reasoning. Most famously, Columbia law professor, Herbert Wechsler, published an article, *Toward Neutral Principles of Constitutional Law*, 73 Harv. L. Rev. 1 (1959); *see also* Charles L. Black, Jr., *The Lawfulness of the Segregation Decisions*, 69 Yale L.J. 421 (1960) (responding to and criticizing Wechsler). There, Wechsler argued that *Brown* was an example of the Supreme Court failing to articulate a convincing rationale anchored in constitutional principle. Since then, though *Brown* is firmly part of the "constitutional firmament," Michael J. Klarman, *The Puzzling Resistance to Political Process Theory*, 77 Va. L. Rev. 747, 816 (1991), scholars have continued to debate its justification.

Brown is considered part of the "canon of constitutional law," while *Plessy* is part of the anti-canon of constitutional law. *See* Richard A. Primus, Essay, *Canon, Anti-Canon, and Judicial Dissent*, 48 Duke L.J. 243 (1998) (explaining the concepts of constitutional canon and anti-canon); J.M. Balkin & Sanford Levinson, Comment, *The Canons of Constitutional Law*, 111 Harv. L. Rev. 963 (1998) (discussing the concept of "canon"). The canon of constitutional law is the list of Supreme Court cases that form the foundation of constitutional law, while the anti-canon symbolizes alternative visions of the law that are foreclosed. These concepts are useful as ways to structure your understanding of constitutional law, both its internal architecture — the canonical cases — and its boundaries — the anti-canonical cases. What other cases have you studied that fall into the canon and anti-canon?

3. "Reverse Incorporation"

There is no constitutional provision corresponding to the Equal Protection Clause that applies to the federal government. So, does that mean that the Constitution does not limit the federal government's ability to treat people unequally? In a companion case to *Brown*, the Supreme Court held that the Fifth Amendment's Due Process Clause embodied an equal protection component, in a process that has come to be known as "reverse incorporation."

BOLLING v. SHARPE
347 U.S. 497 (1954)

MR. CHIEF JUSTICE WARREN delivered the opinion of the Court.

This case challenges the validity of segregation in the public schools of the District of Columbia. The petitioners, minors of the Negro race, allege that such segregation deprives them of due process of law under the Fifth Amendment.

We have this day held that the Equal Protection Clause of the Fourteenth Amendment prohibits the states from maintaining racially segregated public schools. The legal problem in the District of Columbia is somewhat different, however. The Fifth Amendment, which is applicable in the District of Columbia, does not contain an equal protection clause as does the Fourteenth Amendment which applies only to the states. But the concepts of equal protection and due process, both stemming from our American ideal of fairness, are not mutually exclusive. The "equal protection of the laws" is a more explicit safeguard of prohibited unfairness than "due process of law," and, therefore, we do not imply that the two are always interchangeable phrases. But, as this Court has recognized, discrimination may be so unjustifiable as to be violative of due process.

Although the Court has not assumed to define "liberty" with any great precision, that term is not confined to mere freedom from bodily restraint. Liberty under law extends to the full range of conduct which the individual is free to pursue, and it cannot be restricted except for a proper governmental objective. Segregation in public education is not reasonably related to any proper governmental objective, and thus it imposes on Negro children of the District of Columbia a burden that constitutes an arbitrary deprivation of their liberty in violation of the Due Process Clause.

In view of our decision that the Constitution prohibits the states from maintaining racially segregated public schools, it would be unthinkable that the same Constitution would impose a lesser duty on the Federal Government. We hold that racial segregation in the public schools of the District of Columbia is a denial of the due process of law guaranteed by the Fifth Amendment to the Constitution.

It is so ordered.

EXERCISE 5:

1.   What reason(s) did the Supreme Court give for interpreting the Fifth Amendment's Due Process Clause identical to the Equal Protection Clause? What arguments might one make against the Court's ruling? Which are more persuasive?

E.   EQUAL PROTECTION DOCTRINE TODAY

1.   Introduction

Modern equal protection doctrine shares many affinities with substantive due process. For example, both utilize the means-ends analyses of rational basis and strict scrutiny. The same tests used in the substantive due process context apply here as well. To satisfy rational basis review, the challenger bears the burden of persuading a court that the challenged governmental action is not rationally related to a conceivable legitimate state interest. Similarly, to satisfy strict scrutiny, the government has the burden of showing that the challenged action is necessary to achieve a compelling state interest.

Equal protection doctrine, however, contains a third — in-between — form of analysis labeled intermediate scrutiny. In these cases, the government bears the burden of establishing that the challenged action is "substantially related" to an "important governmental interest."

Modern equal protection law has two basic forms: "suspect classification" and "fundamental rights" equal protection. We will introduce each in turn.

Suspect classification equal protection is the standard form and what one usually thinks of when one thinks of the Equal Protection Clause. It focuses on the manner by which a statute or other governmental activity divides the general population. For example, a state statute that authorizes only those age sixteen years and older to procure a driving license, divides potential drivers by age.

Since the 1940s, the Supreme Court — at first inchoately and later explicitly — identified some classification that are "suspect" and which receive "heightened scrutiny."[40] Those classifications that receive strict scrutiny are race, national origin, and alienage, and those that receive intermediate scrutiny include gender and legitimacy. All other classifications receive rational basis review.

The second form of equal protection — fundamental rights — governs governmental classifications that infringe on the exercise of a fundamental right. For instance, a statute that restricts the fundamental right to vote to those that have state-issued photographic identification divides state citizens into groups and restricts the ability of citizens to exercise the right to vote. Governmental actions that classify based on the exercise of fundamental rights are subject to strict scrutiny.

---

[40] Today, heightened scrutiny includes both strict and intermediate scrutiny.

2. Rational Basis Review

Rational basis review is the baseline standard of review applicable to all classifications. However, its primary use is with classifications that impact economic and social relations. Rational basis review requires that (1) the challenger of the governmental action persuade a court that the classification drawn by the government is (2) not rationally related to a (3) conceivable (4) legitimate government interest.

a. Economic and Social Regulations

RAILWAY EXPRESS AGENCY, INC. v. NEW YORK
336 U.S. 106 (1949)

Mr. Justice Douglas delivered the opinion of the Court.

Section 124 of the Traffic Regulations of the City of New York promulgated by the Police Commissioner provides: "No person shall operate, or cause to be operated, in or upon any street an advertising vehicle; provided that nothing herein contained shall prevent the putting of business notices upon business delivery vehicles, so long as such vehicles are engaged in the usual business or regular work of the owner."

Appellant is engaged in a nation-wide express business. It operates about 1,900 trucks in New York City and sells the space on the exterior sides of these trucks for advertising. That advertising is for the most part unconnected with its own business. It was convicted in the magistrates court and fined.

The question of equal protection of the laws is pressed strenuously on us. It is pointed out that the regulation draws the line between advertisements of products sold by the owner of the truck and general advertisements. It is argued that unequal treatment on the basis of such a distinction is not justified by the aim and purpose of the regulation. It is said, for example, that one of appellant's trucks carrying the advertisement of a commercial house would not cause any greater distraction of pedestrians and vehicle drivers than if the commercial house carried the same advertisement on its own truck. It is therefore contended that the classification which the regulation makes has no relation to the traffic problem since a violation turns not on what kind of advertisements are carried on trucks but on whose trucks they are carried.

That, however, is a superficial way of analyzing the problem, even if we assume that it is premised on the correct construction of the regulation. The local authorities may well have concluded that those who advertised their own wares on their trucks do not present the same traffic problem in view of the nature or extent of the advertising which they use. It would take a degree of omniscience which we lack to say that such is not the case. If that judgment is correct, the advertising displays that are exempt have less incidence on traffic than those of appellants.

We cannot say that that judgment is not an allowable one. Yet if it is, the classification has relation to the purpose for which it is made and does not contain the kind of discrimination against which the Equal Protection Clause affords protection. It is by such practical considerations based on experience rather than by theoretical inconsistencies that the question of equal protection is to be answered. And the fact that New York City sees fit to eliminate from traffic this kind of distraction but does not touch what may be even greater ones in a different category, such as the vivid displays on Times Square, is immaterial. It is no requirement of equal protection that all evils of the same genus be eradicated or none at all.

Affirmed.

MR. JUSTICE RUTLEDGE acquiesces in the Court's opinion and judgment, dubitante on the question of equal protection of the laws.

MR. JUSTICE JACKSON, concurring.

Invocation of the equal protection clause does not disable any governmental body from dealing with the subject at hand. It merely means that the prohibition or regulation must have a broader impact. I regard it as a salutary doctrine that cities, states and the Federal Government must exercise their powers so as not to discriminate between their inhabitants except upon some reasonable differentiation fairly related to the object of regulation. This equality is not merely abstract justice. The framers of the Constitution knew, and we should not forget today, that there is no more effective practical guaranty against arbitrary and unreasonable government than to require that the principles of law which officials would impose upon a minority must be imposed generally. Conversely, nothing opens the door to arbitrary action so effectively as to allow those officials to pick and choose only a few to whom they will apply legislation and thus to escape the political retribution that might be visited upon them if larger numbers were affected. Courts can take no better measure to assure that laws will be just than to require that laws be equal in operation.

This case affords an illustration. Even casual observations from the sidewalks of New York will show that an ordinance which would forbid all advertising on vehicles would run into conflict with many interests, including some, if not all, of the great metropolitan newspapers, which use that advertising extensively. Their blandishment of the latest sensations is not less a cause of diverted attention and traffic hazard than the commonplace cigarette advertisement which this truck-owner is forbidden to display. But any regulation applicable to all such advertising would require much clearer justification in local conditions to enable its enactment than does some regulation applicable to a few.

I think the answer has to be that the hireling may be put in a class by himself and may be dealt with differently than those who act on their own[,] because there is a real difference between doing in self-interest and doing for hire, so that it is one thing to tolerate action from those who act on their own and it is another thing to permit the same action to be promoted for a price.

EXERCISE 6:

1.   What is the challenged governmental classification?

2.   What analysis did the Supreme Court utilize to evaluate the constitutionality of the challenged traffic regulation?

3.   In what ways was the challenged classification over- and/or under-inclusive?

4.   What did the Court mean when it stated that it "is not requirement of equal protection that all evils of the same genus be eradicated or none at all"?

5.   In what ways is the Supreme Court's analysis in *Railway Express Agency* deferential to the City's judgment?

6.   Following the logic of *Carolene Products* Footnote 4, why was the Supreme Court so deferential to the City's judgment?

7.   Is rational basis review, as used here, too generous to the government?

8.   According to Justice Jackson, what is the reason for the City's classification?

9.   Justice Jackson argued that the Supreme Court should more readily utilize the Equal Protection Clause than the Due Process Clause to strike down governmental actions. Articulate his argument. Are you persuaded?

b. Age

MASSACHUSETTS BOARD OF RETIREMENT v. MURGIA
427 U.S. 307 (1976)

PER CURIAM.

This case presents the question whether the provision of Mass. Gen. Laws Ann. c. 32, § 26(3)(a) (1969), that a uniformed state police officer "shall be retired . . . upon his attaining age fifty," denies appellee police officer equal protection of the laws in violation of the Fourteenth Amendment.

Appellee Robert Murgia was an officer in the Uniformed Branch of the Massachusetts State Police. The Massachusetts Board of Retirement retired him upon his 50th birthday. Appellee brought this civil action in the United States District Court for the District of Massachusetts, alleging that the operation of § 26(3)(a) denied him equal protection of the laws. [T]he three-judge court filed an opinion that declared § 26(3)(a) unconstitutional on the ground that "a classification based on age 50 alone lacks a rational basis in furthering any substantial state interest." We now reverse.

The primary function of the Uniformed Branch of the Massachusetts State Police is to protect persons and property and maintain law and order. Specifically, uniformed officers participate in controlling prison and civil disorders, respond to emergencies and natural disasters, patrol highways in marked cruisers, investigate crime, apprehend criminal suspects, and provide backup support for local law enforcement personnel. As the District Court observed, "service in this branch is, or can be, arduous."

These considerations prompt the requirement that uniformed state officers pass a comprehensive physical examination biennially until age 40. After that, until mandatory retirement at age 50, uniformed officers must pass annually a more rigorous examination, including an electrocardiogram and tests for gastro-intestinal bleeding. Appellee Murgia had passed such an examination four months before he was retired, and there is no dispute that, when he retired, his excellent physical and mental health still rendered him capable of performing the duties of a uniformed officer.

I

We need state only briefly our reasons for [holding] that strict scrutiny is not the proper test for determining whether the mandatory retirement provision denies appellee equal protection. *San Antonio School District v. Rodriguez*, 411 U.S. 1, 16 (1973), reaffirmed that equal protection analysis requires strict scrutiny of a legislative classification only when the classification impermissibly interferes with the exercise of a fundamental right or operates to the peculiar disadvantage of a suspect class. Mandatory retirement at age 50 under the Massachusetts statute involves neither situation.

This Court's decisions give no support to the proposition that a right of governmental employment per se is fundamental. *See San Antonio School District v. Rodriguez*. Accordingly, we have expressly stated that a standard less than strict scrutiny "has consistently been applied to state legislation restricting the availability of employment opportunities."

Nor does the class of uniformed state police officers over 50 constitute a suspect class for purposes of equal protection analysis. *Rodriguez*, 411 U.S. at 28, observed that a suspect class is one "saddled with such disabilities, or subjected to such a history of purposeful unequal treatment, or relegated to such a position of political powerlessness as to command extraordinary protection from the majoritarian political process." While the treatment of the aged in this Nation has not been wholly free of discrimination, such persons, unlike, say, those who have been discriminated against on the basis of race or national origin, have not experienced a "history of purposeful unequal treatment" or been subjected to unique disabilities on the basis of stereotyped characteristics not truly indicative of their abilities. The class subject to the compulsory retirement feature of the Massachusetts statute consists of uniformed state police officers over the age of 50. It cannot be said to discriminate only against the elderly. Rather, it draws the line at a certain age in middle life. But even old age does not define a "discrete and insular" group, *United States v. Carolene Products Co.*, 304 U.S. 144, 152–153, n. 4 (1938), in need of "extraordinary protection from the majoritarian political process." Instead, it marks a stage that each of us will reach if we live out our normal span. Even if the statute could be said to impose a penalty upon a class defined as the aged, it would not impose a distinction sufficiently akin to those classifications that we have found suspect to call for strict judicial scrutiny.

Under the circumstances, it is unnecessary to subject the State's resolution of competing interests in this case to the degree of critical examination that our cases under the Equal Protection Clause recently have characterized as "strict judicial scrutiny."

II

We turn then to examine this state classification under the rational-basis standard. This inquiry employs a relatively relaxed standard reflecting the Court's awareness that the drawing of lines that create distinctions is peculiarly a legislative task and an unavoidable one. Perfection in making the necessary classifications is neither possible nor necessary. Such action by a legislature is presumed to be valid.

In this case, the Massachusetts statute clearly meets the requirements of the Equal Protection Clause, for the State's classification rationally furthers the purpose identified by the State: Through mandatory retirement at age 50, the legislature seeks to protect the public by assuring physical preparedness of its uniformed police. Since physical ability generally declines with age, mandatory retirement at 50 serves to remove from police service those whose fitness for uniformed work presumptively has diminished with age. This clearly is rationally related to the State's objective. There is no indication that § 26(3)(a) has the effect of excluding from service so few officers who are in fact unqualified as to render age 50 a criterion wholly unrelated to the objective of the statute.

That the State chooses not to determine fitness more precisely through individualized testing after age 50 is not to say that the objective of assuring physical fitness is not rationally furthered by a maximum-age limitation. It is only to say that with regard to the interest of all concerned, the State perhaps has not chosen the best means to accomplish this purpose. But where rationality is the test, a State "does not violate the Equal Protection Clause merely because the classifications made by its laws are imperfect."

"[W]e do not decide today that the [Massachusetts statute] is wise, that it best fulfills the relevant social and economic objectives that [Massachusetts] might ideally espouse, or that a more just and humane system could not be revised." We decide only that the system enacted by the Massachusetts Legislature does not deny appellee equal protection of the laws.

The judgment is reversed.

Mr. Justice Stevens took no part in the consideration or decision of this case.

Mr. Justice Marshall, dissenting.

I

Although there are signs that its grasp on the law is weakening, the rigid two-tier model still holds sway as the Court's articulated description of the equal protection test. Again, I must object to its perpetuation. The model's two fixed modes of analysis, strict scrutiny and mere rationality, simply do not describe the inquiry the Court has undertaken or should undertake in equal protection cases. It has focused upon the character of the classification in question, the relative importance to individuals in the class discriminated against of the governmental benefits that they do not receive, and the state interests asserted in support of the classification.

II

The danger of the Court's verbal adherence to the rigid two-tier test is demonstrated by its efforts here. There is simply no reason why a statute that tells able-bodied police officers, ready and willing to work, that they no longer have the right to earn a living in their chosen profession merely because they are 50 years old should be judged by the same minimal standards of rationality that we use to test economic legislation that discriminates against business interests. See *Williamson v. Lee Optical Co.*, 348 U.S. 483 (1955). Yet, the Court today not only invokes the minimal level of scrutiny, it wrongly adheres to it.

While depriving any government employee of his job is a significant deprivation, it is particularly burdensome when the person deprived is an older citizen. Once terminated, the elderly cannot readily find alternative employment. The lack of work is not only economically damaging, but emotionally and physically draining. Deprived of his status in the community and of the opportunity for meaningful activity, fearful of becoming dependent on others for his support, and lonely in his new-found isolation, the involuntarily retired person is susceptible to physical and emotional ailments as a direct consequence of his enforced idleness.

Not only are the elderly denied important benefits when they are terminated on the basis of age, but the classification of older workers is itself one that merits judicial attention. Whether older workers constitute a "suspect" class or not, it cannot be disputed that they constitute a class subject to repeated and arbitrary discrimination in employment[, a]s Congress found in passing the Age Discrimination in Employment Act of 1967.

Of course, the Court is quite right in suggesting that distinctions exist between the elderly and traditional suspect classes such as Negroes, and between the elderly and "quasi-suspect" classes such as women or illegitimates. The elderly are protected not only by certain anti-discrimination legislation, but by legislation that provides them with positive benefits not enjoyed by the public at large. Moreover, the elderly are not isolated in society, and discrimination against them is not pervasive but is centered primarily in employment. The advantage of a flexible equal protection standard, however, is that it can readily accommodate such variables. The elderly are undoubtedly discriminated against, and when legislation denies them an important benefit I conclude that to sustain the legislation appellants must show a reasonably substantial interest and a scheme reasonably closely tailored to achieving that interest.

Turning, then, to appellants' arguments, I agree that the purpose of the mandatory retirement law is legitimate, and indeed compelling. [T]he Commonwealth has every reason to assure that its state police officers are of sufficient physical strength and health to perform their jobs.

In my view, however, the means chosen, the forced retirement of officers at age 50, is so over-inclusive that it must fall. All potential officers must pass a rigorous physical examination. Until age 40, this same examination must be passed every two years when the officer re-enlists and, after age 40, every year. Thus, the only members of the state police still on the force at age 50 are those who have been determined repeatedly by the Commonwealth to be physically fit for the job. Yet, all of these physically fit officers are automatically terminated at age 50. Appellants do not seriously assert that their testing is no longer effective at age 50, nor do they claim that continued testing would serve no purpose because officers over 50 are no longer physically able to perform their jobs. Thus the Commonwealth is in the position of already individually testing its police officers for physical fitness, conceding that such testing is adequate to determine the physical ability of an officer to continue on the job, and conceding that that ability may continue after age 50. In these circumstances, I see no reason at all for automatically terminating those officers who reach the age of 50; indeed, that action seems the height of irrationality.

EXERCISE 7:

1.   What is the challenged governmental classification?

2.   On what basis did the Supreme Court rule that government employment is not a fundamental right, meriting strict scrutiny? Was that ruling correct?

3.   On what basis did the Supreme Court rule that age was not a suspect classification? Did the Supreme Court arrive at the correct conclusion, or was Justice Marshall correct?

4.   Explain why the Supreme Court ruled that Massachusetts' mandatory retirement law met the rational basis test.

5.   In what ways was the challenged classification both over- and under-inclusive? Was this level of over- and under-inclusiveness acceptable? Articulate arguments from the Court's and Justice Marshall's perspectives.

6.   In place of rational basis review, what form of analysis did Justice Marshall suggest? Which is a better approach, the majority's or Justice Marshall's?

7.   The Supreme Court opinion in *Murgia* is *per curiam*, or by the Court. In such cases, the opinion's author is not noted, though concurring and dissenting opinion authorship is noted. Typically, per curiam opinions are used for relatively minor decisions, such as dismissing a case as lacking jurisdiction. Although it is relatively rare today for the Supreme Court to issue a substantive *per curiam* opinion, during the 1970s, use of *per curiam* opinions was relatively more frequent, perhaps to insulate individual justices from criticism for controversial rulings. For histories of *per curiam* opinions see Laura Krugman Ray, *The Road to* Bush v. Gore: *The History of the Supreme Court's Use of the* Per Curiam *Opinion*, 79 NEB. L. REV. 517, 521 (2000); Stephen L. Wasby, et al., *The* Per Curiam *Opinion: Its Nature and Functions*, 76 JUDICATURE 29, 33 (1992).

c. Disability

CITY OF CLEBURNE, TEXAS v.
CLEBURNE LIVING CENTER
473 U.S. 432 (1985)

JUSTICE WHITE delivered the opinion of the Court.

I

In July 1980, respondent Jan Hannah purchased a building at 201 Featherston Street in the city of Cleburne, Texas, with the intention of leasing it to Cleburne Living Center, Inc. (CLC), for the operation of a group home for the mentally retarded. It was anticipated that the home would house 13 retarded men and women, who would be under the constant supervision of CLC staff members. CLC planned to comply with all applicable state and federal regulations.

The city informed CLC that a special use permit would be required for the operation of a group home at the site, and CLC accordingly submitted a permit application. [T]he city explained that under the zoning regulations applicable to the site, a special use permit was required for the construction of "[h]ospitals for the insane or feeble-minded, or alcoholic [sic] or drug addicts, or penal or correctional institutions." The city had determined that the proposed group home should be classified as a "hospital for the feebleminded." After holding a public hearing on CLC's application, the City Council voted 3 to 1 to deny a special use permit.

CLC then filed suit in Federal District Court alleging that the zoning ordinance was invalid because it discriminated against the mentally retarded in violation of the equal protection rights of CLC and its potential residents. The Court of Appeals for the Fifth Circuit determin[ed] that mental retardation was a quasi-suspect classification[,] and the court held that the ordinance was invalid because it did not substantially further any important governmental interests.

II

The Equal Protection Clause of the Fourteenth Amendment commands that no State shall "deny to any person within its jurisdiction the equal protection of the laws," which is essentially a direction that all persons similarly situated should be treated alike. The general rule is that legislation is presumed to be valid and will be sustained if the classification drawn by the statute is rationally related to a legitimate state interest. When social or economic legislation is at issue, the Equal Protection Clause allows the States wide latitude, and the Constitution presumes that even improvident decisions will eventually be rectified by the democratic processes.

The general rule gives way, however, when a statute classifies by race, alienage, or national origin. These factors are so seldom relevant to the achievement of any legitimate state interest that laws grounded in such considerations are deemed to reflect prejudice and antipathy. For these reasons and because such discrimination is unlikely to be soon rectified by legislative means, these laws are subjected to strict scrutiny and will be sustained only if they are suitably tailored to serve a compelling state interest. Similar oversight by the courts is due when state laws impinge on personal rights protected by the Constitution. *Skinner v. Oklahoma*, 316 U.S. 535 (1942).

Legislative classifications based on gender also call for a heightened standard of review. That factor generally provides no sensible ground for differential treatment. *Frontiero v. Richardson*, 411 U.S. 677, 686 (1973). Rather than resting on meaningful considerations, statutes distributing benefits and burdens between the sexes in different ways very likely reflect outmoded notions of the relative capabilities of men and women. Because illegitimacy is beyond the individual's control and bears "no relation to the individual's ability to participate in and contribute to society," official discriminations resting on that characteristic are also subject to somewhat heightened review.

We have declined, however, to extend heightened review to differential treatment based on age: *Massachusetts Board of Retirement v. Murgia*, 427 U.S. 307, 313 (1976). The lesson of *Murgia* is that where individuals in the group affected by a law have distinguishing characteristics relevant to interests the State has the authority to implement, the courts have been very reluctant, as they should be in our federal system and with our respect for the separation of powers, to closely scrutinize legislative choices as to whether, how, and to what extent those interests should be pursued. In such cases, the Equal Protection Clause requires only a rational means to serve a legitimate end.

III

Against this background, we conclude that the Court of Appeals erred in holding mental retardation a quasi-suspect classification. First, it is undeniable that those who are mentally retarded have a reduced ability to cope with and function in the everyday world. Nor are they all cut from the same pattern: as the testimony in this record indicates, they range from those whose disability is not immediately evident to those who must be constantly cared for. They are thus different, immutably so, in relevant respects, and the States' interest in dealing with and providing for them is plainly a legitimate one. How this large and diversified group is to be treated under the law is a difficult and often a technical matter, very much a task for legislators guided by qualified professionals and not by the perhaps ill-informed opinions of the judiciary. Heightened scrutiny inevitably involves substantive judgments about legislative decisions, and we doubt that the predicate for such judicial oversight is present where the classification deals with mental retardation.

Second, the distinctive legislative response, both national and state, to the plight of those who are mentally retarded demonstrates that the lawmakers have been addressing their difficulties in a manner that belies a continuing antipathy or prejudice and a corresponding need for more intrusive oversight by the judiciary. Thus, the Federal Government has not only outlawed discrimination against the mentally retarded in federally funded programs, but it has also provided the retarded with the right to receive "appropriate treatment, services, and habilitation" in a setting that is "least restrictive of [their] personal liberty." The State of Texas has similarly enacted legislation that acknowledges the special status of the mentally retarded.

Such legislation thus singling out the retarded for special treatment reflects the real and undeniable differences between the retarded and others. That a civilized and decent society expects and approves such legislation indicates that governmental consideration of those differences in the vast majority of situations is not only legitimate but also desirable. It may be, as CLC contends, that legislation designed to benefit, rather than disadvantage, the retarded would generally withstand examination under a test of heightened scrutiny. The relevant inquiry, however, is whether heightened scrutiny is constitutionally mandated in the first instance. Even assuming that many of these laws could be shown to be substantially related to an important governmental purpose, merely requiring the legislature to justify its efforts in these terms may lead it to refrain from acting at all. Much recent legislation intended to benefit the retarded also assumes the need for measures that might be perceived to disadvantage them. Especially given the wide variation in the abilities and needs of the retarded themselves, governmental bodies must have a certain amount of flexibility and freedom from judicial oversight in shaping and limiting their remedial efforts.

Third, the legislative response, which could hardly have occurred and survived without public support, negates any claim that the mentally retarded are politically powerless. Fourth, if the large and amorphous class of the mentally retarded were deemed quasi-suspect, it would be difficult to find a principled way to distinguish a variety of other groups who have perhaps immutable disabilities setting them off from others, who cannot themselves mandate the desired legislative responses, and who can claim some degree of prejudice from at least part of the public at large. One need mention in this respect only the aging, the disabled, the mentally ill, and the infirm. We are reluctant to set out on that course, and we decline to do so.

Doubtless, there have been and there will continue to be instances of discrimination against the retarded that are in fact invidious, and that are properly subject to judicial correction under constitutional norms. But the appropriate method of reaching such instances is not to create a new quasi-suspect classification and subject all governmental action based on that classification to more searching evaluation. Rather, we should look to the likelihood that governmental action premised on a particular classification is valid as a general matter, not merely to the specifics of the case before us.

Our refusal to recognize the retarded as a quasi-suspect class does not leave them entirely unprotected from invidious discrimination. To withstand equal protection review, legislation that distinguishes between the mentally retarded and others must be rationally related to a legitimate governmental purpose. The State may not rely on a classification whose relationship to an asserted goal is so attenuated as to render the distinction arbitrary or irrational. See *United States Dept. of Agriculture v. Moreno*, 413 U.S. 528, 535 (1973). Furthermore, some objectives-such as "a bare . . . desire to harm a politically unpopular group," *id.*, at 534 -are not legitimate state interests.

IV

We turn to the issue of the validity of the zoning ordinance insofar as it requires a special use permit for homes for the mentally retarded. The city does not require a special use permit in an R-3 zone for apartment houses, multiple dwellings, boarding and lodging houses, fraternity or sorority houses, dormitories, apartment hotels, hospitals, sanitariums, nursing homes for convalescents or the aged (other than for the insane or feebleminded or alcoholics or drug addicts), private clubs or fraternal orders, and other specified uses. It does, however, insist on a special permit for the Featherston home, and it does so, as the District Court found, because it would be a facility for the mentally retarded. May the city require the permit for this facility when other care and multiple-dwelling facilities are freely permitted?

Because in our view the record does not reveal any rational basis for believing that the Featherston home would pose any special threat to the city's legitimate interests, we affirm the judgment below insofar as it holds the ordinance invalid as applied in this case.

First, the Council was concerned with the negative attitude of the majority of property owners located within 200 feet of the Featherston facility, as well as with the fears of elderly residents of the neighborhood. But mere negative attitudes, or fear, unsubstantiated by factors which are properly cognizable in a zoning proceeding, are not permissible bases for treating a home for the mentally retarded differently from apartment houses, multiple dwellings, and the like.

Second, the Council had two objections to the location of the facility. It was concerned that the facility was across the street from a junior high school, and it feared that the students might harass the occupants of the Featherston home. But the school itself is attended by about 30 mentally retarded students, and denying a permit based on such vague, undifferentiated fears is again permitting some portion of the community to validate what would otherwise be an equal protection violation. The other objection to the home's location was that it was located on "a five hundred year flood plain." This concern with the possibility of a flood, however, can hardly be based on a distinction between the Featherston home and, for example, nursing homes, homes for convalescents or the aged, or sanitariums or hospitals, any of which could be located on the Featherston site without obtaining a special use permit. The same may be said of another concern of the Council-doubts about the legal responsibility for actions which the mentally retarded might take. If there is no concern about legal responsibility with respect to other uses that would be permitted in the area, such as boarding and fraternity houses, it is difficult to believe that the groups of mildly or moderately mentally retarded individuals who would live at 201 Featherston would present any different or special hazard.

Fourth, the Council was concerned with the size of the home and the number of people that would occupy it. The District Court found that "[i]f the potential residents of the Featherston Street home were not mentally retarded, but the home was the same in all other respects, its use would be permitted under the city's zoning ordinance." Given this finding, there would be no restrictions on the number of people who could occupy this home as a boarding house, nursing home, family dwelling, fraternity house, or dormitory. At least this record does not clarify how, in this connection, the characteristics of the intended occupants of the Featherston home rationally justify denying to those occupants what would be permitted to groups occupying the same site for different purposes.

In the courts below the city also urged that the ordinance is aimed at avoiding concentration of population and at lessening congestion of the streets. These concerns obviously fail to explain why apartment houses, fraternity and sorority houses, hospitals and the like, may freely locate in the area without a permit. So, too, the expressed worry about fire hazards, the serenity of the neighborhood, and the avoidance of danger to other residents fail rationally to justify singling out a home such as 201 Featherston for the special use permit, yet imposing no such restrictions on the many other uses freely permitted in the neighborhood.

The short of it is that requiring the permit in this case appears to us to rest on an irrational prejudice against the mentally retarded, including those who would occupy the Featherston facility and who would live under the closely supervised and highly regulated conditions expressly provided for by state and federal law.

The judgment of the Court of Appeals is affirmed insofar as it invalidates the zoning ordinance as applied to the Featherston home. The judgment is otherwise vacated, and the case is remanded.

It is so ordered.

JUSTICE STEVENS, with whom THE CHIEF JUSTICE joins, concurring. [Opinion omitted.]

JUSTICE MARSHALL, with whom JUSTICE BRENNAN and JUSTICE BLACKMUN join, concurring in the judgment in part and dissenting in part.

I

[T]he Court's heightened-scrutiny discussion is puzzling given that Cleburne's ordinance is invalidated only after being subjected to precisely the sort of probing inquiry associated with heightened scrutiny. To be sure, the Court does not label its handiwork heightened scrutiny. But however labeled, the rational basis test invoked today is most assuredly not the rational-basis test of *Williamson v. Lee Optical of Oklahoma, Inc.*, 348 U.S. 483 (1955).

*   *   *

II

I have long believed the level of scrutiny employed in an equal protection case should vary with "the constitutional and societal importance of the interest adversely affected and the recognized invidiousness of the basis upon which the particular classification is drawn." *San Antonio Independent School District v. Rodriguez*, 411 U.S. 1, 99 (1973) (MARSHALL, J., dissenting). When a zoning ordinance works to exclude the retarded from all residential districts in a community, these two considerations require that the ordinance be convincingly justified as substantially furthering legitimate and important purposes.

First, the interest of the retarded in establishing group homes is substantial. * * * Second, the mentally retarded have been subject to a "lengthy and tragic history," of segregation and discrimination that can only be called grotesque. * * *

In light of the importance of the interest at stake and the history of discrimination the retarded have suffered, the Equal Protection Clause requires us to do more than review the distinctions drawn by Cleburne's zoning ordinance as if they appeared in a taxing statute or in economic or commercial legislation. The searching scrutiny I would give to restrictions on the ability of the retarded to establish community group homes leads me to conclude that Cleburne's vague generalizations for classifying the "feeble-minded" with drug addicts, alcoholics, and the insane, and excluding them where the elderly, the ill, the boarder, and the transient are allowed, are not substantial or important enough to overcome the suspicion that the ordinance rests on impermissible assumptions or outmoded and perhaps invidious stereotypes.

III

[T]he Court offers several justifications as to why the retarded do not warrant heightened judicial solicitude. These justifications, however, find no support in our heightened-scrutiny precedents and cannot withstand logical analysis.

The Court downplays the lengthy "history of purposeful unequal treatment" of the retarded by pointing to recent legislative action. Building on this point, the Court similarly concludes that the retarded are not "politically powerless."

Courts, however, do not sit or act in a social vacuum. Moral philosophers may debate whether certain inequalities are absolute wrongs, but history makes clear that constitutional principles of equality, like constitutional principles of liberty, property, and due process, evolve over time; what once was a "natural" and "self-evident" ordering later comes to be seen as an artificial and invidious constraint on human potential and freedom. Compare *Plessy v. Ferguson*, 163 U.S. 537 (1896), and *Bradwell v. Illinois* [83 U.S. (16 Wall.) 130,] 141 [(1872)] (Bradley, J., concurring in judgment), with *Brown v. Board of Education*, 347 U.S. 483 (1954), and *Reed v. Reed*, 404 U.S. 71 (1971). Shifting cultural, political, and social patterns at times come to make past practices appear inconsistent with fundamental principles upon which American society rests, an inconsistency legally cognizable under the Equal Protection Clause. It is natural that evolving standards of equality come to be embodied in legislation. When that occurs, courts should look to the fact of such change as a source of guidance on evolving principles of equality.

For the retarded, just as for Negroes and women, much has changed in recent years, but much remains the same; out-dated statutes are still on the books, and irrational fears or ignorance, traceable to the prolonged social and cultural isolation of the retarded, continue to stymie recognition of the dignity and individuality of retarded people. Heightened judicial scrutiny of action appearing to impose unnecessary barriers to the retarded is required in light of increasing recognition that such barriers are inconsistent with evolving principles of equality embedded in the Fourteenth Amendment.

The Court also offers a more general view of heightened scrutiny, a view focused primarily on when heightened scrutiny does *not* apply as opposed to when it does apply. Two principles appear central to the Court's theory. First, heightened scrutiny is said to be inapplicable where *individuals* in a group have distinguishing characteristics that legislatures properly may take into account in some circumstances. Heightened scrutiny is also purportedly inappropriate when many legislative classifications affecting the *group* are likely to be valid.

If the Court's first principle were sound, heightened scrutiny would have to await a day when people could be cut from a cookie mold. Women are hardly alike in all their characteristics, but heightened scrutiny applies to them because legislatures can rarely use gender itself as a proxy for these other characteristics. Permissible distinctions between persons must bear a reasonable relationship to their *relevant* characteristics, and gender *per se* is almost never relevant. Similarly, that some retarded people have reduced capacities in some areas does not justify using retardation as a proxy for reduced capacity in areas where relevant individual variations in capacity do exist.

The Court's second assertion is similarly flawed. Our heightened-scrutiny precedents belie the claim that a characteristic must virtually always be irrelevant to warrant heightened scrutiny. Heightened but not strict scrutiny is considered appropriate in areas such as gender, illegitimacy, or alienage because the Court views the trait as relevant under some circumstances but not others. Because the government also may not take this characteristic into account in many circumstances, such as those presented here, careful review is required to separate the permissible from the invalid in classifications relying on retardation.

Discrimination, in the Fourteenth Amendment sense, connotes a substantive constitutional judgment that two individuals or groups are entitled to be treated equally with respect to something. With regard to economic and commercial matters, no basis for such a conclusion exists, for as Justice Holmes urged the *Lochner* Court, the Fourteenth Amendment was not "intended to embody a particular economic theory. . . ." *Lochner v. New York*, 198 U.S. [45], 75, [(1905)] (dissenting). The structure of economic and commercial life is a matter of political compromise, not constitutional principle, and no norm of equality requires that there be as many opticians as optometrists, see *Williamson v. Lee Optical of Oklahoma, Inc.*, 348 U.S. 483 (1955).

But the Fourteenth Amendment does prohibit other results under virtually all circumstances, such as castes created by law along racial or ethnic lines, see *Loving v. Virginia*, 388 U.S. 1 (1967), and significantly constrains the range of permissible government choices where gender or illegitimacy, for example, are concerned. Where such constraints, derived from the Fourteenth Amendment, are present, and where history teaches that they have systemically been ignored, a "more searching judicial inquiry" is required. *United States v. Carolene Products Co.*, 304 U.S. 144, 153, n. 4 (1938).

As the history of discrimination against the retarded and its continuing legacy amply attest, the mentally retarded have been, and in some areas may still be, the targets of action the Equal Protection Clause condemns. With respect to a liberty so valued as the right to establish a home in the community, and so likely to be denied on the basis of irrational fears and outright hostility, heightened scrutiny is surely appropriate.

EXERCISE 8:

1.   What was the challenged governmental classification?

2.   Upon what factors did the Supreme Court rely to justify its ruling that disability was not a suspect classification? Who had the better argument, the majority or Justice Marshall?

3.   The Supreme Court also argued that it should not readily label a classification "suspect" because of the principle of separation of powers. Flesh-out the Court's reasoning. Why might that be the case?

4.   What harm would there be, according to the majority, if it adopted heightened scrutiny of disability classifications?

5.   The Court stated that the Equal Protection Clause is "essentially a direction that all persons similarly situated should be treated alike." Is that interpretation faithful to the Clause's text? Is it faithful to the Clause's original meaning?

6.   Explain the Court's application of rational basis review in *Cleburne*.

7.   The *Cleburne* majority stated that it used rational basis review to evaluate the City's denial of a zoning permit. Is that true? In what ways did the majority's use of rational basis review differ from, for instance, *Railway Express Agency*, above?

8.   Many have dubbed the *Cleburne* Court's use of rational basis review as "rational basis with bite" to signify that it is somewhat more stringent than traditional or normal rational basis review. Why might the Court have utilized rational basis "with bite"? Is it a good idea to have such an additional "tier" of scrutiny?

9.   From what source(s) did Justice Marshall draw his interpretation of the Equal Protection Clause as embodying "evolving principles of equality"?

10.   What is the basis of Justice Marshall's distinction between "economic and commercial matters," where the Equal Protection Clause does not require heightened scrutiny, and race, gender, and illegitimacy, where the Clause requires heightened scrutiny? Is that a persuasive basis?

d.   Sexual Orientation

ROMER v. EVANS
517 U.S. 620 (1996)

JUSTICE KENNEDY delivered the opinion of the Court.

One century ago, the first Justice Harlan admonished this Court that the Constitution "neither knows nor tolerates classes among citizens." *Plessy v. Ferguson*, 163 U.S. 537, 559 (1896) (dissenting opinion). Unheeded then, those words now are understood to state a commitment to the law's neutrality where the rights of persons are at stake. The Equal Protection Clause enforces this principle and today requires us to hold invalid a provision of Colorado's Constitution.

I

The enactment challenged in this case is an amendment to the Constitution of the State of Colorado, adopted in a 1992 statewide referendum. The parties and the state courts refer to it as "Amendment 2." The impetus for the amendment and the contentious campaign that preceded its adoption came in large part from ordinances that had been passed in various Colorado municipalities. What gave rise to the statewide controversy was the protection the ordinances afforded to persons discriminated against by reason of their sexual orientation. Amendment 2 repeals these ordinances to the extent they prohibit discrimination on the basis of "homosexual, lesbian or bisexual orientation, conduct, practices or relationships." Colo. Const., Art. II, § 30b.

Yet Amendment 2, in explicit terms, does more than repeal or rescind these provisions. It prohibits all legislative, executive or judicial action at any level of state or local government designed to protect the named class, a class we shall refer to as homosexual persons or gays and lesbians. The amendment reads:

> "No Protected Status Based on Homosexual, Lesbian or Bisexual Orientation. Neither the State of Colorado, through any of its branches or departments, nor any of its agencies, political subdivisions, municipalities or school districts, shall enact, adopt or enforce any statute, regulation, ordinance or policy whereby homosexual, lesbian or bisexual orientation, conduct, practices or relationships shall constitute or otherwise be the basis of or entitle any person or class of persons to have or claim any minority status, quota preferences, protected status or claim of discrimination."

Soon after Amendment 2 was adopted, this litigation to declare its invalidity and enjoin its enforcement was commenced in the District Court for the City and County of Denver. [T]he State Supreme Court held that Amendment 2 was subject to strict scrutiny under the Fourteenth Amendment[, which the state failed to meet]. We granted certiorari and now affirm the judgment, but on a rationale different from that adopted by the State Supreme Court.

II

The State's principal argument in defense of Amendment 2 is that it puts gays and lesbians in the same position as all other persons. So, the State says, the measure does no more than deny homosexuals special rights. This reading of the amendment's language is implausible. Sweeping and comprehensive is the change in legal status effected by this law. Homosexuals, by state decree, are put in a solitary class with respect to transactions and relations in both the private and governmental spheres. The amendment withdraws from homosexuals, but no others, specific legal protection from the injuries caused by discrimination, and it forbids reinstatement of these laws and policies.

The change Amendment 2 works in the legal status of gays and lesbians in the private sphere is far reaching. Th[is] is well illustrated by contemporary statutes and ordinances prohibiting discrimination by providers of public accommodations. These statutes and ordinances enumerat[e] the groups or persons within their ambit of protection. Enumeration is the essential device used to make the duty not to discriminate concrete and to provide guidance for those who must comply. In following this approach, Colorado's state and local governments have set forth an extensive catalog of traits which cannot be the basis for discrimination, including, in recent times, sexual orientation.

Amendment 2 bars homosexuals from securing protection against the injuries that these public-accommodations laws address. That in itself is a severe consequence, but there is more. Amendment 2, in addition, nullifies specific legal protections for this targeted class in all transactions in housing, sale of real estate, insurance, health and welfare services, private education, and employment. Not confined to the private sphere, Amendment 2 also operates to repeal and forbid all laws or policies providing specific protection for gays or lesbians from discrimination by every level of Colorado government.

[W]e cannot accept the view that Amendment 2's prohibition on specific legal protections does no more than deprive homosexuals of special rights. To the contrary, the amendment imposes a special disability upon those persons alone. Homosexuals are forbidden the safeguards that others enjoy or may seek without constraint. They can obtain specific protection against discrimination only by enlisting the citizenry of Colorado to amend the State Constitution. This is so no matter how local or discrete the harm, no matter how public and widespread the injury. We find nothing special in the protections Amendment 2 withholds. These are protections taken for granted by most people either because they already have them or do not need them; these are protections against exclusion from an almost limitless number of transactions and endeavors that constitute ordinary civic life in a free society.

III

The Fourteenth Amendment's promise that no person shall be denied the equal protection of the laws must coexist with the practical necessity that most legislation classifies for one purpose or another, with resulting disadvantage to various groups or persons. We have attempted to reconcile the principle with the reality by stating that, if a law neither burdens a fundamental right nor targets a suspect class, we will uphold the legislative classification so long as it bears a rational relation to some legitimate end.

Amendment 2 fails, indeed defies, even this conventional inquiry. First, the amendment has the peculiar property of imposing a broad and undifferentiated disability on a single named group, an exceptional and, as we shall explain, invalid form of legislation. Second, its sheer breadth is so discontinuous with the reasons offered for it that the amendment seems inexplicable by anything but animus toward the class it affects; it lacks a rational relationship to legitimate state interests.

Taking the first point, [i]n the ordinary case, a law will be sustained if it can be said to advance a legitimate government interest, even if the law seems unwise or works to the disadvantage of a particular group, or if the rationale for it seems tenuous. See *Williamson v. Lee Optical of Okla., Inc.*, 348 U.S. 483 (1955); *Railway Express Agency, Inc. v. New York*, 336 U.S. 106 (1949).

Amendment 2 confounds this normal process of judicial review. It is at once too narrow and too broad. It identifies persons by a single trait and then denies them protection across the board. The resulting disqualification of a class of persons from the right to seek specific protection from the law is unprecedented in our jurisprudence.

It is not within our constitutional tradition to enact laws of this sort. Central both to the idea of the rule of law and to our own Constitution's guarantee of equal protection is the principle that government and each of its parts remain open on impartial terms to all who seek its assistance. Respect for this principle explains why laws singling out a certain class of citizens for disfavored legal status or general hardships are rare. A law declaring that in general it shall be more difficult for one group of citizens than for all others to seek aid from the government is itself a denial of equal protection of the laws in the most literal sense.

A second and related point is that laws of the kind now before us raise the inevitable inference that the disadvantage imposed is born of animosity toward the class of persons affected. "[I]f the constitutional conception of 'equal protection of the laws' means anything, it must at the very least mean that a bare . . . desire to harm a politically unpopular group cannot constitute a *legitimate* governmental interest." *Department of Agriculture v. Moreno*, 413 U.S. 528, 534 (1973). Even laws enacted for broad and ambitious purposes often can be explained by reference to legitimate public policies which justify the incidental disadvantages they impose on certain persons. Amendment 2, however, in making a general announcement that gays and lesbians shall not have any particular protections from the law, inflicts on them immediate, continuing, and real injuries that outrun and belie any legitimate justifications that may be claimed for it. We conclude that, in addition to the far-reaching deficiencies of Amendment 2 that we have noted, the principles it offends, in another sense, are conventional and venerable; a law must bear a rational relationship to a legitimate governmental purpose, and Amendment 2 does not.

The primary rationale the State offers for Amendment 2 is respect for other citizens' freedom of association, and in particular the liberties of landlords or employers who have personal or religious objections to homosexuality. Colorado also cites its interest in conserving resources to fight discrimination against other groups. The breadth of the amendment is so far removed from these particular justifications that we find it impossible to credit them. We cannot say that Amendment 2 is directed to any identifiable legitimate purpose or discrete objective. It is a status-based enactment divorced from any factual context from which we could discern a relationship to legitimate state interests; it is a classification of persons undertaken for its own sake, something the Equal Protection Clause does not permit.

We must conclude that Amendment 2 classifies homosexuals not to further a proper legislative end but to make them unequal to everyone else. This Colorado cannot do. A State cannot so deem a class of persons a stranger to its laws. Amendment 2 violates the Equal Protection Clause, and the judgment of the Supreme Court of Colorado is affirmed.

It is so ordered.

JUSTICE SCALIA, with whom THE CHIEF JUSTICE and JUSTICE THOMAS join, dissenting.

The Court has mistaken a Kulturkampf for a fit of spite. The constitutional amendment before us here is not the manifestation of a " 'bare . . . desire to harm' " homosexuals, but is rather a modest attempt by seemingly tolerant Coloradans to preserve traditional sexual mores against the efforts of a politically powerful minority to revise those mores through use of the laws. Since the Constitution of the United States says nothing about this subject, it is left to be resolved by normal democratic means. I vigorously dissent.

I

Let me first discuss Part II of the Court's opinion. [T]he principle underlying the Court's opinion is that one who is accorded equal treatment under the laws, but cannot as readily as others obtain *preferential* treatment under the laws, has been denied equal protection of the laws. If merely stating this alleged "equal protection" violation does not suffice to refute it, our constitutional jurisprudence has achieved terminal silliness. The world has never heard of such a principle, which is why the Court's opinion is so long on emotive utterance and so short on relevant legal citation. And it seems to me most unlikely that any multilevel democracy can function under such a principle. For *whenever* a disadvantage is imposed, or conferral of a benefit is prohibited, at one of the higher levels of democratic decisionmaking, the affected group has (under this theory) been denied equal protection. To take the simplest of examples, consider a state law prohibiting the award of municipal contracts to relatives of mayors or city councilmen. Once such a law is passed, the group composed of such relatives must, in order to get the benefit of city contracts, persuade the state legislature-unlike all other citizens, who need only persuade the municipality. It is ridiculous to consider this a denial of equal protection, which is why the Court's theory is unheard of.

II

I turn next to whether there was a legitimate rational basis for the substance of the constitutional amendment. It is unsurprising that the Court avoids discussion of this question, since the answer is so obviously yes. The case most relevant to the issue before us today is not even mentioned in the Court's opinion: In *Bowers v. Hardwick*, 478 U.S. 186 (1986), we held that the Constitution does not prohibit what virtually all States had done from the founding of the Republic until very recent years-making homosexual conduct a crime. That holding is unassailable, except by those who think that the Constitution changes to suit current fashions. But in any event it is a given in the present case: Respondents' briefs did not urge overruling *Bowers*. If it is constitutionally permissible for a State to make homosexual conduct criminal, surely it is constitutionally permissible for a State to enact other laws merely *disfavoring* homosexual conduct. And *a fortiori* it is constitutionally permissible for a State to adopt a provision *not even* disfavoring homosexual conduct, but merely prohibiting all levels of state government from bestowing *special protections* upon homosexual conduct.

III

No principle set forth in the Constitution, nor even any imagined by this Court in the past 200 years, prohibits what Colorado has done here. But the case for Colorado is much stronger than that. What it has done is not only unprohibited, but eminently reasonable.

First, as to its eminent reasonableness. The Court's opinion contains grim, disapproving hints that Coloradans have been guilty of "animus" or "animosity" toward homosexuality, as though that has been established as un-American. But I had thought that one could consider certain conduct reprehensible-murder, for example, or polygamy, or cruelty to animals-and could exhibit even "animus" toward such conduct. Surely that is the only sort of "animus" at issue here: moral disapproval of homosexual conduct, the same sort of moral disapproval that produced the centuries-old criminal laws that we held constitutional in *Bowers*. The Colorado amendment does not, to speak entirely precisely, prohibit giving favored status to people who are *homosexuals;* they can be favored for many reasons-for example, because they are senior citizens or members of racial minorities. But it prohibits giving them favored status *because of their homosexual conduct*-that is, it prohibits favored status *for homosexuality.*

But though Coloradans are, as I say, *entitled* to be hostile toward homosexual conduct, the fact is that the degree of hostility reflected by Amendment 2 is the smallest conceivable. The Court's portrayal of Coloradans as a society fallen victim to pointless, hate-filled "gay-bashing" is so false as to be comical. Colorado not only is one of the 25 States that have repealed their antisodomy laws, but was among the first to do so. But the society that eliminates criminal punishment for homosexual acts does not necessarily abandon the view that homosexuality is morally wrong and socially harmful.

There is a problem which arises when criminal sanction of homosexuality is eliminated but moral and social disapprobation of homosexuality is meant to be retained. The problem (a problem, that is, for those who wish to retain social disapprobation of homosexuality) is that, because those who engage in homosexual conduct tend to reside in disproportionate numbers in certain communities, and, of course, care about homosexual-rights issues much more ardently than the public at large, they possess political power much greater than their numbers, both locally and statewide. Quite understandably, they devote this political power to achieving not merely a grudging social toleration, but full social acceptance, of homosexuality. See, e.g., [Andrew M.] Jacobs, The Rhetorical Construction of Rights: The Case of the Gay Rights Movement, 1969–1991, 72 NEB. L. REV. 723, 724 (1993) ("[T]he task of gay rights proponents is to move the center of public discourse along a continuum from the rhetoric of disapprobation, to rhetoric of tolerance, and finally to affirmation").

By the time Coloradans were asked to vote on Amendment 2, [t]hree Colorado cities-Aspen, Boulder, and Denver-had enacted ordinances that listed "sexual orientation" as an impermissible ground for discrimination, equating the moral disapproval of homosexual conduct with racial and religious bigotry. The phenomenon had even appeared statewide: The Governor of Colorado had signed an executive order directing state agency-heads to "ensure non-discrimination" in hiring and promotion based on, among other things, "sexual orientation." I do not mean to be critical of these legislative successes; homosexuals are as entitled to use the legal system for reinforcement of their moral sentiments as is the rest of society. But they are subject to being countered by lawful, democratic countermeasures as well.

That is where Amendment 2 came in. It sought to counter both the geographic concentration and the disproportionate political power of homosexuals by (1) resolving the controversy at the statewide level, and (2) making the election a single-issue contest for both sides. It put directly, to all the citizens of the State, the question: Should homosexuality be given special protection? They answered no. The Court today asserts that this most democratic of procedures is unconstitutional.

[T]his is proved false every time a state law prohibiting or disfavoring certain conduct is passed, because such a law prevents the adversely affected group-whether drug addicts, or smokers, or gun owners, or motorcyclists-from changing the policy thus established in "each of [the] parts" of the State. What the Court says is even demonstrably false at the constitutional level. The Establishment Clause of the First Amendment prevents theocrats from having their way by converting their fellow citizens at the local, state, or federal statutory level.

But there is a much closer analogy, one that involves precisely the effort by the majority of citizens to preserve its view of sexual morality statewide, against the efforts of a geographically concentrated and politically powerful minority to undermine it. The Constitutions of the States of Arizona, Idaho, New Mexico, Oklahoma, and Utah *to this day* contain provisions stating that polygamy is "forever prohibited." Polygamists, and those who have a polygamous "orientation," have been "singled out" by these provisions for much more severe treatment than merely denial of favored status; and that treatment can only be changed by achieving amendment of the state constitutions. The Court's disposition today suggests that these provisions are unconstitutional.

IV

The Court today employs a constitutional theory heretofore unknown to frustrate Colorado's reasonable effort to preserve traditional American moral values. [T]he Court today has done so, not only by inventing a novel and extravagant constitutional doctrine to take the victory away from traditional forces, but even by verbally disparaging as bigotry adherence to traditional attitudes. To suggest, for example, that this constitutional amendment springs from nothing more than " 'a bare . . . desire to harm a politically unpopular group,' " is nothing short of insulting. (It is also nothing short of preposterous to call "politically unpopular" a group which enjoys enormous influence in American media and politics, and which, as the trial court here noted, though composing no more than 4% of the population had the support of 46% of the voters on Amendment 2.)

When the Court takes sides in the culture wars, it tends to be with the knights rather than the villeins — and more specifically with the Templars, reflecting the views and values of the lawyer class from which the Court's Members are drawn.

EXERCISE 9:

1.   What was the challenged governmental classification?

2.   Why did the Supreme Court majority not utilize heightened scrutiny to evaluate Amendment 2?

3.   The *Romer* majority stated that it used rational basis review to evaluate Amendment 2. Is that true?

4.   Explain the Court's application of rational basis review in *Romer*.

5.   Many have dubbed the *Romer* Court's use of rational basis review as "rational basis with bite" to signify that it is somewhat more stringent than traditional or normal rational basis review. Why might the Court have utilized rational basis "with bite"?

6.   Justice Kennedy, for the Court, concluded that Amendment 2 was the product of "the disadvantage imposed is born of animosity toward the class of persons affected." What is the evidence upon which one would draw to determine whether Amendment 2 was the product of "animosity"? Does that evidence support Justice Kennedy's claim?

7.   In the lower courts, Colorado argued that Amendment 2 was justified by the state's interest in preserving traditional morality. Articulate that argument. Why did the state not make that argument to the Supreme Court? If it had made the argument, would it have been successful?

8.   Justice Scalia chided the majority for failing to distinguish or overrule, much less follow, *Bowers v. Hardwick*. Was that a fair criticism? Does the Supreme Court have an obligation to explain a holding's relationship to previous case law, assuming the precedent is relevant?

9.   Who, the majority or dissent, had the better of the argument regarding whether Amendment 2's restrictions on antidiscrimination laws that included sexual orientation

as a protected class violated equal protection? What limiting principle did the majority, or could the majority, articulate to distinguish Justice Scalia's examples?

10. Justice Scalia lodged a familiar (for him) charge against the *Romer* majority: the majority was taking "sides in the culture wars," and, in particular, on the side of cultural elites. Is that true and, if so, so what?

3. Strict Scrutiny

a. What Makes a Classification Suspect?

Up to this point, we have reviewed the rational basis component of the Supreme Court's Equal Protection Clause jurisprudence. For the remainder of this Chapter, we will cover those situations where the Clause requires "heightened scrutiny." Heightened scrutiny, as we will see below, includes both strict scrutiny and intermediate scrutiny review. A lot rests on the distinction between rational basis review and heightened scrutiny, so the distinction is crucial to properly understanding the Supreme Court's equal protection case law.

Over a number of decades, the Supreme Court — inchoately at first, and later explicitly — treated some legal classifications more stringently than others. Beginning in the early 1940s, the Supreme Court utilized a number of related labels to describe its approach to what today we would call suspect classifications or fundamental rights. *Korematsu v. United States*, 323 U.S. 214, 216 (1944); *Murdock v. Pennsylvania*, 319 U.S. 105, 115 (1943); *Skinner v. Oklahoma*, 316 U.S. 535, 541 (1942). In the equal protection context, this practice slowly solidified into modern strict scrutiny by 1984, *Palmore v. Sidoti*, 466 U.S. 429 (1984), though *Bolling v. Sharpe*, 347 U.S. 497, 499 (1954), had earlier suggested strict scrutiny.

At the same time, the Supreme Court, both implicitly and explicitly, relied on a number of factors to determine whether a particular classification was "suspect" and hence subject to heightened scrutiny. The four most commonly utilized factors are: (1) whether there is a history of discrimination based on the classification; (2) whether the classification is ever, or rarely, relevant to legitimate policy goals; (3) whether the classified group is able to fully participate in the political process; and (4) whether the classified characteristic is immutable.[41] You have already seen the Supreme Court applying these factors when it ruled that age and disability were not suspect classifications.

Much of the Supreme Court's most important Equal Protection Clause cases arose in the context of racial discrimination, so looking at the Court's equal protection doctrines from that lens is helpful. Applying the four factors to race classifications shows that: (1) there is a long and deep history of discrimination based on race; (2) race is rarely a legitimate basis upon which to legally classify; (3) racial minorities have historically been subject to exclusion from the political process; and (4) race is immutable. It is this type of analysis that moved the Supreme Court to label race a

---

[41] On occasions, the Supreme Court has also relied on a fifth factor: the obviousness, or lack thereof, of the characteristic. Race, for instance, is usually obvious, while alienage (citizenship-status), is not.

"suspect classification" that receives strict scrutiny.

The Supreme Court employed these factors when it determined that the classifications we review below — race, alienage, gender, and legitimacy — were suspect.

b. Distinguishing Suspect from Non-Suspect Classifications

(i) Introduction

Once we know what factors the Supreme Court took into account when it ruled that race, alienage, gender, and legitimacy classifications were suspect, we must still determine whether a particular law employs a suspect classification. This subsection describes how that is done.

(ii) Facially Discriminatory Classifications

In some cases, this is relatively easy: the law textually classifies based on a suspect classification. For example, in *Plessy* and *Brown*, the challenged state laws explicitly divided people based on race: Which train cars and schools people attended depended on their race. Another example is reprinted below.

LOVING v. VIRGINIA
388 U.S. 1 (1967)

Mr. Chief Justice Warren delivered the opinion of the Court.

This case presents a constitutional question: whether a statutory scheme adopted by the State of Virginia to prevent marriages between persons solely on the basis of racial classifications violates the Equal Protection Clause.

I.

[T]he State argues that the meaning of the Equal Protection Clause is only that state penal laws containing an interracial element as part of the definition of the offense must apply equally to whites and Negroes in the sense that members of each race are punished to the same degree. Thus, the State contends that, because its miscegenation statutes punish equally both the white and the Negro participants in an interracial marriage, these statutes, despite their reliance on racial classifications do not constitute an invidious discrimination based upon race. The second argument advanced by the State is that, if the Equal Protection Clause does not outlaw miscegenation statutes because of their reliance on racial classifications, the question of constitutionality would thus become whether there was any rational basis for a State to treat interracial marriages differently from other marriages. On this question, the State argues, this Court should defer to the wisdom of the state legislature.

Because we reject the notion that the mere "equal application" of a statute containing racial classifications is enough to remove the classifications from the Fourteenth Amendment's proscription of all invidious racial discriminations, we do not accept the State's contention that these statutes should be upheld if there is any possible basis for concluding that they serve a rational purpose. The mere fact of equal application does not mean that our analysis of these statutes should follow the approach we have taken in cases involving no racial discrimination where the Equal Protection Clause has been arrayed against a statute discriminating between the kinds of advertising which may be displayed on trucks in New York City, *Railway Express Agency, Inc. v. People of State of New York*, 336 U.S. 106 (1949). In these cases, involving distinctions not drawn according to race, the Court has merely asked whether there is any rational foundation for the discriminations, and has deferred to the wisdom of the state legislatures. In the case at bar, however, we deal with statutes containing racial classifications, and the fact of equal application does not immunize the statute from the very heavy burden of justification which the Fourteenth Amendment has traditionally required of state statutes drawn according to race.

The State argues that statements in the Thirty-ninth Congress about the time of the passage of the Fourteenth Amendment indicate that the Framers did not intend the Amendment to make unconstitutional state miscegenation laws. Many of the statements alluded to by the State concern the debates over the Freedmen's Bureau Bill, which President Johnson vetoed, and the Civil Rights Act of 1866, enacted over his veto. As for the various statements directly concerning the Fourteenth Amendment, we have said in connection with a related problem, that although these historical sources "cast some light" they are not sufficient to resolve the problem; "[a]t best, they are inconclusive." *Brown v. Board of Education*, 347 U.S. 483, 489 (1954). The clear and central purpose of the Fourteenth Amendment was to eliminate all official state sources of invidious racial discrimination in the States. *Slaughter-House Cases*, [83 U.S. (16 Wall.)] 36, 71 (1873); *Strauder v. West Virginia*, 100 U.S. 303, 307–308 (1880).

There can be no question but that Virginia's miscegenation statutes rest solely upon distinctions drawn according to race. The statutes proscribe generally accepted conduct if engaged in by members of different races. At the very least, the Equal Protection Clause demands that racial classifications be subjected to the "most rigid scrutiny," *Korematsu v. United States*, 323 U.S. 214, 216 (1944), and they must be shown to be necessary to the accomplishment of some permissible state objective, independent of the racial discrimination which it was the object of the Fourteenth Amendment to eliminate.

There is patently no legitimate overriding purpose independent of invidious racial discrimination which justifies this classification. The fact that Virginia prohibits only interracial marriages involving white persons demonstrates that the racial classifications must stand on their own justification, as measures designed to maintain White Supremacy. We have consistently denied the constitutionality of measures which restrict the rights of citizens on account of race. There can be no doubt that restricting the freedom to marry solely because of racial classifications violates the central meaning of the Equal Protection Clause.

II.

[The Supreme Court ruled that the Due Process Clause also prohibited state bans on interracial marriage.]

Reversed.

Mr. Justice Stewart, concurring. [opinion omitted]

EXERCISE 10:

1. On what basis did the Court rule that racial classifications should be subject to strict scrutiny?

2. Explain the Supreme Court's application of strict scrutiny to Virginia's statute.

3. Is the Court's description of the Equal Protection Clause's history accurate?

4. Under the Clause's original meaning, how would this case have come out?

Virginia's anti-miscegenation statute explicitly employed a racial classification. Such facially discriminatory statutes have become exceedingly rare because of changed legal and social views regarding racial discrimination. Consequently, the Supreme Court has explained what conditions must exist for a facially neutral law to invoke strict scrutiny.

(iii)   Facially Neutral Classifications

Most laws do not explicitly employ suspect classifications. *Yick Wo v. Hopkins*, 118 U.S. 356 (1886), noted earlier, exemplifies this. The challenged San Francisco city ordinance prohibited operating laundries in wooden building without permission. Though the ordinance did not explicitly mention Chinese ethnicity, the vast majority of wooden laundries were owned by people of Chinese descent. In fact, after the demise of segregation in the South, facially discriminatory laws have become rare (outside of the context of affirmative action, which we will cover below).

To deal with these facially neutral laws, the Supreme Court instructed that a challenger must establish that the law has a discriminatory purpose *and* a discriminatory effect.[42] In other words, only a discriminatory purpose, or only a discriminatory effect, will not violate the Equal Protection Clause.[43] The Court issued this ruling in *Washington v. Davis*, 426 U.S. 229 (1976). There, black job applicants sued the District of Columbia police department commissioner when they were not promoted alleging that the department's promotion policies were racially discriminatory. *Id.* at 232. In particular, they argued that the department's use of a written test, which disproportionately excluded black police officers from promotion, violated equal protection. *Id.* at 233–35.

---

[42] The common labels for discriminatory purpose discrimination and discriminatory effect discrimination is disparate treatment and disparate impact, respectively.

[43] Keep in mind, however, that, just because the Equal Protection Clause does not prohibit non-intentional discriminatory effects, that does not mean that discriminatory effect is legal. There are other legal norms that a plaintiff can frequently look to for relief. In particular, the 1964 Civil Rights Act prohibits discriminatory effects, without proof of discriminatory intent. Griggs v. Duke Power Co., 401 U.S. 424, 429–30 (1971).

The Supreme Court ruled that, to bring a successful claim for violation of equal protection, a plaintiff must show purposeful discrimination. *Id.* at 239–40. The Court reviewed its precedent and concluded that: "we have not held that a law, neutral on its face and serving ends otherwise within the power of government to pursue, is invalid under the Equal Protection Clause simply because it may affect a greater proportion of one race than of another. Disproportionate impact is not irrelevant, but it is not the sole touchstone of an invidious racial discrimination forbidden by the Constitution. Standing alone, it does not trigger the rule . . . that racial classifications are to be subjected to the strictest scrutiny and are justifiable only by the weightiest of considerations." *Id.* at 242. The following year, the Court explained *how* a plaintiff can establish the necessary discriminatory purpose.

VILLAGE OF ARLINGTON HEIGHTS v. METROPOLITAN HOUSING DEVELOPMENT CORPORATION
429 U.S. 252 (1977)

Mr. Justice Powell delivered the opinion of the Court.

I

Arlington Heights is a suburb of Chicago. Most of the land in Arlington Heights is zoned for detached single-family homes. The Village experienced substantial growth during the 1960's, but, like other communities in northwest Cook County, its population of racial minority groups remained quite low. According to the 1970 census, only 27 of the Village's 64,000 residents were black.

The Clerics of St. Viator, a religious order (Order), own an 80-acre parcel just east of the center of Arlington Heights. Part of the site is occupied by the Viatorian high school, and part by the Order's three-story novitiate building. Much of the site, however, remains vacant. Since 1959, when the Village first adopted a zoning ordinance, all the land surrounding the Viatorian property has been zoned R-3, a single-family specification with relatively small minimum lot-size requirements.

The Order decided in 1970 to devote some of its land to low- and moderate-income housing. Investigation revealed that the most expeditious way to build such housing was to work through a nonprofit developer. MHDC is such a developer. It was organized in 1968 by several prominent Chicago citizens for the purpose of building low- and moderate-income housing throughout the Chicago area.

After some negotiation, MHDC and the Order entered into a 99-year lease and an accompanying agreement of sale covering a 15-acre site in the southeast corner of the Viatorian property. MHDC became the lessee immediately, but the sale agreement was contingent upon MHDC's securing zoning clearances from the Village.

MHDC engaged an architect and proceeded with the project, to be known as Lincoln Green. The plans called for 20 two-story buildings with a total of 190 units.

The planned development did not conform to the Village's zoning ordinance and could not be built unless Arlington Heights rezoned the parcel to R-5, its multiple-family housing classification. Accordingly, MHDC filed with the Village Plan Commission a petition for rezoning. The materials made clear that one requirement under [the federal housing program] is an affirmative marketing plan designed to assure that a subsidized development is racially integrated.

During the spring of 1971, the Plan Commission considered the proposal at a series of three public meetings, which drew large crowds. Some of the comments, both from opponents and supporters, addressed what was referred to as the "social issue" the desirability or undesirability of introducing at this location in Arlington Heights low- and moderate-income housing, housing that would probably be racially integrated.

Many of the opponents, however, focused on the zoning aspects of the petition, stressing two arguments. First, the area always had been zoned single-family, and the neighboring citizens had built or purchased there in reliance on that classification. Rezoning threatened to cause a measurable drop in property value for neighboring sites. Second, the Village's apartment policy called for R-5 zoning primarily to serve as a buffer between single-family development and land uses thought incompatible, such as commercial or manufacturing districts. Lincoln Green did not meet this requirement, as it adjoined no commercial or manufacturing district.

At the close of the third meeting, the Plan Commission adopted a motion to recommend to the Village's Board of Trustees that it deny the request. The Village Board met on September 28, 1971, to consider MHDC's request and the recommendation of the Plan Commission. After a public hearing, the Board denied the rezoning by a 6-1 vote.

The following June MHDC and three Negro individuals filed this lawsuit against the Village, seeking declaratory and injunctive relief. [T]he District Court held that the petitioners were not motivated by racial discrimination or intent to discriminate against low-income groups when they denied rezoning, but rather by a desire "to protect property values and the integrity of the Village's zoning plan."

A divided Court of Appeals reversed. It first approved the District Court's finding that the defendants were motivated by a concern for the integrity of the zoning plan, rather than by racial discrimination. [T]he Court of Appeals [also] ruled that the denial of the Lincoln Green proposal had racially discriminatory effects and could be tolerated only if it served compelling interests. Neither the buffer policy nor the desire to protect property values met this exacting standard. The court therefore concluded that the denial violated the Equal Protection Clause of the Fourteenth Amendment.

III

Our decision last Term in *Washington v. Davis*, 426 U.S. 229 (1976), made it clear that official action will not be held unconstitutional solely because it results in a racially disproportionate impact. Proof of racially discriminatory intent or purpose is required to show a violation of the Equal Protection Clause.

Davis does not require a plaintiff to prove that the challenged action rested solely on racially discriminatory purposes. Rarely can it be said that a legislature or administrative body operating under a broad mandate made a decision motivated solely by a single concern, or even that a particular purpose was the "dominant" or "primary" one. In fact, it is because legislators and administrators are properly concerned with balancing numerous competing considerations that courts refrain from reviewing the merits of their decisions, absent a showing of arbitrariness or irrationality. But racial discrimination is not just another competing consideration. When there is a proof that a discriminatory purpose has been a motivating factor in the decision, this judicial deference is no longer justified.

Determining whether invidious discriminatory purpose was a motivating factor demands a sensitive inquiry into such circumstantial and direct evidence of intent as may be available. The impact of the official action [and] whether it "bears more heavily on one race than another," *Washington v. Davis*, 426 U.S., at 242, may provide an important starting point. Sometimes a clear pattern, unexplainable on grounds other than race, emerges from the effect of the state action even when the governing legislation appears neutral on its face. *Yick Wo v. Hopkins*, 118 U.S. 356 (1886). But such cases are rare. Absent a pattern as stark as that in *Yick Wo*, impact alone is not determinative, and the Court must look to other evidence.

The historical background of the decision is one evidentiary source, particularly if it reveals a series of official actions taken for invidious purposes. The specific sequence of events leading up the challenged decision also may shed some light on the decisionmaker's purposes. For example, if the property involved here always had been zoned R-5 but suddenly was changed to R-3 when the town learned of MHDC's plans to erect integrated housing, we would have a far different case. Departures from the normal procedural sequence also might afford evidence that improper purposes are playing a role. Substantive departures too may be relevant, particularly if the factors usually considered important by the decisionmaker strongly favor a decision contrary to the one reached.

The legislative or administrative history may be highly relevant, especially where there are contemporary statements by members of the decisionmaking body, minutes of its meetings, or reports. In some extraordinary instances the members might be called to the stand at trial to testify concerning the purpose of the official action.

With these in mind, we now address the case before us.

IV

In making its findings on this issue, the District Court held that the evidence "does not warrant the conclusion that this motivated the defendants." The Court of Appeals approved the District Court's findings.

We also have reviewed the evidence. The impact of the Village's decision does arguably bear more heavily on racial minorities. Minorities constitute 18% of the Chicago area population, and 40% of the income groups said to be eligible for Lincoln Green. But there is little about the sequence of events leading up to the decision that would spark suspicion. The area around the Viatorian property has been zoned R-3 since Arlington Heights first adopted a zoning map. Single-family homes surround the 80-acre site, and the Village is undeniably committed to single-family homes as its dominant residential land use. The rezoning request progressed according to the usual procedures. The Plan Commission even scheduled two additional hearings, at least in part to accommodate MHDC and permit it to supplement its presentation with answers to questions generated at the first hearing.

The statements by the Plan Commission and Village Board members, as reflected in the official minutes, focused almost exclusively on the zoning aspects of the MHDC petition, and the zoning factors on which they relied are not novel criteria in the Village's rezoning decisions. There is no reason to doubt that there has been reliance by some neighboring property owners on the maintenance of single-family zoning in the vicinity. The Village originally adopted its buffer policy long before MHDC entered the picture and has applied the policy too consistently for us to infer discriminatory purpose from its application in this case. Finally, MHDC called one member of the Village Board to the stand at trial. Nothing in her testimony supports an inference of invidious purpose.

In sum, Respondents simply failed to carry their burden of proving that discriminatory purpose was a motivating factor in the Village's decision.

V

Respondents' complaint also alleged that the refusal to rezone violated the Fair Housing Act of 1968. We remand the case for further consideration of respondents' statutory claims.

Reversed and remanded.

Mr. Justice Stevens took no part in the consideration or decision of this case.

Mr. Justice Marshall, with whom Mr. Justice Brennan joins, concurring in part and dissenting in part. [Opinion omitted.]

Mr. Justice White, dissenting. [Opinion omitted.]

EXERCISE 11:

1.   According to the *Arlington Heights* Court, what counts as a discriminatory "purpose" sufficient to invoke strict scrutiny under the Equal Protection Clause?

2.   How does one establish a discriminatory purpose?

3.   Is there even such a thing as "purpose" of a multi-member body like a city council?

4.   Is requiring a discriminatory purpose faithful to the Equal Protection Clause? Is it a good idea? What are the arguments pro and con the purpose requirement?

c.   Race and National Origin

The rule that race and national origin classifications are subject to strict scrutiny traces its origin, ironically, to one of the Supreme Court's most criticized cases, reprinted below.

KOREMATSU v. UNITED STATES
323 U.S. 214 (1944)

MR. JUSTICE BLACK delivered the opinion of the Court.

The petitioner, an American citizen of Japanese descent, was convicted in a federal district court for remaining in San Leandro, California, a "Military Area", contrary to Civilian Exclusion Order No. 34 of the Commanding General of the Western Command, U.S. Army, which directed that after May 9, 1942, all persons of Japanese ancestry should be excluded from that area. No question was raised as to petitioner's loyalty to the United States.

It should be noted, to begin with, that all legal restrictions which curtail the civil rights of a single racial group are immediately suspect. That is not to say that all such restrictions are unconstitutional. It is to say that courts must subject them to the most rigid scrutiny. Pressing public necessity may sometimes justify the existence of such restrictions; racial antagonism never can.

In the instant case prosecution of the petitioner was begun by information charging violation of an Act of Congress, of March 21, 1942, which provides that

> "* * * whoever shall enter, remain in, leave, or commit any act in any military area or military zone prescribed, under the authority of an Executive order of the President, by the Secretary of War, or by any military commander designated by the Secretary of War, contrary to the restrictions applicable to any such area or zone or contrary to the order of the Secretary of War or any such military commander, shall, if it appears that he knew or should have known of the existence and extent of the restrictions or order and that his act was in violation thereof, be guilty of a misdemeanor."

Exclusion Order No. 34, which the petitioner knowingly and admittedly violated was one of the series of orders and proclamations which was promulgated pursuant to Executive Order 9066. As is the case with the exclusion order here, [a] prior curfew order was designed as a "protection against espionage and against sabotage." In *Hirabayashi v. United States*, 320 U.S. 81 [(1943)], we sustained a conviction obtained for violation of the curfew order. The Hirabayashi conviction and this one thus rest on the same 1942 Congressional Act and the same basic executive and military orders, all of which orders were aimed at the twin dangers of espionage and sabotage. We upheld the curfew order as an exercise of the power of the government to take steps necessary to prevent espionage and sabotage in an area threatened by Japanese attack.

In the light of the principles we announced in the *Hirabayashi* case, we are unable to conclude that it was beyond the war power of Congress and the Executive to exclude those of Japanese ancestry from the West Coast war area at the time they did. True, exclusion from the area in which one's home is located is a far greater deprivation than constant confinement to the home from 8 p.m. to 6 a.m. Nothing short of apprehension by the proper military authorities of the gravest imminent danger to the public safety can constitutionally justify either. But exclusion from a threatened area, no less than curfew, has a definite and close relationship to the prevention of espionage and sabotage. The military authorities, charged with the primary responsibility of defending our shores, concluded that curfew provided inadequate protection and ordered exclusion. They did so in accordance with Congressional authority to the military to say who should, and who should not, remain in the threatened areas.

In this case the petitioner challenges the assumptions upon which we rested our conclusions in the *Hirabayashi* case. He also urges that by May 1942, when Order No. 34 was promulgated, all danger of Japanese invasion of the West Coast had disappeared. After careful consideration of these contentions we are compelled to reject them.

Here, as in the *Hirabayashi* case, 320 U.S. at page 99, "we cannot reject as unfounded the judgment of the military authorities and of Congress that there were disloyal members of that population, whose number and strength could not be precisely and quickly ascertained. We cannot say that the war-making branches of the Government did not have ground for believing that in a critical hour such persons could not readily be isolated and separately dealt with, and constituted a menace to the national defense and safety, which demanded that prompt and adequate measures be taken to guard against it."

Like curfew, exclusion of those of Japanese origin was deemed necessary because of the presence of an unascertained number of disloyal members of the group, most of whom we have no doubt were loyal to this country. It was because we could not reject the finding of the military authorities that it was impossible to bring about an immediate segregation of the disloyal from the loyal that we sustained the validity of the curfew order as applying to the whole group. In the instant case, temporary exclusion of the entire group was rested by the military on the same ground. The judgment that exclusion of the whole group was for the same reason a military imperative answers the contention that the exclusion was in the nature of group punishment based on antagonism to those of Japanese origin. That there were members of the group who retained loyalties to Japan has been confirmed by investigations made subsequent to the exclusion. Approximately five thousand American citizens of Japanese ancestry refused to swear unqualified allegiance to the United States and to renounce allegiance to the Japanese Emperor, and several thousand evacuees requested repatriation to Japan.

We uphold the exclusion order. In doing so, we are not unmindful of the hardships imposed by it upon a large group of American citizens. But hardships are part of war, and war is an aggregation of hardships. All citizens alike, both in and out of uniform, feel the impact of war in greater or lesser measure. Citizenship has its responsibilities as well as its privileges, and in time of war the burden is always heavier. Compulsory exclusion of large groups of citizens from their homes, except under circumstances of direst emergency and peril, is inconsistent with our basic governmental institutions. But when under conditions of modern warfare our shores are threatened by hostile forces, the power to protect must be commensurate with the threatened danger.

Our task would be simple, our duty clear, were this a case involving the imprisonment of a loyal citizen in a concentration camp because of racial prejudice. [W]e are dealing specifically with nothing but an exclusion order. To cast this case into outlines of racial prejudice, without reference to the real military dangers which were presented, merely confuses the issue. Korematsu was not excluded from the Military Area because of hostility to him or his race. He was excluded because we are at war with the Japanese Empire, because the properly constituted military authorities feared an invasion of our West Coast and felt constrained to take proper security measures, because they decided that the military urgency of the situation demanded that all citizens of Japanese ancestry be segregated from the West Coast temporarily, and finally, because Congress, reposing its confidence in this time of war in our military leaders determined that they should have the power to do just this. There was evidence of disloyalty on the part of some, the military authorities considered that the need for action was great, and time was short. We cannot — by availing ourselves of the calm perspective of hindsight — now say that at that time these actions were unjustified.

Affirmed.

MR. JUSTICE FRANKFURTER, concurring. [Opinion omitted.]

MR. JUSTICE ROBERTS. [Dissenting opinion omitted.]

MR. JUSTICE MURPHY, dissenting.

This exclusion of "all persons of Japanese ancestry, both alien and non-alien," from the Pacific Coast area on a plea of military necessity in the absence of martial law ought not to be approved. Such exclusion goes over "the very brink of constitutional power" and falls into the ugly abyss of racism.

In dealing with matters relating to the prosecution and progress of a war, we must accord great respect and consideration to the judgments of the military authorities who are on the scene and who have full knowledge of the military facts. And their judgments ought not to be overruled lightly by those whose training and duties ill-equip them to deal intelligently with matters so vital to the physical security of the nation.

At the same time, however, it is essential that there be definite limits to military discretion. Individuals must not be left impoverished of their constitutional rights on a plea of military necessity that has neither substance nor support. Thus, the military claim must subject itself to the judicial process of having its reasonableness determined and its conflicts with other interests reconciled.

The judicial test of whether the Government, on a plea of military necessity, can validly deprive an individual of any of his constitutional rights is whether the deprivation is reasonably related to a public danger that is so "immediate, imminent, and impending" as not to admit of delay and not to permit the intervention of ordinary constitutional processes to alleviate the danger. Civilian Exclusion Order No. 34 clearly does not meet that test. Being an obvious racial discrimination, the order deprives all those within its scope of the equal protection of the laws as guaranteed by the Fifth Amendment. And that relation is lacking because the exclusion order necessarily must rely for its reasonableness upon the assumption that all persons of Japanese ancestry may have a dangerous tendency to commit sabotage and espionage and to aid our Japanese enemy in other ways.

That this forced exclusion was the result in good measure of this erroneous assumption of racial guilt rather than bona fide military necessity is evidenced by the Commanding General's Final Report on the evacuation from the Pacific Coast area. In it he refers to all individuals of Japanese descent as "subversive," as belonging to "an enemy race" whose "racial strains are undiluted," and as constituting "over 112,000 potential enemies * * * at large today" along the Pacific Coast. In support of this blanket condemnation of all persons of Japanese descent, however, no reliable evidence is cited to show that such individuals were generally disloyal, or had generally so conducted themselves in this area as to constitute a special menace to defense installations or war industries. A military judgment based upon such racial and sociological considerations is not entitled to the great weight ordinarily given the judgments based upon strictly military considerations.

No adequate reason is given for the failure to treat these Japanese Americans on an individual basis by holding investigations and hearings to separate the loyal from the disloyal, as was done in the case of persons of German and Italian ancestry. It is asserted merely that the loyalties of this group "were unknown and time was of the essence." Yet nearly four months elapsed after Pearl Harbor before the first exclusion order was issued; nearly eight months went by until the last order was issued; and the last of these "subversive" persons was not actually removed until almost eleven months had elapsed.

Moreover, there was no adequate proof that the Federal Bureau of Investigation and the military and naval intelligence services did not have the espionage and sabotage situation well in hand during this long period. It seems incredible that under these circumstances it would have been impossible to hold loyalty hearings for the mere 112,000 persons involved especially when a large part of this number represented children and elderly men and women.[16]

I dissent, therefore, from this legalization of racism. Racial discrimination in any form and in any degree has no justifiable part whatever in our democratic way of life. It is unattractive in any setting but it is utterly revolting among a free people who have embraced the principles set forth in the Constitution of the United States. All residents of this nation are kin in some way by blood or culture to a foreign land. Yet they are primarily and necessarily a part of the new and distinct civilization of the

---

[16] During a period of six months, the 112 alien tribunals or hearing boards set up by the British Government shortly after the outbreak of the present war summoned and examined approximately 74,000 German and Austrian aliens. These tribunals determined whether each individual enemy alien was a real enemy of the Allies or only a "friendly enemy." About 64,000 were freed from internment and from any special restrictions, and only 2,000 were interned.

United States. They must accordingly be treated at all times as the heirs of the American experiment and as entitled to all the rights and freedoms guaranteed by the Constitution.

MR. JUSTICE JACKSON, dissenting.

* * *

The military reasonableness of these orders can only be determined by military superiors. If the people ever let command of the war power fall into irresponsible and unscrupulous hands, the courts wield no power equal to its restraint. The chief restraint upon those who command the physical forces of the country must be their responsibility to the political judgments of their contemporaries and to the moral judgments of history.

My duties as a justice as I see them do not require me to make a military judgment as to whether General DeWitt's evacuation and detention program was a reasonable military necessity. I do not suggest that the courts should have attempted to interfere with the Army in carrying out its task. But I do not think they may be asked to execute a military expedient that has no place in law under the Constitution. I would reverse the judgment and discharge the prisoner.

EXERCISE 12:

1. What legal classification was at issue?

2. What analysis did the Supreme Court utilize to evaluate that classification?

3. Describe the Court's application of that analysis.

4. What role did the context play in the Court's analysis; in particular, the on-going war and the military's judgment? How did this context make it difficult to fit this case into the *Carolene Products* Footnote 4 paradigm?

5. Looking at the case from an institutional perspective, what role, if any, should the judgments of Congress in passing Act of Congress, of March 21, 1942, President Roosevelt in signing Executive Order 9066, and General DeWitt in issuing Exclusion Order 34, have played in the Court's analysis of Korematsu's claim? What were the respective positions of the majority and Justice Murphy? Who was right? Or was Justice Jackson correct when he argued that the military was subject only to political checks via the elected branches?

6. The Supreme Court still regularly cites *Korematsu*, usually for the proposition that racial classifications are subject to strict scrutiny. *E.g., Adarand Constructors, Inc. v. Pena*, 515 U.S. 200, 214–17 (1995). Is it appropriate for the Court to cite a case for a legal proposition when the case reached such a bad result?

7. Prior to his appointment to the Supreme Court by President Franklin Roosevelt, in 1941, Robert Jackson — an extremely strong supporter of President Roosevelt, the New Deal, and the Democratic Party — served in a number of executive positions, until President Roosevelt appointed him to serve as Attorney General in

1940. President Roosevelt appointed Justice Jackson to the Supreme Court with the expectation that he would support the President's policies, especially war policies, when on the Court. Justice Jackson dissented in *Korematsu*. Few doubt that, as Attorney General, he would have vigorously advocated for the government's position. What, if anything, does Justice Jackson's dissent in *Korematsu* show about the independence of Supreme Court justices?

8.　In 1988, the United States formally apologized for the Japanese internment with the passage of the Civil Liberties Act of 1988, 102 Stat. 904 (1988). The Act also provided compensation to surviving internees.

———————

One of the most controversial aspects of constitutional law is the case law regarding affirmative action. From its first encounter with affirmative action in 1978, the Supreme Court has struggled to chart a consistent path. The first major case was *Regents of the Univ. of Cal. v. Bakke*, 438 U.S 265 (1978). There, the Court faced a challenge under the Equal Protection Clause brought by a white applicant who was denied admission to the University of Davis medical school. The plaintiff argued that he was denied admission because of the school's affirmative action program, which admitted lower qualified non-white students in place of him.

The Court badly fractured. Justice Powell wrote for himself, in what is usually taken to be the case's controlling opinion.[44] He concluded that the use of race in affirmative action programs is subject to review under the Equal Protection Clause, that U.C. Davis' affirmative action program was subject to strict scrutiny, and that educational diversity in higher education was a compelling state interest. *Id.* at 289–315. However, Justice Powell then ruled that Davis' use of race was not narrowly tailored to its compelling interest because it used race as a quota, and not as one factor among many in building a diverse student body. *Id.* at 319–20.

Four other justices joined an opinion authored by Justice Brennan who concluded that the Equal Protection Clause applied to Davis' use of race in its affirmative action program, but that Davis' "benign" use of race was subject only to intermediate scrutiny because of the Clause's overriding purpose of equality. *Id.* at 359 (Brennan, J., concurring). Thereafter, they argued that Davis' affirmative action program was substantially related to an important state interest of overcoming the lingering effects of past societal discrimination. *Id.* at 362–79.

The other four justices joined an opinion written by Justice Stevens who concluded that Davis' affirmative action program violated Title VI of the 1964 Civil Rights Act. *Id.* at 412–17. Relying on the traditional norm of avoiding constitutional issues, these four justices did not discuss the constitutionality of affirmative action.

Following *Bakke*, the Supreme Court faced a number of challenges to affirmative action, and the key issue was the level of scrutiny to which the Court should subject the

———————

[44]　*See* Marks v. United States, 430 U.S. 188, 193 (1977) ("When a fragmented Court decides a case and no single rationale explaining the result enjoys the assent of five Justices, 'the holding of the Court may be viewed as that position taken by those Members who concurred in the judgments on the narrowest grounds.' ").

use of race in this context. The Court settled this issue in two cases, *Richmond v. J.A. Croson*, 488 U.S. 469 (1989), and *Adarand Constructors, Inc. v. Pena*, 515 U.S. 200 (1995).

CITY OF RICHMOND v. J.A. CROSON COMPANY
488 U.S. 469 (1989)

JUSTICE O'CONNOR announced the judgment of the Court and delivered the opinion of the Court with respect to Parts I, III-B, and IV, an opinion with respect to Part II, in which THE CHIEF JUSTICE and JUSTICE WHITE join, and an opinion with respect to Parts III-A and V, in which THE CHIEF JUSTICE, JUSTICE WHITE, and JUSTICE KENNEDY join.

In this case, we confront once again the tension between the Fourteenth Amendment's guarantee of equal treatment to all citizens, and the use of race-based measures to ameliorate the effects of past discrimination on the opportunities enjoyed by members of minority groups in our society.

I

On April 11, 1983, the Richmond City Council adopted the Minority Business Utilization Plan (the Plan). The Plan required prime contractors to whom the city awarded construction contracts to subcontract at least 30% of the dollar amount of the contract to one or more Minority Business Enterprises (MBE's). The Plan defined an MBE as "[a] business at least fifty-one (51) percent of which is owned and controlled . . . by minority group members." "Minority group members" were defined as "[c]itizens of the United States who are Blacks, Spanish-speaking, Orientals, Indians, Eskimos, or Aleuts." [A] qualified MBE from anywhere in the United States could avail itself of the 30% set-aside. The Plan declared that it was "remedial" in nature.

The Plan was adopted by the Richmond City Council after a public hearing. Proponents of the set-aside provision relied on a study which indicated that, while the general population of Richmond was 50% black, only 0.67% of the city's prime construction contracts had been awarded to minority businesses in the 5-year period from 1978 to 1983. It was also established that a variety of contractors' associations had virtually no minority businesses within their membership. There was no direct evidence of race discrimination on the part of the city in letting contracts or any evidence that the city's prime contractors had discriminated against minority-owned subcontractors.

J.A. Croson Company (Croson), a mechanical plumbing and heating contractor, brought this action under 42 U.S.C. § 1983 in the Federal District Court for the Eastern District of Virginia, arguing that the Richmond ordinance was unconstitutional. The District Court upheld the Plan in all respects. The Court of Appeals [held] that even if the city had demonstrated a compelling interest in the use of a race-based quota, the 30% set-aside was not narrowly tailored to accomplish a remedial purpose. We affirm the judgment.

II

The parties and their supporting *amici* fight an initial battle over the scope of the city's power to adopt legislation designed to address the effects of past discrimination. Congress, unlike any State or political subdivision, has a specific constitutional mandate to enforce the dictates of the Fourteenth Amendment. The power to "enforce" may at times also include the power to define situations which *Congress* determines threaten principles of equality and to adopt prophylactic rules to deal with those situations. See *Katzenbach v. Morgan*, 384 U.S. [641,] 651 [(1966)] ("Correctly viewed, § 5 is a positive grant of legislative power authorizing Congress to exercise its discretion in determining whether and what legislation is needed to secure the guarantees of the Fourteenth Amendment").

That Congress may identify and redress the effects of society-wide discrimination does not mean that, *a fortiori*, the States and their political subdivisions are free to decide that such remedies are appropriate. Section 1 of the Fourteenth Amendment is an explicit *constraint* on state power, and the States must undertake any remedial efforts in accordance with that provision. To hold otherwise would be to cede control over the content of the Equal Protection Clause to the 50 state legislatures and their myriad political subdivisions. The mere recitation of a benign or compensatory purpose for the use of a racial classification would essentially insulate any racial classification from judicial scrutiny under § 1. We believe that such a result would be contrary to the intentions of the Framers of the Fourteenth Amendment, who desired to place clear limits on the States' use of race as a criterion for legislative action.

It would seem equally clear, however, that a state or local subdivision has the authority to eradicate the effects of private discrimination within its own legislative jurisdiction. This authority must, of course, be exercised within the constraints of § 1 of the Fourteenth Amendment. As a matter of state law, the city of Richmond has legislative authority over its procurement policies, and can use its spending powers to remedy private discrimination, if it identifies that discrimination with the particularity required by the Fourteenth Amendment. Thus, if the city could show that it had essentially become a "passive participant" in a system of racial exclusion practiced by elements of the local construction industry, we think it clear that the city could take affirmative steps to dismantle such a system.

III

A

The Equal Protection Clause of the Fourteenth Amendment provides that "[n]o State shall . . . deny to *any person* within its jurisdiction the equal protection of the laws." (Emphasis added.) As this Court has noted in the past, the "rights created by the first section of the Fourteenth Amendment are, by its terms, guaranteed to the individual." The Richmond Plan denies certain citizens the opportunity to compete for a fixed percentage of public contracts based solely upon their race. To whatever racial group these citizens belong, their "personal rights" to be treated with equal dignity and respect are implicated by a rigid rule erecting race as the sole criterion in an aspect of public decisionmaking.

Absent searching judicial inquiry into the justification for such race-based measures, there is simply no way of determining what classifications are "benign" or "remedial" and what classifications are in fact motivated by illegitimate notions of racial inferiority or simple racial politics. Indeed, the purpose of strict scrutiny is to "smoke out" illegitimate uses of race by assuring that the legislative body is pursuing a goal important enough to warrant use of a highly suspect tool. The test also ensures that the means chosen "fit" this compelling goal so closely that there is little or no possibility that the motive for the classification was illegitimate racial prejudice or stereotype.

Classifications based on race carry a danger of stigmatic harm. Unless they are strictly reserved for remedial settings, they may in fact promote notions of racial inferiority and lead to a politics of racial hostility. See *University of California Regents v. Bakke*, 438 U.S. [265,] 298 [(1978)] (opinion of Powell, J.) ("[P]referential programs may only reinforce common stereotypes holding that certain groups are unable to achieve success without special protection based on a factor having no relation to individual worth"). We thus []affirm the view that the standard of review under the Equal Protection Clause is not dependent on the race of those burdened or benefited by a particular classification. See also *San Antonio Independent School Dist. v. Rodriguez*, 411 U.S. 1, 105 (1973) (MARSHALL, J., dissenting) ("The highly suspect nature of classifications based on race, nationality, or alienage is well established").

Our continued adherence to [strict scrutiny] does not, as JUSTICE MARSHALL'S dissent suggests, indicate that we view "racial discrimination as largely a phenomenon of the past." As we indicate, States and their local subdivisions have many legislative weapons at their disposal both to punish and prevent present discrimination and to remove arbitrary barriers to minority advancement. Rather, our interpretation of § 1 stems from our agreement with the view expressed by Justice Powell in *Bakke* that "[t]he guarantee of equal protection cannot mean one thing when applied to one individual and something else when applied to a person of another color." *Bakke*, 438 U.S., at 289–290. The dissent's watered-down version of equal protection review effectively assures that race will always be relevant in American life, and that the "ultimate goal" of "eliminat[ing] entirely from governmental decisionmaking such irrelevant factors as a human being's race," will never be achieved.

Even were we to accept a reading of the guarantee of equal protection under which the level of scrutiny varies according to the ability of different groups to defend their interests in the representative process, heightened scrutiny would still be appropriate in the circumstances of this case. One of the central arguments for applying a less exacting standard to "benign" racial classifications is that such measures essentially involve a choice made by dominant racial groups to disadvantage themselves. If one aspect of the judiciary's role under the Equal Protection Clause is to protect "discrete and insular minorities" from majoritarian prejudice or indifference, see *United States v. Carolene Products Co.*, 304 U.S. 144, 153, n. 4 (1938), some maintain that these concerns are not implicated when the "white majority" places burdens upon itself. See J[ohn Hart] Ely, Democracy and Distrust 170 (1980).

In this case, blacks constitute approximately 50% of the population of the city of Richmond. Five of the nine seats on the city council are held by blacks. The concern that a political majority will more easily act to the disadvantage of a minority based on unwarranted assumptions or incomplete facts would seem to militate for, not against, the application of heightened judicial scrutiny in this case.

B

We think it clear that the factual predicate offered in support of the Richmond Plan suffers from two defects. [A] generalized assertion that there has been past discrimination in an entire industry provides no guidance for a legislative body to determine the precise scope of the injury it seeks to remedy. It "has no logical stopping point." "Relief" for such an ill-defined wrong could extend until the percentage of public contracts awarded to MBE's in Richmond mirrored the percentage of minorities in the population as a whole.

Appellant argues that it is attempting to remedy various forms of past discrimination that are alleged to be responsible for the small number of minority businesses in the local contracting industry. This past discrimination has prevented them "from following the traditional path from laborer to entrepreneur." While there is no doubt that the sorry history of both private and public discrimination in this country has contributed to a lack of opportunities for black entrepreneurs, this observation, standing alone, cannot justify a rigid racial quota in the awarding of public contracts in Richmond, Virginia.

It is sheer speculation how many minority firms there would be in Richmond absent past societal discrimination. Defining these sorts of injuries as "identified discrimination" would give local governments license to create a patchwork of racial preferences based on statistical generalizations about any particular field of endeavor.

None of [Richmond's] "findings," singly or together, provide the city of Richmond with a "strong basis in evidence for its conclusion that remedial action was necessary." There is nothing approaching a prima facie case of a constitutional or statutory violation by *anyone* in the Richmond construction industry.

The District Court relied on the highly conclusionary statement of a proponent of the Plan that there was racial discrimination in the construction industry "in this area, and the State, and around the nation." These statements are of little probative value in establishing identified discrimination in the Richmond construction industry. The factfinding process of legislative bodies is generally entitled to a presumption of regularity and deferential review by the judiciary. See *Williamson v. Lee Optical of Oklahoma, Inc.*, 348 U.S. 483, 488–489 (1955). But when a legislative body chooses to employ a suspect classification, it cannot rest upon a generalized assertion as to the classification's relevance to its goals. The history of racial classifications in this country suggests that blind judicial deference to legislative or executive pronouncements of necessity has no place in equal protection analysis. See *Korematsu v. United States*, 323 U.S. 214, 235–240 (1944) (Murphy, J., dissenting).

Reliance on the disparity between the number of prime contracts awarded to minority firms and the minority population of the city of Richmond is similarly misplaced. In this case, the city does not even know how many MBE's in the relevant market are qualified to undertake prime or subcontracting work in public construction projects. Nor does the city know what percentage of total city construction dollars minority firms now receive as subcontractors on prime contracts let by the city.

To a large extent, the set-aside of subcontracting dollars seems to rest on the unsupported assumption that white prime contractors simply will not hire minority firms.[3] Indeed, there is evidence in this record that overall minority participation in city contracts in Richmond is 7 to 8%, and that minority contractor participation in Community Block Development Grant *construction* projects is 17 to 22%. Without any information on minority participation in subcontracting, it is quite simply impossible to evaluate overall minority representation in the city's construction expenditures.

The city and the District Court also relied on evidence that MBE membership in local contractors' associations was extremely low. Again, standing alone this evidence is not probative of any discrimination in the local construction industry. There are numerous explanations for this dearth of minority participation, including past societal discrimination in education and economic opportunities as well as both black and white career and entrepreneurial choices. Blacks may be disproportionately attracted to industries other than construction. The mere fact that black membership in these trade organizations is low, standing alone, cannot establish a prima facie case of discrimination.

JUSTICE MARSHALL apparently views the requirement that Richmond identify the discrimination it seeks to remedy in its own jurisdiction as a mere administrative headache. We cannot agree. "[B]ecause racial characteristics so seldom provide a relevant basis for disparate treatment, and because classifications based on race are potentially so harmful to the entire body politic, it is especially important that the reasons for any such classification be clearly identified and unquestionably legitimate." The "evidence" relied upon by the dissent, the history of school desegregation in Richmond and numerous congressional reports, does little to define the scope of any injury to minority contractors in Richmond or the necessary remedy. The factors relied upon by the dissent could justify a preference of any size or duration.

In sum, none of the evidence presented by the city points to any identified discrimination in the Richmond construction industry. We, therefore, hold that the city has failed to demonstrate a compelling interest in apportioning public contracting opportunities on the basis of race. To accept Richmond's claim that past societal discrimination alone can serve as the basis for rigid racial preferences would be to open the door to competing claims for "remedial relief" for every disadvantaged group. The dream of a Nation of equal citizens in a society where race is irrelevant to personal opportunity and achievement would be lost in a mosaic of shifting preferences based on inherently unmeasurable claims of past wrongs. We think such a result would be

---

[3] Since 1975 the city of Richmond has had an ordinance on the books prohibiting both discrimination in the award of public contracts and employment discrimination by public contractors. The city points to no evidence that its prime contractors have been violating the ordinance in either their employment or subcontracting practices.

contrary to both the letter and spirit of a constitutional provision whose central command is equality.

The foregoing analysis applies only to the inclusion of blacks within the Richmond set-aside program. There is *absolutely no evidence* of past discrimination against Spanish-speaking, Oriental, Indian, Eskimo, or Aleut persons in any aspect of the Richmond construction industry. It may well be that Richmond has never had an Aleut or Eskimo citizen. The random inclusion of racial groups that, as a practical matter, may never have suffered from discrimination in the construction industry in Richmond suggests that perhaps the city's purpose was not in fact to remedy past discrimination. If a 30% set-aside was "narrowly tailored" to compensate black contractors for past discrimination, one may legitimately ask why they are forced to share this "remedial relief" with an Aleut citizen who moves to Richmond tomorrow? The gross overinclusiveness of Richmond's racial preference strongly impugns the city's claim of remedial motivation.

IV

As noted by the court below, it is almost impossible to assess whether the Richmond Plan is narrowly tailored to remedy prior discrimination since it is not linked to identified discrimination in any way. We limit ourselves to two observations in this regard.

First, there does not appear to have been any consideration of the use of race-neutral means to increase minority business participation in city contracting. Many of the barriers to minority participation in the construction industry relied upon by the city to justify a racial classification appear to be race neutral. If MBE's disproportionately lack capital or cannot meet bonding requirements, a race-neutral program of city financing for small firms would, *a fortiori*, lead to greater minority participation.

Second, the 30% quota cannot be said to be narrowly tailored to any goal, except perhaps outright racial balancing. It rests upon the "completely unrealistic" assumption that minorities will choose a particular trade in lockstep proportion to their representation in the local population.

Under Richmond's scheme, a successful black, Hispanic, or Oriental entrepreneur from anywhere in the country enjoys an absolute preference over other citizens based solely on their race. We think it obvious that such a program is not narrowly tailored to remedy the effects of prior discrimination.

V

Nothing we say today precludes a state or local entity from taking action to rectify the effects of identified discrimination within its jurisdiction. If the city of Richmond had evidence before it that nonminority contractors were systematically excluding minority businesses from subcontracting opportunities it could take action to end the discriminatory exclusion. Where there is a significant statistical disparity between the number of qualified minority contractors willing and able to perform a particular service and the number of such contractors actually engaged by the locality or the locality's prime contractors, an inference of discriminatory exclusion could arise. Under such circumstances, the city could act to dismantle the closed business system by taking appropriate measures against those who discriminate on the basis of race or other illegitimate criteria. In the extreme case, some form of narrowly tailored racial preference might be necessary to break down patterns of deliberate exclusion.

Even in the absence of evidence of discrimination, the city has at its disposal a whole array of race-neutral devices to increase the accessibility of city contracting opportunities to small entrepreneurs of all races.

Proper findings are necessary to define both the scope of the injury and the extent of the remedy necessary to cure its effects. Such findings also serve to assure all citizens that the deviation from the norm of equal treatment of all racial and ethnic groups is a temporary matter, a measure taken in the service of the goal of equality itself. Absent such findings, there is a danger that a racial classification is merely the product of unthinking stereotypes or a form of racial politics.

Accordingly, the judgment of the Court of Appeals for the Fourth Circuit is

Affirmed.

JUSTICE STEVENS, concurring in part and concurring in the judgment.

I do not agree with the premise that seems to underlie today's decision, that a governmental decision that rests on a racial classification is never permissible except as a remedy for a past wrong. I do, however, agree with the Court's explanation of why the Richmond ordinance cannot be justified as a remedy for past discrimination, and therefore join Parts I, III-B, and IV of its opinion.

JUSTICE KENNEDY, concurring in part and concurring in the judgment.

I join all but Part II of JUSTICE O'CONNOR'S opinion and give this further explanation.

The moral imperative of racial neutrality is the driving force of the Equal Protection Clause. JUSTICE SCALIA'S opinion underscores that proposition, quite properly in my view. The rule suggested in his opinion, which would strike down all preferences which are not necessary remedies to victims of unlawful discrimination, would serve important structural goals, as it would eliminate the necessity for courts to pass upon each racial preference that is enacted. Structural protections may be necessities if moral imperatives are to be obeyed. His opinion would make it crystal clear to the political branches, at least those of the States, that legislation must be based on criteria other than race.

Nevertheless, given that a rule of automatic invalidity for racial preferences in almost every case would be a significant break with our precedents that require a case-by-case test, I am not convinced we need adopt it at this point. On the assumption that it will vindicate the principle of race neutrality found in the Equal Protection Clause, I accept the less absolute rule contained in JUSTICE O'CONNOR's opinion, a rule based on the proposition that any racial preference must face the most rigorous scrutiny by the courts.

JUSTICE SCALIA, concurring in the judgment.

I agree with much of the Court's opinion, and, in particular, with JUSTICE O'CONNOR'S conclusion that strict scrutiny must be applied to all governmental classification by race, whether or not its asserted purpose is "remedial" or "benign." I do not agree, however, with JUSTICE O'CONNOR'S dictum suggesting that, despite the Fourteenth Amendment, state and local governments may in some circumstances discriminate on the basis of race in order (in a broad sense) "to ameliorate the effects of past discrimination." The benign purpose of compensating for social disadvantages, whether they have been acquired by reason of prior discrimination or otherwise, can no more be pursued by the illegitimate means of racial discrimination than can other assertedly benign purposes we have repeatedly rejected. The difficulty of overcoming the effects of past discrimination is as nothing compared with the difficulty of eradicating from our society the source of those effects, which is the tendency-fatal to a Nation such as ours-to classify and judge men and women on the basis of their country of origin or the color of their skin. A solution to the first problem that aggravates the second is no solution at all. I share the view expressed by Alexander Bickel that "[t]he lesson of the great decisions of the Supreme Court and the lesson of contemporary history have been the same for at least a generation: discrimination on the basis of race is illegal, immoral, unconstitutional, inherently wrong, and destructive of democratic society." A[lexander] Bickel, The Morality of Consent 133 (1975). At least where state or local action is at issue, only a social emergency rising to the level of imminent danger to life and limb-for example, a prison race riot, requiring temporary segregation of inmates-can justify an exception to the principle embodied in the Fourteenth Amendment that "[o]ur Constitution is color-blind, and neither knows nor tolerates classes among citizens," *Plessy v. Ferguson*, 163 U.S. 537, 559 (1896) (Harlan, J., dissenting).

In my view there is only one circumstance in which the States may act *by race* to "undo the effects of past discrimination": where that is necessary to eliminate their own maintenance of a system of unlawful racial classification. If, for example, a state agency has a discriminatory pay scale compensating black employees in all positions at 20% less than their nonblack counterparts, it may assuredly promulgate an order raising the salaries of "all black employees" to eliminate the differential. This distinction explains our school desegregation cases, in which we have made plain that States and localities sometimes have an obligation to adopt race-conscious remedies. While there is no doubt that those cases have taken into account the continuing "effects" of previously mandated racial school assignment, we have held those effects to justify a race-conscious remedy only because we have concluded, in that context, that they perpetuate a "dual school system." While thus permitting the use of race to *de* classify racially classified students, teachers, and educational resources, however, we have also made it clear that the remedial power extends no further than the scope of the continuing constitutional violation. And it is implicit in our cases that after the dual school system has been completely disestablished, the States may no longer assign students by race.

A State can, of course, act "to undo the effects of past discrimination" in many permissible ways that do not involve classification by race. Such programs may well have racially disproportionate impact, but they are not based on race. And, of course, a State may "undo the effects of past discrimination" in the sense of giving the identified victim of state discrimination that which it wrongfully denied him-for example, giving to a previously rejected black applicant the job that, by reason of discrimination, had been awarded to a white applicant, even if this means terminating the latter's employment. In such a context, the white job-holder is not being selected for disadvantageous treatment because of his race, but because he was wrongfully awarded a job to which another is entitled. That is worlds apart from the system here, in which those to be disadvantaged are identified solely by race.

In his final book, Professor Bickel wrote:

> "[A] racial quota derogates the human dignity and individuality of all to whom it is applied; it is invidious in principle as well as in practice. Moreover, it can easily be turned against those it purports to help. The history of the racial quota is a history of subjugation, not beneficence. Its evil lies in its effects: a quota is a divider of society, a creator of castes, and it is all the worse for its racial base, especially in a society desperately striving for an equality that will make race irrelevant." [Alexander] Bickel, The Morality of Consent 133 [(1975)].

Those statements are true and increasingly prophetic. Apart from their societal effects, however, it is important not to lose sight of the fact that even "benign" racial quotas have individual victims, whose very real injustice we ignore whenever we deny them enforcement of their right not to be disadvantaged on the basis of race. When we depart from this American principle we play with fire, and much more than an occasional Croson burns.

It is plainly true that in our society blacks have suffered discrimination immeasurably greater than any directed at other racial groups. But those who believe that racial preferences can help to "even the score" display, and reinforce, a manner of thinking by race that was the source of the injustice and that will, if it endures within our society, be the source of more injustice still. The relevant proposition is not that it was blacks, or Jews, or Irish who were discriminated against, but that it was individual men and women, "created equal," who were discriminated against. And the relevant resolve is that that should never happen again. Racial preferences appear to "even the score" (in some small degree) only if one embraces the proposition that our society is appropriately viewed as divided into races, making it right that an injustice rendered in the past to a black man should be compensated for by discriminating against a white. Nothing is worth that embrace.

Since I believe that the appellee here had a constitutional right to have its bid succeed or fail under a decisionmaking process uninfected with racial bias, I concur in the judgment of the Court.

JUSTICE MARSHALL, with whom JUSTICE BRENNAN and JUSTICE BLACKMUN join, dissenting.

It is a welcome symbol of racial progress when the former capital of the Confederacy acts forthrightly to confront the effects of racial discrimination in its midst. In my view, nothing in the Constitution can be construed to prevent Richmond, Virginia, from allocating a portion of its contracting dollars for businesses owned or controlled by members of minority groups.

A majority of this Court holds today, however, that the Equal Protection Clause of the Fourteenth Amendment blocks Richmond's initiative. I find deep irony in second-guessing Richmond's judgment on this point. As much as any municipality in the United States, Richmond knows what racial discrimination is; a century of decisions by this and other federal courts has richly documented the city's disgraceful history of public and private racial discrimination. In any event, the Richmond City Council *has* supported its determination that minorities have been wrongly excluded from local construction contracting.

More fundamentally, today's decision marks a deliberate and giant step backward in this Court's affirmative-action jurisprudence. Cynical of one municipality's attempt to redress the effects of past racial discrimination in a particular industry, the majority launches a grapeshot attack on race-conscious remedies in general. The majority's unnecessary pronouncements will inevitably discourage or prevent governmental entities, particularly States and localities, from acting to rectify the scourge of past discrimination. This is the harsh reality of the majority's decision, but it is not the Constitution's command.

I

As an initial matter, the majority takes an exceedingly myopic view of the factual predicate on which the Richmond City Council relied when it passed the Minority Business Utilization Plan. In so doing, the majority downplays the fact that the city council had before it a rich trove of evidence that discrimination in the Nation's construction industry had seriously impaired the competitive position of businesses owned or controlled by members of minority groups. It is only against this backdrop of documented national discrimination, however, that the local evidence adduced by Richmond can be properly understood.

The city council's members heard testimony that, although minority groups made up half of the city's population, only 0.67% of the $24.6 million which Richmond had dispensed in construction contracts during the five years ending in March 1983 had gone to minority-owned prime contractors. They heard testimony that the major Richmond area construction trade associations had virtually no minorities among their hundreds of members. Finally, they heard testimony from city officials as to the exclusionary history of the local construction industry. So long as one views Richmond's local evidence of discrimination against the backdrop of systematic nationwide racial discrimination which Congress had so painstakingly identified in this very industry, this case is readily resolved.

III

A

Today, for the first time, a majority of this Court has adopted strict scrutiny as its standard of Equal Protection Clause review of race-conscious remedial measures. This is an unwelcome development. A profound difference separates governmental actions that themselves are racist, and governmental actions that seek to remedy the effects of prior racism.

Racial classifications "drawn on the presumption that one race is inferior to another or because they put the weight of government behind racial hatred and separatism" warrant the strictest judicial scrutiny because of the very irrelevance of these rationales. By contrast, racial classifications drawn for the purpose of remedying the effects of discrimination that itself was race based have a highly pertinent basis: the tragic and indelible fact that discrimination against blacks and other racial minorities in this Nation has pervaded our Nation's history and continues to scar our society.

In concluding that remedial classifications warrant no different standard of review under the Constitution, a majority of this Court signals that it regards racial discrimination as largely a phenomenon of the past, and that government bodies need no longer preoccupy themselves with rectifying racial injustice. I, however, do not believe this Nation is anywhere close to eradicating racial discrimination or its vestiges.

B

I am also troubled by the majority's assertion that, even if it did not believe generally in strict scrutiny of race-based remedial measures, "the circumstances of this case" require this Court to look upon the Richmond City Council's measure with the strictest scrutiny. The sole such circumstance which the majority cites, however, is the fact that blacks in Richmond are a "dominant racial grou[p]" in the city.

It cannot seriously be suggested that nonminorities in Richmond have any "history of purposeful unequal treatment." Nor is there any indication that they have any of the disabilities that have characteristically afflicted those groups this Court has deemed suspect. Indeed, the numerical and political dominance of nonminorities within the State of Virginia and the Nation as a whole provides an enormous political check against the "simple racial politics" at the municipal level which the majority fears.

In my view, the "circumstances of this case," underscore the importance of *not* subjecting to a strict scrutiny straitjacket the increasing number of cities which have recently come under minority leadership and are eager to rectify, or at least prevent the perpetuation of, past racial discrimination.

C

Today's decision, finally, is particularly noteworthy for the daunting standard it imposes upon States and localities contemplating the use of race-conscious measures to eradicate the present effects of prior discrimination and prevent its perpetuation.

Nothing in the Constitution or in the prior decisions of this Court supports limiting state authority to confront the effects of past discrimination to those situations in which a prima facie case of a constitutional or statutory violation can be made out. As for § 1, it is too late in the day to assert seriously that the Equal Protection Clause prohibits States from enacting race-conscious remedies. Our cases in the areas of school desegregation, voting rights, and affirmative action have demonstrated time and again that race is constitutionally germane, precisely because race remains dismayingly relevant in American life. The fact is that Congress' concern in passing the Reconstruction Amendments, and particularly their congressional authorization provisions, was that States would *not* adequately respond to racial violence or discrimination against newly freed slaves. To interpret any aspect of these Amendments as proscribing state remedial responses to these very problems turns the Amendments on their heads.

JUSTICE BLACKMUN, with whom JUSTICE BRENNAN joins, dissenting. [Opinion omitted.]

EXERCISE 13:

1.   What was the classification at issue?

2.   What level of scrutiny did the Supreme Court utilize to evaluate Richmond's classification? Why?

3.   Justice O'Connor argued that the use of race-based affirmative action has the potential to cause "stigmatic harm." What is that, is it likely to occur and, even if it is likely to occur, does that harm outweigh the benefits of affirmative action?

4.   The dissent argued that different standards of review should apply to malign and benign use of racial classifications. What reasons did the dissent offer for this distinction? How did Justice O'Connor respond? Which standard of review — strict or intermediate scrutiny — would be better in the affirmative action context?

5.   *J.A. Croson* is a key case because it shifted the focus of Equal Protection jurisprudence away from an historically disadvantaged group, such as black Americans, and toward the classification itself, race. What are the arguments, given by the justices, for and against this move?

6.   Do the reasons for the Court's use of strict scrutiny apply equally to state governments and the federal government?

7.   What interests did Richmond proffer to satisfy strict scrutiny? According to the Court, were those interests compelling?

8.   Was Richmond's use of race to advance its proffered interests narrowly tailored, according to the Court?

9.   Following this case, if you were Richmond's attorney, what would you advise Richmond to do in order to enact another affirmative action program in this context?

10.   Justice O'Connor argued that strict scrutiny was necessary to enable the Court to distinguish those uses of race that harm from those that benefit racial minorities. Is that true?

11.   Justice O'Connor cited to *Korematsu* for the proposition that the Supreme Court should not defer to the judgments of the other branches and the states when they utilize racial classifications. Is that a fair use of *Korematsu*?

12.   Justice Scalia argued that the Equal Protection Clause bars nearly all use of racial classifications. From where did he draw that claim? Is it consistent with the Clause's original meaning? *Compare* Jed Rubenfeld, *Affirmative Action*, 107 YALE L.J. 427 (1997) (reviewing the Clause's original meaning and concluding that it permitted affirmative action).

13.   When, according to Justice Scalia, may racial classifications be used? How are those permitted usages consistent with his suggested blanket rule against use of racial classifications?

14.   Is Justice Scalia's nearly-absolute rule against governmental use of racial classifications more or less attractive than Justice O'Connor's position? Justice Marshall's?

15.   Explain why Justice Kennedy declined to adopt Justice Scalia's position.

16.   What limits would Justice Marshall's reasoning impose on state use of affirmative action?

J.A. Croson concerned state employment of affirmative action; what about federal use of affirmative action? The Supreme Court ruled, in *Adarand Constructors, Inc. v. Pena*, 515 U.S. 200 (1995), that the same strict scrutiny analysis applied to the federal government. To reach this conclusion, the Court reviewed its case law governing constitutional restrictions on the federal government in the area of race. It summarized this law:

> Despite lingering uncertainty in the details, however, the Court's cases through *Croson* had established three general propositions with respect to governmental racial classifications. First, skepticism: " 'Any preference based on racial or ethnic criteria must necessarily receive a most searching examination.' " Second, consistency: "[T]he standard of review under the Equal Protection Clause is not dependent on the race of those burdened or benefited by a particular classification," *i.e.*, all racial classifications reviewable under the Equal Protection Clause must be strictly scrutinized. And third, congruence: "Equal protection analysis in the Fifth Amendment area is the same as that under the Fourteenth Amendment[.]" Taken together, these three propositions lead to the conclusion that any person, of whatever race, has the right to demand that any governmental actor subject to the Constitution justify any racial classification subjecting that person to unequal treatment under the strictest judicial scrutiny.

Id. at 223–24. The Court, as in *J.A. Croson* speaking through Justice O'Connor, grounded these three propositions in the more "basic principle that the Fifth and Fourteenth Amendments to the Constitution protect *persons*, not *groups*. It follows from that principle that all governmental action based on race-a *group* classification long recognized as 'in most circumstances irrelevant and therefore prohibited,' should be subjected to detailed judicial inquiry to ensure that the *personal* right to equal protection of the laws has not been infringed. These ideas have long been central to this Court's understanding of equal protection, and holding 'benign' state and federal racial classifications to different standards does not square with them." *Id.* at 227.

After *Adarand*, lower courts, scholars, and legislators struggled within the strict scrutiny analysis to articulate what interests, if any, justified affirmative action programs and what means were sufficiently narrowly tailored. In an important pair of cases, the Supreme Court applied strict scrutiny to the affirmative action policies of the University of Michigan and its law school.

The Supreme Court struck down the University's use of affirmative action in *Gratz v. Bollinger*, 539 U.S. 244 (2003). The University's affirmative action policy gave 20 points (when 100 points caused applicants to be automatically admitted) out of a 150-point scale to applicants of an "underrepresented minority." *Id.* at 255. The Court, in a six-three decision, ruled that the University's use of an automatic 20 points based on race, was not narrowly tailored. *Id.* at 275.

In the companion case of *Grutter v. Bollinger*, 539 U.S. 306 (2003), however, the Supreme Court upheld the law school's affirmative action policy.

GRUTTER v. BOLLINGER
539 U.S. 306 (2003)

JUSTICE O'CONNOR delivered the opinion of the Court.

This case requires us to decide whether the use of race as a factor in student admissions by the University of Michigan Law School (Law School) is unlawful.

I

A

The Law School ranks among the Nation's top law schools. It receives more than 3,500 applications each year for a class of around 350 students. [T]he Law School seeks "a mix of students with varying backgrounds and experiences who will respect and learn from each other."

The hallmark of th[e Law School's admissions] policy is its focus on academic ability coupled with a flexible assessment of applicants' talents, experiences, and potential "to contribute to the learning of those around them." The policy requires admissions officials to evaluate each applicant based on all the information available in the file. In reviewing an applicant's file, admissions officials must consider the applicant's undergraduate grade point average (GPA) and Law School Admission Test (LSAT) score because they are important predictors of academic success in law school. The policy makes clear, however, that even the highest possible score does not guarantee admission to the Law School. Nor does a low score automatically disqualify an applicant.

The policy aspires to "achieve that diversity which has the potential to enrich everyone's education and thus make a law school class stronger than the sum of its parts." The policy reaffirm[s] the Law School's longstanding commitment to "one particular type of diversity," that is, "racial and ethnic diversity with special reference to the inclusion of students from groups which have been historically discriminated against, like African-Americans, Hispanics and Native Americans, who without this commitment might not be represented in our student body in meaningful numbers." By enrolling a " 'critical mass' of [underrepresented] minority students," the Law School seeks to "ensur[e] their ability to make unique contributions to the character of the Law School."

B

Petitioner Barbara Grutter is a white Michigan resident who applied to the Law School in 1996 with a 3.8 GPA and 161 LSAT score. The Law School rejected her application. In December 1997, petitioner filed suit in the United States District Court for the Eastern District of Michigan against the Law School. Petitioner alleged that respondents discriminated against her on the basis of race in violation of the Fourteenth Amendment.

[T]he District Court concluded that the Law School's use of race as a factor in admissions decisions was unlawful. Sitting en banc, the Court of Appeals reversed the District Court's judgment. We granted certiorari to resolve the disagreement among the Courts of Appeals on a question of national importance: Whether diversity is a compelling interest that can justify the narrowly tailored use of race in selecting applicants for admission to public universities.

II

A

We last addressed the use of race in public higher education over 25 years ago [i]n the landmark [*Regents of Univ. of Cal. v. Bakke*, 438 U.S. 265 (1978)] case. Since this Court's splintered decision in *Bakke*, Justice Powell's opinion announcing the judgment of the Court has served as the touchstone for constitutional analysis of race-conscious admissions policies. Public and private universities across the Nation have modeled their own admissions programs on Justice Powell's views on permissible race-conscious policies. [F]or the reasons set out below, today we endorse Justice Powell's view that student body diversity is a compelling state interest that can justify the use of race in university admissions.

B

The Equal Protection Clause provides that no State shall "deny to any person within its jurisdiction the equal protection of the laws." U.S. Const., Amdt. 14, § 2. Because the Fourteenth Amendment "protect[s] *persons*, not *groups*," all "governmental action based on race . . . should be subjected to detailed judicial inquiry to ensure that the *personal* right to equal protection of the laws has not been infringed." *Adarand Constructors, Inc. v. Peña*, 515 U.S. 200, 227 (1995).

We have held that all racial classifications imposed by government "must be analyzed by a reviewing court under strict scrutiny." This means that such classifications are constitutional only if they are narrowly tailored to further compelling governmental interests. "Absent searching judicial inquiry into the justification for such race-based measures," we have no way to determine what "classifications are 'benign' or 'remedial' and what classifications are in fact motivated by illegitimate notions of racial inferiority or simple racial politics." *Richmond v. J.A. Croson Co.*, 488 U.S. 469, 493 (1989).

Strict scrutiny is not "strict in theory, but fatal in fact." *Adarand Constructors, Inc.*, at 237. Context matters when reviewing race-based governmental action under the Equal Protection Clause. Not every decision influenced by race is equally objectionable, and strict scrutiny is designed to provide a framework for carefully examining the importance and the sincerity of the reasons advanced by the governmental decisionmaker for the use of race in that particular context.

III

A

With these principles in mind, we turn to the question whether the Law School's use of race is justified by a compelling state interest. Before this Court, respondents assert only one justification for their use of race in the admissions process: obtaining "the educational benefits that flow from a diverse student body."

We first wish to dispel the notion that the Law School's argument has been foreclosed, either expressly or implicitly, by our affirmative-action cases decided since *Bakke*. It is true that some language in those opinions might be read to suggest that remedying past discrimination is the only permissible justification for race-based governmental action. See, *e.g.*, *Richmond v. J.A. Croson Co.*, at 493 (stating that unless classifications based on race are "strictly reserved for remedial settings, they may in fact promote notions of racial inferiority and lead to a politics of racial hostility"). But we have never held that the only governmental use of race that can survive strict scrutiny is remedying past discrimination. Nor, since *Bakke*, have we directly addressed the use of race in the context of public higher education.

The Law School's educational judgment that such diversity is essential to its educational mission is one to which we defer. The Law School's assessment that diversity will, in fact, yield educational benefits is substantiated by respondents and their *amici*. Our scrutiny of the interest asserted by the Law School is no less strict for taking into account complex educational judgments in an area that lies primarily within the expertise of the university.

We have long recognized that, given the important purpose of public education and the expansive freedoms of speech and thought associated with the university environment, universities occupy a special niche in our constitutional tradition. In announcing the principle of student body diversity as a compelling state interest, Justice Powell invoked our cases recognizing a constitutional dimension, grounded in the First Amendment, of educational autonomy. From this premise, Justice Powell reasoned that by claiming "the right to select those students who will contribute the most to the 'robust exchange of ideas,' " a university "seek[s] to achieve a goal that is of paramount importance in the fulfillment of its mission." [*Bakke*,] 438 U.S., at 313. Our conclusion that the Law School has a compelling interest in a diverse student body is informed by our view that attaining a diverse student body is at the heart of the Law School's proper institutional mission, and that "good faith" on the part of a university is "presumed" absent "a showing to the contrary." [*Bakke*,] 438 U.S., at 318–319.

[T]he Law School seeks to "enroll a 'critical mass' of minority students." The Law School's interest is not simply "to assure within its student body some specified percentage of a particular group merely because of its race or ethnic origin." That would amount to outright racial balancing, which is patently unconstitutional. *Richmond v. J.A. Croson Co.*, 488 U.S., at 507. Rather, the Law School's concept of critical mass is defined by reference to the educational benefits that diversity is designed to produce.

These benefits are substantial. As the District Court emphasized, the Law School's admissions policy promotes "cross-racial understanding," helps to break down racial stereotypes, and "enables [students] to better understand persons of different races." These benefits are "important and laudable," because "classroom discussion is livelier, more spirited, and simply more enlightening and interesting" when the students have "the greatest possible variety of backgrounds."

The Law School's claim of a compelling interest is further bolstered by its *amici*, who point to the educational benefits that flow from student body diversity. In addition to the expert studies and reports entered into evidence at trial, numerous studies show that student body diversity promotes learning outcomes, and "better prepares students for an increasingly diverse workforce and society, and better prepares them as professionals."

These benefits are not theoretical but real, as major American businesses have made clear that the skills needed in today's increasingly global marketplace can only be developed through exposure to widely diverse people, cultures, ideas, and viewpoints. What is more, high-ranking retired officers and civilian leaders of the United States military assert that, "[b]ased on [their] decades of experience," a "highly qualified, racially diverse officer corps . . . is essential to the military's ability to fulfill its principle mission to provide national security."

We have repeatedly acknowledged the overriding importance of preparing students for work and citizenship, describing education as pivotal to "sustaining our political and cultural heritage" with a fundamental role in maintaining the fabric of society.

Brown v. Board of Education, 347 U.S. 483, 493 (1954). For this reason, the diffusion of knowledge and opportunity through public institutions of higher education must be accessible to all individuals regardless of race or ethnicity. Effective participation by members of all racial and ethnic groups in the civic life of our Nation is essential if the dream of one Nation, indivisible, is to be realized.

Moreover, universities, and in particular, law schools, represent the training ground for a large number of our Nation's leaders. *Sweatt v. Painter*, 339 U.S. 629, 634 (1950). Individuals with law degrees occupy roughly half the state governorships, more than half the seats in the United States Senate, and more than a third of the seats in the United States House of Representatives.

In order to cultivate a set of leaders with legitimacy in the eyes of the citizenry, it is necessary that the path to leadership be visibly open to talented and qualified individuals of every race and ethnicity. All members of our heterogeneous society must have confidence in the openness and integrity of the educational institutions that provide this training. Access to legal education (and thus the legal profession) must be inclusive of talented and qualified individuals of every race and ethnicity, so that all members of our heterogeneous society may participate in the educational institutions that provide the training and education necessary to succeed in America.

The Law School does not premise its need for critical mass on "any belief that minority students always (or even consistently) express some characteristic minority viewpoint on any issue." To the contrary, diminishing the force of such stereotypes is both a crucial part of the Law School's mission, and one that it cannot accomplish with only token numbers of minority students. Just as growing up in a particular region or having particular professional experiences is likely to affect an individual's views, so too is one's own, unique experience of being a racial minority in a society, like our own, in which race unfortunately still matters.

B

Even in the limited circumstance when drawing racial distinctions is permissible to further a compelling state interest, government is still "constrained in how it may pursue that end: [T]he means chosen to accomplish the [government's] asserted purpose must be specifically and narrowly framed to accomplish that purpose." The purpose of the narrow tailoring requirement is to ensure that "the means chosen 'fit' th[e] compelling goal so closely that there is little or no possibility that the motive for the classification was illegitimate racial prejudice or stereotype." *Richmond v. J.A. Croson Co.*, 488 U.S., at 493.

To be narrowly tailored, a race-conscious admissions program cannot use a quota system — it cannot "insulat[e] each category of applicants with certain desired qualifications from competition with all other applicants." *Bakke*, 438 U.S., at 315 (opinion of Powell, J.). Instead, a university may consider race or ethnicity only as a "'plus' in a particular applicant's file," without "insulat[ing] the individual from comparison with all other candidates for the available seats."

We are satisfied that the Law School's admissions program does not operate as a quota. The Law School's goal of attaining a critical mass of underrepresented minority students does not transform its program into a quota. [T]here is of course "some relationship between numbers and achieving the benefits to be derived from a diverse student body, and between numbers and providing a reasonable environment for those students admitted." Between 1993 and 1998, the number of African-American, Latino, and Native-American students in each class at the Law School varied from 13.5 to 20.1 percent, a range inconsistent with a quota.

That a race-conscious admissions program does not operate as a quota does not, by itself, satisfy the requirement of individualized consideration. When using race as a "plus" factor in university admissions, a university's admissions program must remain flexible enough to ensure that each applicant is evaluated as an individual and not in a way that makes an applicant's race or ethnicity the defining feature of his or her application.

Here, the Law School engages in a highly individualized, holistic review of each applicant's file, giving serious consideration to all the ways an applicant might contribute to a diverse educational environment. The Law School affords this individualized consideration to applicants of all races. There is no policy, either *de jure* or *de facto*, of automatic acceptance or rejection based on any single "soft" variable.

We also find that the Law School's race-conscious admissions program adequately ensures that all factors that may contribute to student body diversity are meaningfully considered alongside race in admissions decisions. With respect to the use of race itself, all underrepresented minority students admitted by the Law School have been deemed qualified. By virtue of our Nation's struggle with racial inequality, such students are both likely to have experiences of particular importance to the Law School's mission, and less likely to be admitted in meaningful numbers on criteria that ignore those experiences.

What is more, the Law School actually gives substantial weight to diversity factors besides race. The Law School frequently accepts nonminority applicants with grades and test scores lower than underrepresented minority applicants (and other nonminority applicants) who are rejected. This shows that the Law School seriously weighs many other diversity factors besides race that can make a real and dispositive difference for nonminority applicants as well.

Petitioner and the United States argue that the Law School's plan is not narrowly tailored because race-neutral means exist to obtain the educational benefits of student body diversity that the Law School seeks. We disagree. Narrow tailoring does not require exhaustion of every conceivable race-neutral alternative. Nor does it require a university to choose between maintaining a reputation for excellence or fulfilling a commitment to provide educational opportunities to members of all racial groups. Narrow tailoring does, however, require serious, good faith consideration of workable race-neutral alternatives that will achieve the diversity the university seeks. [T]hese alternatives would require a dramatic sacrifice of diversity, the academic quality of all admitted students, or both.

Because a lottery would make that kind of nuanced judgment impossible, it would effectively sacrifice all other educational values, not to mention every other kind of diversity. So too with the suggestion that the Law School simply lower admissions standards for all students, a drastic remedy that would require the Law School to become a much different institution and sacrifice a vital component of its educational mission. The United States advocates "percentage plans," recently adopted by public undergraduate institutions in Texas, Florida, and California, to guarantee admission to all students above a certain class-rank threshold in every high school in the State. [E]ven assuming such plans are race-neutral, they may preclude the university from conducting the individualized assessments necessary to assemble a student body that is not just racially diverse, but diverse along all the qualities valued by the university. We are satisfied that the Law School adequately considered race-neutral alternatives currently capable of producing a critical mass without forcing the Law School to abandon the academic selectivity that is the cornerstone of its educational mission.

We acknowledge that "there are serious problems of justice connected with the idea of preference itself." *Bakke*, 438 U.S., at 298 (opinion of Powell, J.). Narrow tailoring, therefore, requires that a race-conscious admissions program not unduly harm members of any racial group. Even remedial race-based governmental action generally "remains subject to continuing oversight to assure that it will work the least harm possible to other innocent persons competing for the benefit." We are satisfied that the Law School's admissions program does not. Because the Law School considers "all pertinent elements of diversity," it can (and does) select nonminority applicants who have greater potential to enhance student body diversity over underrepresented minority applicants.

We are mindful, however, that "[a] core purpose of the Fourteenth Amendment was to do away with all governmentally imposed discrimination based on race." *Palmore v. Sidoti*, 466 U.S. 429, 432 (1984). Accordingly, race-conscious admissions policies must be limited in time. This requirement reflects that racial classifications, however compelling their goals, are potentially so dangerous that they may be employed no more broadly than the interest demands. Enshrining a permanent justification for racial preferences would offend this fundamental equal protection principle. We see no reason to exempt race-conscious admissions programs from the requirement that all governmental use of race must have a logical end point. In the context of higher education, the durational requirement can be met by sunset provisions in race-conscious admissions policies and periodic reviews to determine whether racial preferences are still necessary to achieve student body diversity.

It has been 25 years since Justice Powell first approved the use of race to further an interest in student body diversity in the context of public higher education. Since that time, the number of minority applicants with high grades and test scores has indeed increased. We expect that 25 years from now, the use of racial preferences will no longer be necessary to further the interest approved today.

IV

The judgment of the Court of Appeals for the Sixth Circuit, accordingly, is affirmed.

It is so ordered.

JUSTICE GINSBURG, with whom JUSTICE BREYER joins, concurring.

It is well documented that conscious and unconscious race bias, even rank discrimination based on race, remain alive in our land, impeding realization of our highest values and ideals. As to public education, data for the years 2000–2001 show that 71.6% of African-American children and 76.3% of Hispanic children attended a school in which minorities made up a majority of the student body. And schools in predominantly minority communities lag far behind others measured by the educational resources available to them.

[I]t remains the current reality that many minority students encounter markedly inadequate and unequal educational opportunities. Despite these inequalities, some minority students are able to meet the high threshold requirements set for admission to the country's finest undergraduate and graduate educational institutions. As lower school education in minority communities improves, an increase in the number of such students may be anticipated. From today's vantage point, one may hope, but not firmly forecast, that over the next generation's span, progress toward nondiscrimination and genuinely equal opportunity will make it safe to sunset affirmative action.

JUSTICE SCALIA, with whom JUSTICE THOMAS joins, concurring in part and dissenting in part.

The "educational benefit" that the University of Michigan seeks to achieve by racial discrimination consists, according to the Court, of " 'cross-racial understanding,' " and " 'better prepar[ation of] students for an increasingly diverse workforce and society,' " all of which is necessary not only for work, but also for good "citizenship." This is not, of course, an "educational benefit" on which students will be graded on their law school transcript (Works and Plays Well with Others: B+) or tested by the bar examiners (Q: Describe in 500 words or less your cross-racial understanding). For it is a lesson of life rather than law — essentially the same lesson taught to people three feet shorter and 20 years younger than the full-grown adults at the University of Michigan Law School, in institutions ranging from Boy Scout troops to public-school kindergartens. If properly considered an "educational benefit" at all, it is surely not one that is either uniquely relevant to law school or uniquely "teachable" in a formal educational setting. *And therefore:* If it is appropriate for the University of Michigan Law School to use racial discrimination for the purpose of putting together a "critical mass" that will convey generic lessons in socialization and good citizenship, surely it is no less appropriate for the civil service system of the State of Michigan to do so. There, also, those exposed to "critical masses" of certain races will presumably become better Americans, better Michiganders, better civil servants. And surely private employers cannot be criticized if they also "teach" good citizenship to their adult employees through a patriotic, all-American system of racial discrimination in hiring. The nonminority individuals who are deprived of a legal education, a civil service job, or any job at all by reason of their skin color will surely understand.

Unlike a clear constitutional holding that racial preferences in state educational institutions are impermissible, or even a clear anticonstitutional holding that racial preferences in state educational institutions are OK, today's *Grutter-Gratz* split double header seems perversely designed to prolong the controversy and the litigation. I do not look forward to any of these cases.

JUSTICE THOMAS, with whom JUSTICE SCALIA joins as to Parts I-VII, concurring in part and dissenting in part.

Frederick Douglass, speaking to a group of abolitionists almost 140 years ago, delivered a message lost on today's majority:

> "[I]n regard to the colored people, there is always more that is benevolent, I perceive, than just, manifested towards us. What I ask for the negro is not benevolence, not pity, not sympathy, but simply *justice*. The American people have always been anxious to know what they shall do with us. . . . I have had but one answer from the beginning. Do nothing with us! Your doing with us has already played the mischief with us. Do nothing with us! If the apples will not remain on the tree of their own strength, if they are worm eaten at the core, if they are early ripe and disposed to fall, let them fall! . . . And if the negro cannot stand on his own legs, let him fall also. All I ask is, give him a chance to stand on his own legs! Let him alone! . . . [Y]our interference is doing him positive injury." What the Black Man Wants: An Address Delivered in Boston, Massachusetts, on 26 January 1865, reprinted in 4 The Frederick Douglass Papers 59, 68 (J. Blassingame & J. McKivigan eds.1991).

Like Douglass, I believe blacks can achieve in every avenue of American life without the meddling of university administrators. Because I wish to see all students succeed whatever their color, I share, in some respect, the sympathies of those who sponsor the type of discrimination advanced by the University of Michigan Law School (Law School). The Constitution does not, however, tolerate institutional devotion to the status quo in admissions policies when such devotion ripens into racial discrimination.

No one would argue that a university could set up a lower general admissions standard and then impose heightened requirements only on black applicants. Similarly, a university may not maintain a high admissions standard and grant exemptions to favored races. The Law School, of its own choosing, and for its own purposes, maintains an exclusionary admissions system that it knows produces racially disproportionate results. Racial discrimination is not a permissible solution to the self-inflicted wounds of this elitist admissions policy.

The majority upholds the Law School's racial discrimination not by interpreting the people's Constitution, but by responding to a faddish slogan of the cognoscenti. Nevertheless, I concur in part in the Court's opinion. First, I agree with the Court insofar as its decision, which approves of only one racial classification, confirms that further use of race in admissions remains unlawful. Second, I agree with the Court's holding that racial discrimination in higher education admissions will be illegal in 25 years. I respectfully dissent from the remainder of the Court's opinion and the judgment, however, because I believe that the Law School's current use of race violates the Equal Protection Clause and that the Constitution means the same thing today as it will in 300 months.

II

The Law School's argument can only be understood in one way: Classroom aesthetics yields educational benefits, racially discriminatory admissions policies are required to achieve the right racial mix, and therefore the policies are required to achieve the educational benefits. It is the *educational benefits* that are the end, or allegedly compelling state interest, not "diversity." One must consider the Law School's refusal to entertain changes to its current admissions system that might produce the same educational benefits. In other words, the Law School seeks to improve marginally the education it offers without sacrificing too much of its exclusivity and elite status. Unless each constituent part of this state interest is of pressing public necessity, the Law School's use of race is unconstitutional. I find each of them to fall far short of this standard.

III

B

1

While legal education at a public university may be good policy or otherwise laudable, it is obviously not a pressing public necessity. The fact that some fraction of the States reject a particular enterprise creates a presumption that the enterprise itself is not a compelling state interest. In this sense, the absence of a public, American Bar Association (ABA) accredited, law school in Alaska, Delaware, Massachusetts, New Hampshire, and Rhode Island provides evidence that Michigan's maintenance of the Law School does not constitute a compelling state interest.

2

Still, even assuming that a State may demonstrate a cognizable interest in having an elite law school, Michigan has failed to do so here. This Court has limited the scope of equal protection review to interests and activities that occur within that State's jurisdiction. The only cognizable state interests vindicated by operating a public law school are, therefore, the education of that State's citizens and the training of that State's lawyers. The Law School today, however, does precious little training of those attorneys who will serve the citizens of Michigan. In 2002, graduates of the Law School made up less than 6% of applicants to the Michigan bar, even though the Law School's graduates constitute nearly 30% of all law students graduating in Michigan. Less than 16% of the Law School's graduating class elects to stay in Michigan after law school.

It does not take a social scientist to conclude that it is precisely the Law School's status as an elite institution that causes it to be a waystation for the rest of the country's lawyers, rather than a training ground for those who will remain in Michigan. The Law School's decision to be an elite institution does little to advance the welfare of the people of Michigan or any cognizable interest of the State of Michigan.

Again, the fact that few States choose to maintain elite law schools raises a strong inference that there is nothing compelling about elite status.

3

Finally, even if the Law School's racial tinkering produces tangible educational benefits, a marginal improvement in legal education cannot justify racial discrimination where the Law School has no compelling interest either in its existence or in its current educational and admissions policies.

IV

The interest in remaining elite and exclusive that the majority thinks so obviously critical requires the use of admissions "standards" that, in turn, create the Law School's "need" to discriminate on the basis of race. [T]he Law School should be forced to choose between its classroom aesthetic and its exclusionary admissions system — it cannot have it both ways.

With the adoption of different admissions methods, such as accepting all students who meet minimum qualifications, the Law School could achieve its vision of the racially aesthetic student body without the use of racial discrimination. The Law School concedes this, but the Court holds, implicitly and under the guise of narrow tailoring, that the Law School has a compelling state interest in doing what it wants to do. I cannot agree. First, under strict scrutiny, the Law School's assessment of the benefits of racial discrimination and devotion to the admissions status quo are not entitled to any sort of deference. Second, even if its "academic selectivity" must be maintained at all costs along with racial discrimination, the Court ignores the fact that other top law schools have succeeded in meeting their aesthetic demands without racial discrimination.

VI

The absence of any articulated legal principle supporting the majority's principal holding suggests another rationale. I believe what lies beneath the Court's decision today are the benighted notions that one can tell when racial discrimination benefits (rather than hurts) minority groups, and that racial discrimination is necessary to remedy general societal ills.

The Law School tantalizes unprepared students with the promise of a University of Michigan degree and all of the opportunities that it offers. These overmatched students take the bait, only to find that they cannot succeed in the cauldron of competition. And this mismatch crisis is not restricted to elite institutions. See T[homas] Sowell, Race and Culture 176–177 (1994) ("Even if most minority students are able to meet the normal standards at the 'average' range of colleges and universities, the systematic mismatching of minority students begun at the top can mean that such students are generally overmatched throughout all levels of higher education"). Indeed, to cover the tracks of the aestheticists, this cruel farce of racial discrimination must continue — in selection for the Michigan Law Review, see

University of Michigan Law School Student Handbook 2002–2003, pp. 39–40 (noting the presence of a "diversity plan" for admission to the review), and in hiring at law firms and for judicial clerkships — until the "beneficiaries" are no longer tolerated.

Beyond the harm the Law School's racial discrimination visits upon its test subjects, no social science has disproved the notion that this discrimination "engender[s] attitudes of superiority or, alternatively, provoke[s] resentment among those who believe that they have been wronged by the government's use of race." *Adarand*, 515 U.S., at 241 (THOMAS, J., concurring in part and concurring in judgment). It is uncontested that each year, the Law School admits a handful of blacks who would be admitted in the absence of racial discrimination. Who can differentiate between those who belong and those who do not? The majority of blacks are admitted to the Law School because of discrimination, and because of this policy all are tarred as undeserving. This problem of stigma does not depend on determinacy as to whether those stigmatized are actually the "beneficiaries" of racial discrimination. When blacks take positions in the highest places of government, industry, or academia, it is an open question today whether their skin color played a part in their advancement. The question itself is the stigma — because either racial discrimination did play a role, in which case the person may be deemed "otherwise unqualified," or it did not, in which case asking the question itself unfairly marks those blacks who would succeed without discrimination. Is this what the Court means by "visibly open"?

* * *

It has been nearly 140 years since Frederick Douglass asked the intellectual ancestors of the Law School to "[d]o nothing with us!" and the Nation adopted the Fourteenth Amendment. Now we must wait another 25 years to see this principle of equality vindicated. I therefore respectfully dissent from the remainder of the Court's opinion and the judgment.

CHIEF JUSTICE REHNQUIST, with whom JUSTICE SCALIA, JUSTICE KENNEDY, and JUSTICE THOMAS join, dissenting.

I do not believe that the University of Michigan Law School's (Law School) means are narrowly tailored to the interest it asserts. The Law School claims it must take the steps it does to achieve a " 'critical mass' " of underrepresented minority students. But its actual program bears no relation to this asserted goal. Stripped of its "critical mass" veil, the Law School's program is revealed as a naked effort to achieve racial balancing.

From 1995 through 2000, the Law School admitted between 1,130 and 1,310 students. Of those, between 13 and 19 were Native American, between 91 and 108 were African-American, and between 47 and 56 were Hispanic. If the Law School is admitting between 91 and 108 African-Americans in order to achieve "critical mass," thereby preventing African-American students from feeling "isolated or like spokespersons for their race," one would think that a number of the same order of magnitude would be necessary to accomplish the same purpose for Hispanics and Native Americans. Similarly, even if all of the Native American applicants admitted in a given year matriculate, which the record demonstrates is not at all the case, how can this possibly constitute a "critical mass" of Native Americans in a class of over 350 students? In order for this pattern of admission to be consistent with the Law School's explanation of "critical mass," one would have to believe that the objectives of "critical mass" offered by respondents are achieved with only half the number of Hispanics and one-sixth the number of Native Americans as compared to African-Americans.

These different numbers, moreover, come only as a result of substantially different treatment among the three underrepresented minority groups. [T]he Law School states that "[s]ixty-nine minority applicants were rejected between 1995 and 2000 with at least a 3.5 [Grade Point Average (GPA)] and a [score of] 159 or higher on the [Law School Admission Test (LSAT)]" while a number of Caucasian and Asian-American applicants with similar or lower scores were admitted. Review of the record reveals only 67 such individuals. Of these 67 individuals, *56* were Hispanic, while only 6 were African-American, and only 5 were Native American. This discrepancy reflects a consistent practice. For example, in 2000, 12 Hispanics who scored between a 159–160 on the LSAT and earned a GPA of 3.00 or higher applied for admission and only 2 were admitted. Meanwhile, 12 African-Americans in the same range of qualifications applied for admission and all 12 were admitted. Likewise, that same year, 16 Hispanics who scored between a 151–153 on the LSAT and earned a 3.00 or higher applied for admission and only 1 of those applicants was admitted. Twenty-three similarly qualified African-Americans applied for admission and 14 were admitted. Respondents have *never* offered any race-specific arguments explaining why significantly more individuals from one underrepresented minority group are needed in order to achieve "critical mass" or further student body diversity.

[T]he correlation between the percentage of the Law School's pool of applicants who are members of the three minority groups and the percentage of the admitted applicants who are members of these same groups is far too precise to be dismissed as merely the result of the school paying "some attention to [the] numbers." For example, in 1995, when 9.7% of the applicant pool was African-American, 9.4% of the admitted class was African-American. By 2000, only 7.5% of the applicant pool was African-American, and 7.3% of the admitted class was African-American. The tight correlation between the percentage of applicants and admittees of a given race, therefore, must result from careful race based planning by the Law School. It suggests a formula for admission based on the aspirational assumption that all applicants are equally qualified academically, and therefore that the proportion of each group admitted should be the same as the proportion of that group in the applicant pool.

The Law School has offered no explanation for its actual admissions practices and, unexplained, we are bound to conclude that the Law School has managed its admissions program, not to achieve a "critical mass," but to extend offers of admission to members of selected minority groups in proportion to their statistical representation in the applicant pool. But this is precisely the type of racial balancing that the Court itself calls "patently unconstitutional."

Justice Kennedy, dissenting. [Opinion omitted.]

EXERCISE 14:

1. Did the *Grutter* majority really utilize strict scrutiny or some other — less rigorous — mode of analysis?

2. Is the Court's ruling that educational diversity in higher education is a compelling state interest consistent with prior case law governing what constitutes a compelling interest?

3. Does educational diversity in higher education and, in particular, racial and ethnic diversity in that context, create better learning outcomes? If so, do those benefits outweigh the costs of affirmative action, for example, the costs claimed by Justice Thomas? Is the Supreme Court the best governmental institution to evaluate these questions?

4. The *Grutter* Court emphasized the particular context presented by the case. Is the Court's critical mass rationale limited to that context or, as Justice Scalia contended, does it extend to and justify race-based affirmative action in many areas of American life?

5. Is *Grutter* consistent with *J.A. Croson*?

6. The majority stated that it deferred to the Law School's judgment regarding whether diversity in higher education is a compelling state interest. Is that deference appropriate? From where did the majority derive that rule? Should the Court defer to other institutions as well?

7. Explain the Court's reasoning that the Law School's use of race-based affirmative action was narrowly tailored. Did Chief Justice Rehnquist's opinion persuade you that it was?

8. How was the Law School's use of race different from a "quota"?

9. Justice Thomas argued that the Law School's use of race was not narrowly tailored because it could have achieved its goals, without the use of race, through the race-neutral method of lowering its admissions standards (and, with it, presumably, the Law School's elite status). What was the majority's response? Who had the better of the argument?

10. One of the most controversial aspects of the Court's opinion was the claim that race-based affirmative action programs "must have a logical end point" and that the majority believed that twenty-five years would be that point. Evaluate the Court's claim both as a legal and empirical matter.

11. The *Grutter* majority acknowledged what it called "problems of justice" with race-based affirmative action. What did it have in mind? Why did those problems not persuade the justices to rule differently?

12. Is *Grutter* sufficiently different from *Gratz* to justify the different result?

The most recent Supreme Court affirmative action case was *Parents Involved in Cmty. Schs. v. Seattle Sch. Dist. No. 1*, 551 U.S. 701 (2007). This consolidated case involved lawsuits brought by the parents of students in the Seattle and Louisville school districts challenging, under the Equal Protection Clause, the districts' voluntary use of race in student school assignments. The schools adopted their respective race-based school assignment schemes in order to maintain the racial balance in their schools within a predetermined range.

The Supreme Court struck down the districts' use of race. Chief Justice Roberts wrote the Court's opinion and, applying strict scrutiny, ruled that neither of the previously established compelling state interests — remedying identified past discrimination or diversity in higher education — supported the districts' programs. *Id.* at 720–25. Furthermore, while the minimal impact of the districts' use of race ensured that the programs were narrowly tailored, it also showed that the use of race to achieve the desired racial balance was not compelling. *Id.* at 733–35. Invoking *Brown*, the Chief Justice stated:

> Before *Brown*, schoolchildren were told where they could and could not go to school based on the color of their skin. The school districts in these cases have not carried the heavy burden of demonstrating that we should allow this once again — even for very different reasons. For schools that never segregated on the basis of race, such as Seattle, or that have removed the vestiges of past segregation, such as Jefferson County, the way "to achieve a system of determining admission to the public schools on a nonracial basis," is to stop assigning students on a racial basis. The way to stop discrimination on the basis of race is to stop discriminating on the basis of race.

Id. at 747–48.

d. Alienage

Alienage is the status of being a noncitizen.[45] There is a long history of distinguishing between citizens and noncitizens. The Constitution itself explicitly utilizes this distinction. For example, the Privileges or Immunities Clause protects only citizens. U.S. Const. amend. XIV, § 1; *see also, e.g., id.* art. I, § 2, cl. 2 (limiting members of the House to those who have "been seven Years a citizen"). Many laws today continue to distinguish between aliens and citizens.

For most of American history, the Supreme Court regularly rejected challenges to state laws differentiating between citizens and aliens. The Court utilized the "special public interest" doctrine under which a state could exclude aliens from, for instance, passing land intestate, if the state articulated a public interest behind its exclusion. *Hauenstein v. Lynham*, 100 U.S. (10 Otto) 483 (1879).

Beginning with *Graham v. Richardson*, 403 U.S. 365 (1971), however, the Supreme Court, through its interpretation of the Equal Protection Clause — which applies to "person[s]" — subjected alienage classifications to a bifurcated form of analysis. The standard level of scrutiny for state alienage classifications is strict scrutiny. However, as we will see below, the Court has also carved out an exception for those alienage

---

[45] Alienage is different from national origin because national origin classifications focus on a person's country of origin rather than a person's current citizenship status.

classifications that pertain to state political processes or state governmental functions. In those situations, the Court employs rational basis review. The key issue, in many of these cases, is whether strict scrutiny or rational basis applies. On this axis, the Supreme Court's cases are difficult to synthesize.

AMBACH v. NORWICK
441 U.S. 68 (1979)

MR. JUSTICE POWELL delivered the opinion of the Court.

This case presents the question whether a State, consistently with the Equal Protection Clause of the Fourteenth Amendment, may refuse to employ as elementary and secondary school teachers aliens who are eligible for United States citizenship but who refuse to seek naturalization.

I

New York Education Law § 3001(3) (McKinney 1970) forbids certification as a public school teacher of any person who is not a citizen of the United States, unless that person has manifested an intention to apply for citizenship. Unless a teacher obtains certification, he may not work in a public elementary or secondary school in New York.

Appellee Norwick was born in Scotland and is a subject of Great Britain. She has resided in this country since 1965 and is married to a United States citizen. Appellee Norwick currently meet[s] all of the educational requirements New York has set for certification as a public school teacher, but [she has] consistently refused to seek citizenship in spite of [her] eligibility to do so. Norwick applied in 1973 for a teaching certificate covering nursery school through sixth grade. [Her] application[was] denied because of appellee[']s[] failure to meet the requirements of § 3001(3). Norwick then filed this suit seeking to enjoin the enforcement of § 3001(3).

A three-judge District Court was convened. Applying the "close judicial scrutiny" standard of *Graham v. Richardson*, 403 U.S. 365, 372 (1971), the court held that § 3001(3) discriminated against aliens in violation of the Equal Protection Clause. We now reverse.

II

A

The decisions of this Court regarding the permissibility of statutory classifications involving aliens have not formed an unwavering line over the years. State regulation of the employment of aliens long has been subject to constitutional constraints. In *Yick Wo v. Hopkins*, 118 U.S. 356 (1886), the Court struck down an ordinance which was applied to prevent aliens from running laundries. At the same time, however, the Court also has recognized a greater degree of latitude for the States when aliens were sought to be excluded from public employment.

Over time, the Court's decisions gradually have restricted the activities from which States are free to exclude aliens. This process of withdrawal from the former doctrine culminated in *Graham v. Richardson*, which for the first time treated classifications based on alienage as "inherently suspect and subject to close judicial scrutiny." Applying *Graham*, this Court has held invalid statutes that prevented aliens from entering a State's classified civil service, working as an engineer, and receiving state educational benefits.

Although our more recent decisions have departed substantially from the [earlier] public-interest doctrine, they have not abandoned the general principle that some state functions are so bound up with the operation of the State as a governmental entity as to permit the exclusion from those functions of all persons who have not become part of the process of self-government.

The exclusion of aliens from such governmental positions would not invite as demanding scrutiny from this Court. Applying the rational-basis standard, we held last Term that New York could exclude aliens from the ranks of its police force. *Foley v. Connelie*, 435 U.S. 291 (1978). Because the police function fulfilled "a most fundamental obligation of government to its constituency" and by necessity cloaked policemen with substantial discretionary powers, we view the police force as being one of those appropriately defined classes of positions for which a citizenship requirement could be imposed. Accordingly, the State was required to justify its classification only "by a showing of some rational relationship between the interest sought to be protected and the limiting classification."

The rule for governmental functions, which is an exception to the general standard applicable to classifications based on alienage, rests on important principles inherent in the Constitution. The distinction between citizens and aliens, though ordinarily irrelevant to private activity, is fundamental to the definition and government of a State. The Constitution itself refers to the distinction no less than 11 times, indicating that the status of citizenship was meant to have significance in the structure of our government. The assumption of that status, denotes an association with the polity which, in a democratic republic, exercises the powers of governance. The form of this association is important: an oath of allegiance or similar ceremony cannot substitute for the unequivocal legal bond citizenship represents. It is because of this special significance of citizenship that governmental entities, when exercising the functions of government, have wider latitude in limiting the participation of noncitizens.

B

In determining whether, for purposes of equal protection analysis, teaching in public schools constitutes a governmental function, we look to the role of public education and to the degree of responsibility and discretion teachers possess in fulfilling that role.

Public education, like the police function, "fulfills a most fundamental obligation of government to its constituency." The importance of public schools in the preparation of individuals for participation as citizens, and in the preservation of the values on which our society rests, long has been recognized by our decisions[.] *Brown v. Board of Education*, 347 U.S. 483, 493 (1954). Other authorities have perceived public schools as an "assimilative force" by which diverse and conflicting elements in our society are brought together on a broad but common ground. See, *e. g.*, J[ohn] Dewey, Democracy and Education 26 (1929). These perceptions of the public schools as inculcating fundamental values necessary to the maintenance of a democratic political system have been confirmed by the observations of social scientists.[8]

Within the public school system, teachers play a critical part in developing students' attitude toward government and understanding of the role of citizens in our society. Alone among employees of the system, teachers are in direct, day-to-day contact with students both in the classrooms and in the other varied activities of a modern school. In shaping the students' experience to achieve educational goals, teachers by necessity have wide discretion over the way the course material is communicated to students. They are responsible for presenting and explaining the subject matter in a way that is both comprehensible and inspiring. Further, a teacher serves as a role model for his students, exerting a subtle but important influence over their perceptions and values.

Furthermore, it is clear that all public school teachers should help fulfill the broader function of the public school system. Teachers, regardless of their specialty, may be called upon to teach other subjects, including those expressly dedicated to political and social subjects. More importantly, a State properly may regard all teachers as having an obligation to promote civic virtues and understanding in their classes, regardless of the subject taught. Certainly a State also may take account of a teacher's function as an example for students, which exists independently of particular classroom subjects. In light of the foregoing considerations, we think it clear that public school teachers come well within the "governmental function" principle. Accordingly, the Constitution requires only that a citizenship requirement applicable to teaching in the public schools bear a rational relationship to a legitimate state interest. See *Massachusetts Board of Retirement v. Murgia*, 427 U.S. 307, 314 (1976).

III

As the legitimacy of the State's interest in furthering the educational goals outlined above is undoubted, it remains only to consider whether § 3001(3) bears a rational relationship to this interest. The restriction is carefully framed to serve its purpose, as it bars from teaching only those aliens who have demonstrated their unwillingness to obtain United States citizenship. Appellee, and aliens similarly situated, in effect have chosen to classify themselves. They prefer to retain citizenship in a foreign country with the obligations it entails of primary duty and loyalty. They have rejected the open invitation extended to qualify for eligibility to teach by applying for citizenship in this

---

[8] The curricular requirements of New York's public school system reflect some of the ways a public school system promotes the development of the understanding that is prerequisite to intelligent participation in the democratic process. The schools are required to provide instruction "to promote a spirit of patriotic and civic service and obligation and to foster in the children of the state moral and intellectual qualities which are essential in preparing to meet the obligations of citizenship in peace or in war . . . ." Flag and other patriotic exercises also are prescribed, as loyalty is a characteristic of citizenship essential to the preservation of a country. In addition, required courses include classes in civics, United States and New York history, and principles of American government.

country. The people of New York, acting through their elected representatives, have made a judgment that citizenship should be a qualification for teaching the young of the State in the public schools, and § 3001(3) furthers that judgment.

Reversed.

Mr. Justice BLACKMUN, with whom Mr. Justice BRENNAN, Mr. Justice MARSHALL, and Mr. Justice STEVENS join, dissenting. [Dissent omitted.]

EXERCISE 15:

1. The Supreme Court utilized a lesser standard of review in *Ambach.* What is the test the Court used to identify when rational basis review applies and when it does not?

2. Is that test one that courts can apply in a principled manner?

3. Why did the Court rule that rational basis review applied in governmental function cases, instead of ruling that, in those cases, states meet strict scrutiny?

4. Should there be an exception for governmental functions?

5. Did the Court correctly conclude that public school teachers fell within the governmental functions exception to strict scrutiny?

6. Describe the Court's application of rational basis review to the challenged New York statute.

The discussion thus far has assumed that the aliens in question are lawfully in the United States. What about state alienage classifications regarding aliens *un*lawfully in the United States? In *Plyler v. Doe,* 457 U.S. 202 (1982), the Supreme Court ruled that a Texas statute that denied funding for public school education for children not legally admitted to the United States, violated the Equal Protection Clause. The Court first ruled that the Clause protected "person[s]," including illegal aliens. *Id.* at 210. Second, after concluding that illegal aliens were not a suspect class and that education was not a fundamental right, *id.* at 223, the Court nonetheless seemed to employ heightened scrutiny by requiring Texas to show a "substantial goal." *Id.* at 224. *Plyler* is a difficult to situate case because it does not fall neatly into the standard doctrinal categories. Therefore, it is unclear what impact, if any, *Plyler* will have in the future.

Unlike state alienage classifications, which are presumptively subject to strict scrutiny, the Supreme Court has ruled that federal alienage classifications are subject to rational basis review. In *Mathews v. Diaz,* 426 U.S. 67 (1976), a case involving a challenge to the Social Security Act's exclusion of some aliens from the program, the Court distinguished *Graham v. Richardson* and ruled that such federal alienage classifications are subject to rational basis review. The Court did so on three bases: (1) the Constitution textually delegated powers over immigration and naturalization to Congress, *id.* at 80; (2) federal alienage classifications implicate international relations, at which courts are not adept, *id.* at 81; and (3) federal alienage classifications must respond to varied and changing circumstances, again, at which courts are not institutionally suited. *Id.*

4. Intermediate Scrutiny

a. Introduction

Thus far, we have reviewed two standards of review employed by the Supreme Court to evaluate governmental classifications: rational basis and strict scrutiny. In this subsection, we will cover a third "tier" of scrutiny: intermediate scrutiny. Intermediate scrutiny is most commonly associated with and used in relation to gender classifications, but it also applies to legitimacy classifications; we will cover both, below.

Intermediate scrutiny places the burden on the government to establish that the challenged classification substantially advances an important governmental interest.

b. Gender

Gender classifications have a long history in American and Western law more generally, and continue today. For most of its history, the Supreme Court did not strictly scrutinize gender classifications. For example, *Bradwell v. Illinois*, 83 U.S. (16 Wall.) 130 (1873), upheld Illinois' exclusion of women from the bar. *See also Goesaert v. Cleary*, 335 U.S. 464 (1948) (upholding Michigan's ban on women bartenders (who were not the wife or daughter of a male owner of a bar)).

Then, in 1971, for the first time, the Supreme Court struck down a gender classification. The state statute at issue in *Reed v. Reed*, 404 U.S. 71 (1971), required that a probate court choose a man over an equally qualified woman to administer a decedent's estate. The unanimous Supreme Court ruled that the gender distinction was "arbitrary," and therefore violated the Equal Protection Clause. *Id.* at 76–77.

Following *Reed*, there was disagreement on the Court over whether gender classifications were suspect and, if so, what level of scrutiny such classifications should receive. Initially, it appeared that the Court was moving toward strict scrutiny. *Frontiero v. Richardson*, 411 U.S. 677, 682 (1973). However, five years after *Reed*, the Supreme Court determined that intermediate scrutiny applied to gender classifications.

CRAIG v. BOREN
429 U.S. 190 (1976)

Mr. Justice Brennan delivered the opinion of the Court.

The interaction of two sections of an Oklahoma statute prohibits the sale of "nonintoxicating" 3.2% beer to males under the age of 21 and to females under the age of 18. The question to be decided is whether such a gender-based differential constitutes a denial to males 18–20 years of age of the equal protection of the laws in violation of the Fourteenth Amendment.

This action was brought in the District Court for the Western District of Oklahoma by appellant Craig, a male then between 18 and 21 years of age. A three-judge court sustained the constitutionality of the statutory differential and dismissed the action. We reverse.

II

A

Analysis may appropriately begin with the reminder that *Reed* [*v. Reed*, 404 U.S. 71 (1971),] emphasized that statutory classifications that distinguish between males and females are "subject to scrutiny under the Equal Protection Clause." To withstand constitutional challenge, classifications by gender must serve important governmental objectives and must be substantially related to achievement of those objectives.

Reed v. Reed has provided the underpinning for decisions that have invalidated statutes employing gender as an inaccurate proxy for other, more germane bases of classification. Hence, "archaic and overbroad" generalizations concerning the financial position of servicewomen, and working women, could not justify use of a gender line in determining eligibility for certain governmental entitlements. Similarly, increasingly outdated misconceptions concerning the role of females in the home rather than in the "marketplace and world of ideas" were rejected as loose-fitting characterizations incapable of supporting state statutory schemes that were premised upon their accuracy. In light of the weak congruence between gender and the characteristic or trait that gender purported to represent, it was necessary that the legislatures choose either to realign their substantive laws in a gender-neutral fashion, or to adopt procedures for identifying those instances where the sex-centered generalization actually comported with fact.

We turn then to the question whether the difference between males and females with respect to the purchase of 3.2% beer warrants the differential in age drawn by the Oklahoma statute. We conclude that it does not.

C

We accept for purposes of discussion the District Court's identification of the objective underlying ss 241 and 245 as the enhancement of traffic safety. Clearly, the protection of public health and safety represents an important function of state and local governments. However, appellees' statistics in our view cannot support the conclusion that the gender-based distinction closely serves to achieve that objective.

The appellees introduced a variety of statistical surveys. First, an analysis of arrest statistics for 1973 demonstrated that 18-20-year-old male arrests for "driving under the influence" and "drunkenness" substantially exceeded female arrests for that same age period. Similarly, youths aged 17–21 were found to be overrepresented among those killed or injured in traffic accidents, with males again numerically exceeding females in this regard. Third, a random roadside survey in Oklahoma City revealed that young males were more inclined to drive and drink beer than were their female counterparts. Fourth, Federal Bureau of Investigation nationwide statistics exhibited a notable increase in arrests for "driving under the influence." Finally, statistical evidence gathered in other jurisdictions, particularly Minnesota and Michigan, was offered to corroborate Oklahoma's experience by indicating the pervasiveness of youthful participation in motor vehicle accidents following the imbibing of alcohol.

Even were this statistical evidence accepted as accurate, it nevertheless offers only a weak answer to the equal protection question presented here. The most focused and relevant of the statistical surveys, arrests of 18-20-year-olds for alcohol-related driving offenses, exemplifies the ultimate unpersuasiveness of this evidentiary record. Viewed in terms of the correlation between sex and the actual activity that Oklahoma seeks to regulate[,] the statistics broadly establish that .18% of females and 2% of males in that age group were arrested for that offense. While such a disparity is not trivial in a statistical sense, it hardly can form the basis for employment of a gender line as a classifying device. Certainly if maleness is to serve as a proxy for drinking and driving, a correlation of 2% must be considered an unduly tenuous "fit."

Moreover, the statistics exhibit a variety of other shortcomings that seriously impugn their value to equal protection analysis. [T]he surveys do not adequately justify the salient features of Oklahoma's gender-based traffic-safety law. None purports to measure the use and dangerousness of 3.2% beer as opposed to alcohol generally, a detail that is of particular importance since, in light of its low alcohol level, Oklahoma apparently considers the 3.2% beverage to be "nonintoxicating." Moreover, many of the studies, while graphically documenting the unfortunate increase in driving while under the influence of alcohol, make no effort to relate their findings to age-sex differentials as involved here.

There is no reason to belabor this line of analysis. It is unrealistic to expect either members of the judiciary or state officials to be well versed in the rigors of experimental or statistical technique. But this merely illustrates that proving broad sociological propositions by statistics is a dubious business. We hold, therefore, that Oklahoma's 3.2% beer statute invidiously discriminates against males 18–20 years of age.

It is so ordered.

MR. JUSTICE POWELL, concurring. [Opinion omitted.]

MR. JUSTICE STEVENS, concurring. [Opinion omitted.]

MR. JUSTICE BLACKMUN, concurring in part. [Opinion omitted.]

MR. JUSTICE STEWART, concurring in the judgment. [Opinion omitted.]

MR. CHIEF JUSTICE BURGER, dissenting. [Opinion omitted.]

MR. JUSTICE REHNQUIST, dissenting.

The Court's disposition of this case is objectionable on two grounds. First is its conclusion that men challenging a gender-based statute which treats them less favorably than women may invoke a more stringent standard of judicial review than pertains to most other types of classifications. Second is the Court's enunciation of this standard, without citation to any source, as being that "classifications by gender must serve important governmental objectives and must be substantially related to achievement of those objectives." I think the Oklahoma statute challenged here need pass only the "rational basis" equal protection analysis expounded in cases such as *Williamson v. Lee Optical Co.*, 348 U.S. 483 (1955), and I believe that it is constitutional under that analysis.

In *Frontiero v. Richardson*, [411 U.S. 677 (1973)], the opinion for the plurality sets forth the reasons of four Justices for concluding that sex should be regarded as a suspect classification. These reasons center on our Nation's "long and unfortunate history of sex discrimination," which has been reflected in a whole range of restrictions on the legal rights of women. Noting that the pervasive and persistent nature of the discrimination experienced by women is in part the result of their ready identifiability, the plurality rested its invocation of strict scrutiny largely upon the fact that "statutory distinctions between the sexes often have the effect of invidiously relegating the entire class of females to inferior legal status without regard to the actual capabilities of its individual members."

[T]he Court's application here of "intermediate" scrutiny raises the question of why the statute here should be treated any differently from countless legislative classifications unrelated to sex which have been upheld under a minimum rationality standard. *Williamson v. Lee Optical Co.*, 348 U.S., at 488–489. Most obviously unavailable to support any kind of special scrutiny in this case, is a history or pattern of past discrimination. There is no suggestion in the Court's opinion that males in this age group are in any way peculiarly disadvantaged, subject to systematic discriminatory treatment, or otherwise in need of special solicitude from the courts.

The Court's conclusion that a law which treats males less favorably than females "must serve important governmental objectives and must be substantially related to achievement of those objectives" apparently comes out of thin air. The Equal Protection Clause contains no such language, and none of our previous cases adopt that standard. I would think we have had enough difficulty with the two standards of review which our cases have recognized — the norm of "rational basis," and the "compelling state interest" required where a "suspect classification" is involved — so as to counsel weightily against the insertion of still another "standard" between those two. How is this Court to divine what objectives are important? How is it to determine whether a particular law is "substantially" related to the achievement of such objective, rather than related in some other way to its achievement? Both of the phrases used are so diaphanous and elastic as to invite subjective judicial preferences or prejudices.

[T]he introduction of the adverb "substantially" requires courts to make subjective judgments as to operational effects, for which neither their expertise nor their access to data fits them. And even if we manage to avoid both confusion and the mirroring of our own preferences in the development of this new doctrine, the thousands of judges in other courts who must interpret the Equal Protection Clause may not be so fortunate.

*   *   *

EXERCISE 16:

1. The Supreme Court in *Craig* adopted intermediate scrutiny for gender classifications. Utilizing the standard factors utilized by the Court to determine if a classification is "suspect," how do they apply in this context?

2. Justice Rehnquist argued, in dissent, that the Equal Protection Clause, even if interpreted to provide heightened scrutiny to gender classifications that disadvantage women, should not do so with regard to classifications that disadvantage men. Evaluate Justice Rehnquist's claim. We saw an analogous claim in the affirmative action context, where some justices argued that racial classifications that benefit racial minorities should be subject to lesser scrutiny. Even if one were to accept the distinction in one context, does one also have to accept it in the other?

3. From what source(s) did the *Craig* Court draw the rule that gender classifications are subject to intermediate scrutiny?

4. Is intermediate scrutiny for gender classifications consistent with the Equal Protection Clause's original meaning?

5. What was Oklahoma's proffered state interest? Was it "important"?

6. The majority rejects Oklahoma's argument that its gender classification substantially furthered the goal of traffic safety. It did so by rejecting the import of the statistical evidence proffered by the state. Was the Court right to do so? What would have satisfied the majority? Is that an appropriate standard to which to hold a state legislature?

7. Justice Rehnquist criticized the Court's adoption of intermediate scrutiny because it would "invite subjective judicial preferences or prejudices relating to particular types of legislation, masquerading as judgments whether such legislation is directed at 'important' objectives or, whether the relationship to those objectives is 'substantial' enough." Is he correct?

The most important application of intermediate scrutiny to gender classifications occurred in *United States v. Virginia*, 518 U.S. 515 (1996), reprinted below.

UNITED STATES v. VIRGINIA
518 U.S. 515 (1996)

JUSTICE GINSBURG delivered the opinion of the Court.

Virginia's public institutions of higher learning include an incomparable military college, Virginia Military Institute (VMI). The United States maintains that the Constitution's equal protection guarantee precludes Virginia from reserving exclusively to men the unique educational opportunities VMI affords. We agree.

I

Founded in 1839, VMI is today the sole single-sex school among Virginia's 15 public institutions of higher learning. VMI's distinctive mission is to produce "citizen-soldiers," men prepared for leadership in civilian life and in military service. VMI has notably succeeded in its mission to produce leaders; among its alumni are military generals, Members of Congress, and business executives. The school's alumni overwhelmingly perceive that their VMI training helped them to realize their personal goals. VMI's endowment reflects the loyalty of its graduates; VMI has the largest per-student endowment of all public undergraduate institutions in the Nation.

Virginia has elected to preserve exclusively for men the advantages and opportunities a VMI education affords.

II

A

VMI today enrolls about 1,300 men as cadets. Its academic offerings in the liberal arts, sciences, and engineering are also available at other public colleges and universities in Virginia. In contrast to the federal service academies, institutions maintained "to prepare cadets for career service in the armed forces," VMI's program "is directed at preparation for both military and civilian life"; "[o]nly about 15% of VMI cadets enter career military service."

VMI produces its "citizen-soldiers" through "an adversative, or doubting, model of education" which features "[p]hysical rigor, mental stress, absolute equality of treatment, absence of privacy, minute regulation of behavior, and indoctrination in desirable values." VMI cadets live in spartan barracks where surveillance is constant and privacy nonexistent; they wear uniforms, eat together in the mess hall, and regularly participate in drills. Entering students are incessantly exposed to the rat line, "an extreme form of the adversative model," comparable in intensity to Marine Corps boot camp. Tormenting and punishing, the rat line bonds new cadets to their fellow sufferers and, when they have completed the 7-month experience, to their former tormentors.

VMI's "adversative model" is further characterized by a hierarchical "class system" of privileges and responsibilities, a "dyke system" for assigning a senior class mentor to each entering class "rat," and a stringently enforced "honor code," which prescribes that a cadet " 'does not lie, cheat, steal nor tolerate those who do.' "

VMI attracts some applicants because of its reputation as an extraordinarily challenging military school, and "because its alumni are exceptionally close to the school." "[W]omen have no opportunity anywhere to gain the benefits of [the system of education at VMI]."

B

In 1990, prompted by a complaint filed with the Attorney General by a female high-school student seeking admission to VMI, the United States sued the Commonwealth of Virginia alleging that VMI's exclusively male admission policy violated the Equal Protection Clause of the Fourteenth Amendment.

[I]t was established [at trial] that "some women are capable of all of the individual activities required of VMI cadets." In addition, experts agreed that if VMI admitted women, "the VMI ROTC experience would become a better training program from the perspective of the armed forces, because it would provide training in dealing with a mixed-gender army."

The District Court ruled in favor of VMI. The Court of Appeals for the Fourth Circuit disagreed and vacated the District Court's judgment. Remanding the case, the appeals court assigned to Virginia, in the first instance, responsibility for selecting a remedial course.

C

In response to the Fourth Circuit's ruling, Virginia proposed a parallel program for women: Virginia Women's Institute for Leadership (VWIL). The 4-year, state-sponsored undergraduate program would be located at Mary Baldwin College, a private liberal arts school for women, and would be open, initially, to about 25 to 30 students. Although VWIL would share VMI's mission — to produce "citizen-soldiers" — the VWIL program would differ, as does Mary Baldwin College, from VMI in academic offerings, methods of education, and financial resources.

D

Virginia returned to the District Court seeking approval of its proposed remedial plan, and the court decided the plan met the requirements of the Equal Protection Clause. A divided Court of Appeals affirmed the District Court's judgment.

III

The cross-petitions in this suit present two ultimate issues. First, does Virginia's exclusion of women from the educational opportunities provided by VMI deny to women the equal protection of the laws guaranteed by the Fourteenth Amendment? Second, if VMI offends the Constitution's equal protection principle, what is the remedial requirement?

IV

We note, once again, the core instruction of this Court's pathmarking decisions: Parties who seek to defend gender-based government action must demonstrate an "exceedingly persuasive justification" for that action. Today's skeptical scrutiny of official action denying rights or opportunities based on sex responds to volumes of history. As a plurality of this Court acknowledged a generation ago, "our Nation has had a long and unfortunate history of sex discrimination." *Frontiero v. Richardson*, 411 U.S. 677, 684 (1973). Through a century plus three decades and more of that history, women did not count among voters composing "We the People." And for a half century thereafter, it remained the prevailing doctrine that government, both federal and state, could withhold from women opportunities accorded men so long as any "basis in reason" could be conceived for the discrimination.

In 1971, for the first time in our Nation's history, this Court ruled in favor of a woman who complained that her State had denied her the equal protection of its laws. *Reed v. Reed*, 404 U.S. 71, 73 [(1971)]. Since *Reed*, the Court has repeatedly recognized that neither federal nor state government acts compatibly with the equal protection principle when a law or official policy denies to women, simply because they are women, full citizenship stature — equal opportunity to aspire, achieve, participate in and contribute to society based on their individual talents and capacities.

To summarize the Court's current directions for cases of official classification based on gender: Focusing on the differential treatment for denial of opportunity for which relief is sought, the reviewing court must determine whether the proffered justification is "exceedingly persuasive." The burden of justification is demanding and it rests entirely on the State. See *Mississippi Univ. for Women [v. Hogan]*, 458 U.S., [718,] 724 [(1982)]. The State must show "at least that the [challenged] classification serves 'important governmental objectives and that the discriminatory means employed' are 'substantially related to the achievement of those objectives.'" The justification must be genuine, not hypothesized or invented *post hoc* in response to litigation. And it must not rely on overbroad generalizations about the different talents, capacities, or preferences of males and females.

The heightened review standard our precedent establishes does not make sex a proscribed classification. Supposed "inherent differences" are no longer accepted as a ground for race or national origin classifications. See *Loving v. Virginia*, 388 U.S. 1 (1967). Physical differences between men and women, however, are enduring. "Inherent differences" between men and women, we have come to appreciate, remain cause for celebration, but not for denigration of the members of either sex or for artificial constraints on an individual's opportunity. Sex classifications may be used to compensate women "for particular economic disabilities [they have] suffered," to "promot[e] equal employment opportunity," to advance full development of the talent and capacities of our Nation's people.[7] But such classifications may not be used, as they once were, to create or perpetuate the legal, social, and economic inferiority of women.

---

[7] Several *amici* have urged that diversity in educational opportunities is an altogether appropriate governmental pursuit and that single-sex schools can contribute importantly to such diversity. Indeed, it is the mission of some single-sex schools "to dissipate, rather than perpetuate, traditional gender classifications." See Brief for Twenty-six Private Women's Colleges as *Amici Curiae* 5. We do not question the Commonwealth's prerogative evenhandedly to support diverse educational opportunities. We address specifically and only an educational opportunity recognized as "unique," an opportunity available only at Virginia's premier military institute, the Commonwealth's sole single-sex public university or college.

V

Virginia asserts two justifications in defense of VMI's exclusion of women. First, the Commonwealth contends, "single-sex education provides important educational benefits," and the option of single-sex education contributes to "diversity in educational approaches." Second, the Commonwealth argues, "the unique VMI method of character development and leadership training," the school's adversative approach, would have to be modified were VMI to admit women. We consider these two justifications in turn.

A

Single-sex education affords pedagogical benefits to at least some students, Virginia emphasizes, and that reality is uncontested in this litigation. Similarly, it is not disputed that diversity among public educational institutions can serve the public good. But Virginia has not shown that VMI was established, or has been maintained, with a view to diversifying, by its categorical exclusion of women, educational opportunities within the Commonwealth. In cases of this genre, our precedent instructs that "benign" justifications proffered in defense of categorical exclusions will not be accepted automatically; a tenable justification must describe actual state purposes, not rationalizations for actions in fact differently grounded.

Neither recent nor distant history bears out Virginia's alleged pursuit of diversity through single-sex educational options. In 1839, when the Commonwealth established VMI, a range of educational opportunities for men and women was scarcely contemplated. Higher education at the time was considered dangerous for women; reflecting widely held views about women's proper place, the Nation's first universities and colleges admitted only men. VMI was not at all novel in this respect: In admitting no women, VMI followed the lead of the Commonwealth's flagship school, the University of Virginia, founded in 1819.

Virginia eventually provided for several women's seminaries and colleges. Farmville Female Seminary became a public institution in 1884. Two women's schools, Mary Washington College and James Madison University, were founded in 1908; another, Radford University, was founded in 1910. Ultimately, in 1970, the University of Virginia, introduced coeducation.

[W]e find no persuasive evidence in this record that VMI's male-only admission policy "is in furtherance of a state policy of 'diversity.' " A purpose genuinely to advance an array of educational options is not served by VMI's historic and constant plan to "affor[d] a unique educational benefit only to males." However "liberally" this plan serves the Commonwealth's sons, it makes no provision whatever for her daughters. That is not *equal* protection.

B

Virginia next argues that VMI's adversative method of training provides educational benefits that cannot be made available, unmodified, to women. Alterations to accommodate women would necessarily be "radical," so "drastic," Virginia asserts, as to transform, indeed "destroy," VMI's program. Neither sex would be favored by the transformation, Virginia maintains: Men would be deprived of the unique opportunity currently available to them; women would not gain that opportunity because their participation would "eliminat[e] the very aspects of [the] program that distinguish [VMI] from . . . other institutions of higher education in Virginia."

The District Court forecast from expert witness testimony, and the Court of Appeals accepted, that coeducation would materially affect "at least these three aspects of VMI's program — physical training, the absence of privacy, and the adversative approach." And it is uncontested that women's admission would require accommodations, primarily in arranging housing assignments and physical training programs for female cadets. It is also undisputed, however, that "the VMI methodology could be used to educate women." The District Court even allowed that some women may prefer it to the methodology a women's college might pursue. The parties, furthermore, agree that "*some* women can meet the physical standards [VMI] now impose[s] on men." In sum, "neither the goal of producing citizen soldiers," VMI's *raison d'être*, "nor VMI's implementing methodology is inherently unsuitable to women."

The United States does not challenge any expert witness estimation on average capacities or preferences of men and women. Instead, the United States emphasizes that time and again since this Court's turning point decision in *Reed v. Reed*, 404 U.S. 71 (1971), we have cautioned reviewing courts to take a "hard look" at generalizations or "tendencies" of the kind pressed by Virginia, and relied upon by the District Court. See [Sandra Day] O'Connor, *Portia's Progress*, 66 N.Y.U. L. Rev. 1546, 1551 (1991).

It may be assumed, for purposes of this decision, that most women would not choose VMI's adversative method. [I]t is also probable that "many men would not want to be educated in such an environment." Education, to be sure, is not a "one size fits all" business. The issue, however, is not whether "women — or men — should be forced to attend VMI"; rather, the question is whether the Commonwealth can constitutionally deny to women who have the will and capacity, the training and attendant opportunities that VMI uniquely affords.

The notion that admission of women would downgrade VMI's stature, destroy the adversative system and, with it, even the school, is a judgment hardly proved, a prediction hardly different from other "self-fulfilling prophec[ies]," once routinely used to deny rights or opportunities. When women first sought admission to the bar and access to legal education, concerns of the same order were expressed.

Women's successful entry into the federal military academies, and their participation in the Nation's military forces, indicate that Virginia's fears for the future of VMI may not be solidly grounded. The Commonwealth's justification for excluding all women from "citizen-soldier" training for which some are qualified, in any event, cannot rank as "exceedingly persuasive," as we have explained and applied that standard.

The Commonwealth's misunderstanding is apparent from VMI's mission: to produce "citizen-soldiers." Surely that goal is great enough to accommodate women, who today count as citizens in our American democracy equal in stature to men. Just as surely, the Commonwealth's great goal is not substantially advanced by women's categorical exclusion, in total disregard of their individual merit, from the Commonwealth's premier "citizen-soldier" corps. Virginia, in sum, "has fallen far short of establishing the 'exceedingly persuasive justification,' " that must be the solid base for any gender-defined classification.

VI

A

A remedial decree, this Court has said, must closely fit the constitutional violation; it must be shaped to place persons unconstitutionally denied an opportunity or advantage in "the position they would have occupied in the absence of [discrimination]." The constitutional violation in this suit is the categorical exclusion of women from an extraordinary educational opportunity afforded men. A proper remedy for an unconstitutional exclusion, we have explained, aims to "eliminate [so far as possible] the discriminatory effects of the past" and to "bar like discrimination in the future."

Virginia chose not to eliminate, but to leave untouched, VMI's exclusionary policy. For women only, however, Virginia proposed a separate program, different in kind from VMI and unequal in tangible and intangible facilities.

VWIL affords women no opportunity to experience the rigorous military training for which VMI is famed. Instead, the VWIL program "deemphasize[s]" military education, and uses a "cooperative method" of education "which reinforces self-esteem." VWIL students participate in ROTC and a "largely ceremonial" Virginia Corps of Cadets, but Virginia deliberately did not make VWIL a military institute. The VWIL House is not a military-style residence and VWIL students need not live together throughout the 4-year program, eat meals together, or wear uniforms during the schoolday. VWIL students thus do not experience the "barracks" life "crucial to the VMI experience," the spartan living arrangements designed to foster an "egalitarian ethic."

VWIL students receive their "leadership training" in seminars, externships, and speaker series, episodes and encounters lacking the "[p]hysical rigor, mental stress, . . . minute regulation of behavior, and indoctrination in desirable values" made hallmarks of VMI's citizen-soldier training. Kept away from the pressures, hazards, and psychological bonding characteristic of VMI's adversative training, VWIL students will not know the "feeling of tremendous accomplishment" commonly experienced by VMI's successful cadets.

Virginia maintains that these methodological differences are "justified pedagogically," based on "important differences between men and women in learning and developmental needs," "psychological and sociological differences." The Task Force charged with developing the leadership program for women "determined that a military model and, especially VMI's adversative method, would be wholly inappropriate for educating and training *most women.*"

As earlier stated, generalizations about "the way women are," estimates of what is appropriate for *most women*, no longer justify denying opportunity to women whose talent and capacity place them outside the average description. Notably, Virginia never asserted that VMI's method of education suits *most men*. It is also revealing that Virginia accounted for its failure to make the VWIL experience "the entirely militaristic experience of VMI" on the ground that VWIL "is planned for women who do not necessarily expect to pursue military careers." By that reasoning, VMI's "entirely militaristic" program would be inappropriate for men in general or *as a group*, for "[o]nly about 15% of VMI cadets enter career military service."

In contrast to the generalizations about women on which Virginia rests, we note again these dispositive realities: VMI's "implementing methodology" is not "inherently unsuitable to women," "some women . . . do well under [the] adversative model"; "some women, at least, would want to attend [VMI] if they had the opportunity," "some women are capable of all of the individual activities required of VMI cadets," and "can meet the physical standards [VMI] now impose[s] on men." It is on behalf of these women that the United States has instituted this suit, and it is for them that a remedy must be crafted, a remedy that will end their exclusion from a state-supplied educational opportunity for which they are fit, a decree that will "bar like discrimination in the future."

B

In myriad respects other than military training, VWIL does not qualify as VMI's equal. VWIL's student body, faculty, course offerings, and facilities hardly match VMI's. Nor can the VWIL graduate anticipate the benefits associated with VMI's 157-year history, the school's prestige, and its influential alumni network. Mary Baldwin College, whose degree VWIL students will gain, enrolls first-year women with an average combined SAT score about 100 points lower than the average score for VMI freshmen. The Mary Baldwin faculty holds "significantly fewer Ph.D.'s," and receives substantially lower salaries than the faculty at VMI.

Mary Baldwin does not offer a VWIL student the range of curricular choices available to a VMI cadet. VMI awards baccalaureate degrees in liberal arts, biology, chemistry, civil engineering, electrical and computer engineering, and mechanical engineering. VWIL students attend a school that "does not have a math and science focus," they cannot take at Mary Baldwin any courses in engineering or the advanced math and physics courses VMI offers.

For physical training, Mary Baldwin has "two multi-purpose fields" and "[o]ne gymnasium." VMI has "an NCAA competition level indoor track and field facility; a number of multi-purpose fields; baseball, soccer and lacrosse fields; an obstacle course; large boxing, wrestling and martial arts facilities; an 11-laps-to-the-mile indoor running course; an indoor pool; indoor and outdoor rifle ranges; and a football stadium that also contains a practice field and outdoor track."

Although Virginia has represented that it will provide equal financial support for in-state VWIL students and VMI cadets, and the VMI Foundation has agreed to endow VWIL with $5.4625 million, the difference between the two schools' financial reserves is pronounced. Mary Baldwin's endowment, currently about $19 million, will gain an additional $35 million based on future commitments; VMI's current endowment, $131 million — the largest public college per-student endowment in the Nation — will gain $220 million.

The VWIL student does not graduate with the advantage of a VMI degree. Her diploma does not unite her with the legions of VMI "graduates [who] have distinguished themselves" in military and civilian life. A VWIL graduate cannot assume that the "network of business owners, corporations, VMI graduates and non-graduate employers . . . interested in hiring VMI graduates," will be equally responsive to her search for employment.

[W]e rule here that Virginia has not shown substantial equality in the separate educational opportunities the Commonwealth supports at VWIL and VMI.

C

Virginia's remedy does not match the constitutional violation; the Commonwealth has shown no "exceedingly persuasive justification" for withholding from women qualified for the experience premier training of the kind VMI affords.

For the reasons stated, the initial judgment of the Court of Appeals is affirmed, the final judgment of the Court of Appeals is reversed, and the case is remanded for further proceedings consistent with this opinion.

It is so ordered.

JUSTICE THOMAS took no part in the consideration or decision of these cases.

CHIEF JUSTICE REHNQUIST, concurring in the judgment. [Opinion omitted.]

JUSTICE SCALIA, dissenting.

Today the Court shuts down an institution that has served the people of the Commonwealth of Virginia with pride and distinction for over a century and a half. To achieve that desired result, it rejects (contrary to our established practice) the factual findings of two courts below, sweeps aside the precedents of this Court, and ignores the history of our people. As to facts: It explicitly rejects the finding that there exist "gender-based developmental differences" supporting Virginia's restriction of the "adversative" method to only a men's institution, and the finding that the all-male composition of the Virginia Military Institute (VMI) is essential to that institution's character. As to precedent: It drastically revises our established standards for reviewing sex-based classifications. And as to history: It counts for nothing the long tradition, enduring down to the present, of men's military colleges supported by both States and the Federal Government.

Much of the Court's opinion is devoted to deprecating the closed-mindedness of our forebears with regard to women's education, and even with regard to the treatment of women in areas that have nothing to do with education. Closed-minded they were —

as every age is, including our own, with regard to matters it cannot guess, because it simply does not consider them debatable. The virtue of a democratic system with a First Amendment is that it readily enables the people, over time, to be persuaded that what they took for granted is not so, and to change their laws accordingly. That system is destroyed if the smug assurances of each age are removed from the democratic process and written into the Constitution. So to counterbalance the Court's criticism of our ancestors, let me say a word in their praise: They left us free to change. The same cannot be said of this most illiberal Court, which has embarked on a course of inscribing one after another of the current preferences of the society (and in some cases only the counter-majoritarian preferences of the society's law-trained elite) into our Basic Law. Today it enshrines the notion that no substantial educational value is to be served by an all-men's military academy. Since it is entirely clear that the Constitution of the United States — the old one — takes no sides in this educational debate, I dissent.

EXERCISE 17:

1. Granting the Supreme Court's historical review of legal and social obstacles to women's equality, what role, if any, should the current status of women in America have in determining what level of scrutiny is appropriate for gender classifications? Since women receive, relative to earlier periods, more equal treatment, should that fact (assuming, of course, that you agree with that assessment) push the Supreme Court's doctrine toward rational basis review?

2. What analysis did the Supreme Court employ to evaluate Virginia's gender classification?

3. Did the Supreme Court alter the analysis it used to evaluate Virginia's gender classification?

4. What interests did Virginia proffer to support its educational system? How did the Court rule regarding those interests?

5. Virginia argued that admission of women to VMI would change its character. Flesh-out Virginia's argument. How did the Court respond?

6. The *V.M.I.* majority contended that Virginia did not, as a historical matter, pursue educational diversity. Assuming that is true, should more recent history "trump" earlier history? Also, why should the Court exclude a *current* state purpose, assuming it would otherwise satisfy intermediate scrutiny?

7. Is ascertaining Virginia's "purpose," especially from 1839, a coherent inquiry? How does one reconstruct a state's purpose from 150 years earlier? Do state's even have purposes?

8. Since the standard of review is intermediate scrutiny, why is the fact that some — though an admittedly small number of — women would be willing and able to attend VMI sufficient to show that VMI is not substantially related to Virginia's objective?

9. Why did the Supreme Court reject Virginia's proposed remedy of WVIL?

10.   A common thread in the Supreme Court's gender classification case law, including *V.M.I.*, is that laws based on stereotypes about women violate the Equal Protection Clause. In this case, what role did this argument play?

11.   Did the Court's ruling expressly or implicitly prohibit separate-but-equal education for gender? For example, after this ruling, could Virginia — assuming good faith and sufficient resources — create a women's VMI? If you conclude that *V.M.I.*, at least as a practical matter, precludes separate women's colleges, is that an attractive consequence?

12.   Justice Ginsburg's majority opinion, controversially, contended that men and women are different and that these differences justify less-than-strict scrutiny. Are those claims true? How are they relevant to the Court's equal protection analysis?

13.   Is the Court's ruling consistent with the Equal Protection Clause's original meaning? With the Court's own precedent?

14.   Justice Ginsburg's authorship of the *V.M.I.* opinion was the culmination of her professional activities prior to elevation to the Supreme Court. During her time as a law professor, Justice Ginsburg briefed and argued, on behalf of the ACLU's Women's Rights Project, many of the seminal gender classification cases, such as *Reed v. Reed*, 404 U.S. 71 (1971).

One of the key themes in this area of law is that laws that utilize gender classifications either as a result of or to further stereotypes regarding women violate the Equal Protection Clause. If the Supreme Court perceives that a gender stereotype is at operation in a classification, it will strike down the law. *Mississippi Univ. for Women v. Hogan*, 458 U.S. 718 (1982), exemplified this.

There, the plaintiff was denied entry to a woman's state nursing university because he was a man. The Court, in an opinion written by Justice O'Connor, emphasized the disfavored place of gender stereotypes:

> Although the test for determining the validity of a gender-based classification is straightforward, it must be applied free of fixed notions concerning the roles and abilities of males and females. Care must be taken in ascertaining whether the statutory objective itself reflects archaic and stereotypic notions. Thus, if the statutory objective is to exclude or "protect" members of one gender because they are presumed to suffer from an inherent handicap or to be innately inferior, the objective itself is illegitimate.

> If the State's objective is legitimate and important, we next determine whether the requisite direct, substantial relationship between objective and means is present. The purpose of requiring that close relationship is to assure that the validity of a classification is determined through reasoned analysis rather than through the mechanical application of traditional, often inaccurate, assumptions about the proper roles of men and women. The need for the requirement is amply revealed by reference to the broad range of statutes already invalidated by this Court; statutes that relied upon the simplistic, outdated assumption that gender could be used as a "proxy for other, more

germane bases of classification," *Craig v. Boren*, 429 U.S. 190, 198 (1976), to establish a link between objective and classification.

Id. at 724–26.

Though simple in theory, the ability of the Supreme Court to accurately determine whether a stereotype is at work is complicated by another line of cases that upholds gender classifications when they reflect biological differences between men and women. As noted by Justice Ginsburg, in her *V.M.I.* opinion, there are " '[i]nherent differences' between men and women." The challenge faced by the Court is discerning when the classification reflects an "inherent difference[]" or a stereotype.

One of many cases where the Court fractured on this point was *Nguyen v. I.N.S.*, 533 U.S. 53 (2001). At issue in *Nguyen* was a gender distinction in federal immigration law that made it easier for a child born overseas to an unmarried citizen mother and noncitizen father to establish U.S. citizenship than for a child born to an unmarried noncitizen mother and citizen father. *Id.* at 59–60.

The majority of the Court ruled that the gender classification was substantially related to the government's important interests because of the biological differences between mothers and fathers, in particular, that mothers are present at birth while fathers need not be. *Id.* at 62–69. By contrast, the dissent, authored by Justice Ginsburg, argued that the federal government's use of a gender classification reflected gender stereotypes because it had available to it less restrictive means of pursuing its goals. *Id.* at 78–92.

c. Legitimacy

Another classification that the Supreme Court has ruled receives heightened scrutiny is legitimacy classifications. (Other labels for these classifications include non-marital children, illegitimacy, and the older "bastardy" label.) A legitimate child is one born to married parents while an illegitimate child is born outside that context.

Anglo-American law has a long history of treating legitimate and illegitimate children differently. For example, many states did not permit an illegitimate child to inherit via intestate succession.

Beginning with *Levy v. Louisiana*, 391 U.S. 68 (1968), the Supreme Court subjected legitimacy classifications to intermediate review by requiring governments to establish that the classification was substantially related to an important governmental interest. Below, the Supreme Court unanimously re-affirmed its use of this standard.

CLARK v. JETER
486 U.S. 456 (1988)

JUSTICE O'CONNOR delivered the opinion of the Court.

Under Pennsylvania law, an illegitimate child must prove paternity before seeking support from his or her father, and a suit to establish paternity ordinarily must be brought within six years of an illegitimate child's birth. By contrast, a legitimate child may seek support from his or her parents at any time.

I

On September 22, 1983, petitioner Cherlyn Clark filed a support complaint in the Allegheny County Court of Common Pleas on behalf of her minor daughter, Tiffany, who was born out of wedlock on June 11, 1973. Clark named respondent Gene Jeter as Tiffany's father.

Jeter moved to dismiss the complaint on the ground that it was barred by the 6-year statute of limitations for paternity actions. In her response, Clark contended that this statute is unconstitutional under the Equal Protection Clause of the Fourteenth Amendment.

The trial court upheld the statute of limitations. The Superior Court affirmed the trial court's conclusions. The Pennsylvania Supreme Court denied her petition for allowance of appeal.

II

In considering whether state legislation violates the Equal Protection Clause of the Fourteenth Amendment, U.S. Const., Amdt. 14, § 1, we apply different levels of scrutiny to different types of classifications. At a minimum, a statutory classification must be rationally related to a legitimate governmental purpose. *San Antonio Independent School Dist. v. Rodriguez*, 411 U.S. 1, 17 (1973). Classifications based on race or national origin, *e.g.*, *Loving v. Virginia*, 388 U.S. 1, 11 (1967), and classifications affecting fundamental rights, are given the most exacting scrutiny. Between these extremes of rational basis review and strict scrutiny lies a level of intermediate scrutiny, which generally has been applied to discriminatory classifications based on sex or illegitimacy. See, *Craig v. Boren*, 429 U.S. 190, 197 (1976).

To withstand intermediate scrutiny, a statutory classification must be substantially related to an important governmental objective. Consequently we have invalidated classifications that burden illegitimate children for the sake of punishing the illicit relations of their parents, because "visiting this condemnation on the head of an infant is illogical and unjust." *Weber v. Aetna Casualty & Surety Co.*, 406 U.S. 164, 175 (1972). Yet, in the seminal case concerning the child's right to support, this Court acknowledged that it might be appropriate to treat illegitimate children differently in the support context because of "lurking problems with respect to proof of paternity." *Gomez v. Perez*, 409 U.S. 535, 538 (1973).

This Court has developed a particular framework for evaluating equal protection challenges to statutes of limitations that apply to suits to establish paternity, and thereby limit the ability of illegitimate children to obtain support.

> "First, the period for obtaining support . . . must be sufficiently long in duration to present a reasonable opportunity for those with an interest in such children to assert claims on their behalf. Second, any time limitation placed on that opportunity must be substantially related to the State's interest in avoiding the litigation of stale or fraudulent claims."

[W]e conclude that Pennsylvania's 6-year statute of limitations violates the Equal Protection Clause. Even six years does not necessarily provide a reasonable opportunity to assert a claim on behalf of an illegitimate child. "The unwillingness of the mother to file a paternity action on behalf of her child, which could stem from her relationship with the natural father or . . . from the emotional strain of having an illegitimate child, or even from the desire to avoid community and family disapproval, may continue years after the child is born. The problem may be exacerbated if, as often happens, the mother herself is a minor." Not all of these difficulties are likely to abate in six years. A mother might realize only belatedly "a loss of income attributable to the need to care for the child." Furthermore, financial difficulties are likely to increase as the child matures and incurs expenses for clothing, school, and medical care. Thus it is questionable whether a State acts reasonably when it requires most paternity and support actions to be brought within six years of an illegitimate child's birth.

We do not rest our decision on this ground, however, for it is not entirely evident that six years would necessarily be an unreasonable limitations period for child support actions involving illegitimate children. We are, however, confident that the 6-year statute of limitations is not substantially related to Pennsylvania's interest in avoiding the litigation of stale or fraudulent claims. In a number of circumstances, Pennsylvania permits the issue of paternity to be litigated more than six years after the birth of an illegitimate child. The statute itself permits a suit to be brought more than six years after the child's birth if it is brought within two years of a support payment made by the father. And in other types of suits, Pennsylvania places no limits on when the issue of paternity may be litigated. For example, the intestacy statute permits a child born out of wedlock to establish paternity as long as "there is clear and convincing evidence that the man was the father of the child." Likewise, no statute of limitations applies to a father's action to establish paternity. Recently, the Pennsylvania Legislature enacted a statute that tolls most other civil actions during a child's minority. [This] tolling statute[] cast[s] doubt on the State's purported interest in avoiding the litigation of stale or fraudulent claims.

A more recent indication that Pennsylvania does not consider proof problems insurmountable is the enactment by the Pennsylvania Legislature in 1985 of an 18-year statute of limitations for paternity and support actions. [T]he new statute is a tacit concession that proof problems are not overwhelming. [I]ncreasingly sophisticated tests for genetic markers permit the exclusion of over 99% of those who might be accused of paternity, regardless of the age of the child. This scientific evidence is available throughout the child's minority, and it is an additional reason to doubt that Pennsylvania had a substantial reason for limiting the time within which paternity and support actions could be brought.

We conclude that the Pennsylvania statute does not withstand heightened scrutiny under the Equal Protection Clause. The judgment of the Superior Court is reversed, and the case is remanded for further proceedings not inconsistent with this opinion.

It is so ordered.

EXERCISE 18:

1. The Supreme Court affirmed that intermediate scrutiny is the appropriated analysis for legitimacy classifications. Utilizing the standard factors utilized by the Court to determine if a classification is "suspect," how do they apply in this context? Should legitimacy classifications receive greater or lesser scrutiny?

2. Explain the Court's reasoning holding that the Pennsylvania statute of limitations violated the Equal Protection Clause. Are you persuaded?

5. "Fundamental Rights Equal Protection"

a. Introduction

The equal protection material we covered thus far is the standard method of analysis under the Supreme Court's equal protection jurisprudence. In this section, we will cover the case law that utilized a related analysis under the Equal Protection Clause (and the Fifth Amendment's equal protection component) labeled: Fundamental Rights Equal Protection.

There are four fundamental rights protected under equal protection: marriage, voting, access to courts, and travel. For example, the most prominent fundamental rights equal protection cases dealt with statutes that described who could and could not vote. These statutes divided people in various ways regarding their ability to and the weight of their vote.

Fundamental rights equal protection analysis has these components: (1) is there a fundamental right at issue?; (2) is the government classification significantly infringing the right?; and (3) is the infringement of a fundamental right (A) necessary to (B) a compelling state interest? The government has the burden of supporting its infringement of the right.

You may be wondering why, given your study of substantive due process in **Chapter 3**, the Supreme Court created this analogous form of analysis. There are a number of suggested explanations. One is that the Court used fundamental rights equal protection as a substitute for the more-controversial substantive due process doctrine. *See* Michael J. Klarman, *An Interpretative History of Modern Equal Protection*, 90 MICH. L. REV. 213, 285 (1991) (arguing that the Burger Court limited the fundamental rights equal protection strand because of concerns over too much judicial discretion and potential wealth redistribution).

Since the early 1970s, the Court has generally refused to expand the scope of fundamental rights equal protection analysis. Usually, the Court will utilize substantive due process in place of equal protection analysis if it wishes to move in a more expansive doctrinal direction. This fact, in some sense, makes this area of law a relic, though, as with all legal doctrine, it has the potential to become reanimated given the right conditions.

As a practical matter, there is little difference between the substantive due process and fundamental rights equal protection cases other than the labels. The label "fundamental right," whether under due process or equal protection doctrine, is what does the analytical work of placing the burden on the government to establish narrow tailoring and a compelling interest. *See* Robert C. Farrell, *An Excess of Methods: Identifying Implied Fundamental Rights in the Supreme Court*, 26 St. Louis U. Pub. L. Rev. 203, 210 (2007) ("[T]he Court commonly cites implied fundamental rights equal protection cases in support of due process conclusions and implied fundamental rights due process cases in support of equal protection conclusions.").

b. Marriage

In **Chapter 3**, we saw that the Supreme Court ruled that there was a substantive due process right to marriage. *Loving v. Virginia*, 388 U.S. 1 (1967). The Court in *Loving* also protected the right to marriage from racial discrimination under the Equal Protection Clause.

In a subsequent case, the Supreme Court more fully explained the contours of the right to marry. In *Zablocki v. Redhail*, 434 U.S. 374 (1978), the plaintiff was denied marriage, pursuant to a Wisconsin statute. The statute prohibited marriage by anyone with a child support order for minor children not in that person's custody, without court permission. *Id.* at 375. The state's statutory purpose was to ensure that children who are supported by noncustodial-parent child support payments do not become public dependents because of the parent's marriage. *Id.*

In an opinion by Justice Marshall, the Court reaffirmed the right to marry and located the right in the Equal Protection Clause, though it cited both its substantive due process and equal protection precedent. *Id.* at 393–96. Then, the Court found that the Wisconsin statute infringed on Redhail's right to marry because of the substantial — and likely insurmountable — obstacle the statute placed in the way of his marriage, and subjected the statute to strict scrutiny. *Id.* at 386–88. The Court found that the statute failed:

> Appellant asserts that two interests are served by the challenged statute: the permission-to-marry proceeding furnishes an opportunity to counsel the applicant as to the necessity of fulfilling his prior support obligations; and the welfare of the out-of-custody children is protected. We may accept for present purposes that these are legitimate and substantial interests, but, since the means selected by the State for achieving these interests unnecessarily impinge on the right to marry, the statute cannot be sustained.
>
> The statute does not expressly require or provide for any counseling whatsoever, and thus it can hardly be justified as a means for ensuring counseling of the persons within its coverage. Even assuming that counseling does take place[,] this interest obviously cannot support the withholding of court permission to marry once counseling is completed.
>
> With regard to safeguarding the welfare of the out-of-custody children, appellant's brief does not make clear the connection between the State's interest and the statute's requirements. At argument, appellant's counsel suggested that, since permission to marry cannot be granted unless the applicant shows that he has satisfied his court-determined support obligations to the prior children and that those children will not become public charges,

the statute provides incentive for the applicant to make support payments to his children. This "collection device" rationale cannot justify the statute's broad infringement on the right to marry.

First, with respect to individuals who are unable to meet the statutory requirements, the statute merely prevents the applicant from getting married, without delivering any money at all into the hands of the applicant's prior children. More importantly, regardless of the applicant's ability or willingness to meet the statutory requirements, the State already has numerous other means for exacting compliance with support obligations, means that are at least as effective as the instant statute's and yet do not impinge upon the right to marry. Under Wisconsin law, whether the children are from a prior marriage or were born out of wedlock, court-determined support obligations may be enforced directly via wage assignments, civil contempt proceedings, and criminal penalties.

Id. at 388–90.

EXERCISE 19:

1.   Why did the challenged statute fail strict scrutiny?

2.   How would you distinguish the numerous regulations of marriage that remain unchallenged? For example, the requirement to obtain a marriage license or, in some states, a blood test?

c.   Voting

For most of its history, the Supreme Court steadfastly refused to entertain challenges to the constitutionality of voting restrictions and regulations. Most famously, the Court ruled that such challenges under the Guarantee Clause in Article IV, § 4, were nonjusticiable. *Luther v. Borden*, 48 U.S. (7 How.) 1 (1849). In 1962, however, the Court reversed course and ruled that such suits brought under the Equal Protection Clause were justiciable. *Baker v. Carr*, 369 U.S. 186 (1962). This opened the door to the Supreme Court's articulation of one of the most famous rules of constitutional law: one-person-one-vote, below.

REYNOLDS v. SIMS
377 U.S. 533 (1964)

MR. CHIEF JUSTICE WARREN delivered the opinion of the Court.

Involved in these cases are an appeal and two cross-appeals from a decision of the Federal District Court for the Middle District of Alabama holding invalid, under the Equal Protection Clause of the Federal Constitution, the apportionment of seats in the two houses of the Alabama Legislature.

I.

On August 26, 1961, the original plaintiffs, residents, taxpayers and voters of Jefferson County, Alabama, filed a complaint in the United States District Court for the Middle District of Alabama, in their own behalf and on behalf of all similarly situated Alabama voters, challenging the apportionment of the Alabama Legislature. The complaint alleged a deprivation of rights under the Equal Protection Clause of the Fourteenth Amendment.

Plaintiffs below alleged that the last apportionment of the Alabama Legislature was based on the 1900 federal census, despite the requirement of the State Constitution that the legislature be reapportioned decennially. They asserted that, since the population growth in the State from 1900 to 1960 had been uneven, Jefferson and other counties were now victims of serious discrimination with respect to the allocation of legislative representation. The complaint asserted that plaintiffs had no other adequate remedy, and that they had exhausted all forms of relief other than that available through the federal courts. They alleged that representation at any future constitutional convention would be established by the legislature, making it unlikely that the membership of any such convention would be fairly representative; and that, while the Alabama Supreme Court had found that the legislature had not complied with the State Constitution in failing to reapportion according to population decennially, that court had nevertheless indicated that it would not interfere with matters of legislative reapportionment.

No effective political remedy to obtain relief against the alleged malapportionment of the Alabama Legislature appears to have been available. No initiative procedure exists under Alabama law. Amendment of the State Constitution can be achieved only after a proposal is adopted by three-fifths of the members of both houses of the legislature and is approved by a majority of the people, or as a result of a constitutional convention convened after approval by the people of a convention call initiated by a majority of both houses of the Alabama Legislature.

II.

Undeniably the Constitution of the United States protects the right of all qualified citizens to vote, in state as well as in federal elections. A consistent line of decisions by this Court in cases involving attempts to deny or restrict the right of suffrage has made this indelibly clear. The right to vote can neither be denied outright, nor destroyed by alteration of ballots, nor diluted by ballot-box stuffing. Racially based gerrymandering, and the conducting of white primaries, *Nixon v. Herndon*, 273 U.S. 536 [(1927)], *Nixon v. Condon*, 286 U.S. 73 [(1932)], *Terry v. Adams*, 345 U.S. 461 [(1953)], both of which result in denying to some citizens their right to vote, have been held to be constitutionally impermissible. And history has seen a continuing expansion of the scope of the right of suffrage in this country.[28] The right to vote freely for the candidate of one's choice is of the essence of a democratic society, and any restrictions

---

[28] The Fifteenth, Seventeenth, Nineteenth, Twenty-third and Twenty-fourth Amendments to the Federal Constitution all involve expansions of the right of suffrage.

on that right strike at the heart of representative government. And the right of suffrage can be denied by a debasement or dilution of the weight of a citizen's vote just as effectively as by wholly prohibiting the free exercise of the franchise.

[T]he fundamental principle of representative government in this country is one of equal representation for equal numbers of people, without regard to race, sex, economic status, or place of residence within a State. Our problem, then, is to ascertain, in the instant cases, whether there are any constitutionally cognizable principles which would justify departures from the basic standard of equality among voters in the apportionment of seats in state legislatures.

Undoubtedly, the right of suffrage is a fundamental matter in a free and democratic society. Especially since the right to exercise the franchise in a free and unimpaired manner is preservative of other basic civil and political rights, any alleged infringement of the right of citizens to vote must be carefully and meticulously scrutinized. Almost a century ago, in *Yick Wo v. Hopkins*, 118 U.S. 356 [(1886)], the Court referred to "the political franchise of voting" as "a fundamental political right, because preservative of all rights."

Legislators represent people, not trees or acres. Legislators are elected by voters, not farms or cities or economic interests. As long as ours is a representative form of government, and our legislatures are those instruments of government elected directly by and directly representative of the people, the right to elect legislators in a free and unimpaired fashion is a bedrock of our political system. It could hardly be gainsaid that a constitutional claim had been asserted by an allegation that certain otherwise qualified voters had been entirely prohibited from voting for members of their state legislature. And, if a State should provide that the votes of citizens in one part of the State should be given two times, or five times, or 10 times the weight of votes of citizens in another part of the State, it could hardly be contended that the right to vote of those residing in the disfavored areas had not been effectively diluted. The resulting discrimination against those individual voters living in disfavored areas is easily demonstrable mathematically. Their right to vote is simply not the same right to vote as that of those living in a favored part of the State. Two, five, or 10 of them must vote before the effect of their voting is equivalent to that of their favored neighbor. Weighting the votes of citizens differently, by any method or means, merely because of where they happen to reside, hardly seems justifiable.[41]

State legislatures are, historically, the fountainhead of representative government in this country. A number of them have their roots in colonial times, and substantially antedate the creation of our Nation and our Federal Government. But representative government is in essence self-government through the medium of elected representatives of the people, and each and every citizen has an inalienable right to full and

---

[41] James Wilson, a delegate to the Constitutional Convention and later an Associate Justice of this Court, stated:

"[A]ll elections ought to be equal. Elections are equal, when a given number of citizens, in one part of the state, choose as many representatives, as are chosen by the same number of citizens, in any other part of the state. In this manner, the proportion of the representatives and of the constituents will remain invariably the same." 2 The Works of James Wilson (Andrews ed. 1896) 15.

effective participation in the political processes of his State's legislative bodies. Most citizens can achieve this participation only as qualified voters through the election of legislators to represent them. Full and effective participation by all citizens in state government requires, therefore, that each citizen have an equally effective voice in the election of members of his state legislature. Modern and viable state government needs, and the Constitution demands, no less.

Logically, in a society ostensibly grounded on representative government, it would seem reasonable that a majority of the people of a State could elect a majority of that State's legislators. To conclude differently, and to sanction minority control of state legislative bodies, would appear to deny majority rights in a way that far surpasses any possible denial of minority rights that might otherwise be thought to result. Since legislatures are responsible for enacting laws by which all citizens are to be governed, they should be bodies which are collectively responsive to the popular will. And the concept of equal protection has been traditionally viewed as requiring the uniform treatment of persons standing in the same relation to the governmental action questioned or challenged. With respect to the allocation of legislative representation, all voters, as citizens of a State, stand in the same relation regardless of where they live. Any suggested criteria for the differentiation of citizens are insufficient to justify any discrimination, as to the weight of their votes, unless relevant to the permissible purposes of legislative apportionment. Since the achieving of fair and effective representation for all citizens is concededly the basic aim of legislative apportionment, we conclude that the Equal Protection Clause guarantees the opportunity for equal participation by all voters in the election of state legislators. Diluting the weight of votes because of place of residence impairs basic constitutional rights under the Fourteenth Amendment just as much as invidious discriminations based upon factors such as race, *Brown v. Board of Education*, 347 U.S. 483 [(1954)], or economic status, *Griffin v. People of State of Illinois*, 351 U.S. 12 [(1956)], *Douglas v. People of State of California*, 372 U.S. 353 [(1963)]. Our constitutional system amply provides for the protection of minorities by means other than giving them majority control of state legislatures. And the democratic ideals of equality and majority rule, which have served this Nation so well in the past, are hardly of any less significance for the present and the future.

We are told that the matter of apportioning representation in a state legislature is a complex and many-faceted one. We are advised that States can rationally consider factors other than population in apportioning legislative representation. We are admonished not to restrict the power of the States to impose differing views as to political philosophy on their citizens. We are cautioned about the dangers of entering into political thickets and mathematical quagmires. Our answer is this: a denial of constitutionally protected rights demands judicial protection; our oath and our office require no less of us.

To the extent that a citizen's right to vote is debased, he is that much less a citizen. The fact that an individual lives here or there is not a legitimate reason for overweighting or diluting the efficacy of his vote. The complexions of societies and civilizations change, often with amazing rapidity. A nation once primarily rural in character becomes predominantly urban. Representation schemes once fair and equitable become archaic and outdated. But the basic principle of representative government remains, and must remain, unchanged — the weight of a citizen's vote cannot be made to depend on where he lives. Population is, of necessity, the starting point for consideration and the controlling criterion for judgment in legislative apportionment controversies. A citizen, a qualified voter, is no more nor no less so because he lives in the city or on the farm. This is the clear and strong command of our Constitution's Equal Protection Clause. This is an essential part of the concept of a government of laws and not men. This is at the heart of Lincoln's vision of "government of the people, by the people, (and) for the people." The Equal Protection Clause demands no less than substantially equal state legislative representation for all citizens, of all places as well as of all races.

IV.

We hold that, as a basic constitutional standard, the Equal Protection Clause requires that the seats in both houses of a bicameral state legislature must be apportioned on a population basis. Simply stated, an individual's right to vote for state legislators is unconstitutionally impaired when its weight is in a substantial fashion diluted when compared with votes of citizens living on other parts of the State. Since, under neither the existing apportionment provisions nor either of the proposed plans was either of the houses of the Alabama Legislature apportioned on a population basis, the District Court correctly held that all three of these schemes were constitutionally invalid.[45]

Legislative apportionment in Alabama is signally illustrative and symptomatic of the seriousness of this problem in a number of the States. At the time this litigation was commenced, there had been no reapportionment of seats in the Alabama Legislature for over 60 years. Legislative inaction, coupled with the unavailability of any political or judicial remedy, had resulted, with the passage of years, in the perpetuated scheme becoming little more than an irrational anachronism. Consistent failure by the Alabama Legislature to comply with state constitutional requirements as to the frequency of reapportionment and the bases of legislative representation resulted in a minority strangle hold on the State Legislature.

V.

Since neither of the houses of the Alabama Legislature was apportioned on a population basis, we would be justified in proceeding no further. However, one of the proposed plans, that contained in the so-called 67-Senator Amendment, at least superficially resembles the scheme of legislative representation followed in the Federal Congress. Under this plan, each of Alabama's 67 counties is allotted one

---

[45] Under the existing scheme, Marshall County, with a 1960 population of 48,018, Baldwin County, with 49,088, and Houston County, with 50,718, are each given only one seat in the Alabama House, while Bullock County, with only 13,462, Henry County, with 15,286, and Lowndes County, with 15,417, are allotted two representatives each. And in the Alabama Senate, under the existing apportionment, a district comprising Lauderdale and Limestone Counties had a 1960 population of 98,135, and another composed of Lee and Russell Counties had 96,105. Conversely, Lowndes County, with only 15,417, and Wilcox County, with 18,739, are nevertheless single-county senatorial districts given one Senate seat each.

senator, and no counties are given more than one Senate seat. Arguably, this is analogous to the allocation of two Senate seats, in the Federal Congress, to each of the 50 States, regardless of population. Seats in the Alabama House, under the proposed constitutional amendment, are distributed by giving each of the 67 counties at least one, with the remaining 39 seats being allotted among the more populous counties on a population basis. This scheme, at least at first glance, appears to resemble that prescribed for the Federal House of Representatives, where the 435 seats are distributed among the States on a population basis, although each State, regardless of its population, is given at least one Congressman.

We find the federal analogy inapposite and irrelevant to state legislative districting schemes. Attempted reliance on the federal analogy appears often to be little more than an after-the-fact rationalization offered in defense of maladjusted state apportionment arrangements. The original constitutions of 36 of our States provided that representation in both houses of the state legislatures would be based completely, or predominantly, on population. And the Founding Fathers clearly had no intention of establishing a pattern or model for the apportionment of seats in state legislatures when the system of representation in the Federal Congress was adopted.[53] Demonstrative of this is the fact that the Northwest Ordinance, adopted in the same year, 1787, as the Federal Constitution, provided for the apportionment of seats in territorial legislatures solely on the basis of population.

The system of representation in the two Houses of the Federal Congress is one ingrained in our Constitution, as part of the law of the land. It is one conceived out of compromise and concession indispensable to the establishment of our federal republic. Arising from unique historical circumstances, it is based on the consideration that in establishing our type of federalism a group of formerly independent States bound themselves together under one national government. [A]t the heart of our constitutional system remains the concept of separate and distinct governmental entities which have delegated some, but not all, of their formerly held powers to the single national government. The fact that almost three-fourths of our present States were never in fact independently sovereign does not detract from our view that the so-called federal analogy is inapplicable as a sustaining precedent for state legislative apportionments. The developing history and growth of our republic cannot cloud the fact that, at the time of the inception of the system of representation in the Federal Congress, a compromise between the larger and smaller States on this matter averted a deadlock in the Constitutional Convention which had threatened to abort the birth of our Nation.

Political subdivisions of States — counties, cities, or whatever — never were and never have been considered as sovereign entities. Rather, they have been traditionally regarded as subordinate governmental instrumentalities created by the State to assist in the carrying out of state governmental functions. The relationship of the States to

---

[53] Thomas Jefferson repeatedly denounced the inequality of representation provided for under the 1776 Virginia Constitution and frequently proposed changing the State Constitution to provide that both houses be apportioned on the basis of population. In 1816 he wrote that "a government is republican in proportion as every member composing it has his equal voice in the direction of its concerns * * * by representatives chosen by himself * * *." Letter to Samuel Kercheval, 10 Writings of Thomas Jefferson (Ford ed. 1899) 38.

the Federal Government could hardly be less analogous.

The right of a citizen to equal representation and to have his vote weighted equally with those of all other citizens in the election of members of one house of a bicameral state legislature would amount to little if States could effectively submerge the equal-population principle in the apportionment of seats in the other house. If such a scheme were permissible, an individual citizen's ability to exercise an effective voice in the only instrument of state government directly representative of the people might be almost as effectively thwarted as if neither house were apportioned on a population basis.

We do not believe that the concept of bicameralism is rendered anachronistic and meaningless when the predominant basis of representation in the two state legislative bodies is required to be the same — population. A prime reason for bicameralism, modernly considered, is to insure mature and deliberate consideration of, and to prevent precipitate action on, proposed legislative measures. Simply because the controlling criterion for apportioning representation is required to be the same in both houses does not mean that there will be no differences in the composition and complexion of the two bodies. Different constituencies can be represented in the two houses. One body could be composed of single-member districts while the other could have at least some multimember districts. The length of terms of the legislators in the separate bodies could differ. The numerical size of the two bodies could be made to differ, even significantly, and the geographical size of districts from which legislators are elected could also be made to differ.

VI.

By holding that as a federal constitutional requisite both houses of a state legislature must be apportioned on a population basis, we mean that the Equal Protection Clause requires that a State make an honest and good faith effort to construct districts, in both houses of its legislature, as nearly of equal population as is practicable. We realize that it is a practical impossibility to arrange legislative districts so that each one has an identical number of residents, or citizens, or voters. Mathematical exactness or precision is hardly a workable constitutional requirement.

A State may legitimately desire to maintain the integrity of various political subdivisions, insofar as possible, and provide for compact districts of contiguous territory in designing a legislative apportionment scheme. Valid considerations may underlie such aims. Indiscriminate districting, without any regard for political subdivision or natural or historical boundary lines, may be little more than an open invitation to partisan gerrymandering. Single-member districts may be the rule in one State, while another State might desire to achieve some flexibility by creating multimember districts. Whatever the means of accomplishment, the overriding objective must be substantial equality of population among the various districts, so that the vote of any citizen is approximately equal in weight to that of any other citizen in the State.

So long as divergences from a strict population standard are based on legitimate considerations incident to the effectuation of a rational state policy, some deviations from the equal-population principle are constitutionally permissible with respect to the apportionment of seats in either or both of the two houses of a bicameral state legislature. But neither history alone, nor economic or other sorts of group interests, are permissible factors in attempting to justify disparities from population-based representation.

Affirmed and remanded.

MR. JUSTICE CLARK, concurring in the affirmance. [Opinion omitted.]

MR. JUSTICE STEWART. [Opinion omitted.]

MR. JUSTICE HARLAN, dissenting.

Whatever may be thought of [today's] holding as a piece of political ideology[,] I think it demonstrable that the Fourteenth Amendment does not impose this political tenet on the States or authorize this Court to do so. The Court's constitutional discussion is remarkable for its failure to address itself at all to the Fourteenth Amendment as a whole or to the legislative history of the Amendment pertinent to the matter at hand. Stripped of aphorisms, the Court's argument boils down to the constitutionally frail tautology that "equal" means "equal."

Had the Court paused to probe more deeply into the matter, it would have found that the Equal Protection Clause was never intended to inhibit the States in choosing any democratic method they pleased for the apportionment of their legislatures. Since it can, I think, be shown beyond doubt that state legislative apportionments, as such, are wholly free of constitutional limitations, save such as may be imposed by the Republican Form of Government Clause (Const., Art. IV, s 4), the Court's action now bringing them within the purview of the Fourteenth Amendment amounts to nothing less than an exercise of the amending power by this Court.

I.

A. *The Language of the Fourteenth Amendment.*

The Amendment is a single text. Whatever one might take to be the application of these cases of the Equal Protection Clause if it stood alone, I am unable to understand the Court's utter disregard of the second section which expressly recognizes the States' power to deny "or in any way" abridge the right of their inhabitants to vote for "the members of the (State) Legislature," and its express provision of a remedy for such denial or abridgment. The comprehensive scope of the second section and its particular reference to the state legislatures preclude the suggestion that the first section was intended to have the result reached by the Court today.

B. Proposal and Ratification of the Amendment.

The history of the adoption of the Fourteenth Amendment provides conclusive evidence that neither those who proposed nor those who ratified the Amendment believed that the Equal Protection Clause limited the power of the States to apportion their legislatures as they saw fit. Moreover, the history demonstrate that the intention to leave this power undisturbed was deliberate and was widely believed to be essential to the adoption of the Amendment.

(i) Proposal of the amendment in Congress. —

*   *   *

In the House, Thaddeus Stevens introduced debate on the resolution on May 8. In his opening remarks, Stevens explained the power of a State to withhold the right to vote:

> "If any State shall exclude any of her adult male citizens from the elective franchise, or abridge that right, she shall forfeit her right to representation in the same proportion. The effect of this provision will be either to compel the States to grant universal suffrage or so to shear them of their power as to keep them forever in a hopeless minority in the national Government, both legislative and executive."

*   *   *

Toward the end of the debate three days later, Mr. Bingham, the author of the first section in the Reconstruction Committee and its leading proponent, concluded his discussion of it with the following: "The amendment does not give, as the second section shows, the power to Congress of regulating suffrage in the several States." He immediately continued: "The second section excludes the conclusion that by the first section suffrage is subjected to congressional law."

*   *   *

(ii) Ratification by the "loyal" States. — Reports of the debates in the state legislatures on the ratification of the Fourteenth Amendment are not generally available. There is, however, compelling indirect evidence. Of the 23 loyal States which ratified the Amendment before 1870, five had constitutional provisions for apportionment of at least one house of their respective legislatures which wholly disregarded the spread of population. Ten more had constitutional provisions which gave primary emphasis to population, but which applied also other principles, such as partial ratios and recognition of political subdivisions, which were intended to favor sparsely settled areas. Can it be seriously contended that the legislatures of these States, almost two-thirds of those concerned, would have ratified an amendment which might render their own States' constitutions unconstitutional?

*   *   *

(iii) Ratification by the "reconstructed" States. — Each of the 10 "reconstructed" States was required to ratify the Fourteenth Amendment before it was readmitted to the Union. The Constitution of each was scrutinized in Congress. Debates over readmission were extensive. The Constitutions of six of the 10 States contained provisions departing substantially from the method of apportionment now held to be required by the Amendment.

*   *   *

C. After 1868.

The years following 1868, far from indicating a developing awareness of the applicability of the Fourteenth Amendment to problems of apportionment, demonstrate precisely the reverse: that the States retained and exercised the power independently to apportion their legislatures.

*   *   *

D. Today.

As of 1961, the Constitutions of all but 11 States recognized bases of apportionment other than geographic spread of population, and to some extent favored sparsely populated areas by a variety of devices, ranging from straight area representation or guaranteed minimum area representation to complicated schemes.

*   *   *

E. Other Factors.

*   *   *

II.

The consequence of today's decision is that in all but the handful of States which may already satisfy the new requirements the local District Court are given blanket authority to supervise apportionment of the State Legislatures. It is difficult to imagine a more intolerable and inappropriate interference by the judiciary with the independent legislatures of the States.

Generalities cannot obscure the cold truth that cases of this type are not amenable to the development of judicial standards. No set of standards can guide a court which has to decide how many legislative districts a State shall have, or what the shape of the districts shall be, or where to draw a particular district line. No judicially manageable standard can determine whether a State should have single-member districts or multimember districts or some combination of both. No such standard can control the balance between keeping up with population shifts and having stable districts. In all these respects, the courts will be called upon to make particular decisions with respect to which a principle of equally populated districts will be of no assistance whatsoever. Quite obviously, there are limitless possibilities for districting consistent with such a principle. Nor can these problems be avoided by judicial reliance on legislative judgments so far as possible. Reshaping or combining one or two districts, or modifying just a few district lines, is no less a matter of choosing among many possible solutions, with varying political consequences, than reapportionment broadside.

[T]he Court excludes virtually every basis for the formation of electoral districts. So far as presently appears, the only factor which a State may consider, apart from numbers, is political subdivisions. I know of no principle of logic or practical or theoretical politics, still less any constitutional principle, which establishes all or any of these exclusions. Certain it is that the Court's opinion does not establish them. So far as the Court says anything at all on this score, it says only that "legislators represent people, not trees or acres." All this may be conceded. But it is surely equally obvious, and, in the context of elections, more meaningful to note that legislators can represent their electors only by speaking for their interests — economic, social, political — many of which do reflect the place where the electors live. The Court does not establish, or indeed even attempt to make a case for the proposition that conflicting interests within a State can only be adjusted by disregarding them when voters are grouped for purposes of representation.

EXERCISE 20:

1.   What analysis did the Supreme Court utilize to evaluate the plaintiffs' equal protection claim?

2.   Is voting a "fundamental right"? Why is it, according to the Supreme Court?

3.   Justice Harlan argued that the Equal Protection Clause did not protect the right to vote. What was his argument? Evaluate it.

4.   The Supreme Court ruled relatedly that the fundamental right to vote is the right to "equal representation for equal numbers of people." What is(are) the source(s) of that claim, for the Court?

5.   What is vote dilution and how, according to the Court, did it infringe on the fundamental right to vote?

6.   Chief Justice Warren famously stated that: "Legislators represent people, not trees or acres. Legislators are elected by voters, not farms or cities or economic interests." Is it part of the concept of democratic representation, as Chief Justice Warren claimed, that *nothing* can interfere with numerical voter equality in legislative apportionment? For instance, many states followed the federal example, and members of their upper legislative chambers represented the state's counties. Is that undemocratic? Is it irrational?

7.   At the end of its opinion, the majority stated that: "neither history alone, nor economic or other sorts of group interests" justify deviation from one-person-one-vote. Is that claim in tension with the Court's rationale in *Grutter v. Bollinger*, discussed above?

8.   Are nations, both presently and in the past, that used criteria other than pure numerical voter equality, to that extent, undemocratic? In particular, some states limited the franchise to those who could read. Others, to those with a minimum level of property. Great Britain gave additional weight to voters who were graduates of the

United Kingdom's major universities. Were these practices undemocratic? Were they irrational?

9.   The Court rejected what it called "the federal analogy." What was that analogy? Upon what basis did the Court reject it? Are you persuaded?

10.   What interests did the state advance to support its classification (its districting method)?

11.   How does *Reynolds*, if at all, fit within the parameters of *Carolene Products* Footnote 4?

12.   If you are critical of the *Reynolds* decision, like Justice Harlan, what do you suggest that the plaintiffs should have done in response to the legislative refusal to redistrict?

13.   Justice Harlan criticized the Court for inserting federal courts into an area that courts would find it difficult to navigate in a principled manner. For example, how much deviation from one-man-one-vote was too much? What was the majority's response? Who had the better of the argument?

14.   Justice Harlan charged the Court majority with ignoring the text and history of the Fourteenth Amendment, along with the Court's own precedent. Is that true? If it is true, why did the Court do so and what is the import of that gap?

15.   Today, *Reynolds'* one-man-one-vote rule of constitutional law is one that Americans almost universally favor. Assuming, as most scholars argue, that this rule is not consistent with the Equal Protection Clause's original meaning, does this fact pose a problem for originalism?

The Supreme Court decided *Lucas v. Forty-Fourth General Assembly of the State of Colo.*, 377 U.S. 713 (1964), on the same day as *Reynolds*. Leading up to *Lucas*, the citizens of Colorado had adopted a state constitutional amendment that governed legislative districting. This amendment apportioned the state senate largely on a geographic basis. The Supreme Court ruled that this state constitutional amendment violated the Equal Protection Clause, despite its adoption by a majority of Coloradoans, including a majority in every county:

> An individual's constitutionally protected right to cast an equally weighted vote cannot be denied even by a vote of a majority of a State's electorate, if the apportionment scheme adopted by the voters fails to measure up to the requirements of the Equal Protection Clause. Manifestly, the fact that an apportionment plan is adopted in a popular referendum is insufficient to sustain its constitutionality or to induce a court of equity to refuse to act. 'One's right to life, liberty, and property * * * and other fundamental rights may not be submitted to vote; they depend on the outcome of no elections.' A citizen's constitutional rights can hardly be infringed simply because a majority of the people choose that it be. We hold that the fact that a challenged legislative apportionment plan was approved by the electorate is without

federal constitutional significance, if the scheme adopted fails to satisfy the basic requirements of the Equal Protection Clause, as delineated in our opinion in Reynolds v. Sims.

Id. at 736–37.

EXERCISE 21:

1.   Is *Lucas* consistent with *Reynolds*?

2.   How might one distinguish voting from the Court's analogy to "other fundamental rights"?

3.   It is a generally established principle that one can waive one's rights. Articulate and critique the argument that the citizens of Colorado waived their *Reynolds* one-person-one-vote right.

The Supreme Court also faced the question of whether state-crafted federal congressional districts were subject to restrictions. In *Wesberry v. Sanders*, 376 U.S. 1 (1964), the Court ruled that Article I, § 2, which states that members of the House must be chosen "by the People of the several States," required "that as nearly as is practicable one man's vote in a congressional election is to be worth as much as another's." *Id.* at 7–8. To support its ruling, the Supreme Court appealed to both political morality and history:

> We do not believe that the Framers of the Constitution intended to permit . . . vote-diluting discrimination to be accomplished through the device of districts containing widely varied numbers of inhabitants. To say that a vote is worth more in one district than in another would not only run counter to our fundamental ideas of democratic government, it would cast aside the principle of a House of Representatives elected 'by the People,' a principle tenaciously fought for and established at the Constitutional Convention. The history of the Constitution, particularly that part of it relating to the adoption of Art. I, s 2, reveals that those who framed the Constitution meant that, no matter what the mechanics of an election, whether statewide or by districts, it was population which was to be the basis of the House of Representatives.

Id. at 8.

d.   Access to Courts

In a series of difficult-to-synthesize cases, the Supreme Court ruled that access to courts, at least in some contexts, is a fundamental right. These cases are hard to fit together because the Court was not explicit about its reasoning in many of the cases, and the rationale for a right of access to the courts changed over time in response to, among other things, concerns that the initial rationale was too broad.

The first major case is *Griffin v. Illinois*, 351 U.S. 12 (1956), where the Court ruled that a state had to provide a trial transcript to indigent criminal defendants for their first appeal-as-of-right. The source of the *Griffen* Court's ruling, in either the Due

Process or Equal Protection Clauses, was unclear. *Id.* at 17. However, the plurality opinion's rationale was potentially very broad because it was premised, not on deliberate state discrimination, but on the disparate impact of wealth. *Id.* at 17–18. *See also Mayer v. Chicago*, 404 U.S. 189 (1971) (holding that the right to transcripts for a first appeal applied to indigent defendants charged with nonfelony crimes). The Court expanded the right of access to courts in *Gideon v. Wainwright*, 372 U.S. 335 (1963), and *Douglas v. California*, 372 U.S. 353 (1963), when it ruled that states must provide indigent criminal defendants with counsel in trials and first appeals-as-of-right.

Then, in 1971, the Supreme Court changed and limited the right of access to courts in *Boddie v. Connecticut*, 401 U.S. 371 (1971). *Boddie* concerned a state requirement that a petitioner for a divorce pay court fees and costs of service of process, without an exception for indigent petitioners. The Court ruled that the requirement violated procedural due process because court action was the only mechanism the state allowed to dissolve a marriage which the state could not condition on sufficient wealth. *Id.* at 381–82. In other words, according to *Boddie*, the right of access to courts is protected by the Due Process Clause (alone), and it protects indigent parties only when the state monopolized access to a right. Below is a portion of the most recent case where the Supreme Court attempted to synthesize the law in this area:

M.L.B. v. S.L.J.
519 U.S. 102 (1996)

JUSTICE GINSBURG delivered the opinion of the Court.

By order of a Mississippi Chancery Court, petitioner M.L.B.'s parental rights to her two minor children were forever terminated. M.L.B. sought to appeal from the termination decree, but Mississippi required that she pay in advance record preparation fees estimated at $2,352.36. Because M.L.B. lacked funds to pay the fees, her appeal was dismissed. We hold that Mississippi may not deny M.L.B., because of her poverty, appellate review of the sufficiency of the evidence on which the trial court found her unfit to remain a parent.

II

Courts have confronted, in diverse settings, the "age-old problem" of "[p]roviding equal justice for poor and rich, weak and powerful alike." *Griffin v. Illinois*, 351 U.S. 12, 16 (1956). "[T]o deny adequate review to the poor," the plurality observed, "means that many of them may lose their life, liberty or property because of unjust convictions which appellate courts would set aside." [T]he *Griffin* plurality drew support from the Due Process and Equal Protection Clauses.

In contrast to the "flat prohibition" of "bolted doors" that the *Griffin* line of cases securely established, the right to counsel at state expense, as delineated in our decisions, is less encompassing. A State must provide trial counsel for an indigent defendant charged with a felony, *Gideon v. Wainwright*, 372 U.S. 335, 339 (1963), but that right does not extend to nonfelony trials if no term of imprisonment is actually imposed. A State's obligation to provide appellate counsel to poor defendants faced with incarceration applies to appeals of right. *Douglas v. California*, 372 U.S. 353, 357 (1963).

III

We have also recognized a narrow category of civil cases in which the State must provide access to its judicial processes without regard to a party's ability to pay court fees. In *Boddie v. Connecticut*, 401 U.S. 371 (1971), we held that the State could not deny a divorce to a married couple based on their inability to pay approximately $60 in court costs. Crucial to our decision in *Boddie* was the fundamental interest at stake. "[G]iven the basic position of the marriage relationship in this society's hierarchy of values and the concomitant state monopolization of the means for legally dissolving this relationship," we said, due process "prohibit[s] a State from denying, solely because of inability to pay, access to its courts to individuals who seek judicial dissolution of their marriages."

In sum, this Court has not extended *Griffin* to the broad array of civil cases. But tellingly, the Court has consistently set apart from the mine run of cases those involving state controls or intrusions on family relationships.

IV

Choices about marriage, family life, and the upbringing of children are among associational rights this Court has ranked as "of basic importance in our society," *Boddie*, 401 U.S., at 376, rights sheltered by the Fourteenth Amendment against the State's unwarranted usurpation, disregard, or disrespect. See, for example, *Loving v. Virginia*, 388 U.S. 1 (1967) (marriage); *Skinner v. Oklahoma*, 316 U.S. 535 (1942) (procreation); *Pierce v. Society of Sisters*, 268 U.S. 510 (1925), and *Meyer v. Nebraska*, 262 U.S. 390 (1923) (raising children). M.L.B.'s case, involving the State's authority to sever permanently a parent-child bond, demands the close consideration the Court has long required when a family association so undeniably important is at stake.

V

M.L.B. maintains that the accusatory state action she is trying to fend off is barely distinguishable from criminal condemnation in view of the magnitude and permanence of the loss she faces. For the purpose at hand, M.L.B. asks us to treat her parental termination appeal as we have treated petty offense appeals; she urges us to rule that Mississippi may not withhold the transcript M.L.B. needs to gain review of the order ending her parental status.

We observe first that the Court's decisions concerning access to judicial processes, reflect both equal protection and due process concerns. The equal protection concern relates to the legitimacy of fencing out would-be appellants based solely on their inability to pay core costs. The due process concern homes in on the essential fairness of the state-ordered proceedings anterior to adverse state action. Nevertheless, "[m]ost decisions in this area," we have recognized, "res[t] on an equal protection framework," for, as we earlier observed, due process does not independently require that the State provide a right to appeal. We place this case within the framework established by our past decisions in this area. In line with those decisions, we inspect the character and intensity of the individual interest at stake, on the one hand, and the State's justification for its exaction, on the other.

[T]he stakes for petitioner M.L.B. — forced dissolution of her parental rights — are large, "more substantial than mere loss of money." [P]arental status termination is "irretrievabl[y] destructi[ve]" of the most fundamental family relationship. And the risk of error is considerable.

Mississippi has, by statute, adopted a "clear and convincing proof" standard for parental status termination cases. Nevertheless, the Chancellor's termination order in this case simply recites statutory language; it describes no evidence, and otherwise details no reasons for finding M.L.B. "clear[ly] and convincing [ly]" unfit to be a parent. Only a transcript can reveal to judicial minds other than the Chancellor's the sufficiency, or insufficiency, of the evidence to support his stern judgment.

The countervailing government interest is financial. Mississippi urges, as the justification for its appeal cost prepayment requirement, the State's legitimate interest in offsetting the costs of its court system. But in the tightly circumscribed category of parental status termination cases, appeals are few, and not likely to impose an undue burden on the State. See Brief for Petitioner 20, 25 (observing that only 16 reported appeals in Mississippi from 1980 until 1996 referred to the State's termination statute, and only 12 of those decisions addressed the merits of the grant or denial of parental rights).

In States providing criminal appeals an indigent's access to appeal, through a transcript of relevant trial proceedings, is secure under our precedent. That equal access right holds for petty offenses as well as for felonies. But counsel at state expense, we have held, is a constitutional requirement, even in the first instance, only when the defendant faces time in confinement. When deprivation of parental status is at stake, however, counsel is sometimes part of the process that is due. It would be anomalous to recognize a right to a transcript needed to appeal a misdemeanor conviction — though trial counsel may be flatly denied — but hold, at the same time, that a transcript need not be prepared for M.L.B. — though were her defense sufficiently complex, state-paid counsel would be designated for her.

In aligning M.L.B.'s case — parental status termination decrees and criminal convictions that carry no jail time — for appeal access purposes, we do not question the general rule that fee requirements ordinarily are examined only for rationality. The State's need for revenue to offset costs, in the mine run of cases, satisfies the rationality requirement; States are not forced by the Constitution to adjust all tolls to account for "disparity in material circumstances." *Griffin*, 351 U.S., at 23 (Frankfurter, J., concurring in judgment).

It is so ordered.

JUSTICE KENNEDY, concurring in the judgment. [Opinion omitted.]

CHIEF JUSTICE REHNQUIST, dissenting. [Opinion omitted.]

JUSTICE THOMAS, with whom JUSTICE SCALIA joins, and with whom THE CHIEF JUSTICE joins except as to Part II, dissenting. [Opinion omitted.]

EXERCISE 22:

1. What does the *M.L.B.* Court describe as the source of the right of access to courts?

2. What is the scope of the right to access courts, as described by *M.L.B.*?

3. Does *M.L.B.* change the law from *Boddie*?

4. What are the limits to the right of access to courts, as articulated in *M.L.B.*?

5. You covered the State Action Doctrine in **Chapter 1**. Make an argument that the State Action Doctrine precludes M.L.B.'s claim in the case. How would the Court respond?

e. Right to Travel

Like the right of access to courts, the Supreme Court's case law on the right to travel also poses a challenge to fit together. These cases have their source in different provisions of the Constitution, and they span a wide variety of factual contexts. Some of the cases that fall under the rubric of right to travel have their source in the Privileges and Immunities Clause and the Privileges or Immunities Clause, others in due process, and others in equal protection. Furthermore, states impose a wide variety of burdens on travel including residency requirements, taxation, and travel regulations.

The foundational case for the equal protection component of the right to travel is *Shapiro v. Thompson*, 394 U.S. 618 (1969), excerpted below.

SHAPIRO v. THOMPSON
394 U.S. 618 (1969)

MR. JUSTICE BRENNAN delivered the opinion of the Court.

These three appeals [are] from a decision of a three-judge District Court holding unconstitutional a State or District of Columbia statutory provision which denies welfare assistance to residents of the State or District who have not resided within their jurisdictions for at least one year immediately preceding their applications for such assistance. We affirm the judgments of the District Courts in the three cases.

II.

There is no dispute that the effect of the waiting-period requirement in each case is to create two classes of needy resident families indistinguishable from each other except that one is composed of residents who have resided a year or more, and the second of residents who have resided less than a year, in the jurisdiction. On the basis of this sole difference the first class is granted and the second class is denied welfare aid upon which may depend the ability of the families to obtain the very means to subsist — food, shelter, and other necessities of life. In each case, the District Court found that appellees met the test for residence in their jurisdictions, as well as all other eligibility requirements except the requirement of residence for a full year prior to their applications. On reargument, appellees' central contention is that the statutory prohibition of benefits to residents of less than a year creates a classification which constitutes an invidious discrimination denying them equal protection of the laws. We agree.

III.

Primarily, appellants justify the waiting-period requirement as a protective device to preserve the fiscal integrity of state public assistance programs. It is asserted that people who require welfare assistance during their first year of residence in a State are likely to become continuing burdens on state welfare programs. Therefore, the argument runs, if such people can be deterred from entering the jurisdiction by denying them welfare benefits during the first year, state programs to assist long-time residents will not be impaired by a substantial influx of indigent newcomers.

We do not doubt that the one-year waiting period device is well suited to discourage the influx of poor families in need of assistance. An indigent who desires to migrate, resettle, find a new job, and start a new life will doubtless hesitate if he knows that he must risk making the move without the possibility of falling back on state welfare assistance during his first year of residence, when his need may be most acute. But the purpose of inhibiting migration by needy persons into the State is constitutionally impermissible.

This Court long ago recognized that the nature of our Federal Union and our constitutional concepts of personal liberty unite to require that all citizens be free to travel throughout the length and breadth of our land uninhibited by statutes, rules, or regulations which unreasonably burden or restrict this movement. That proposition was early stated by Chief Justice Taney in the *Passenger Cases*, [48 U.S. (7 How.)] 283, 492 (1849): "For all the great purposes for which the Federal government was formed, we are one people, with one common country. We are all citizens of the United States; and, as members of the same community, must have the right to pass and repass through every part of it without interruption, as freely as in our own States." We have no occasion to ascribe the source of this right to travel interstate to a particular constitutional provision.

Thus, the purpose of deterring the in-migration of indigents cannot serve as justification for the classification created by the one-year waiting period, since that purpose is constitutionally impermissible. If a law has "no other purpose * * * than to chill the assertion of constitutional rights by penalizing those who choose to exercise them, then it [is] patently unconstitutional."

Alternatively, appellants argue that even if it is impermissible for a State to attempt to deter the entry of all indigents, the challenged classification may be justified as a permissible state attempt to discourage those indigents who would enter the State solely to obtain larger benefits. We observe first that none of the statutes before us is tailored to serve that objective. Rather, the class of barred newcomers is all-inclusive, lumping the great majority who come to the State for other purposes with those who come for the sole purpose of collecting higher benefits. In actual operation, therefore, the three statutes enact what in effect are non-rebuttable presumptions that every applicant for assistance in his first year of residence came to the jurisdiction solely to obtain higher benefits.

Appellants argue further that the challenged classification may be sustained as an attempt to distinguish between new and old residents on the basis of the contribution they have made to the community through the payment of taxes. We have difficulty seeing how long-term residents who qualify for welfare are making a greater present contribution to the State in taxes than indigent residents who have recently arrived. Appellants' reasoning would logically permit the State to bar new residents from schools, parks, and libraries or deprive them of police and fire protection. Indeed it would permit the State to apportion all benefits and services according to the past tax contributions of its citizens. The Equal Protection Clause prohibits such an apportionment of state services.

We recognize that a State has a valid interest in preserving the fiscal integrity of its programs. It may legitimately attempt to limit its expenditures, whether for public assistance, public education, or any other program. But a State may not accomplish such a purpose by invidious distinctions between classes of its citizens. It could not, for example, reduce expenditures for education by barring indigent children from its schools. Similarly, in the cases before us, appellants must do more than show that denying welfare benefits to new residents saves money. The saving of welfare costs cannot justify an otherwise invidious classification.

[W]e reject appellants' argument that a mere showing of a rational relationship between the waiting period and these admittedly permissible state objectives will suffice to justify the classification. The waiting-period provision denies welfare benefits to otherwise eligible applicants solely because they have recently moved into the jurisdiction. But in moving from State to State or to the District of Columbia appellees were exercising a constitutional right, and any classification which serves to penalize the exercise of that right, unless shown to be necessary to promote a compelling governmental interest, is unconstitutional. Cf. *Skinner v. Oklahoma*, 316 U.S. 535, 541 (1942); Korematsu v. United States, 323 U.S. 214, 216 (1944).

Affirmed.

MR. JUSTICE STEWART, concurring. [Opinion omitted.]

MR. CHIEF JUSTICE WARREN, with whom MR. JUSTICE BLACK joins, dissenting. [Opinion omitted.]

MR. JUSTICE HARLAN, dissenting. [Opinion omitted.]

EXERCISE 23:

1.	What was the classification at issue?

2.	How did that classification implicate the right to travel since the plaintiffs had already ceased traveling and were settled in their respective states?

3.	What is the source of that right in the Constitution? Is that an adequate justification?

4.	What analysis did the Supreme Court utilize to evaluate the challenged classification?

5.	What were the states' proffered interests, and why did the Court reject them?

———————

The most recent important discussion of the right to travel occurred in *Saenz v. Roe*, 526 U.S. 489 (1999). The Court's opinion, written by Justice Stevens, self-consciously attempted to summarize and clarify the case law governing the right to travel. The Court stated that:

> The "right to travel" discussed in our cases embraces at least three different components. It protects the right of a citizen of one State to enter and to leave another State, the right to be treated as a welcome visitor rather than an unfriendly alien when temporarily present in the second State, and, for those travelers who elect to become permanent residents, the right to be treated like other citizens of that State.

Id. at 500. The first component of the right to travel, the Court stated, originated in the nature of the federal union itself, and not from a particular constitutional provision. *Id.* at 501. The second aspect derived from the Privileges and Immunities Clause. *Id.* The third component of the right to travel — the facet at issue in *Shapiro* — was described by the *Saenz* Court as originating in the Privileges or Immunities Clause, which we covered in **Chapter 2[D]**.

Though the Court in *Saenz* frequently cited to *Shapiro*, it appeared that the Court meant for the *Saenz* privileges or immunities rationale to supplant *Shapiro*'s equal protection focus. Thus, though the holdings of the prior right to travel cases continue to stand, the privileges or immunities reasoning may govern future cases.

TABLE OF CASES

[References are to pages]

TABLE OF CASES

[References are to pages]

[References are to pages]

INDEX

[References are to sections.]

[References are to sections.]